Contents

III. GLOBALIZATION AND SOCIAL WELFARE

Foreword

Since 1994, when the undersigned was elected as the Hony. Secretary and Treasurer of the IEA, efforts were made to publish theme-wise edited volumes of IEA Conference/Seminar papers as due to space constraint, it is not possible to include many good papers in the Annual Conference Volumes. Ultimately in 1997, during 80 years of the IEA, a plan was formulated to publish such volumes since 1994 Conference which, with active co-operation of IEA Presidents Dr. G.S. Monga and Prof. Ajit Kumar Sinha, could materialise in 1999. This is continuing till now with co-operation from successive IEA Presidents and Secretaries. The present volume is an outcome of such papers contributed to the IEA 85th Conference held at the Kerala University, Thiruvananthapuram in 2002.

Globalization and Decentralised Development is an edited volume consisting of 38 selected papers contributed in one of the technical sessions of the IEA 85th Conference. These are grouped in three sections viz.: (a) Theories and Philosophy of Globalization and Decentralised Development, (b) Sectoral, Region-Specific and Goods-Specific Issues of Globalization, and (c) Globalization and Social Welfare. One can obtain an idea of the growing literature in this emerging and important area of economics from this volume.

We are thankful to the contributors of these articles without whose co-operation the publication of this volume could not be possible. Thanks are due to Prof. Gyana Chandra Kar for the editorial process and the introduction. We also thank Shri G.S.

Bhatia of Deep & Deep Publications Pvt. Ltd., New Delhi for publishing this volume in an elegant manner.

Kolkata

PROFESSOR RAJ KUMAR SEN
President (2003-04)
Indian Economic Association

Editorial Introduction

Globalization as a concept is yet to have a clear definition. The Uruguay rounds of talk followed by the setting-up of the third leg of the tripod of the UN system under the banner of World Trade Organization have opened-up endless debates in countries that have joined the organization as well as those who have not joined or yet to join. India faced with a crisis had probably no option but to accept globalization by signing the agreements and joining the WTO.

Long period of near isolation with all kinds of trade barriers and a socialistic pattern of democracy with domestic policy and with commanding heights of public sector was almost a way of life making none too happy—neither the socialists nor the capitalists. The Marxist-Leninist's philosophy was imbedded firmly in the minds of equally large number of politicians as well as social thinkers and workers. An equally powerful group was feeling restless in an environment of License Raj, Quota and a predominantly high place of the public sector both in industrial as well as commercial segments of the economy. The collapse of the Soviet Union exposed several serious weaknesses of a control economy. The Chinese opened their economy to a considerable extent in sixties allowing overseas investment and all the subsequent prosperity in terms of the growth of the economy were mostly ascribed to globalization. Some of the Indian economists even were lamenting as to why the pulses of quick growth could not be felt by the power that be in the early 60s and 70s.

The World is divided sharply between South, North, East and

West. The countries either due to their typical location, or due to their cultural heritage or historical reasons are dissimilar. The difference is sometimes moderate and, more often, severe. Within each country, there exist also sharp dissimilarities among the federating States (if it is a federal state) or among the regions (if it is an unitary state). Group or regional interests vary. Conflicts do exist for which different economic or political doctrines have continued to exist even within the boundary of a political economy. India, a union of states with unitary features provides the typical example of such conflicts of interests backed by powerful economic and political doctrines. Although majority believe in one philosophy, there are others who sharply differ from the majority belief. Adherence to a particular economic system or arrangement, however, depends squarely on the political system that either accepts and promotes the economic principles imbedded in the system, or rejects it outright considering it to be irrelevant or out of place. No economic doctrine, however strong logic may support it, has relevance only when it confers benefits on the society at large. Leonard Silk in his article 'Economics for the Perplexed' (*Span*, January 1976) has rightly quoted Kenneth Boulding who observed that "I have been gradually coming under the conviction, disturbing for a professional theorist, that there is no such thing as economics; there is only social science applied to economic problems. Indeed, there may only be general science applied to the problems of society".

The strength and weaknesses of the system are vividly explained and expressed within a country particularly when the party in power at different levels of governance are different. In such a situation, each unit acts as a watchdog over the other and, more often than not, the avid principles of the system gets diluted. Such has become the fate of globalization. Recognising the internal conflicts among the 'Isms' and wide variance in the social and economic endowments among the countries, provision of certain relaxations and flexibilities have been incorporated in the WTO arrangements.

Globalization essentially means free flow of resources among the countries—not all resources but mostly financial resources. The flow of raw material and men is only technical in the sense that it eventually becomes either 'outsourcing' or cause foreign direct investments in other countries. This has been the present status of globalization. Countries that are signatories to the WTO arrangement have either totally changed their fiscal, monetary and economic policies or are in the process of bringing about changes in smaller yet effective doses in order to fulfil the ultimate requirements under globalization.

The debate is still on. The questions that are raised are many. Is globalization the best alternative path for economic development? What is the trade off between 'growth' and 'social welfare' and 'social justice'?

Will globalization bring in decentralised development? What are the serious trade-offs between 'Globalization' and 'Decentralised Development'? In what best way the conflicts can be reconciled within the framework of WTO? What will happen to specific sectors within an economy that pursues globalization? What happens to labour?

The papers presented in the Indian Economic Conference at Thiruvananthapuram on the theme have tried to dwell on the different questions raised. While a few of the papers have dealt with the basic philosophy and theories behind globalization examining its relevance in the context of a particular socio-economic arrangement, others have dealt with specific issues such as international trade in goods, services and finance. A few researchers have also gone further by examining the effects of globalization on money capital, physical resources and labour, in particular. Questions have been raised whether decentralised development is possible or furthered in a globalization scenario. A few writers have gone a little further in dealing with some of the commodities that have international market. Still a few have even tried to link globalization with the working of the Panchayati Raj Institutions in India. A few papers have also dealt with impact of globalization of specific states of India and are in the nature of case studies.

The number of papers received were more than 100. But each of the paper writers has done a very good job in presenting the point he or she wants to highlight. My most revered teacher Professor D.C. Mishra, former Vice-Chancellor, Sambalpur University has greatly helped me in the selection of papers for which I express my sincere gratitude to him. As the editor, it is necessary to make a candid confession that going through all the papers was a Herculean task. It was considered wise to refrain from discussing individual papers as this would be not only a lengthy process but also may carry an overtone of the bias of the editor. It is not claimed that the papers selected for this volume are the best nor is it claimed that the papers that have not found place in this volume are anyway inferior. Some amount of judgement was necessary in selecting the papers which the editor has a right to pronounce without hurting anybody's academic pride. The papers chosen are representative in nature and have bearing on the major issues spelt out here under the broad head of globalization.

The papers have been arranged into three broad sections. Section I deals with papers that are theoretical and deal with the philosophy of globalization. Section II contains the papers that are sector-specific, region-specific or goods-specific in nature while Section-III deals with papers that focussed on welfare issues.

It is hoped that the readers would appreciate the issues. As a concluding observation all that could be said that it is probably too early to pass any judgement on the subject.

Bhubaneswar

DR. GYANA CHANDRA KAR
Editor

List of Contributors

1. **Dr. D. Narasimha Reddy,** Professor of Economics, University of Hyderabad, Hyderabad.
2. **Dr. Ram Binod Singh,** Darbhanga, Bihar.
3. **Sri Sukumar Basu,** S.B. College (Retd.) Magra, West Bengal.
4. **Dr. J. Lenka,** Department of Economics, Bhadrak College, Bhadrak, Orissa.
5. **Dr. S.K. Dhage,** Department of Economics, Waghire College, Saswad, Maharashtra.
6. **Mrs. R. Meera,** Department of Economics, S.N.M.V. College of Arts and Science, Malumachampetti, Tamil Nadu.
7. **Dr. V. Radja Ramane,** Department of Economics, S.N.M.V. College of Arts and Science, Malumachampetti, Tamil Nadu.
8. **Sri C. Rajendran,** Department of Economics, S.N.M.V. College of Arts and Science, Malumachampetti, Tamil Nadu.
9. **Dr. A. Meenakshisundararajan,** PG Department of Economics and Research Centre, S.T. Hindu College, Nagercoil, Tamil Nadu.
10. **Dr. P.N. Rao,** Department of Economics, Nagarjuna University, Guntoor, Andhra Pradesh.
11. **Sri Debasis Chakraborty,** International Trade and Development Division, JNU, New Delhi.
12. **Sri Arup Guha,** International Trade and Development Division, JNU, New Delhi.
13. **Ms. Suchismita Mondal** (Research Scholar), Department of Economics, Burdwan University, Burdwan, West Bengal.

14. **Dr. Pinaki Chakraborti,** Professor of Economics, Burdwan University, Burdwan, West Bengal.
15. **Dr. Md. Abdus Salam,** Department of Economics, A.M.U., Aligarh, U.P.
16. **Dr. Saundarjya Borbora,** Department of Humanities and Social Sciences, IIT, Guwahati, Assam.
17. **Sri Ratul Mahanta** (Research Scholar), Department of Humanities and Social Sciences, IIT, Guwahati, Assam.
18. **Dr. R. Annapoorani,** Department of Economics, Avinashilingam University, Coimbatore, Tamil Nadu.
19. **Sri K. Nirmaladevi** (PG Student), Department of Economics, Avinashilingam University, Coimbatore, Tamil Nadu.
20. **Dr. Paramjit Nanda** (Reader), Punjab School of Economics, Guru Nanak Dev University, Amritsar, Punjab.
21. **Dr. P.S. Raikhy** (Professor), Punjab School of Economics, Guru Nanak Dev University, Amritsar, Punjab.
22. **Dr. K. Sai Haragopal,** Department of Economics, Osmania University, Hyderabad.
23. **Dr. S. Perumalsamy,** Professor of Economics, Bharathiar University, Coimbatore, Tamil Nadu.
24. **Mrs. P. Krishna Thulasimani,** Department of Economics, NGM College, Pollachi, Tamil Nadu.
25. **Dr. U.B. Kondewar,** Sharda College, Parbhaur, Maharashtra.
26. **Dr. Kapildeo Singh,** Department of Economics, Magadh University, Bodh Gaya, Bihar.
27. **Dr. P.K. Pal,** Department of Economics, Rabindra Bharati University, Kolkata.
28. **Dr. Pardeep Kumar,** Department of Economics, MCM DAV College, Kangra, Himachal Pradesh.
29. **Dr. S. Chinnammai,** Department of Economics, University of Madras PG Extension Centre, Vellore, Tamil Nadu.
30. **Sri Kanaga Sabesan Nagarajan,** Muladore, Chennai.
31. **Dr. Inderpal Kaur,** PSE, Guru Nanak Dev University, Amritsar, Punjab.
32. **Dr. V.S. Ganesamurthy,** Department of Economics, Sri Vasavi College, Erode, Tamil Nadu.
33. **Sri K. Mariappan,** Department of Economics, Sri Vasavi College, Erode, Tamil Nadu.

34. **Dr. Uday Kumar Lal Das,** Institute of Education and Rural Development Research, Darbhanga, Bihar.
35. **Prof. V.P. Tripathi,** DDU Institute of Rural Development, Agra, U.P.
36. **Dr. V. Prakash,** Department of Economics, Government PG College, Morena, M.P.
37. **Mr. Arun Bhadauria,** (Research Scholar), DDU Institute of Rural Development, Agra, U.P.
38. **Sri B.P. Chandramohan,** Department of Economics, Presidency College, Chennai.
39. **Dr. Gajavelli V. Swamy,** SDM Institute for Management Development, Mysore, Karnataka.
40. **Dr. A.R. Veeramani,** Professor of Economics, University of Madras, Chennai.
41. **Sri K. Ramesh,** Department of Economics, Government Arts College, Chennai.
42. **Dr. Davinder Kumar Madaan,** Economics Department, Guru Kashi College, Daur Charan Sahib, Punjab.
43. **Prof. S. Vijayalakshmi,** Department of Econometrics, Madurai Kamraj University, Madurai, Tamil Nadu.
44. **Dr. A.P. Pandey,** Economics Department, BHU, Varanasi.
45. **Dr. S.K. Mishra,** Economics Department, PG College, Sakaldiha, U.P.
46. **Dr. I.D. Singh,** Economics Department, PG College, Sakaldiha, U.P.
47. **Dr. Anil Kumar Choudhary,** Economics Department, Government PG College, Ambikapur, Chhattisgarh.
48. **Dr. L. Rathakrishnan,** Gandhigram Rural Institute, Gandhigram, Tamil Nadu.
49. **Sri N. Krishnakumar** (Research Scholar), Gandhigram Rural Institute, Gandhigram, Tamil Nadu.
50. **Sri S.K. Pant,** G.B. Pant Social Science Institute, Jhansi, U.P.
51. **Sri S.P. Saha,** JMDPL Mahila College, Madhubani, Bihar.
52. **Sri V.S. Paswan,** Research Scholar, LNM University, Darbhanga, Bihar.
53. **Ms. Supriya,** M.Phil. Student, Patna University, Patna.
54. **Ms. Nivedita Chaturvedi,** Research Scholar, MG Kashi Vidyapith, Varanasi, U.P.

SECTION I

THEORIES AND PHILOSOPHY OF GLOBALIZATION AND DECENTRALISED DEVELOPMENT

1

Globalization and Decentralised Development: Bringing Back the Nation-state

D. Narasimha Reddy

The main objective of this paper is to contextualise the present phase of globalization and to explore the possibility of realization of emanicipatory decentralized development under the present context. The paper is divided into three parts. After a brief survey of various interpretations, the first part sets out with the basic proposition that, globalization is a hegemonic process at the behest of the interests typically neo-imperialist. The second part explores the onslaught of globalization on development discourse. The third part tries to show from a few exemplar instances, as to how decentralized development needs enabling intervention by the state committee to national development.

The author is grateful to C.T. Kurien for his comments on an earlier draft.

I
GLOBALIZATION: WHY AND FOR WHOM?

Over the past two decades, globalization has been the topic of extensive debate. There has been wide variations in the definition of globalization, often causing confusion. At times attempts are made to theorise globalization in a manner, that only add to building myths around the concept. The growing interpretations of globalization has prompted many to build a taxonomy of 'glob-talk'. Schuurman (2001b) talks of nine different types of 'glob-talk', ranging from the 'true globalists' who consider globality as a new era which is still awaiting adequate concepts to describe it, to 'cyber space globalists', for whom it is the computer age effect on production, consumption and interpersonal relations. In this classification, there are, in between, 'neo-liberal globalists', who believe in the global spread of market logic as the end of history, as much as the 'diehard modernists' for whom globalization is coming to an end after the spread of modernity. The Neo-Marxist, post-modernist, historical and other varieties too habit this taxonomy, which only goes to show the range of possibilities of confusing the gullible.

However, most of the writings of those who have been explaining globalization as a process are grouped into two approaches, viz., 'open pluralism' and 'structured pluralism' (*Wilkin*, 1996). 'Open Pluralism' is attributed to those, who are influenced by Weberian theory of history and here globalization is depicted "as a process, that is contingent and multicentred in such a way, that there is no single site of power and transformation, that serves as a mechanism to drive it". In contrast, 'Structured Pluralism' is attributed to approaches based on historical materialsm, and these writings generally agree upon the proposition that the driving mechanisms of globalization are to be found in the structure of capitalism as a world-system and its logic. Whether all these writings have a template of 'pluralism' is doubtful, but the two-way competing explanations of the process of globalization is helpful in demystifying the debate.

First, let us consider the neo-liberal approach that, 'globalization' is an inevitable process that is unfolding from everywhere at once, with no centre and no discernible power structure. The 'fashionable' proponents of 'globalization' like

Michael Hardt and Antonio Negri in the *Empire* refer to global reality as one of "a fluid, infinitely expanding and highly organized system that encompasses the world's entire population without any privileged positions or places of power" or the one like Thomas Friedman in his, *The Lexus and the Olive Tree*, where he describes globalization as a new technological economic system, based in the microchip and ruled by an "electronic herd" of financial investors and multinational corporations, free from any nation state or power structure and beholden to none (for a critique of these works, see *Foster*, 2001, 2002). The peak of this process of propaganda that, 'globalization' has no manifest 'agent' is reached when the World Bank in its *World Development Report, 1996* attempts to enlist in its favour Marx and Engels by quoting from *The Communist Manifesto*: "Constant revolutionizing of production, uninterrupted disturbance of social conditions, everlasting uncertainty and agitation. . . . All fixed, fast frozen relations, with their train of ancient and venerable prejudices and opinions, are swept away, all new-formed ones become antiquated before they can ossify. All that is solid melts into air. . .". This is just one of those neo-liberal fallacies of appeal to authority, in this case to wrong ones, to argue, that the transition from planned to market economies under the present phase of globalization is an inseparable, elemental process, lacking any visible hand behind it (*Foster*, 2002). And an attempt to din the message that there is no alternative. Nothing can be more further from truth.

Approaches based on historical materialism would consider a process of expansion similar to what is described as 'globalization' have always been associated with the development of capitalism. Economic globalization is perceived not as a self-induced or natural process but as a process driven by mechanisms of capitalist expansion. These mechanisms could be either direct exercise of political power of domination and control as in the past, or indirect imposition of a set of policies that would bring out structural transformation to facilitate easier penetration of capital (*Bagchi*, 1999). Broadly, the 'materialist European expansion' of 1500-1800 and the 'imperialist expansion' of 1800-1950 are part of capitalist expansion (*Amin*, 2001), although the 'imperialist phase' is known for the faster pace and spread of capital, which is akin to the present 'globalization'. A comparison between these two phases is available elsewhere (*Economist*, 1997;

Reddy, 2002a), but presently we confine here to the 'globalization' of the present, a phenomenon unfolding during the last quarter of the Twentieth century, beginning with late 1970s. The idea, that the present phase of globalization is *not* a neutral or natural or inevitable process is essential for understanding its implications. Globalization is to be seen as one of the most hegemonic concepts for understanding the political economy of international capitalism (*Harvey*, 2000). In fact globalization has come to be regarded as the mother of all ideologically charged contemporary expressions (*Kurien*, 1994). The present era is defined by a fundamental reorganization of international relations, propped by processes of globalization, in which the form and the functions of the sovereign territorial nation-state are being redefined and reconstituted (*McGrew*, 1998). It is the very transformation in the nature of state power, rather than statehood *per se*, which constitutes a hindrance to substantive progress in many parts of the world. It is not as much as neutralizing nation-state but converting "the state into an agency for adjusting national economic practices and policies to the perceived exigencies of the global economy" (*Cox*, 2000). The present phase of 'globalization' is widely seen as "another word for the reach of American imperialism, the power of financial markets, the spread of capitalist social relations, the intensification of exploitation and a vast growth in social inequality" (*Panitch*, 2000). Without much difficulty, one could garner substantial evidence to show that it is the USA and its foreign military and commercial policies (*Harvey*, 2000) and the implicit consensus of the other capitalist powers and the multilateral institutions at their behest,—a consensus, that is now widely known as the "Washington Consensus"—that has put globalization on the agenda.

The critical questions are, as to why and how, during the last two decades, 'globalization' has become a key concept in the discussions on the way the world works. "1. Why is it that the world 'globalization' has recently entered into our discourses in the way it has? Who put it there and why and by means of what political project? . . . 2. How has the conception of globalization been used politically? Has the adoption of the term signaled a confession of powerlessness on the part of national, regional and local working class or other anti-capitalist movements? Has the belief in the term operated as a powerful deterrent to local and even national 'political action'? . . ." (*Harvey*, 2000). David Harvey suggests four important and interrelated shifts at the global level. The financial deregulation beginning in the US in the early 1970s, the profound technological innovations since mid-1960s, the "information revolution" that has facilitated a dematerialized cyberspace globally, and the steep fall in the cost and time of moving commodities and people, have all contributed towards globalizing production and finance (*Harvey*, 2000). To this, we could add the compulsions of the crisis following the 1945-73 'golden age' of capitalism.

First was the crisis in capitalism, which was sparked-off by the first oil crisis on 1973. The developed capitalist countries had a virtual 'golden age' during 1945-73 with unprecedented growth and prosperity. During this period, substantial flows of investment and trade was within the block of developed capitalist countries. Trade and investment in the Third World was only of supplementary interest. But, the steep hike in the oil prices by the OPEC at the behest of the Arab countries in 1973 in the wake of Arba-Israel war, severely affected the economies of the industrial countries which were heavily dependent on hydrocarbon-based energy. The balance of payments situation of these industrial countries were adversely affected, beginning with 1973-74 (*Krishna Kumar*, 1993). With this, production costs inflated and efficiency plummeted. Closely on the heels of the first, there was a 'second shock' in 1979 by way of further steep rise in oil prices, which precipitated into a global economic crisis, affecting the developed countries too adversely.

Second, closely on the heels of the 1973 economic crisis, there was 'deindustrialization' in 1980s showing contraction of output or employment in the manufacturing employment, which was experiencing marginal decline from 1950s, accelerated from 1973, and declined from 32 percent to 27 percent in 1981. Between 1973 and 1983, manufacturing employment had fallen in almost all industrial countries. The share of manufacturing output in the GDP of the industrial countries continuously increased during the long boom of 1945-73 and reached a peak by the end of this period. But during 1973-83, the growth of manufacturing output was much slower than even the slow GDP growth. The widely held view about de-industrialization is that, it has been caused by the industrialization of the South, especially the newly industrializing countries (NIC) like Korea, Taiwan, Brazil, Mexico, India (*Ajit Singh*, 1991).

Third, there has been substantial increase in the share of developing countries in the global manufacturing output. It was projected that by the end of the century, the developing countries will account for more than half of the share. It is projected that by 2020, the share of developing countries in manufacturing will be over 60 percent, and three out of five major manufacturing countries in the world would be from the present developing countries (*Economist*, 1994).

Fourth, there were critical changes in the structure of output and employment, in the developed countries in the last three decades. Beginning with 1970s, there have been drastic changes in technology, particularly in biotechnology and microchip-based technology. This has brought about a sea change not only in the very nature and composition of the production in the developed capitalist countries, but also in the organization of production. It is this technology, that made post-Fordist decentred organization of work and net-working possible. By 1990s, in the highly developed G-7 countries, 70 to 80% of national income and employment were generated in non-goods producing sector. The share of agricultural output and employment contracted to 2 to 10%. The share of manufacturing sector contracted to 15 to 20% in the national income and employment. So much so, the highly developed economies have come to be described as "service economies". These economies are now characterized by widely diversified service activities, which include both producer services, especially business services, financial and social services, entertainment and the all pervasive information technology to their aid.

Further, during the Cold War era, one of the key elements of the US political strategy was strengthening of local capitalisms. But with the fall of socialism in the Eastern Bloc and the disintegration of the Soviet Union, the rationale for such support to national or local capitalisms dissolved (*Baker* 2000) and turned into a rhetoric against any form of intervention as distorionist obstruction to global development.

II
GLOBALIZATION AND 'DEVELOPMENT'

The unfolding of the process of globalization is accompanied by a vehement *attack on the very world view of development* and with it the *institutional premises* which served as the foundation of mainstream, development theories and strategies in the third world countries during the three decades following the second world war. The image or worldview of development or what may be called the dream of 'development' embedded in the mainstream approach, has been 'becoming like West'. For the realization of this development dream, especially in the context of the Third World, where the markets are far from being perfect, the nation-state, playing the role of accumulator, as well as dynamic entrepreneurs, is conceived as the essential intervening institution. With globalization in 1980s and 1990s, the criticism against these mainstream notions of development came from two sources, which apparently appear to be opposed to each other, viz. (i) a variety of alternative or post-development critiques which, for the sake of convenience, we shall call post-modernism, and (ii) the neo-liberalism. While post-modernism attacks both the images of 'development' as 'becoming like the West' and the institutional premises viz., the nation-state, neo-liberalism in the name of 'counter revolution', retains the 'Eurocentric' image of development but targets the role of nation-state. We shall briefly consider the implications of these critiques, which have come to the fore with the present phase of globalization.

(i) Post-modernism, Post-Development and Alternative Development[1]

Since there is a considerable overlap of the post-modern and certain radical populist criticism of development, these are brought together for the sake of convenience. We shall first analyze, what could be distinguished as post-modern critique in the name of 'post-development' or 'anti-development' and then turn to the populist 'alternative development'.

After the post-modern cultural turn has upset most social sciences, it finally has come to economics and the bundle of practices called development. The most scathing critique is from those inclined towards post-structuralism and post-modernism.

A particular mention may be made here of the 'post-development' or 'anti-development' critics. **'Post-development'** is a radical reaction to the dilemmas of development. It is a cultural critique of economics as a foundational basis of modernity, including the formulation of a culture-based political economy (*Escobar*, 1995). A keen analyst of development summarizes the critique of 'development' by 'post-development' writers as follows: "Perplexity and extreme dissatisfaction with business as usual and standard development rhetoric and practice, and illusion with alternative development are keynotes of this perspective. Development is rejected, because it is the 'new religion of the West' (*Rist*, 1998), it means cultural westernization and homogenization (*Constantino*, 1985) and brings environmental destruction. It is rejected not merely on account of its results, but because of its intentions, its world view and mindset. The mindset of economism implies a rejectionist taking on existence. Thus, according to Sachs, 'it is not the failure of development, which is to be feared, but its success' (*Sachs*, 1992)" (*Pieterse*, 2001).

The post-modernists construct the post-Second World War development paradigm as consisting of three shared characteristics (*Shuuriman*, 2001a). One is essentialization of the entire. Third World as a homogenous entity. Second is unconditional belief in 'progress' or make ability of society or simply 'development'. Third is the importance of nation-state as an analytical frame of reference and the political and scientific confidence in the role of the State to realize progress. All these characteristics are rejected by the post-modernists. The idea of homogenous Third World is easy to deconstruct. The idea of 'progress' is seen as an imposition of an external construct to subjugate 'other' people. And the State is hollowed out as powerless in the face of global onslaught and local government is projected as an example of good governance.

'Post-development' starts out from a basic realization: that attaining middle class lifestyle for the majority of the world population is impossible. And moving towards this modal middle class life, indeed is the mainstream notion of development. In time, this contrast had led to the post-modern position of total rejection of development. Post-development overlaps with the Western critic of modernity. It parallels alternative development and cultural critics of development. It stands against development as "deep ecology does to environmental management". The emphasis of the criticism is on the construction of development economics as a tool to control the underdeveloped by raising unreasonable hopes. There are many such critical voices against 'development'. "Post-development is not alone in looking at the shadow of development, of critical approaches to development dealing with its dark sides. As shown earlier, dependency theory raises the question of inequity. Alternative development focuses on the lack of popular participation. Human development addresses the need to invest in people Post-development focuses on the underlying premises and motives of development, and what sets it apart from other critical approaches is its rejection of development" (*Pieterse*, 2001). But, it is the rejection of development, without any alternative that makes 'post-development' more as a culture critique than as a constructive alternative.

A clear line of distinction may have to drawn between 'post-development' and 'alternative development'. While the former rejects 'development', the latter desires a different development. Those who argue for 'alternative development' also direct their criticism on the mainstream notion of development as becoming like the West as well as the role of state. 'Alternative Development' is a generic expression to capture several activist critiques of development. One may include under this rubric '**Alternative Development**' emphasizing increased NGO action in certain spaces, hitherto occupied by the State, those who insist on '**Endogenous Development**' insisting that development is endogensus and that there are no front runners to be followed; those who refer to **Ethno-Development** with tribes and nations as the basic units of development; and those who insist on '**Human Development**' focusing on qualitative and distributional aspects are also drawn into the rubric. '**Alternative Development**' could be seen as redefinition of development as "a process, by which the members of a society increase their personal and institutional capacities to mobilize and manage resources to produce sustainable and justly distributed improvements in their quality of life consistent with their own aspirations" (*Pieterse*, 2001). 'Alternative Development' to a large extent emphasizes the need for appropriate and sustainable development but does not totally reject development as a goal for the Third World.

Implications for Third World Development[2]

What needs to be understood is that the substantive part of the post-modern criticism is directed at the business civilization of multinational corporations with links to nation-state and against the covert world of invisible manipulation carried out by dominant world powers and international crime networks, which have come to increasingly replace the political space. Therefore, the whole range of post-modern concerns like new social movements or civil society-based counter hegemonic struggles like gender, sexuality, family and social care, environmental issues and various kinds of social identity are directly *anti-political* and focused on the "life world" (*Baker,* 2000). Indeed these struggles are focused on the developed world. In the Third World the situation is different. People still have growing, than failing, aspirations to make use of state power for socio-economic goals. The mobilizations have often been *political* and there has been a surge of nationalism. There is realization of the need to use nation-state as a site of resistance to the global onslaught.

(ii) Neoliberal Counter-Revolution[3]

In the wake of globalization, the second major source of attack on 'development', came from the 'Counter Revolution' (CR) in development theory, and it is based on regrouping of bits and pieces of neo-classical critique of dirigisme. The very expression 'CR' is intended to contrast with the Keynesian 'revolution in economics by way of bringing State intervention'. An excellent summary of the antecedents of 'CR' in development theory is provided by Toye (1987). We shall briefly summarize here the nature of the 'CR' critique of 'development'. The strands that are drawn from the so-called New Political Economy (NPE), to constitute the 'Counter Revolution' are essentially the theory of 'rent-seeking' (*Krueger,* 1974) or 'directly unproductive profit-seeking (DUP) activities' (*Bhagwati,* 1982). The basic proposition of 'rent-seeking' theory is that State intervention by way of controls or restrictions on the economic activity generates a variety of rents—some legal and many illegal. And people often compete for these rents. For instance, State intervention by way of licensing may provide monopoly advantage to the one obtaining a license and thereby enable earning of profits, which have substantial unearned or rental element. In the face of State intervention by way of quantitating restrictions or regulations, rent seeking may take other forms, such as bribery, corruption, smuggling, and black markets. These rents are likely to generate competition for unproductive activities associated with rents and thus represent the inefficient utilization of resources. It is generalized that the poor performance of developing countries is due to the pervasive State intervention inspired by the strategies of 'development'. Krueger's analysis was restricted to the competitive rent-seeking arising out of quantitative restriction upon international trade in India and Turkey. Bhagwati (1982), with some modification, extended rent-seeking as a generalized theory. He introduces the concept of 'directly unproductive profit seeking (DUP) activities', which include rent-seeking and other forms of premium and revenue seeking. DUP activities represent ways of making a profit by undertaking activities, which are directly unproductive. They yield pecuniary returns but do not produce goods or services. When resources are devoted to DUPs these resources are diverted from productive activities and to that extent, represent inefficient use of resources. He refers to DUPs of different types like policy triggered (rent-seeking), policy evading (smuggling) and policy influencing (demanding tariffs on certain imports) (*Dasgupta*, 1997). All these DUPs are described as State intervention induced ones that cause welfare loss. The generalized 'economic reform' strategy has, thus, found 'rent seeking' and DUPs proposition as the central theoretical arguments against the intervening State or dirigisme in 'development'.

Thus, equipped, by mid-1980, the 'Counter-Revolution' paradigm tried to equate the mainstream development theory and development economics with State intervention or dirigisme. The extreme formulations under 'Counter Revolution' like that of Deepak Lal (1983) go to the extent of suggesting that all ills of developing economies are due to the interventionist policies of the State and suggested, that the demise of 'development economics', meaning State intervention, is good for economics and developing economies' (*Toye*, 1987). The 'Counter Revolution' is an effort to restore the markets, the role of efficient allocation of resources and with that, pave the way for structural adjustment from the primacy of State towards market-oriented economic reforms.

Implications for the Third World Development

The implications of neoliberal counter revolution in development theory are quite clear. It serves as the foundation of globalization which emphasizes markets as the only alternative for efficient growth and a neutral state is conducive to maximize private prosperity. It views 'inequality' is, in itself, a good thing, as it creates progress and wealth. But the experience of globalization during the last two decades has shown devastating effects in the form of growing inequality between and within countries, falling incomes and employment of those with less skills and failure of social security of the growing marginalized and vulnerable groups (*Reddy,* 2002a). The question is, how to resist these adverse effects of globalization and restore development on to the main agenda of the Third World that still needs it most.

III
DECENTRALISED DEVELOPMENT: NEED FOR STATE

This part of the paper provides a brief appraisal of the limitations of both the post-modern and neoliberal approaches which take globalization as an inevitable process and project decentralization as the alternative strategy of development and good governance as local governments. One of the defining features of the present phase of globalization is the post-Fordist decentralized production and centralized control. The neoliberal argument reins that, decentralized globalization provides a great deal of impetus for production in different parts of the world. The 'alternative development' and 'post-development' arguments appear to lend an argument on the political and cultural grounds that decentralization and local governance is a progressive process benefiting the poor. The question is whether globalization really result in spread of decentralized production? Whether spatial unbundling of production under globalization results in decentralized development by way of improved employment generation and income distribution in the local areas brought under the network? Or, does the process of decentralization as a part of the global networking of production and foot-loose investment actually disempower progressive elements in the civil society and disable the state to intervene in favour of equity and social justice. In other words, in minimizing state, doesn't decentralization aid in removing whatever remaining obstacles to the global presence of capitalism? After a brief discussion of these issues, attention is drawn to a few instances of successful decentralized development which is made possible through appropriate state initiative in the face of globalization.

It may be helpful to discern the economic, political and cultural dimensions of globalization and the related coalition in favour of decentralization (*Schuurman*, 1997). The two sides of the neo-liberal economic agenda of globalization is the 'hollowing out the state' through Structural Adjustment Programme (SAP) on the one hand, and the post-Fordist reorganization of flexible production on the other. The SAP with an emphasis on deregulation of state intervention, privatization of state assets, curtailment of subsidies on some of the basic services, promotion of export-led industrialization, and an opening up of the economy to international capital has provided a politico-economic channel for dissemination of the decentralization discourse to the Third World (*Schuurman*, 1997). The thrust of the SAPs is on 'rolling back the state'. A similar process is seen in the developed capitalist countries with dismantling of the Fordist welfare state. It is the unfolding of the post-Fordist flexible productions, a flexible workforce, differentiation of the production of goods and services, technological innovation as the guiding principle of production and the rolling back of the regulatory powers of the state that have come to emphasize decentralized development as the local dimension of globalization.

One of the important political dimensions of globalization beginning with 1980s is the so-called "transition to democracy" from dictatorships in Latin America and Africa, and from erstwhile East-European centrality of state. The social movements and the popularity of Gramsci's writings among the Left provided an ideological basis for embracing decentralization in Latin America. Basismo was seen as an "alternative development". The lack of pronounced national identity and persistence of regional solidarity, often ethnic or clan-based, served as the basis for gaining ground, for decentralization in Africa (*Schuurman*, 1997). The cultural dimension of globalization emphasized by the post-modernism lends support to the decentralization discourse. There are two terms of post-modern reasoning: "The first is that post-modern discourse, like decentralization discourse emphasizes the particular, in contradistinction to the modernist emphasis on the universal. The other, to use the post-modern term, has increasingly come under the global spotlight along with the hitherto untold stories of the excluded in the Third World. The local, then, is the spatial frame of reference for the other in Third World to tell his or her story. As such post-modernism unwittingly supported a centralization discourse.

"The second link comes from those post-modernists (a minority) who are interested in giving the 'other' a political as well as a cultural voice. In this case, decentralization provides a suitable local political context in which the other can effectively organize and confront the political powerholders. The newly emerging school of communitarians . . . is making headway in post-modernist circles which favour decentralization" (*Schuurman*, 1997).

Impact of Economic Decentralization[4]

The experience of economic globalization on employment, wages and income distribution has been devastatingly different from the promise of decentralized development. Under the spell of globalization, through casualisation, informalisation, flexibilisation, feminisation, growing wage disparities and reduced opportunities for employment are felt in developed countries as well. The present analysis is confined to some of the experiences in the Third World countries.

Privatization of public sector, decentralized production through sub-contracting and home-based production, deregulation of labour markets, transfer of jobs from the formal to the informal sector undermined the position of labour as a factor of production and labour as a class. The process of sub-contracting with the exception of early Japanese experience, has been highly exploitative as in Southeast Asia where sub-contracting has been widely prevalent. Due to fierce competition among small and informal supplying firms, the large firms, can choose their sub-contractors. The formed sector exploits the existing sharp differentials in job security, wage levels and safety standards by sub-contracting to smaller and informal firms and thereby avoiding costs of social security and high wages. With the emergence of dual production structures, the major proportion of risks, hardships and uncertainties of small enterprises are in turn transferred to hapless workers in these sweatshops (Thomas *et. al.*, 1994).

The forces shaping globalization seem to affect women in ways which suggest increasing feminization of employment, which may not always mean improved employment status for women. Though globally the importance of agriculture for employment is diminishing for women as well as for men, women are moving out of agriculture at a slower pace than men. As a result, women's representation in the agricultural labour force of developing countries is increasing (*Mehra and Gammage*, 1999). During 1980-90, for the developing countries as a whole, it rose from 41 to 43 percent. There has also been an increase of women's employment in manufacturing, particularly in Asia, but only in certain low-paid and low-skilled areas. Standing shows that it is the spread of more flexible and informal employment that accounts for much of the upward trend in the female share of the labour force. The decade spanning the late 1980s and 1990s is one of feminization of flexible labour in industries where profit margins are protected by reducing labour costs, extending hours and decreasing the numbers of formal production workers (*Standing*, 1999). The greatest increase in female share of manufacturing employment is in countries, which adopted export-oriented low-technology high-labour-based industrialization, especially by setting up export processing zones (EPZs) for textiles, garments, shoes and electronics. Women seek employment in these activities, though wages are lower and working hours longer, because alternatives are not much better. Employers, seeking to gain and maintain competitiveness in global markets, are inclined to substitute female for male workers. Governments, seeking employment and foreign exchange gains, exempt them from labour regulations. Often unions are not permitted in EPZs and women have little bargaining power (*Mehra and Gammage*, 1999). There has been fastest growth of women's employment in the South-East Asian export-oriented industries, especially in EPZs, and newer industries. But these are also the locales of widespread sex-based segregation of jobs. The forces of free trade, technological change that divide workers into a small group of highly-skilled highly-paid workers at the one end, and a large number of low-skilled low-paid workers and the resulting organizational changes in the form of sub-contracting and home-based production have driven women into the low-end jobs.

Many of the South-East Asian countries have not even ratified the ILO Convention No. 100 on 'equal pay for equal work'. While feminization of employment is in increasing evidence, the experience has been varied. In India, like Bangladesh and Pakistan, there has been higher growth of female employment compared to male, especially in agriculture. It is happening in the face of stagnation in non-agricultural work, unlike the rapid growth of manufacturing employment in South-East Asian NICs. Much of this female employment is distress-induced supply of female labour than the demand-driven (*Ghosh*, 1999). 'Home workers' is yet another category of degraded labour dominated by female share that is rapidly growing. Employers choose employment contracts with home workers because they are cost-minimizing. These workers actually subsidize capitalist growth by providing infrastructure, tools, equipment and often work below minimum wages (*Chen, et. al.*, 1999). Most of these informal labour markets, under the pressures of the so-called competitiveness as a part of the globalization, are constructed on gendered basis because all the burdens of reproductive economy will be borne largely by women (*Elson*, 1999). Of course, it is true that "the impact of globalization on women's paid labour is far more complex than generally assumed. While it may open up certain opportunities for 'elite' women, it tends to drive many other women into destitution. The economic polarization resulting from globalization sets the dynamics for labour migration as well as its feminization" (*Cheng*, 1999).

During 1980-91, under the influence of globalization, the minimum wages actually declined in several Latin American countries. It fell by 40% in Venezuela, by 60% in Mexico and by 85% in Peru. Besides inflation and weaker union bargaining power, the main reason behind the declining minimum wages is the deliberate policy to abandon minimum wage legislation for the sake of stabilization and adjustment (*Tokman*, 1992). In Africa, real wages became downwardly flexible (*Collier*, 1995). The inequality in income within the countries and across the countries have increased drastically. The wage ratio between developed and developing countries stood at 70 to 1 in 1990. The share of the poorest 50% of the world population in the global income decreased from 7.3% in 1960 to 6.3% in 1986 while the richest 20% of the world improved their share from 71.3% to that of 74.1%.

Increasing unemployment as a consequence of globalization has been one of the major causes for concern all over the world. Among the Latin American countries, there was a surge in unemployment towards two-digit level by 1994-95. Though there is a problem of direct data on unemployment in Africa and parts of Asia, the indications are that there has been persistence of underemployment and poverty in many of these countries (*ILO*, 1996). A review of the employment effects of economic reforms in South Asia (*Islam*, 1996) shows that except for Sri Lanka, the entire South Asian region experienced declining employment growth, especially in the organized private sector, during 1980s and 1990s. Textile, garment, shoe and electronic plants that have spearheaded the 'economic miracle' of Taiwan began to shut down one by one in the 1980s, when globalization took off and capital shifted abroad. Between 1993 and 1995, more than 1,74,000 companies and plants ceased to operate, many leaving their workers without jobs, severance pay or even back wages. More than half of them were women, and due to age-sex discrimination, had to seek low wage work further down the 'flexible' work or remain unemployed (*Cheng*, 1999). There is no wonder that one of the major evaluation of the impact of SAP on the Third World, comes to a very caustic conclusion that it has resulted in growth which is 'Jobless, ruthless, voiceless, rootless and futureless" (*HDR*, 1996).

Political Decentralization?

Under globalization the political dimension of "hollowing out of state", as seen earlier, has presented decentralization seen through democratization or social movements particularly in the context of Latin America and Africa. The experience is illustrated here with the example of Chile (*Schuurman*, 1997). The process shows that many poor regions and municipalities remain very dependent on redistributed national funds. Since they have not attracted much investments, they have no greater financial autonomy. The method of distribution of central resources often fail to break the vicious circle of poverty in poor regions. The social movements and the non-governmental organizations at the regional level are also fragmented and are often coopted by political parties. Poor regions are caught in the disadvantage of lower capabilities for planning which becomes cumulative. The local councils in the decentralized framework are fragmented and the local officialdom as well as the party functionaries neglect these councils. Local party functionaries treat the local council as only a stepping stone to reach more lucrative and powerful positions at the national level. It is observed that as a consequence inequalities in welfare between communities have not diminished. There has been persistence of fragmentation between neofeudal attitude of political parties and the aspirations of social movements. "Decentralization in itself is no guarantee that things will improve for the poor". (*Schuurman*, 1997). The emancipatory potential decentralization is questioned by Mohanty (1995) . . . 'Empowerment', 'civil society' and 'democratisation' form the new package of liberalization discourse which on their own face value respond to the longstanding demand of struggling groups. In practice, however, each of them has been given a restricted meaning and has been oriented to serve the present global drive of western capitalism". (quoted in *Schuurman*, 1997).

Culture and Decentralisation

A glib 'glob-talk' of post-modernism is the 'emancipatory spaces[3] offered by globalization, one of which is local space, sometimes called 'third space', as different from private and public space. There seems to have evolved a global euphoria concerning the economic, political, and cultural emancipatory potentials of local space (*Schuurman*, 2001b). This comes with an acronym 'global' and goes with a slogan "think globally and act locally". It is really to give a misleading impression that post-modern approach would lead to more appropriate locally rooted strategies of well-being. But we are cautioned by experience that emancipatory projects limited to local space are likely to end up as reactionary ones, since these are likely to cause further fragmentation. Such dangers are more likely in the context of time-space compression, i.e. globalization. "We thus approach the central paradox: the less important the spatial barriers, the greater the sensitivity of capital to the variations of place within space, and the greater the incentive for places to be differentiated in ways attractive to capital. The result has been the production of fragmentation, insecurity, and ephemeral uneven development within a highly unified global space economy of capital flows. The historic tension within capitalism between centralization and decentralization is now being worked out in new ways" (Harvey quoted in *Schuurman*, 2001b).What is implied is that in the face of globalization any unprotected decentralization would only uproot the poor. "As long as the current instability of the international economic and financial system lasts, as long as the decentralization disclosure, emphasizing local space, contributes to hollowing out the state, and as long as there is no institutionalized social contract at the global and/or local level, it is rather premature to parade decentralization as the post-Fordist paracea. Concentrating on the emancipatory potential of local space could well turn out to be a neoliberal cul-de-sac for the poor in the Third World". (*Schuurman*, 2001b). Serious doubts are expressed on the possibility of the poor and voiceless local communities gaining through the expected ability to express themselves freely in the transnational space under globalization. The question raised is that of subaltern groups manage to let their voice be heard globally then who is out there listening to them? They might be shouting in a vacuum, because of a crumbling international solidarity (*Schuurman*, 2001b).

There is need for nation-state to serve as the focus of identity and help communities to realize their aspirations. Globalization indeed has undermined the autonomy of nation-state but the promised spread of unbundled post-Fordist decentralized development is nowhere in sight. On the contrary with the erosion of state regulatory authority, the influence of other global actors like the multinational corporations, the international financial institutions and the powerful capitalist countries like the G-7 have been increasingly affecting the social, economic and cultural rights. These agencies are the active promoters of globalization. Global accumulation in all its aspects undermines the value of local diversity and legitimizes the dominant liberal agenda, presenting it as universal, natural and common sense. Yet, it is rooted in a different kind of local, essentially Western, capitalist world view (*Thomas*, 1998). The game of globalization in a world of unequal partners and asymmetrical rules has been accentuating uneven development all over. The need is for nation-states to undertake appropriate policy correctives. The importance of the role of the State lies more as a guarantor of social contracts but not as much as a monopoly law-maker with monopoly of means of violence. Under the globalization, the role of upholding rule of law is relatively independent of those other elements of authoritarian traits that go with it. There are no signs at all of the development of global or local social contracts. Protection of legitimate rights of the citizens and ensuring of equitable development needs states intervention.

Many successful instances of decentralized development in the face of globalization show a clear national strategy. The classic examples in this regard are in the realm of rural transformation. The "Asian successes" (*Xu* and *Tan*, 2001, *Hari*, 1998, *Chang*, 1993) are contrasted with "African failures" (*Haggblade*, 1989) in terms of state's presence and absence in promoting decentralized development. The success of the state-led "Asian model" of development was well acknowledged before the World Bank and the US academic establishment started wrongly blaming 1997 "Asian Crises" as a result of excessive state support or 'crony capitalism' or Asian family capital or whatever (*Biker*, 2000). Returning to the instances of successful state interventions in Asia. Hart (1998) rejects the neoliberal 'new agrarian optimism' that diversification of local rural economies emerges automatically from agricultural growth and fee market expansion. He shows that the spectacular growth of non-farm sector especially in China beginning with 1980s has been due to the institutional innovations at the behest of the state with adequate operational autonomy to local enterprises. The success story of rural industrial development in China is narrated in a different way by Chang (1993), but recognizing the institutional innovativeness of the state industrial policy. Even those who refer to post-Mao reforms as a turning point in the improvement of rural conditions, recognize the role of state strategy. (*Oi*, 1999). Another study of rural transformation in the 1980s and 1990s reveals dynamic process and operating mechanisms of rural economic changes at local level, and the intervening of relationships among the state, local governments, and peasants under the reformed institutional framework of rural development (*Xu* and *Tan*, 2001).

The decentralized industrial development even in Europe point to the need for appropriate state policy, though in tune with local needs and external challenges, globalization has erased 'industrial policy' because it implies pervasive presence of the

State. But successful European experience of decentralized industrial development in the era of globalization shows the need for appropriate orientation of state policy rather than leaving it to the market. The successes in Germany, Northern Italy, Southern France, and Eastern Spain shows the role of creation of social and institutional externalities in promoting competitiveness of decentralized industrial development (*Bianchi*, 1996).

In the era of globalization there have been hardly any instances of sustained decentralized equitable development in the Third World without appropriate state intervention. Paradoxically the degree to which the world economy has internationalized (but not globalized) reinstates the need for the nation state, not in its traditional guise as the sole sovereign power, but as a crucial relay between the international levels of governance and the aspirations of the people of the Third World.

Notes and References

1. This section drawn much from Schuurman (2001a) and Pieterse (2001).
2. Baker (2000) brings out these aspects sharply.
3. For more elaborate discussion see Schuurman (2001b).
4. For an extended discussion of these aspects see Schuurman (1997).

References

Amin, Samin, (2001): "Imperialism and Globalization", *Monthly Review*, June, Vol. 53, No. 2.

Bagchi, A.K., (1999); "Globalization, Liberalization and Vulnerability of India and Third World", *Economic and Political Weekly*, 34(45), 6 November.

Baker, Chris, (2000); "Opportunity and Danger: Globalization; States and Politics in 1990s Asia", Conference on *'Globalization, Income Distribution and Structural Change'*, Chennai, 14-17 December.

Becathini, G. and E. Ruilani, (1996); "Local Systems and Global Connections": The Role of Knowledge in Cossentino (1996).

Bharati, S., (1997); "The Impact of Structural Adjustment on Women": A Governance and Human Rights Agenda", *Human Rights Quarterly*, Vol. 11, pp. 630-665.

Bhagwati, J.N., (1982); "Directly unproductive, Profit-seeking (DUP) Activities", *Journal of Political Economy*, Vol. 90, No. 5.

Bianchi, P., (1996); "New Approaches to Industrial Policies at the Local Level" in Cossentino (1996).

Brusco, S., (1996); "Global Systems and Local Systems" in *Cosseantino* (1996).

Chang, Kyung-Sup., (1993); "The Peasant Family in the Transition from Maoist to Lewisian Rural Industrialisation," *Journal of Development Studies*, Vol. 29, No. 2, January, 220-244.

Chakravarthy, Sukmoy, (1986); "Development Dialogue in the 1980s and Beyond", *Presidential Address to 69th Annual Conference of the Indian Economic Association*, New Delhi.

Chen, M. *et. al.*, (1999); "Counting the Invisible workforce: The Case of Home-based Workers", *World Development*, Vol. 27, No. 3, March, 603-610.

Cheng, L., (1999); "Globalization and Women's Paid Labour in Asia," *International Social Science Journal*, (UNESCO) No. 160.

Collier, Paul, (1995); "On African Labour Markets in "Round Table Discussion on Employment and Development", *Proceedings of the World Bank Annual Conference on Development Economics, 1994*, World Bank, Washington.

Cossentino, F. *et. al.* (eds.) (1996); Local and Regional Response to Global Pressure: The Case of Italy and Its Industrial Districts, Geneva, International Institute for Labour Studies.

Cox, Robert, (2000); "Political Economy and World Order: Problems of Power and Knowledge at the Turn of the Millennium" in *Political Economy and Changing Global Order*, ed. By Richard Stubbs and Geoffrey, R.C. Underbill, Oxford University Press, Ontario.

Dubois, M., (1991); "The Governance of the Third World: A Foncauldian Perspective on Power Relations in Development", *Alternatives*, Vol. 16, No. 1, Winter.

Elson, D., (1999), "Labour Markets as Gendered Institutions: Equality, Efficiency and Empowerment Issues", *World Development*, Vol. 27, No. 3, March 611-627.

Escobar, A., (1995); "Encountering Development", Princeton University Press, Princeton, N.J.

Foster, J.B., (2001); "Imperialism and Empire", *Monthly Review*, Vol. 53, No. 1, December.

Foster, J.B., (2002); "Monopoly Capital and the New Globalization", *Monthly Review*, January, Vol. 53, No. 8.

Frank, Andre Gunder, (1996); "The Underdevelopment of Development" in Chew, S.C. and R.A. Denmark (ed.), *The Underdevelopment of Development*, Sage, London.

Frank, A.G., (1996); "The Underdevelopment of Development" in Chew, S.C. and R.A. Denmark (eds.), *The Underdevelopment of Development*, Sage, London.

Gore, C., (2000); "The Rise and Fall of the Washington Consensus as a Paradigm for Developing Countries", *World Development*, Vol. 28, No. 5.

Gosh, J., (1999); "Macro-economic Trends and Female Employment: India in the Asian Context" in Popola, T.S. and A.N. Sharma (eds.) *Gender and Employment in India*, Vikas Publication House, New Delhi.

Haggblade, S. *et. al.*, (1989); "Farm-Non-form Linkages in Rural Sub-Saharan Africa", *World-Development*, Vol. 17, No. 8, 1173-1201.

Hart, G., (1998); Linkages in the Era of Liberalization: A Critique of the New Agrarian Optimsm", *Development and Change*, Vol. 29, 27-54.

Harey, David, (2000); Spaces of Hope, Edinburgh University Press, Edinburgh.

Hirst, Paul and G. Thompson, (1996); *Globalization in Question*, London, Polity Press.

Hooshand Amirahmadi, (1987); "The Non-Capitalist Way of Development", *Review of Radical Political Economics*, Vol. 19(1).

Islam, R., (1996); "Economic Reforms, Employment and Labour Market in South Asia", *Indian Journal of Labour Economics*, Vol. 39, No. 3, July-September.

ILO, (1996); "World Employment 1996/97: National Policies in a Global Context", ILO, Geneva.

Khor, M., (1996); "Globalization: Implications for Development Policy", Third World Resurgence, No. 74.

Krishna Kumar, T., (1993); "Fund-Bank Policies of Stabilization and Structural Adjustment: A Global and Historical Perspective", *Economic and Political Weekly*, April 23.

Krueger, Anne, (1974); "The Political Economy of the Rent Seeking Society", *The American Economic Review*, June.

Kurien, C.T., (1994); Global Capitalism and the Indian Economy, Hyderabad, Orient Longmen.

McGrew, A.G., (1998); "Human Rights in a Global Age: Coming to Terms with Globalization" in Tony Eavans (ed.), *op. cit*.

Mehra, R. and S. Gummage, (1999); "Trends, Countertrends and Gaps in Women's Employment," *World Development*, Vol. 27, No. 3, March 533-550.

Naqui, Syed Nawale Haider, (1984); "Development Economists in Emperor's Clothes?" *The Pakistan Review*, Vol. XXIII, No. 2 & 3.

Naqui, S.N.H., (2002); "Development Economics: Nature and Significance", New Delhi, Sage Publications.

Oi, J.C., (1993); "Reform and Urban Bias in China", *Journal of Development Studies*, Vol. 29, No. 4, July, 129-148.

Panitch, L., (2000); "Reflections on Strategy for Labour" in Panitch, L. and Colin Leys (ed.) *Working Classes—Global Realities: Socialist Register*, 2001, Merlin Press, London.

Pieterse, J.N., (2001); "Development Theory: Deconstructions/ Reconstruction", Vistar, New Delhi.

Rahnema, M. and Victoria Bawtree (eds.), (1997); The Post-Development Reader, Zed Press, London.

Reddy, D.N., (2002), Development Economics in Disarray, Presidential Address, XX Annual Conference, AP Economic Association, S.K.R. Women's College, Rajahmundary, 9-10 February.

Reddy, D.N., (2002a); "Economic Globalization and Labour Movement: The Challenge and Response", paper presented at the SEPHIS Conference on 'Globalization and Its Discontents, Revisited', Kaula Lumpur, 14-16 June, 2002.

Rodrik, D., (1997), Has Globalization Gone Too Far? Institute for International Economics, Washington.

Schuurman, F.J., (1997); "The Decentralization Discourse: Post-Fordist Paradigm or Neo-liberal Cul-de-Sac?", *The European Journal of Development Research*, Vol. 9, No. 1, June. pp. 150-166.

Schuurman, F.J., (2001); Globalization and Development Studies: Challenges for the 21st Century, New Delhi, Vistar.

Schuurman, F.J., (2001 a); "Introduction" in Schuurman (2001).

Schuurman, F.J., (2001 b); "The Nation-State, Emancipating Spaces and Development Studies in the Global Era" in Schuurman (2001).

Sen, Amartya, (1989); "Food and Freedom", *World Development*, Vol. 17, No. 6, June.

Sen, Amartya, (1999): "Development as Freedom," OUP, New Delhi.

Slater, D., (1992); "Theories of Developments and Politics of the Post-Modern—Exploring a Border Zone", *Development and Change*, Vol. 23, No. 2.

Standing, G., (1999); "Global Feminization Through Flexible Labour: A Theme Revisited", *World Development*, Vol. 27, No. 3, March, 583-602.

Stiglitz, J.E., (1996); "Role of Government in Economic Development", *Annual World Bank Conference* in World Bank, Washington.

Stiglitz, J.E.. (2000): "Development Thinking at the Millennium", *Annual World Bank Conference Economics*, World Bank, Washington.

Taylor, Lance, (1997); "Editorial: The Revival of the Liberal Creed—The IMF and the World Bank in Globalized Economy", *World Development*, Vol. 25, No. 2.

The Economist (1994); "The Global Economy—Survey", October 1.

The Economist (1997); "The World Economy—Survey", September 20.

Thomas, H. *et. al.*, (1994); "Three Highly Differentiated Trajections" in Thomas, H. (ed.) *Globalization and Third World Trade Unions: The Challenges of Rapid Economic Change*, Zed Books.

Thomas, C., (1998); "International Financial Institutions and Social and Economic Human Rights: An Exploration" in Tony Eavans (ed.), Human Rights—Fifty Years: A Reappraisal, Manchester University Press, Manchester.

Tokman, V.E., (1992); "On Freman's Paper" in Proceedings of the World Bank Annual Conference on Development Economics (1992), World Bank, Washington.

UNDP (1996); Human Development Report, 1996, UNDP, OUP, London.

Wallerstein, I., (1996); "Underdevelopment and Its Remedies" in Chew and Denmark (ed.) *op. cit.*

Wilkin, P., (1996); "New Myths for the South; Globalization and the Conflict between Private Power and Freedom", *Third World Quarterly*, Vol. 17, No. 7, June.

World Commission on Dams (WCD), (2000); Dams and Development: A New Framework of Decision Making, *Report of the World Commission on Dams*, Earthscan, London, November.

Xu, Wei and K.C. Tan., (2001); "Reform and the Process of Economic Restructuring in Rural China; A Case Study of Yuhang, Zhejiang", *Journal of Rural Studies*, Vol. 17, pp. 165-181.

2

Decentralization and Globalization: Gandhian Approach

RAM BINOD SINGH

The process of industrialization and growth of mega industries based on capital intensity and high technology, essentially created a situation of centralization. Bigger the better became the dictum of industrial organization. This trend originated with the growth of joint stock company and was facilitated and amply promoted by the Industrial Revolution of the 19th century. Economic rationality in terms of internal and external economies was advanced and taken resort to. This may be relevant under certain circumstances of scarcity of manpower and sufficiency of capital and other resources. Economic concentration leads to political centralization which ultimately erodes and frustrates the basic concept and foundation of democratic polity.

As the process of centralization gathers strength and frustrates people's aspiration for influencing public decisions that vitally affect their life, the demand for decentralization grows strident. Economic concentration and centralization of power and authority create manifold problems leading to systemic distortion and alienation of man from his environment and work. Initiative is stultified and man is turned into mechanical units devoid of sense and sensibility by repetitive works, throughout his engagement in productive units. This breeds discontent among the workmen who are forced to work as a part of big machine doing the same work without applying his acumen and innovative skills and insight. After attaining certain level of growth it creates in-built mechanism for exploitation. Exploitation of man by man owning capital and controlling the giant enterprises becomes inevitable. According to Marxian, doctrine, surplus value is appropriated by the capitalist which ultimately leads to pauperization of the majority workers. This process sows the seed of tension, conflict and clash with the system. Cause of the growth of capitalism is the cause of its crisis of decay in the form of crises and inner contradiction. Violence is bound to erupt, which is to be contained and controlled by greater degree of violence and brute forces. These aspects have been elaborately discussed in 1984 by George Orwell.

With the consequences of centralization, it is obvious that there is a demand for dispersal of industries and devolution of political authority and financial resources to the grass root level to expand the space and opportunities for the local community to decide about what is to be done for the well-being of the community and how it is to be done. It is thus a demand for restoring to the people their sovereignty usurped by the state. Broadly speaking, two different perspectives on the question of decentralization is of interest here. First, there is the Aristotelian perspective which underlines the fact, that man becomes truly human political beings by sharing the responsibilities of public life. For Aristotle, then, full participation in public life is a necessary condition for man to become truly human political being. Such participation can be ensured only in a small community, intimate community. It can also be argued that, the Aristotelian insistence on becoming human is misplaced since it is not participation that makes men good. It is rather good men that lend to the public life dignity and decorum and make it a proper instrument of serving the cause of justice. It is what

M.K. Gandhi essentially argues. For Gandhi what is important is not the making of a blue print of perfect society, but the development in the people, the capacity to resist tyranny and flight arbitrariness.[1] This capacity can develop only when the individual exercise self-rule in the sense provides a solid foundation for political self-rule. This requires an alternative political arrangement in keeping with the true democratic ideal, that is, a radically decentralized and layered arrangements of building-blocks, in which constitutive units yield increasingly specific powers as territory and scope, that is enlarged.[2] Pursuing a simple life, self-reliant and self-governing local communities are to constitute the base of national political life. For Gandhi, the spiritual self-rule is the foundation of political self-rule.

State institutions are often accused of being too remote from the daily realities of common people's life, and decentralization is often recommended as a solution. Decentralization can be powerful for achieving development goals in ways that respond to the needs of local communities, by assigning controlling rights to people who have the information and incentives to make decisions best suited to those needs, and who have the responsibility for the political and economic consequences of their decisions. It is not in itself a goal of development, but a means of improving public sector efficiency. And there are important caveats. The most important is that decentralization can bolster the power of elites in setting with highly unequal power structures. To benefit poor people it must have adequate support and safeguards from the center and effective mechanism of participation.[3]

Decentralization can mean different things to different persons. Here it refers to the formal devolution and power to local decision-makers. Less extensive forms of decentralization include decentralization of the government organization and mechanism and devolution of power or resources to the local units. The size of decentralization to the state in India merely breaks government into the size of many countries. Decentralization to smaller units increases the scope for interaction with the citizenry served.

Decentralization can make state institutions more responsive to poor people, but only if it allows poor people to hold public servants accountable and ensures their participation in the development process. The pace and design of decentralization affect its impact on efficiency, accountability, participation, and ultimately poverty reduction.

Local information has many advantages. It can help to identify more cost-efficient ways of building infrastructure, providing public services and organizing their operation and maintenance. A study in South Africa found that, community involvement reduced the cost of creating jobs and improved the cost effectiveness of transferring resources to poor people at local levels. Moreover, knowing what local needs are most pressing can help the disadvantaged. In Indonesia greater local control over funds, led to more spending on health and education in priority areas for poor people and to more spending on small infrastructure, boosting non-farm employment and income.[4]

Local monitoring and supervision for many types of projects and programmes are more effective and less expensive because of, proximity to the point of provision and better inter-actions at the local level. Decentralization can greatly enhance the state's capacity to accelerate local development and reduce poverty and solve other problems only if it is effectively designed. Local authorities and agencies need considerable autonomy, including fiscal matters, as well as considerable support and safeguards from the centre. Moreover, decentralized government needs mechanisms to ensure high levels of participation in the design and monitoring of programmes and policies by all sections of the population to be served.

Local authorities need to have enough fiscal control to plan their activities. But locally raised revenue are often only a small part of the budget of decentralized units weakening ownership of locally designed policies and threatening their sustainability. While decentralized units need an adequate budget base, enforcing hard budget constraints are also essential, to make them accountable. If *ad-hoc* funds from outside units are available to meet the budget shortfalls, local bodies can lose their incentive to function effectively. Moreover, such funding erodes the real power of the local body and its polity to effect change as time and energy is wasted in extracting these benefits. While certain degree of fiscal devolution is needed for effective decentralization, it carries the risk of exacerbating inequalities between regions. In China, where provinces and local bodies are expected to be self-financing, social services are greatly under funded in poor provinces. Mechanism for redistribution from the central budget can mitigate these inequalities, but this is politically contentious. The problem needs to be addressed through consensus building and tax sharing so that the central government has resources to make transfer, where necessary.

Central support is required to ensure that national policies are adhered to and to coordinate the inter-regional interests of different administrative units—as with highway charges and access to common water resources. Common macro-economic and distributive goals also need to be supported. The danger of decentralization without proper safeguards may threaten the macro-economic stability of the entire country.

Safeguards are also needed to monitor financial probity and discourage the capture of local bodies by powerful elites. One of the most serious pitfalls of decentralization occurs, when power imbalances are large at local levels. In such a situation higher levels of government, less subject to local political pressures, may be more motivated than local bosses, to help the disadvantaged?

PARTICIPATION

Widespread popular participation is vital to successful decentralization because without it, the potential benefits of local information can not be realized. Moreover, participation creates a virtuous circle. Participating in local government helps to build civil society and ensure that, majority needs are heard and goals are achieved. It also helps to increase the voice of the poor people in local affairs. Decentralization of power and resources at the local levels such as neighbourhoods or villages requires special efforts, but benefits can be considerable.[5]

Man-centred approach to development and decentralization is required because every policy is designed to improve the quality of individual life and harmony and cohesion in social system. In this perspective, the dream of paradise on this earth thus depends for its realization on the fulfilment of three vital conditions. First, the individual must exercise complete freedom not only in defining largely his economic purposes but also in executing them. In essence, then, it implies not only the rationality of individual choice but also the making of the choice independently of any external influence. In this context, rationality has only two significant references, i.e. its relationship with individual's well-being as determined by himself, on the one hand, and with the impersonal market process focusing, on the other. It does not necessarily imply the inclusion of the good of the collectivity as a determinant of individual choice. Second, economic activity must gain autonomy from socio-cultural norms and values in order to be an effective tool of individual facility and collective good. And, lastly, the market process must not be interfered with, constrained or restrained.[6] Needless to say that such perspective envisages a social order, which is completely decentralized and which countenance authority over individuals and their interactions, except the impersonal market process. The spirit of commerce that this perspective celebrates, brings with it the spirit of frugality, of economy, of moderation, of work, of tranquility, of order, and of regularity.[7] In addition to instilling good virtues in the individual, the modern economy, as Sir John Stenart claims, "is the most effective bridle ever was invented against the folly of despotism".[8] Yet an element of doubt about the efficiency of the commercial spirit and the virtue of modern economy to keep in leash the tendency towards aggressive pursuits of self-interest and moderate, if not completely, extirpate the disastrous consequences of such a pursuit for social concord persists. Therefore, the sole reliance is not to be put on these virtues alone for inducing man to engage in socially beneficial action. Other factors are claimed to exert salubrious influence on the self-aggrandizing tendency of individuals.

There is no doubt that the above vision is quite attractive and its promise is intellectually irresistible. However, it is this vision that has been responsible for the enormous increase in the power of the state and has pushed the limits of centralization of decision-making to an extent, that chokes democracy to the point of collapse. The prime reason for this, is the irreconcilable tension between freedom and order. When consideration of morality either as personal motivation or as limitation on action are denigrated, self-control no longer constitutes a viable substratum of action. With this, the locus of control on individual action shifts from within the individual to some external agency. It is in this context that we can appreciate the unprecedented accretion in the state's jurisdiction and power over human affairs, not because the state is the most efficient and effective instrument of control but because there is nothing else that stands between the depreciation of the pursuit of self-interest and the utter vulnerability of the collective good to such depreciations.

Here, we encounter certain difficulties. First, the state is seen in a double light, it is considered to be a providential check on human cupidity, bit at the same time it is also a weapon in the hands of powerful interests to keep out the weak and the deprived. Afflicted with this split personality as it were, the state does not prove an effective and efficient instrument of controlling individual behaviour or promoting collective goods. In addition to this, there is also the question of the extent of controlling individual behaviour. Given the central importance of material well-being in man's contemporary existence, to curb individual freedom, especially in the economic realm, is to strike at the very foundation of modern society, what the state can expect that is not to curb or control individual action but only to take care of the consequences of individual action. Even here, the state proves to be of limited usefulness.[9] Although the state has come to be assigned, the important function of regenerating and if possible, controlling the adverse consequences of individual actions, its failure to do so has ironically contributed to the hypertrophy of the state. As the function of the state has expanded and its power has escalated, distortions in political life have mounted. It is this puzzle, that the puzzle of decentralization is expected to overcome and vanquish. But here again pertinent question arises. Can decentralization, it must be asked, cure the hypertrophy of the state and neutralize its adverse consequences, if it is segregated from those factors that are in the first place responsible for centralization? Can it create conditions, which will restore morality both as personal motivation and limitation on action as the basic desideratum of individual action, if it remains conjoined with the fulfilment of ordinary life needs? Can it become an apt instrument of building up an envigorating community life as a ground for situating freedom, if it is conceived as a more effective vehicle to the expression of freedom of homofaber?

There is no doubt that the talk of decentralization is inspired by two salutary objectives, that of a healthy economic growth and of equitable distribution of development benefits favouring particularly weaker sections. It is argued that decentralization will prove a better and more efficient instrument of realizing these objectives. It should be emphasized here that, as long as the pursuit of material well-being that is, the fulfilment of ordinary life-needs remains the central goal in life, decentralization will not make any profound difference in the structure and process of political life that centralization has given rise to. If individual happiness and the progressive unfoldment of human potentialities are to be secured only through fulfilment of ordinary life needs, technologically induced economic growth will retain its primary salience. Proliferation of material needs and homogenization of life style will constitute the two most important planks of any developmental programmes, the first because it is an integral part of modern conception of good life and the second because, confronted with the difficulty of bringing about complete equality, it is homogenization that constitutes the only alternative for moderating discontent triggered off by the heightened perception of inequality. As such, the industrial mode of production with its commitment of centralization and the erosion of the autonomy of local communities will remain the principal means of fulfilling ordinary life-needs of the people, quickening the pace of homogenization.[10]

It is claimed that, it will be possible through decentralization to remove the impediments that currently stymie the deprived and under privileged sections of the population from meaningfully participating in economic and political life. While the empowerment of the weaker sections is laudable objectives, its limitations must be recognised. The removal of the initial disadvantages that the weaker sections suffer from, will not necessarily improve the quality of democratic politics or community life. The process of fulfilment of ordinary life-needs not only requires the expansion of production but also implies the proliferation of needs as well as the upgradation of needs. But as Fred Hirsch puts: For addition to the material goods that can be expanded for all will, in itself, increase the scramble for those goods and facilities, that can be expanded. Taking part in the scramble is fully rational for any individual for his own actions, since in these actions he never confronts the distinction between what is available as a result of getting ahead of these and what is available from a general advance shared by all. The individual who wants to see better, has to stand on tiptoe. In the game of better our neighbour that is what each individual must try to do, even though, not all can.[11] The competition for scarce resources that ensures, introduces a mismatch between private morality and public morality. In this competition, getting ahead of others, for several reasons is the only mode of ensuring individual facility. First, an excessive concern with individual facility remains untouched by the nation of equity, not because, it is impossible to imagine but because it is hard to define. As Hans Kelsen observes: Justice is an irrational ideal. However, indispensable it may be for violation and action, it is not subject to cognition. Regarded from this point of view of rational cognition there are only interest and hence conflicts of interest.[12] Moreover, individual is not in a position to calculate the consequences of his own action for others, he is not in a position to know how does his action influence others and in what ways and actually what constitutes right action in different contests. Since the individual does not possess this information, he is forced to fall back upon his own notion of what is best for him. And what is best for him, is that which maximizes his own facility.

But the search for facility intensifies competition, sharpens conflict and shatters cooperative basis of social interaction. As such, the pursuit of private and essentially individualistic economic goals by enterprises consumers and workers in their market choices—the distinctive capitalistic values that give the system, its drive, must be girded at key points by strict social morality which the system erodes rather than sustains.[13] But the state is incapable of sustaining social morality. It is, therefore, the relative power contenders for scarce material resources which becomes a determining factor, in who gets what, when and how and reliance on power for gaining and retaining access to scarce societal resources, that makes for pervasive social conflict.

To ensure social peace means, that the system must increase its capacity to perform well, not only on the economic but also on political front so that it can meet rising demands for material benefits as well as political participation. This however, becomes difficult for various reasons. First, there are definite limits, both physical and social, to economic growth. Even if these limits can be overcome or reduce, rising affluence itself will stimulate demands for those goods and services which can not be easily satisfied, or can be satisfied only for a few. Thus prosperity for all remains a distant dream. Democratic polity founded on the promissory note of unlimited material well-being for all is, in a sense, the viction of its own propagandas, it evokes demands and pressures that can neither be contained nor met.

Second, liberal democratic order takes cognizance of inequality of opportunity. It is hoped that, the weaker sections of the population will take advantage of the power resource they have, i.e. their numerical strength to influence legislation and through it, correct structural imbalances. However, the outcome of the race of life in which people take part from different points is already heavily loaded in favour of the rich and the privileged. Economic inequality not only persists but also gets aggravated.

Third, with growing affluence the behavioural and motivational premises, on which liberal democracy and theorizing about it rest, have increasingly lost realistic significance. Three crucial assumptions underline empirical democratic theorizing. First, while the pursuits of self-interest constitutes a dynamic element of liberal democracy, this pursuits would be subject to rational control. Individuals in their own action would relate the satisfaction of their own needs to collective purposes. Second, demands for access to societal resources and consequently the level of politicization would rise slowly for the system to respond effectively. And lastly, even if these two assumptions did not work, automatic pressure-basic consensus, rules of the game, etc. integral to the system would prevent the system from going over the brink.

All these assumptions have proved unworkable. As the system responds to rising demands for more and more material benefits, expectations rise precipitously. Of late, the widespread adherence to the philosophy of entitlement that is, expectation of benefits without commensurate efforts,[14] has further queered the pitch. Appeasement strategies by leaders and parties for mobilizing and ensuring electoral support, leads to a spiral of ever greater problems and greater expectations. As a result, disjunction between individual preferences and collective goods occurs. This makes it difficult to find a way to order goals either rationally or democratically.[15]

With this, the need for managing the system becomes even greater. The majority, as the numerical aggregate of minorities tends to break-down under conflicting perspectives and expectations of the coalition partners. Even if the coalition endures, the gap between the perception of the managers and that of the populace increases and strains on the system are generated. More and more popular demands are channeled into the system. But because of reduced capacity of the system to perform, these demands can not be met.[16] Such a situation can be handled either by a resource to populism or authoritarianism. This, however, deepens the crisis of democratic governance. Restricting popular participation to the selection of rules, exacerbated the divergence between what is possible for the individual and what is possible for all individuals. And because of this divergence, insufficient popular support comes forth to protect democracy from a variety of potential threats. Crisis breeds upon crisis.

Modern man is like the peasant who in Lenin's view, possess two souls: One craves for gold that is, affluence, and the other dreams of warmth of an intimate community, both pulling him in opposite direction. Democratization is supposed to unify these two souls. But as long as the goal of affluence untrammeled by any moral value, remains the pivot of human endeavor, neither the object of gold for everybody nor that of strengthening community life as a ground for situating freedom and a falorum of real democracy seems to be feasible. The question remains to haunt us: What is to be done?

Gandhian Plan and economic ideas support the logical basis for decentralized economy in a country like, India. It is clear, that in a country like, India where capital is much the scarcer factor of production than the labour, the optimum adaptation of scarce means to unlimited ends, would be achieved only when we use capital-economizing and labour-intensive methods of production. In other words, we shall have to use less capitalistic methods of production. The protagonists of large scale industrialization do not admit that the problem of unemployment can not be fully solved without providing maximum scope for cottage and decentralized industries, but they deride their inefficiency and crudeness. It must be reiterated that, Gandhi is not against the value of 'efficiency' in production. He would gladly welcome any improvements in the tools and implements used for cottage and village industries, provided they do not cause unemployment. Here Gandhi differentiated between Mechanical Efficiency and Economic Efficiency; an instrument or a machine that is mechanically efficient, need not necessarily be economically efficient as well.[17] For example, huge machines and labour-saving scientific devices are, no doubt efficient from the mechanical and technological stand point, they are capable of producing more with less labour. But they can not be efficient from the viewpoint of economic welfare, in general. Various points may be argued in sport of this contention. Large scale industrialization causes conflict and friction between labour and capital, culminating in strikes or lockouts. It creates unhealthy congestion and slums leading to physical and moral degradation. It causes technological unemployment necessitating social security measures. Unnecessary heavy strain on transport and communication system is for all. There may be over production and glut leading to depression and commitment economic crisis. It creates a chasm between rural and urban centres. It promotes inequality and concentration of economic power not only in a big metropolis centres but also in fewer hands which goes against the spirit of democratic constitution.

Thus, the aim of Gandhian economic planning should be full employment plus maximum mechanical and economic efficiency. Even from the administrative angle, decentralization and devolution of authority is advisable. 'Everybody agrees' writes Prof. Ferdynand Zweig, that planning should be as far as, possible, take the form of decentralized dispersion of function. All local needs, local communication, gas, electricity, water, food supply, industries for local needs trading, the whole of agriculture should be carried out by local authorities within their own framework.[18] The state should seek its ends by trying to influence economic weather, nor by trying to ration rain drops.[19] Gandhi has always held that lasting world peace will be impossible of achievement without economic disarmament which is another name of decentralization of industries. To quote Gandhi, 'I have no manner of doubt that such decentralization of power, both political and economic, would really usher in an era of permanent peace and prosperity. Charan Singh was diehard supporter of Gandhian principles of economic planning. To quote, "If we have the good of the people as a whole at heart, by and large, in a capital poor and labour-rich country like India, there is no escape from an economy, that Mahatma Gandhi advocated. His kind of economy will, not in the present context, produce greater wealth in the total, but will also serve all our other aims, that is, it will provide maximum employment, ensure equitable distribution of national product and promote a democratic way of life."[21]

During the 1990s, decentralization is being prescribed by bilateral donors and major economic players as a solution to the development problems. The World Bank for example, argues for the devolution of power almost as if it were panacea bringing the advancement of good government and fiscal responsibility.[22] Even advocacy of Panchayat reforms in India is equated with decentralization leading to better democracy and more efficient government. It is presumed that, the more a state decentralizes its power, the closer the channels of influence come to the people. This would also give a higher level of legitimacy to public policies and improve the chances of making the political elite directly accountable to the people. In short, decentralization is expected to enhance the efficiency, equality and legitimacy of democracy.[23] Today, however policy-makers recognize that, what determines outcome of decentralization, is a more complicated issue. As one observer puts it, decentralization can in one context lead to improve democratic performance, while in another it can lead to anything from decline in economic growth to "ethic strife and civil war".[24] Increasing responsibility and power at the local level can be disastrous, if local administration is not ready to handle its new role. For example, in Bihar and Uttar Pradesh the local administration suffers severely from inability to carry out development projects and inefficient management of central and state funding. There is a significant risk when the state decreases its sphere of influence or delegates power to local bodies, that the citizens may to a greater extent found themselves under the control of a local leader who does not play according to democratic rules. In its most extreme forms, decentralization in combination with corruption at state level may provide incentive for political movement using violent means. This has been experienced in Jammu and Kashmir.[25] Clearly, if public administration is plagued by corruption, policies and reforms will fail.[26] Against this background, the Panchayat reforms initiated in India in the 1980s and 1990s, which may turn out to be one of the world's largest decentralization schemes, naturally attracts attention.

The Asoka Mehta Committee report presented in 1977, recommended Panchyati Raj institution in India which has been undermined in the sixties and seventies, should become an "organe integral part of the democratic process. West Bengal was the first to implement the recommendation but Karnataka, Andhra Pradesh, and J and K soon followed. In many parts of these states, democratic performance improved as a direct consequence of the reforms and this paved the way for decentralization in other states. A number of constitutional amendments, most of them passed in 1992 established a uniform three-tier system below the state level safeguarding, at least constitutionally, the devolution of power.

One of the main problems impairing the quality of governance in the developing world as well as the industrialized world, is the various forms of corruption. Corruption creates distrust of the public sector and hinders economic growth. And at the most basic level of the structure of a state, corruption impedes education and health programmes, two of the pillars of development.

In this context it is prudent to discuss Jai Prakash Narayan's concept of participating Democracy. He wrote a paper on 'A Reconstruction of Indian Polity', and set forth the arguments and proposals for reforms and reconstruction of the political institutions and processes of this country so as to make them more democratic, efficient, enduring and meaningful. He asserts to emphasize, that the political structure of the country must of necessity be linked intimately to the whole structure of society and the mode of life and thought of its people.[27] He was charged to be enemy of democracy by his critics. To meet his critic, he affirmed his undying and unchanging faith in human freedom and the democratic way to life. To quote: 'Freedom has become a passion of life and I shall not see it compromised for bread, for power, for security, for prosperity, for the glory of the state, or for anything else.'

The Constituent Assembly of India, in the name of the people resolved:

(a) To constitute India into a Sovereign, Democratic, Republic;
(b) To secure to all its citizens justice, social, economic and political; liberty of thought, expression, belief, faith, and worship, equality of status and of opportunity; and
(c) To promote among them all Fraternity assuring the dignity of the individual and the unity of the nation.

These aims and purposes together do make up an inspiring and challenging image of democracy. The people of this country may justly be proud of the fact that, they have deliberately chosen democratic way of life, despite the example of many neighbouring countries having embraced dictatorship of one kind or another. It is an evidence of the people's cultural and spiritual maturity that they have done so. We have experiences of functional democracies in the world and within India as well. Next step beyond government by consent is people's participation in government, or a participating democracy. There is in the West a very healthy and vigorous system of local self-government. While this is to be welcome, local self-government by itself can not satisfy the needs of participating democracy. *There also central government in all powerful*. In the name of strong centre, the concept of participating democracy is being criticized. Devolution of power, so that the centre has only as much of it as required to discharge its central functions, and all the rest is exercised by the lower organs, need not necessarily imply a weak centre. On the other hand, a top-heavy and sprawling centre, poking its finger into every pie, might have the appearance of strength and power but in actual fact, it would be weak, flabby, slow moving, and ineffective.[28]

National unity of strength does not depend upon the list of subjects that a central government deals with, but on such intangible factors as emotional integration, common experiences and aspirations, national ethos, mutual goodwill and the spirit of accommodation, and, above all, upon large hearted wisdom on the part of national leaders. But luckily for us in this country, we have the opportunity to re-fashion, broaden and deepen our democracy under ample, if not full, democratic conditions and get on with the job, so that while there is still time, we might make our democracy invulnerable and satisfying. This may be termed as swaraj from below.

Jai Prakash Narayan laid down certain conditions for the success of a true participating democracy:

1. Education of the people, as understood in the widest sense of the term.
2. Organized political parties refrain from interfering with it trying to convert it into their hand-maiden, and using it as a jumping ground to climb to the power.

3. Real devolution of power and not a make-believe. It is possible to talk of devolution of power without in reality surrendering any power. No one can learn to discharge responsibility unless responsibility is really given to one. For democracy to be a success, it is necessary that the people are prepared and given full opportunity to shoulder responsibility.
4. It is imperative that at each level, the local authority be given its own minimum resources. If control of resources remains in the hands of the state government, the devolution is bound to be rather nominal. He who pays the paper, calls the tune, will be true.
5. Panchayati Raj should be able, as soon as possible to exercise real authority over civil servants under its charge, who should be held fully accountable to it.
6. Of the three-tier structure of Panchayati Raj, the bottom tier, the Gram Panchayat, is obviously the foundation.

But other hindrances and structural constraints are always there in the smooth functioning of the system. The class conflict approach at the village level is likely to help least those very sections of the community that stand most in need of it. It is also clear that village economy must be a small-machine and labour-intensive economy. Secondly, a decentralized economy must aim at relating full utilization of local and regional resources, human and material, to the satisfaction of local and regional needs.

Suffice it to point out that decentralized economy, i.e. development would have benefits of being less dependent that the centralized sector on foreign aid and the centre. Mainly for three reasons: (a) element of voluntary labour would be greater, (b) it would absorb and utilize a larger proportion of small savings, and (c) overhead charges and transport and other social costs would be much lower. Thus, and in this sense too a decentralized economy would be more democratic and nearer the people. In short, a representative that is visible, available to his electorate, and responds to enquiries is close to the people. A representative who is not seen to whom people can not gain access, and who does not reply to queries is distant.

The crux of a decentralized democratic society is a high degree of self-governance at various levels and in diverse sector, and segments of social reality. The Indian people have, in their surroundings to the system, expressed a yearning for this. All that is needed is to galvanise this creative urge of the people is to restructure the relationship between the state and the social order, and, to remember that the Indian social order can not stand the strain of centralized politics. It is a fact that the position of the poor and the weak in the rural areas will not improve so long as power and decision-making remains outside their reach. It is not until the levers of state power move downwards that the poor majorities can aspire to stake a claim in them and use it against their traditional exploiters. Concentration of power and resources at higher levels necessarily limits their availability at lower levels and therefore concentrates them there also. Structure of participation is inherent in the democratic premise on which the Indian polity is supposed to be based. But the pre-existing state did not permit such a polity to evolve. It was a colonial state, drawing its authority from the masters and not from the people. There is a new set of masters in command but many elements of colonial rule still persists and there does exist a large measure of colonial relationship between New Delhi and lower down.

What is necessary is to change the structure of state. This involves a change in power relationship between the centre and the lower echelons. Only a decentralized state can provide the institutional safeguards against both anarchy and autocracy. Everything seems to point to the need for decentralization. It is indeed a historic necessity. The findings of various studies confirm that poverty and inequality are on the increase. Where a dent has been made on them, durability of the achievement is in doubt. The basic reason for failure of rural development and poverty alleviation programmes is in exclusion of the people from participation in the development process and the abandonment of the institutions of democratic decentralization and the related electoral process. The resulting alienation of the people from the most exciting task of development in the post-independent India on the one hand, and the continuation of the colonial pattern of administration, direction from the top and unaccountable to the local population, on the other, have serious implication for both development and democracy.[29]

Globalization is not new, but the present era has distinctive features, shrinking space, shrinking time and disappearing borders are linking people's lives more deeply, more intensely, more immediately than ever before. The concept of global village is coming to reality. Globalization offers great opportunities for human advance, but only with strong governance and well organized economic system.

The challenge of globalization in the present century is not to stop the expansion of global markets. The challenges is to find rules and institution for stronger governance—local, national, regional and global—to preserve the advantages of global markets and competition, but also to provide enough space for human community and environmental resources to ensure that globalization works for people—not just for profit. Globalization with[30]

Ethics	less violation of human rights, not more.
Equity	less disparity within and between nations, not more.
Inclusion	less marginalization of people and countries, not more.
Human security	less instability of societies and less vulnerability of people not more.
Sustainability	less environmental destruction, not more.
Development	less poverty and deprivation, not more.

The opportunities and benefits of globalization need to be shared much more widely. This is laudable objectives and pious declaration of globalization with a human face. The past decade has shown increasing concentration of income, resources and wealth among people corporations and nations. Many people are also missing out on employment opportunities. Inequality has been rising in many countries since the early 1980s. Even in China disparities are rising. OECD countries also registered big increases in inequality after 1980s—especially Sweden, U.K. and the United States.

Inequalities within countries has also increased. The income got between the fifth of the world's people living in the richest countries and the fifth in the poorest was 74 to 1 in 1977, up from 60 to 1 in 1990, 30 to 1 in 1960. In the 19th century too, inequality grew rapidly during the last three decades, in an era of rapid global integration, the income gap between the top and bottom countries increased from 3 to 1 in 1820, 7 to 1 in 1870 and 11 to 1 in 1913.[31]

By the end of 1990s, the fifth of the world's people living in the highest income countries had:

1. 86% of world G.D.P.—the bottom just 1%.
2. 82% of world export markets the bottom fifth just 1%.
3. 68% of foreign direct investment—the bottom fifth just 1%.
4. 74% of World telephone lines—the bottom fifth just 1.5%.[32]

Some have predicted convergence. Yet the past decade has shown increasing concentration of income, resources and wealth among people corporations and countries—

1. OECD countries with 19% of the global population, have 71% of global trade in goods and services, 58% of foreign direct investment and 91% of all Internet users.
2. The World's 200 richest people more than doubled their net worth in four years to 1998, to more than £ 1 trillion. The assets of the top three billionaires are more than the combined GNP of all least developed countries and their 600 million people.
3. The recent waves of mergers and acquisitions in concentrating industrial power in megacorporations at the risk of eroding competition. By 1998 the top 10 companies in pesticides controlled 85% of a $ 31 billion global market and the top 10 in communications, 86% of a $ 262 billion market.
4. In 1993 just 10 countries accounted for 84% of global research and development expenditures and controlled 95% of the U.S. patents of the past two decades. Moreover, more than 80% of the patents granted in developing countries being to residents of industrial countries.[33]

All these trends are not the inevitable consequences of global integration but they have run ahead of global governance. Globalization is creating new threats to human security in rich countries and poor. New information and communications technologies are driving globalization but polarizing the world into connected and isolated. Stronger global cooperation and actions are needed to address the growing problems beyond the scope of national government to manage. It is strong global action which is required to tackle the global threat to human security. Public action must be enhanced and stepped up to develop technologies for human development and the eradication of poverty. Narrowing the gap between rich and poor and the extremes between countries should become explicit global goal. Essential aspect of global governance is responsibility to people—to equity, to justice, to enlarging the choice of all. It is also required to build a more coherent and more democratic architecture of global governance in 21st century.

Despite all claims and pious declaration, empirical evidence available during the last decade of globalization shows that it has an inherent tendency to concentrate wealth, income and resources. Multinational companies and megacorporations are structure-bound for centralizing power, resources and control, otherwise they may be neither viable nor maintainable.

Notes and References

1. *Young India*, 20 January, 1925.
2. Roy, Ramashray, Self and Society: "*A Study in Gandhian Thought Sage*", 1984.
3. *World Development Report*, 2000-01: Oxford University Press.
4. *Ibid.*
5. *Ibid.*
6. Roy, Ramashray: "*The Captive Vision*".
7. Smith, Adam, (1776): "*Wealth of Nations*".
8. Taydor, Charles, (1979): "*Hegel and Modern Soceity*", Cambridge University Press.
9. Roy, Ramashray, (1996): "*Decentralization*", *Madhya Pradesh Journal of Social Science*, Vol. 1, January-June, No. 1.
10. *Ibid.*
11. Hirsch, Fred., (1977): "*Social Limits to Growth*", London, Routtedge & Kegan Paul, p. 10.
12. Hanskelsen, (1958): "*General Theory of Law and State*", Harward University Press, pp. 13-14.

13. *Op. cit.*, p. 117.
14. Robert A. Heilbroner, (1978): *"Beyond Boom and Crash"*, New York, W.W. Norton, p. 44.
15. Roy, Ramashray: *Op. cit.*, p. 35.
16. Badrach, Peter, (1967): *"The Theory of Democratic Elitism"*, Boston: Little Brown and Com.
17. Narayan, Shreeman, (1960): *"Principles of Gandhian Planning"*, Kitab Mahal, Allahabad, p. 75.
18. *The Planning for Fees Society*, p. 252.
19. *The Economist*, (1947): November, 29.
20. *Ibid.*, p. 78.
21. Singh, Charan, (1981): *"Economic Nightmare of India"*, National Publishing House, New Delhi, p. 441.
22. Widmalm, Sten: *"Decentralization and Development," Madhya Pradesh Journal of Social Science*, Vol. 6, July-December 2001, No. 2, Ujjain.
23. Diamond, 1999, p. 20.
24. Yusuf, 1999.
25. Widmalm, *op. cit.*
26. Manor and Crook, 1998.
27. Jai Prakash Narayan, (1961): *"Swaraj for the People"*, Varanasi, pp. 68-69.
28. Jain, L.C., (1985): *"Grass without Roots"*, Rural Development, Sage Publications, New Delhi, p. 15.
29. *Ibid.*
30. *Human Development Report*, 1999, p. 2.
31. *Ibid.*, p.3.
32. *Ibid.*
33. *Ibid.*

3

Globalization and Decentralized Development—A Synthesis

SUKUMAR BASU

I. INTRODUCTION

Most of the developing countries including India adopted the strategy of planted economic development in the fifties of the last century. A concerted effort was made in our country, to accelerate the growth rate of GDP by giving emphasis on public investment in basic and key industries for creating a strong base of rapid industrialization. In the literature on development, the role of state was emphasized for compensation "market failures" in the optimal allocation of scarce resources. The growth rate of GDP in India increased during 1951-65, but after a declining trend during 1966-80, it again began to rise from the 1980's. The rise in GDP; however, did not tricle down to the poorer section and thus the per-capita income could not increase as the expected rate. Such a process of development, instead of reducing inequality in the distribution of income, wealth and power, has benefit a few rich. Elitist and luxury consumption goods are produced at the cost of wage-goods. So, mass poverty and unemployment are the main concerns even after 50 years of planning.

Various "government failures", like, excessive control and regulation, licence-raj, inefficient management in public sector, bureaucratic corruption, etc. have been highlighted by many, for the acute crises and macro-economic disequilibria, in India in 1990. To counter-act those problems, the Government of India had to undertake the new economic strategy of LPG (Liberalization, Privatization and Globalization) in July, 1991, as advised by the World Bank and the IMF.

While some aspects of globalization—both positive and negative, are discussed in the next section, the rational of emphasizing decentralized development through the micro-level planning are explained in the third section of this paper. The last section deals with synthesis between globalization and decentralized development.

II. SOME ASPECTS OF GLOBALIZATION

Globalization of any economy means, its integration with the world economy. It is expected to accelerate Foreign Direct Investment (FDI) and export-led growth by transferring technology, capital and other resources from the developed economies to the developing countries. Globalization created a more competitive environment in the economy, as a means to improve productivity and efficiency of the system. So the development countries are now competing for FDI and offering more attractive terms to the MNCs, which are denied to the domestic firms.[1] Even our domestic industries which had hailed the new economic policy in 1991, have now raised a hue and cry as the government is giving its contracts to the MNCs in preference to the domestic firms. In the interest of the MNCs the government is forced to relax, not only the customs and tariff duties but also labour laws and environment regulations in the name of economic reforms. Even trade union rights are being undermined in order to attract foreign investments.

The developed countries have two strategic advantages;—technologies and investment, over the development ones. New and improved technologies have given them new patent laws under the WTO (World Trade Organization). The patent laws will affect the interests of the domestic industries in our country, specially, the chemicals and pharmaceuticals. Now the MNCs of the developing countries try to bring investment under the WTO. They have both assets—augmenting and asset-exploiting motives. So, like other developing countries, India should demand that both patent and investment should be taken out of the WTO.

The advocates of globalization want to spread the "Hyper-Expansionist" (HE) approach of James Robertson[2] throughout the world, instead of creating an economy for the "same, humane and ecological (SHE) %. A higher rate of growth of the economy, say @ 8-10% per annum would improve the position of top 20% of our population, but it would not solve our basic problems of mass poverty, hunger and unemployment. Even after a decade of the process of globalization about 35% of our population are income-poor. We have failed to provide quality-life to our people, as 71% of total population in rural areas are without access to sanitation; 29% without access to safe drinking water and more that 25% having no access to health care.

So far as the impact of the globalization on unemployment is concerned, we find a "jobless growth" in India. Even the Planning Commission has admitted that employment growth rate has fallen from 2% p.a. in the 1980's to 0.98% in 2000, though during that period the growth rate of GDP increased from 5.8% to 6.7%. Employment growth in the organized sector has slipped down from 2.4% during 1987-93 to 0.45% in 1994-2000 and that of the public sector came down from 0.10% to 0.03%. In the rural sector the employment growth was 0.4% in 1994-2000 as against 2.1% in 1987-93. In 2000-01 there was 1.44 lakhs job-cuts in government and 50,000 in private sector.[3] If this is the picture of the organized sector, we can easily realize the Cyclical effects of such unemployment in the former sector on the lack of jobs in unorganized sector.

Under the above context, let us discuss in brief the impact of so-called Labour Reforms that our government is forced to impose on the labourers in order to attract more foreign investment. To create a flexible labour market of hire and fire policy in India the employers would be given the right to lay-off or retrench in factories having 1000 workers without permission of the government. (Though the Second Labour Commission has recently Recommended that such facility be offered in case of factories employing 300 workers only). Contract labour or temporary job-contract labour system should not be imposed here as a China where workers have no trade union rights and are forced to take jobs at lower wages. It is argued that as more investment would come at lower wages, there would be more employment. At the same time there would be more insecurity and less human welfare. These undermine the motivations of the workers and they cannot be loyal to a company. The Japanese system of flexibility, however, tries to maximize the motivation of the workers which increases the productivity and long-term profit of a company. It promotes family atmosphere within the company. So, in the absence of social security like un-employment insurance, etc. We should adopt the Japanese system for long-term benefits of both employers and workers.[4]

Again, inter-state and intra-state regional disparities are likely to be aggravated as a result of globalization which encourages growth of industries and business centres in economically advanced states or advanced urban areas of weak states of India. Clusters of related firms grow in micro-regions due to globalization. The MNCs have both responded to and influenced the formation of such clusters.[5] The planning Commission itself has acknowledge that "growth has not been as regionally balanced as it should have been".[6] To counter-act increasing urban-rural divergences decentralized development through improvement in agriculture and agro-industries and creation of socio-economic infrastructures in rural areas is necessary. The state has to provide various utility services, like, road construction, irrigation system and environment management, etc. to help the farmers and the people living in the villages.

III. DECENTRALIZED DEVELOPMENT

The Indian economy consists of two sectors: (i) the formal organized modern sector, and (ii) the informal unorganized sector rooted specially in rural areas. In the process of globalization, the modern capitalistic enterprises need to be carefully oriented towards the world market, for it is wise to take into account, assimilate and adapt the latest technologies of advanced countries. Fiscal discipline and other economic reforms within the framework of our constitution are required for rapid expansion and export-led growth of the modern sector. Instead of extending dependency, we must systematically foster self-reliance and the capacity for self-development. While the market and the state have to play leading roles in the formal sector, co-operation and self-reliance must be the hallmarks of the informal sector. So, side by side with modern capitalistic sector, the basis has to be strengthened for an alternative economy depending mainly on the local resources, evolving new forms of co-operation of locally available man-power and producing mainly for local needs in rural areas. This sector will have the character of a "neighbourhood economy" based on 'communitarian' approach, which will sweep aside the barriers of caste, creed and religion. This type of social order cannot be imposed from above but to be built from the base.[7] Decentralized development through decentralized planning with the help of strong panchayat institutions having communitarian outlook is necessary.

The concept of decentralized planning is not new in our country. The Report of the Working Group of District Planning, set-up by the Planning Commission in September 1982, states: "Decentralization enables a better perception of the needs of local areas, makes better informed decision-making possible, gives people a greater voice on decision, concerning their development and welfare which serves to achieve better to be taken into account, ensures active participation of the people, serves to build up a measure of self-reliance by mobilizing resources of the community in kind or in money, making development self-sustaining and enables better exploitation of local resources and growth potentials of the local area for improving productivity and increasing production."[8] Thus to ensure better "trickle-down" benefits of development to the poorest section of people and to tackle unemployment and under-employment problems, decentralized planning is the only way out.

At first, a district was taken as a viable unit of micro-level planning in India because of its infra-structural advantages. Though the district-level planning was first started in Gujarat and Jammu and Kashmir in the 1970s, other states including West Bengal followed it in the 1980's. District and block-level planning have aroused enormous enthusiasm among the people in West Bengal, Kerala, Karnataka, Gujarat, etc.[9] and they have better performance in this respect than in other states specially, BIMARU (Bihar, Madhya Pradesh, Rajasthan, and Uttar Pradesh). Though mounting pressures are coming from the villages and blocks for inclusion of more and more new schemes in district and block plans, unnecessary delay in sanctioning schemes and specially in releasing funds dampen public enthusiasm. The March-fever hampers rural development schemes. So, direct release of funds through constitutional amendments to the grass-roots level re-vitalizing panchayat raj, convergence of various rural development and welfare schemes, proper monitoring of the working of the panchayats, involvement of the NGOs are steps in positive direction. The attitude of the bureaucrats, the local leaders and politicians has to be changed for ensuring smooth functioning of decentralized planning. The local leaders should represent common men and the poor living in villages.

The problems of poverty and unemployment in rural areas and other informal sector of the economy cannot be overcome without substantial development of the "neighbourhood economy".[10] To succeed, we need a model democracy in villages which are now divided into castes, sects, rural political parties and conflicting economic interests. Decisions in the village councils should be taken not by majority votes but by consensus. Already various NGOs, acting as eyes and ears of the people, have started rebuilding village communities even in some remote parts of U.P. and Orissa. Tarun Bharat Sangha in Alwar and Banawasi Seva Ashram in U.P., Gandhi Vichaar Parishad in Bankura in West Bengal, Institute of Social Action and Research Activities in tribal areas of Gajapati district in Orissa, etc. are a few NGOs that are doing laudable work in this respect. The self-help groups and neighbourhood committees are strengthening people's participation in their development and empowerment specially of women. By rebuilding communities at the base, a quit "social revolution" may be possible.

IV. CONCLUSION

From the above discussion we may conclude that in this age of globalization, economic reforms within the framework of our constitution are required for rapid expansion and export-led growth of modern capitalistic enterprises. Reforms with LPG are expected to lead the economy to higher growth with improvement in efficiency and quality of product through competition; but they are not free from social costs. The government has the responsibility to see that the social costs of reforms must be shared by all and provide adequate safety nets and invest a lot in education, training and retaining programmes and create social infrastructures, specially for the un-organized workers.

We must systematically foster self-reliance and self-development. Co-operation and self-development must be the hallmarks of the informal sectors. Side by side, with globalization decentralized development through rebuilding the rural society is required to solve the issues of equity and social justice. In other words, the civil society and the local community have to play leading roles in bringing about a more humane and equitable socio-economic order with the involvement of the NGOs and state-intervention, if necessary.

Notes and References

1. Basu, D., (2002), "Global Questions", *The Statesman*, 18-19-02-2002.
2. Robertson, J., *Future Wealth*; A New Economics for the Twenty-first Century.
3. GOI, *Economic Survey*, 2001.
4. Basu, D. (2002), "Labour Reforms", *The Statesman*, April 2002.
5. Dunning, J.H., (2000), (ed), *"Regions, Globalization and the Knowledge-based Economy*, OUP.
6. GOI, *"Ninth Five Year Plan"*, 1997-2002, Draft, Vol. 1, p. 3.
7. (a) Datta, A., (2000), "One World", *The Statesman*, 15-16.06.2000.
   (b) Datta, A., (2001), "Free Trade", *The Statesman*, 9-10.04.2001.
8. Rao, H., (1982), *Report of the Working Group on District Planning*, Vol. 1, p. 22.
9. (a) Basu, S., (1989), "Decentralized Planning in India: An Experience," *Economic Affairs*, Vol. 34, Qr. 4, Dec., 1989.
   (b) Mohanakumar, S., (2002), "People's Plan sans People", *EPW*, April 20, 2002.
   (c) Aziz, Abdul, (1993), "Decentralized Planning", *The Karnataka Experience*.
10. Datta, A., (2000), *op. cit.*

Appendix

Table I

Some Selected Economic Indicators

Periods	*1993-94*	*1994-95*	*1995-96*	*1996-97*	*1997-98*	*1998-99*	*1999-2000*	*2000-01*	*2001-02*
Value at constant prices % change	5.9	7.3	7.3	7.8	4.8	6.5	6.1	4	5.2
Agriculture (% change)	4.1	5	-0.9	9.6	-2.4	6.2	1.3	-0.2	6.5
Industry (incl. Cons.)	5.2	10.2	11.6	7.1	4.3	3.7	5	6.3	3.5
Services (% change)	7.7	7.1	10.5	7.2	9.8	8.4	9.5	4.8	6.6
Total of Industrial Production (%) change	5.8	9.1	13.1	6.1	6.6	4.1	6.6	5.1	3.5
Employment (Organised)									
Public Sector (million nos.)	19.4	19.5	19.4	19.6	19.4	19.4	—	—	—
Private Sector (million nos.)	7.9	8.1	8.5	8.7	8.7	8.7	—	—	—
Administered Job Seekers (million nos.)	36	36.6	36.8	37.6	39.2	40.2	40.3		41.2

Source: CMIE Various Monthly Review of 2002.

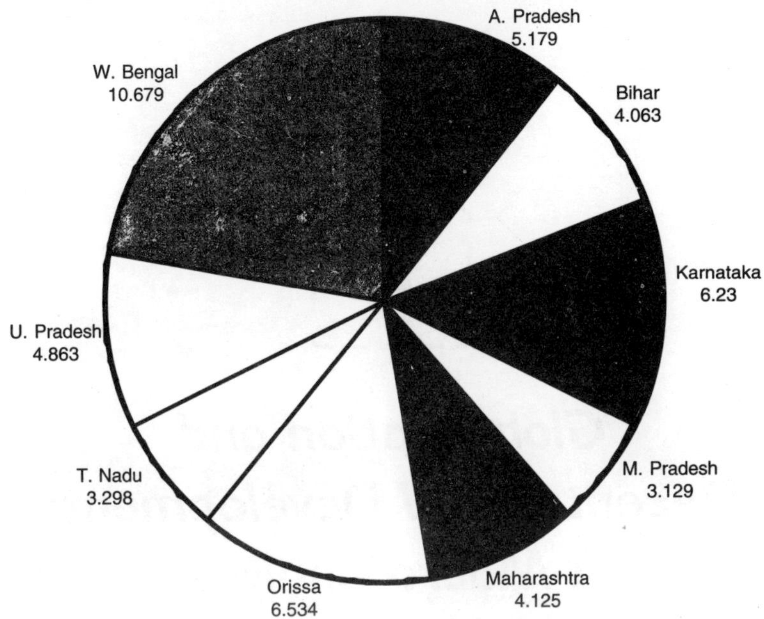

Chart *Source*: Planning Commission

TABLE II

Changes in Employment Growth

Periods	*1960 to 1970-71*	*1960-71 to 1980-81*	*1980-81 to 1990-91*	*1990-91 to 1994-95*	*1960 to 1995*
Employment Growth %	3.77	2.68	1.5	0.71	0.77

Source: Various Issues of Economic Surveys.

4

Globalization and Decentralized Development: A Macro Analysis

J. LENKA

Globalization, if contemplated as collective development of world economy, has made rapid strides in the nineties. Particularly the establishment of World Trade Organization (WTO) in the year 1995 has accelerated its pace. Globalization has brought significant growth in world-wide trade, investment flows and capital transactions. By dismantling economic barriers, it has opened up new vestiges for co-operative development. It is now widely accepted as a development paradigm. Most of the developing countries have in fact shown great urge to globalize their economics. This is indicated by the fact that of the 135 member WTO, 100 are from developing countries.

In the last decade, several countries have lifted their barriers with a view to gaining reciprocal access to the global markets, capital and technologies. These countries perceive globalization as an instrument not just for achieving economic efficiency and competitiveness, but for meeting broader objectives like eradicating poverty and overall advancement.

However, there are doubts whether globalization in its present form has led to a kind of decentralized development, i.e., whether the benefit of globalization has trickled down to more countries and more people within them. The question of decentralized development, therefore, has assumed greater importance in the face of globalization.

'Decentralized development is understood as spreading out of development from large concentrated centres into distant and small peripheries. It is a process or procedure that results in the redistribution of output arising out of specific economic activities. The point here however is, that the fact of decentralization should not be confused with the factors that cause it. What passes for decentralization is simply the result of development. It is suggested that a decentralized pattern of development is instrumental in distributing income and economic power equitably among the people and even among regions thereby contributing to the emergence of an economically sound, politically stable and regionally balanced society. A steadily expanding federation of economic life on a decentralized basis is to be desired not only for maximizing the scope for efficient utilization of human and other resources, but also for making democratic control of economic life possible.

Thus, globalization and decentralized development are not opposed to each other for economic prosperity of the globe and its parts.

The present paper makes a modest attempt to discuss the issue of globalization and decentralized development from a macro stand point. The data used for the analysis are compiled from the World Development Reports—2000-01 and 2002. Macro-economic indicators such as Gross Domestic Product (GDP), Per Capita GDP, Merchandise Export and Import, Foreign Direct Investment (FDI) for the years 1990 and 2000 are used in the present analysis. The comparable data are available for these indicators.

On the basis of the Per Capita Gross National Income the countries are divided into three groups such as: (i) Low income countries ($ 755 or less), (ii) Middle income countries (between $ 756 and $ 9265), and (iii) High income countries ($ 9.266) and more). The classification is made in line with that in the World Development Report (WDR). The classification includes countries with population more than 30,000 only.

GROSS DOMESTIC PRODUCT (GDP)

It is observed in (Table 1), that table world GDP has increased from 213,906 billion dollars in the year 1990 to 313,369 billion dollar in the year 2000, registering an annual average growth rate of 4.65 percent. During the same period, the GDP of low income countries has increased from 8,897 billion dollars to 10,789 billion dollars with an annual average growth of 2.13 per cent. It is heartening to note that the GDP of middle income countries has zoomed from 35,254 billion dollars to 54,908 billion dollars during the study period. The annual average growth rate for these countries stands at 5.58 per cent which is higher than that of the world. Finally, the GDP of high income countries has increased from 1,69,679 billion dollars to 2,47,721 billion dollars with an annual average growth rate of 4.60 per cent. It is evident that low income countries have not made much headway in the process of globalization so far as the growth of their income is concerned.

TABLE 1

Distribution of GDP

(billion dollars)

Countries	*1990*	*2000*	*Annual Average Growth Rate*
Low Income	8,897 (4.16)	10,789 (3.44)	2.13
Middle income	35,254 (16.48)	54,908 (17.72)	5.58
High income	169,679 (79.31)	247,721 (79.05)	4.60
World	213,906 (100)	313,369 (100)	4.65

Figures inside parentheses represent percentage of the column total.
Source: World Development Reports 2000/2001, 2002.

Viewed in another way, it is found that the share of the low income countries in world GDP has decreased from 4.16 per cent in the year 1990 to 3.44 per cent in the year 2000, whereas the share of the middle income countries has increased from 16.48 per cent to 17.72 per cent during the same period. However, the share of the high income countries has marginally declined from 79.31 per cent to 79.05 per cent in the same period. This again confirms the disadvantageous position of the low income countries in the process of globalization.

PER CAPITA GDP

It is observed in (Table 2), that the per capita GDP of low income countries has gone down from 448 dollars in the year 1990 to 439 dollars in the year 2000. However, this does not mean that, there has been no growth in these countries. The fact remains that population growth has overtaken the GDP growth and thereby reducing per capita GDP of low income countries during the study period. In middle income and high income countries, the per capita income has increased while the rate of growth appears to be moderate in middle GDP countries, but it has significantly increased in high income countries. A recent study made by Petar Lindert of University of California and Jeffrey Williamson of Harvard University reveals that, globalization has widened inequalities between nations. It may be noted here that, the annual average growth rates of population stand in the order of 2.39 per cent in low income countries, 1.35 per cent in middle income countries and 0.8 per cent in high income countries during the study period. Therefore, whatever benefits have accrued to the low income countries in the process of globalization has been countermanded by population growth thereby resulting in wider disparities across different income groups.

TABLE 2

Distribution of Per Capita GDP

(dollars)

Countries	*1990*	*2000*	*Annual Average Growth Rate*
Low income	448	439	-0.20
Middle income	1,486	2,039	3.70
High income	20,287	38,288	8.87
World	4,129	5,176	2.54

Source: Compiled from WDR 2000/2001, 2002.

MERCHANDISE EXPORTS

The worth of global merchandise exports has increased from 33,284 billion dollars in the year 1990 to 63,504 billion dollars in the year 2000 with an annual average growth rate of 9.08 per cent. As percentages of world GDP, it has gone up from 15.56 per cent to 20.26 per cent during the study period. Thus, there has been a rise in world trade because of larger market access due to globalization.

TABLE 3

Distribution of Merchandise Exports

(billion dollars)

Countries	*1990*	*% of GDP*	*2000*	*% of GDP*	*Annual Average Growth Rate*
Low income	1,106 (3.32)	12.43	2,176 (3.43)	20.17	9.67
Middle income	6,136 (18.43)	17.41	15,229 (24.09)	27.86	14.93
High income	26,042 (78.24)	15.35	46,029 (72.48)	18.58	7.67
World	33,284 (100)	15.56	63,504 (100)	20.26	9.08

Figures inside parentheses represent percentage of the column total.
Source: World Development Report, 2000/2001, 2002.

It is observed in (Table 3), that the quantum and share of merchandise trade has increased both in lower and middle income countries, the latter doing better. Though the quantum of merchandise exports soared for high income countries, their share has decreased from 78.24 per cent to 72.48 per cent during the period under consideration.

As percentage of their corresponding GDPs, it is seen that the merchandise exports of all categories of countries have increased during the study period. In addition to this, it is also found that the lower and the middle income countries have increased their global share in 2000, when compared to that of 1990. Thus opening up economies has resulted in expanding the volume of world exports. Moreover, the low and middle income countries have managed to capture a larger share, though their aggregate share is still limited to 29 per cent in the year 2000.

TABLE 4

Distribution of Merchandise Imports

(billion dollars)

Countries	*1990*	*% of GDP*	*2000*	*% of GDP*	*Annual Average Growth Rate*
Low income	1,180 -3.46	13.26	2,003 -3.06	18.57	6.97
Middle income	5,729 -16.81	16.25	14,178 21.64	25.82	14.74
High income	27,173 -79.72	16.01	49,327 -75.53	19.91	8.15
World	34,085 -100	15.93	65,507 -100	20.90	9.67

MERCHANDISE IMPORTS

The worth of merchandise imports which was 34.085 billion dollars in the year 1990 has more than doubled at the end of 2000. The annual average growth rate stands at 9.67 per cent. For the low income countries it has increased from 1180 billion dollars to 2003 billion dollars with an annual average growth rate of 6.97 per cent during 1990 and 2000. The growth rate (14.74) per cent for middle income countries appears to be highest in this period. The lowest growth in imports is found for the high income countries.

A close look at the share of their imports in the total merchandise imports it is manifest that, the share of the low and middle income countries have increased whereas that of the high income countries has decreased during the period under reference. Again as percentage of the GDP, the merchandise import is seen to have increased for the world and all income groups. Thus, it is evident that, world trade during the period has increased and the low and middle income countries have become more dependent on the high income countries.

FOREIGN DIRECT INVESTMENT (FDI)

Apart from foreign trade, foreign aid has a direct bearing on the economic growth of a country. It is found (Table 5) that the Foreign Direct Investment (FDI) in low income countries has increased from 22 billion dollars in the year 1999 with an annual average. The amount has increased from 219 billion dollars to 1756 billion dollars with an annual growth rate of 70.18 per cent during the same period. For the high income group, the FDI figures stand at the order of 1692 billion dollars and 7271 billion dollars in the years 1990 and 1999 respectively.

TABLE 5

Distribution of FDI

(billion dollars)

Countries	*1990*	*1999*	*Annual Average Growth Rate*
Low income	22(1.14)	98	34.55
Middle income	219 (11.32)	1756 (19.24)	70.18
High income	1692 (87.49)	7271 (79.68)	32.97
High income	1934 (100)	9215 (100)	37.18

When looked to the share of FDI, it is found that the shares of low income countries and high income countries have decreased, whereas it has increased for the middle income countries. This indicates that the middle income countries have attracted more FDI during the period. It may be due to their overall growth performance. On the other hand, inadequate infrastructural facilities and bottlenecks in low income group and slow down of growth in high income group may be attributed for low FDI in these countries.

CONCLUSION

The above analysis reveals that during 1990 and 2000 the volume of world trade has increased and the low income and middle income countries have managed to increase their shares in world trade though their aggregate volume is still at a low level.

This has happened mainly because of opening up economies and globalization. Moreover, they have invited more Foreign Direct Investment during the period. In contrast with this, the per capita GDP of the low income countries has plummeted and the economic inequality has widened between different income groups. Therefore, one may be tempted to conclude that, globalization has not resulted in decentralized development and the benefit of globalization has not trickled down to the low income countries. In other words, globalization has been confined to developed countries and the developing countries have not been able to participate in the process. This is corroborated by the study of Peter Lindert and Jeffrey Williamson.

However, globalization should not be accused for the failure of the low income groups. These countries suffer from internal problems like rapid rise in population, infrastructure bottlenecks, weak financial markets and so on. More access to globalization and its benefits demand that developing countries first put in place a conducive environment necessary to ensure higher returns and larger markets for foreign investors. To get a share of global capital, technology and output, developing countries have to upgrade their social and economic institutions through administrative, legislative and legal reforms.

Globalization should not be thought of as a solution to everything. It merely provided opportunities. Those who take advantage, they flourish and those who do not, they sink. Globalization is not supposed to produce equality of outcome but it produces equality of opportunity for those with right mindset. Hence the developing countries have to focus on economic restructuring, building market supporting institutions and creating efficient regulatory mechanisms.

Left to themselves the low income countries are helpless. What in fact needed is the international assistance and a support mechanism so as to facilitate their participation in the process of globalization. The challenge of the hour is to make globalization work towards global property through decentralized development. The critical necessity in the context are the collective and co-operative action which should be realised by all countries of the world.

References

Stiglitz, J., (2001); "To a Thirdway Consensus", *The Economic Times*, June, 6.

Prasad, K.N., (1978); "The Strategy of Industrial Dispersal and Decentralized Development", *Wedoli Advertisers*, New Delhi.

Anklesaria Aiyar, S.S., (2002); "Soccer Globalization at Work," *The Economic Times*, October, 2001.

Kausal, N., (2001); "Don't Blame Globalization for Growing Inequalities," *The Economic Times*, October, 2001.

World Development Reports, 2000, 2001, 2002, Oxford University Press.

5

Globalization and its Trends in Indian Economy

S.K. DHAGE

INTRODUCTION

The term globalization has different meanings for different people. In simple words globalization means extending of economic activities across national boundaries. Globalization means, integrating the economy of the country with the world economy. As a result of globalization international markets regarding goods, services, technologies, finance and labour are integrated. National economies are thrown open to the market forces of the world and the scope of government's national macro-economic policies is restricted. In short, globalization is a flow of the processes of economic transactions and their management across the political boundaries of the nations.

INDICATORS OF GLOBALIZATION

Over the last 25 years, the process of globalization has spread rapidly. Rapid expansion of this process has resulted in the following important changes in the economies. These changes are the main indicators of the process of globalization.

I. International Trade

Large volume of world production is entering world trade. Share of world trade in world's Gross Domestic Product (GDP) has risen from 12 percent to 18 percent.

II. International Investment

Percentage of International investment has also looked up. Between 1980 and 1999-2000, Foreign Direct Investment (FDI) has increased from 4.8 percent to 12.6 percent of world production.

III. International Finance

International finance sector has developed very rapidly. According to 1999-2000 statistics, transactions worth $ 1300 billion were taking place daily in this market as against $ 60 billion everyday in 1983.

CAUSES OF GLOBALIZATION

I. Policies of Liberalization

With the removal of constraints road to globalization was all clear. First, impact of openness was witnessed in the trade sector. It was followed by Foreign Direct Investment (FDI). Liberal policies were also adopted towards financial sector subsequently.

II. Technical Revolution

Revolution in the fields of transport and communication has rendered the world a small place to live in. Jet aircrafts, computers, satellites, and information technology all have served to remove frontiers of time and space.

III. Experience of Developing Countries

Over the last two or three decades, centrally planned economies like Russia, Eastern Europe, Eastern Germany, etc. have failed on economic front. These economies were hesitant in adopting the process of globalization. On the contrary, developing economies like Korea, Thailand, Taiwan, Hong Kong, Singapore etc., which adopted the process of globalization achieved new heights of economic success. China also succeeded in achieving high rate of economic growth by resorting to the process of globalization. These successful stories of globalization inspired India and other countries to globalize their economies.

IV. Emergence of United States as a Super Power

Disintegration of Russia and triumph of capitalism rendered America, super power. Political supremacy of America has also been instrumental in hastening the process of globalization. It is the currency of such a super power that facilitates smooth facilitates running of international markets. This role is being played by America.

GLOBALIZATION OF INDIAN ECONOMY

In order to pull the country out of economic crisis, government of India, in 1991 sought financial assistance from International Monetary Fund and World Bank. These two international institutions imposed on India the conditionality of implementation of Stabilization and Structural Adjustment Programme to secure the said assistance. It was to fulfil these conditions, that India introduced New Economic Policy in 1991. The process of globalization in India was the outcome of this policy. Two parts oi the conditions laid down by international institutions were:

I. Stabilization

Stabilization refers to that situation of an economy wherein inflation and balance of payments deficit are kept under control. To achieve this objective, it is essential to scale down fiscal deficit and rate of money supply.

II. Structural Adjustment Programme

It refers to the structural adjustment of the economy on the basis of policy of liberalization. It has two aspects:

(i) *Internal*: In the domestic sector liberal policy should be adopted for adjustment of investment, production, prices, etc. Government controls should be minimised in this regard and ultimately the same be removed.

(ii) *External*: Government controls over the flow of foreign goods, services, capital, technology, investment, etc. should be reduced to the minimum. It implies liberalization of foreign economic policy or globalization of the economy.

CHARACTERISTICS OF GLOBALIZATION OF INDIAN ECONOMY

I. Globalization of Trade

It means reduction of government controls over international trade and adoption of liberal policy in respect of imports and exports. Since 1991, government of India has been pursuing the policy of liberalization to achieve the objective of globalization of trade under new economic policy. In order to liberalize, foreign trade from the control of government and to allow its growth in a free manner, following steps have been taken: (i) In July 1991, Indian rupee was devalued by 22 percent in two instalments so as to let the rupee find its real exchange rate, (ii) In 1993-94, full convertibility on trade account was enforced and integrated exchange rate system was adopted, (iii) In 1994-95 Full convertibility on current account was enforced. It implies freedom to buy and sell foreign currency for international transaction on current account, (iv) Quantum of import duties has been lowered, (v) In the Export-Import Policy 2000-01, restrictions on the import of 715 items have been withdrawn. In 2000-01 import of all goods will be made free.

II. Globalization of Investment

It means removal of restrictions on foreign investment and offering concessions to attract the same. In new economic policy 1991, government has liberalized foreign investment policy and taken following measures in this respect:

(i) In 1991, foreign capital investment upto 51 percent has been allowed in 34 high priority industries, without prior approval of the government.

(ii) In 1996, Foreign Direct Investment (FDI) upto 74 percent has been allowed in 9 industries. Foreign companies are allowed to take profit on investment to the country of origin.

(iii) If foreign companies want full ownership of joint ventures in India or want to set-up subsidiary companies with full ownership, they will be free to do so.

(iv) Restrictions on transference of shares by one non-resident Indian (NRI) to another non-resident Indian have been withdrawn.

(v) Foreign investors are allowed to disinvestment equities at market price. They are free to remit the proceeds of disinvestment to the country of origin.

(vi) Several concessions and facilities have been given on FDI for the development of infrastructure viz. roads, power, communications, etc. Hundred percent equity has been allowed in case of power houses.

(vii) Multinational Companies (MNCs) have been given many concessions to set-up export-oriented units in the country.

(viii) Foreign investment Promotion Board has been established to provide single window facility for approval of foreign investment.

(ix) Non-resident Indians are allowed 100 percent investment in export houses, trade houses, hospitals, export-oriented units, hotels, etc.

(x) In Export-Import Policy, 2000-01, foreign and multinational companies are allowed 100 percent investment in special economic zones.

(xi) New Insurance Act provides for 26 percent foreign investment in the share capital of private sector companies.

III. Globalization of Finance

As a result of Economic Policy, 1991, liberal policy has been adopted in respect of international finance. Following measures have been taken for globalization of international finance:

(i) Companies governed by Foreign Exchange Act have been allowed to borrow or accept deposits without the permission of the Reserve Bank of India.

(ii) Foreign Institutional Investors (FII) are allowed to invest in Indian capital market.

(iii) Efforts are made to mobilize deposits of non-resident Indians.
(iv) Indian Financial Institutions like State Bank of India, have sold India Resurgent Bonds to mobilize foreign capital.
(v) Many facilities have been offered to foreign banks to establish themselves in India.

TRENDS OF GLOBALIZATION OF THE INDIAN ECONOMY

I. Increase in Foreign Trade

As a result of foreign trade policies adopted in the wake of the process of globalization, India's share in the world trade has gone up. In 1990-91, India's share in the world was 0.53 percent. In 1995-96, there was 20 percent increase in it, that is, it rose to 0.60 percent. In 1999-2000 it further increased to 0.62 percent.

TABLE 1

India's Share in World Trade

(Percentage)

Year	*India's Share in World Trade*
1990-91	0.53
1995-96	0.60
1999-2000	0.62

Source: *Southern Economist*, January 2001.

Table 1 shows that as a result of globalization of India's foreign trade, there has been a little increase in India's share in world trade. However, many other countries of the world like China, Hongkong, Singapore, etc. have much larger share in the world trade than India. For instance, share of China in world trade is 3 percent, of Hongkong 3.5 percent and of Singapore 2.5 percent. But India's share is even less than 1 percent. However, share of exports in India's GDP has been constantly rising. In 1990-91, it was 6 percent of GDP that rose in 1999-2000 to 13.5 percent.

II. Increase in Foreign Investment

As a consequence of globalization, there has been a considerable increase in foreign direct investment (FDI) as well as foreign portfolio investment (FPI). In 1991, FDI was barely to the tune of Rs. 174 crore that rose in 2000 to Rs. 9,338 crore. Thus, foreign direct investment has witnessed an increase of 60 times. Similarly, portfolio investment has also increased very much. In 1991, net portfolio investment was merely Rs. 11 crore which in 1999-2000 increased to Rs. 13,112 crore. Between 1991 and 2000, number of foreign collaboration projects was 14,230 with foreign investment amounting to Rs. 32,710 crore. Thanks to the policy of liberalization in 1999-2000, engineering industry had the maximum foreign direct investment amounting to Rs. 1,799 crore.

TABLE 2

Foreign Investment in India

Year	*Foreign Direct Investment (Actual Inflows) (Rs. crore)*	*Net Portfolio Investment (Rs. crore)*	*Total Foreign Investment (Rs. crore)*
1991	174	11	185
2000	9,338	13,112	22,450

Source: Handbook of Statistics on Indian Economy, 2001.

Table 2 shows that in 1991 total foreign investment was Rs. 185 crore that increase in 2000 to Rs. 22,450 crore.

III. Globalization of Capital

India has made enough progress as a result of globalization of capital. (i) In 1990-91, total foreign capital authorised was Rs. 8,123 crore, of which actual utilization was Rs. 6,704 crore. On the contrary, in 2000, total foreign capital authorised was Rs. 20,319 crore as against actual utilization of Rs. 14,405 crore. Rise in the utilization of foreign capital is an indication of the progress of globalization of Indian economy.

(ii) Consequent upon globalization, number of foreign banks in India has been rising constantly. In 1991, there were 26 foreign banks operating in India. In 2000, their number rose to 42.

TABLE 3

External Assistance

Year	*Authorization (Rs. crore)*	*Utilization (Rs. crore)*
1991	8,123	6,704
2000	20,319	14,405

Source: *Handbook of Statistics on Indian Economy*, 2001.

(iii) *Foreign Exchange Reserves*: As a result of globalization of Indian economy, foreign exchange reserves have also increased substantially. In 1991, foreign exchange reserves of India amounted to Rs. 4,822 crore which in 2000 increased to Rs. 1,52,924 crore. Thus, there has been an increase of 26 times in foreign exchange reserves of India.

CONCLUSION

Though globalization and liberalization has its own meaning but it has its goal to attain higher growth rate, self-employment, full employment and better living conditions. Indian Economy is, therefore, supposed to attain growth with equity and just distribution of income and wealth and should try to improve the quality of life of the majority of the people. Besides, the inflow of capital, technology and direct investment haphazardly in the Indian Economy, a consensus is now being emerged that free and wholesale globalization should be replaced by a selective path of globalization, giving due weightage to the National Interest.

REFERENCES

Dhar, P.K. (May 2000), *Indian Economy: its Growing Dimensions*, Kalyani Publishers, New Delhi.

Jain, T.R. (2000-01), *Indian Economy*, V.K. Publications, New Delhi.

Economic Survey (2001-02), Govt. of India, New Delhi.

World Development Report (2002), Oxford University Press, New York.

6

Indian Globalization: A SWOT Analysis

R. Meera, V. Radja Ramane and C. Rajendran

INTRODUCTION

The global economic framework is undergoing metamorphic changes. The impact of this economical change is being felt by nations world over. Globalization is an economy free of restrictions, discrimination, exploitation, and suppression. It is an economy of nations, for nations and by nations. Though globalization in not a new phenomenon, since the process have been happening for ages only of late nations world over have come under its clutches. Thus we can say globalization has become more of a reality than a possibility. Globalization creates a system that upgrades access to the common pool of global resources of finance, markets, technology and information. It is the internationalization of the process in which money, raw materials, goods, services and ideas are exchanged across national borders.

Globalization can be termed as a gradual removal of barriers to trade and investment between nations. It believes that, economic efficiency can be achieved through competitiveness, while seeking the broader objectives of economic and social development. In the meanwhile, common man has misconceived globalization. This is because too much of technical data is being given to him. He is skeptical if globalization would provide better employment, improve current economic conditions, decrease inflation or contrary to the above said. Gain or loss in globalization will depend upon the competitive advantage that one has over the other in all aspects viz. Production, Marketing, Human resource management, Financial management and so on.

Due to this existing scenario the Indian economy is at a crucial turning point. India should go on with the global consensus and intelligently shape its advantage in the future. The Indian industry today stands at a crossroad. Faced, with the problem of survival and growth, the industry seems to be groping for readymade solutions. The Global Competitiveness Report ranks India as 52 with a competitiveness index of (–)1.30 as opposed to the most competitive nation in the world, namely, Singapore whose index is 2.12. With such statistics its high time for India to take globalization seriously.

REASONS FOR INDIA TO GO GLOBAL

Liberalization, privatization, integration of financial markets have made globalization an issue that has to be faced. Private financial markets are deciding exchange and interest rates. India should attract global movement of capital by projecting its natural and human resources. International capital movement improves balance of payments, technology, and level of competitiveness. The standard of our people can be improved only through increased share of exports in world trade. Since globalization has become a compulsion, there has to be revolutionary change in the way we manage our companies. Firms should become internationally competitive in order to improve the economic status as the success of a nation's economy depends on it. An increasing number of industries in India are altering themselves to acquire global position. Firms must uncover or understand if a "Global logic" exists in their businesses, isolate that logic, and develop strategies instead. Here are some of the reasons why India should go global.

Pursuing Potential Customers Abroad

Customers with similar interests and needs can be found world over. Our firms should conduct sufficient market research and find these customers. This in turn means, firms should develop nice marketing. They should also see that they inherit loyalty of these customers. It will also help the companies to pursue geographic diversification.

Exploiting Product Life Cycle Differences

When the market for a firm's product becomes saturated, the firm needs to look out for new opportunities. They have to do this by entering in to foreign markets where the product may not be very well-known. This will also help in market expansion as well as increase profits.

Taking Advantage of Different Growth Rate of Economies

In case the firm is based in a low growth economy, it is likely to suffer competitive disadvantage. In these circumstances, the firm can expand in to faster growing economies and take advantage of the growth opportunity there.

Internal Efficiency

This is an added advantage that a firm can use to co-ordinate its operations for maximum efficiency. This helps them to reduce cost, develop new technological breakthroughs and become more competitive.

Added Synergies

A global firm aims at managing the interdependence between various foreign subsidiaries. This helps them to leverage strong positions in one market to help shore up weak positions in another. This is also called as cross subsidization. This will help the firm to selectively slow a competitors development in markets, where it is more difficult for it to strike back. Thus a global firm will try to maximize its profits for the entire system.

Internationalizing for Defensive Reasons

When a domestic company sees its market being invaded by foreign firms, the domestic company may react by entering the foreign competitors home market in return. As a result, the company can learn valuable information about its competitors that will help in its operations at home.

Opportunities Abroad

This is one of the most common reasons for a firm to go global. Opportunities are vast in foreign markets. So any global company will try and exploit the available opportunities.

The Concept of 'I'

Explosion of identity crisis among nations, religions, regions and ethnic groups is eminent. Cultural identity is on the raise. The raise is likely to become stronger and stronger in the days to come. What can be best dealt at a local level should be addressed at the local level. If our domestic industries can penetrate foreign markets they can hold local positions and traditions from being completely exploited by foreign firms.

OPPORTUNITIES

The policy-makers thus far had camouflaged the Indian business. Now that the reality had struck, intense is the competition. Foreign firms that want to set-up manufacturing bases in India do not have to seek Indian partners. A mediocre Indian is wont to go for goods available at low prices. Foreign firms are offering exactly the same. Its high time that Indian firms use their potentials and make use of the opportunity available. The emphasis is shifting from new product technology to new process technology i.e., low cost. Cheap labour and highly skilled work force will be a powerful competitive weapon. Hypocritical statements should be avoided. The Indian businesses should accept its present status and should strive and learn from the foreign companies.

Globalization is an exciting new social movement led by the people, for the people, challenging a corporate establishment motivated by the power of money and self-interest. This ideology should be drawn in the minds of Indian industries. Some of the opportunities are given below.

Foreign Collaborations

The government of India has allowed 51% of equity participation by foreign companies. This will enable transfer of technology to Indian firms, it will help in improving our managerial talent, upgrade futures, product design and the much required quality. It is incumbent on the part of Indian industries to adopt strategies such as partnerships, joint ventures, collaborative agreements, etc. that will suit global competition.

Build Strong Customer Loyalty

The latest concept of customer relationship management is an efficient tool that helps in building customer relationship, which in turn leads to customer loyalty. Customer loyalty can be obtained through designing a product that adds value to it. Knowing customer experience and perfecting the products. Improving customer's service, improving people to people relationship within the organization and through good internal customer network.

Foreign Direct Investment (FDI)

By its very nature, FDI has a marginal, but crucial role to play. Ever since the initiation of economic reforms, FDI is not very encouraging. The country is in great need of foreign capital to supplement our large national savings, which, in dollar terms, amounts to over 90 billions. India has lot of potential to attract FDI and creation of a conducive environment is the need of the hour. The thrust of the FDI regime must be to channel investments where local capital is inadequate and where from the FDI cannot leave India at will.

Trading Blocks

No national or domestic markets in the traditional sense exist any more. There can be no single factor behind an economic boom, but instead an extraordinary confluence of factors. We are in an unprecedented period of accelerated change, perhaps the most breathtaking of which is the swiftness of our rush to the entire world's becoming a single economy. The advantage of trading block is that the products of member-countries can become more competitive as a result of cost reduction due to economies of scale. Trade blocks can impose tariffs on non-member countries. India can create a new trading block that will be appropriate to its economy and objectives. By doing so, India could negotiate with other trading blocks such as EC, NAFTA, EEA, etc. from a position of strength and equality. Member-countries of the new trading block could be from the Middle East, Australia, ASEAN, Japan and so on.

Access to Global Product Market

Global economy is going to be free of sanctions, quantitative restrictions and trade barriers. This implies that all member countries of WTO can export or import goods among themselves. Indian firms should blend domestic market knowledge with international expertise. Getting global will help the domestic companies to improve economies of scale.

Technological Adaptation

Technology transfer refers to the importation of technology, which is poor in it from one, which is rich in the same. Technology can be acquired through indigenous development or through importation from countries who posses the same. Mr. Lee Kuan Yew, the prime minister of Singapore says, "mankind's progress has been, what it is because of one man's discovery, whether it is the first spark of fire, or the first atomic explosion, does not have to be painfully and painstakingly rediscovered by all those who seek the benefits of the original discovery". In this context, India can even follow the Japanese technique of acquisition, adoption, and adaptation.

Access to Global Capital Market

Firms cannot rely on domestic financial institution alone, because this might jeopardize their business. Today, investors are increasingly looking at investments across borders and currencies. And when they do invest in a foreign country, many of the key traits that they look for are: simplicity, liquidity, and price transparency, in fact, securitization of financial means is the result of selection made in assessing private profit from the point of view of maintaining profit, growth and liquidity, as well as the risk of rearing by individual borrowers, investors, or financial institutions, and constitutes a practice of individual economic entities. India can raise finance through ADR, GDR if the required conditions are met. They can also run advertisements, open sales office and do market research with the above said capital. There have also been major changes in easing the RBI formalities.

STRENGTHS

Though India is not in a position to stand on par with the top countries, it still has lot of potential within itself. It is up to us to tap these potentials and make the best use of it to stand against the tide of globalization. Some of our strengths are discussed below.

Flexible Labour Market

India is one of the world leaders in labour legislation. We have ratified 36 conventions of International Labour Organization (ILO) whereas America has ratified only 11 of them. India has given freedom of association and has given the leader stress to collective bargaining. The availability of cheap and highly skilled work force is an added advantage. Moreover, Indian's are known to be quick learners. Its high time that we use this potential resource.

Economic Reforms

In 1991 due to a precarious foreign exchange situation, adverse balance of payments and huge external debt, the government of India adopted a comprehensive program of macro-economic stipulation and structural adjustments. India's reforms include far reaching trade, fiscal, monetary and industrial policy measures with a major thrust on improvement of competitive efficiency of Indian industries by utilizing foreign investment and technology to a much greater degree than in the past. Issues such as reduction in tariff rates, removal of quantitative restrictions, decentralization of exports and imports with the exception of a few items are some of the notable reforms that the government has taken. This was done to encourage and attract investor's world over.

Channel of Distribution

Every firm that wants to set-up its business in a foreign country, can market its product only if it has an effective distribution channel. Most of the Indian firms have a powerful distribution network. Global firms can tie-up with domestic companies and make the optimum use of this advantage.

Market Share

Purchasing power is one of the factors that determine ones market share. In this context population of our nation determines the potential market. Though the urban markets are flooded with global products there is still a market that can be tapped. It is the rural market, which constitutes about 55% of the entire domestic market share.

Availability of Natural Resources

Natural resource is the actual potential form of wealth supplied by nature. India is a land of abundant resources. Many of its natural resources such as rivers, mines, etc. are not utilized to the best of their ability, because of insufficient finance.

Price Competitiveness

This is another factor that is to our advantage. As said earlier our markets have reasonable purchasing power. Though we are not on par with developed nations, we have the advantage of the huge market. Different types of pricing such as skimming, penetrating pricing, etc. are some of the pricing strategies that have been successful in Indian markets. In agriculture our prices are 1/4th of international market prices. India can use such price competitiveness to its advantage.

MISSING LINKS OF INDIAN ECONOMY

Inspite of strength and opportunities available there are certain areas where we need to make changes so that we can achieve our objectives. Some of them are discussed below.

Control of Fiscal Deficit

Yashwant Sinha's budget for 2002-03 has failed to bring about a solution to control fiscal deficit. This has in turn led to stagnation of the economy.

Glimmer on the Horizon

In 1990-91, the last year of the old economy, agriculture contributed 24 percent and sophisticated manufactures 21.8 percent of exports, while light manufacturing's share having gone up to 54.2%. But 1999-2000, the share if agriculture had declined to 17%, and sophisticated manufactures had gone up to 29.8%. Light manufacturing remained at 54.2%. But compared to the transformation that took place in East Asia in a comparable period in the 1980s, it was only a glimmer. What is more important, very little of the change has been contributed by foreign and joint ventures. Their contribution to exports is not identified separately in official statistics, but is known to be very small. This is because the government failed to reform the structure of the economy in order to assure sustainable growth in the future. This could prove the greater failure in the long-run.

FDI Flow

India's FDI inflows have never exceeded a measly $3.3 billion. India remains a country inveterately hostile to FDI in practice even if not in theory. The FDI inflows into the country in 2001 posted a marginal decline to Rs. 19,265 crores against Rs. 19,341 crores last year, even as faster approvals improved realization rate to 72%, the highest since 1991. Other than some investment in telecommunications and the much-maligned Dabhol power project, the bulk of this has gone into resuming majority shareholding in existing foreign enterprises that were already doing business in India. Proper infrastructure has to be provided and the time taken for issuing permits to the foreign companies by the center and state governments should be minimized. Setting up of one-stop investment promotion agency for all investment purposes could be an ideal one in such causes.

Minimizing Non-labour Cost

Due to the foreign investment flow in 1980's and 1990's like a flood tide because of the asymmetry between the progressive unification of the global product markets and the increasingly rigid separation of the national labour markets. This created wage differentials of 20 to 60 times between the highly industrialized countries on one hand and India, Thailand, Indonesia, China and Vietnam on the other. But for an investor from the mature industrial economy, who wants to exploit this labour cost advantage, he must feel reasonably sure that it will not get offset by higher non-labour costs. All the above countries were able to offer this assurance, India failed.

Failure of EPZ's and SEZ's

The objectives of EPZ's and SEZ's were, to increase foreign exchange earnings, attract FDI and provide employment opportunities. But it failed miserably to achieve any of these objectives. Even though Indian exports witnessed a quantum jump in post-liberalization period, the contribution of EPZ's and SEZ's was pathetic. In 1999-2000, EPZ's and SEZ's contributed to a mere 4.7% of the total exports and the previous years were no better. India should start more EPZ's and SEZ's with new incentives to promote quality exports. Off late FICCI had formed a committee and asked to draft a report on the highly successful Chinese model of EPZ's in Guang Zon, Sen Zhen.

Hands-on, Value-Driven

Can values be taught? The answer is 'yes' or 'no'. What is inborn in every human is a series of negative values, some metaphysicians call this the original sin in all of us. Certainly the child is born with the desire to enhance its share of all that promotes its happiness and thus it learns the positive values. We are struck by the explicit attention people pay to values and by the way in which their leaders have created exiting environments through personal attention, persistence and direct intervention for down the line. The real difference between success and failure of a corporation can very often be traced to the question of how well the organization brings out the great energies and talents of its people. A great organization will owe its resiliency not to its form of organization or administrative skills, but to the power of what we call beliefs and the appeal these beliefs have for its people. An organization should have, sound set of beliefs on which it premises all its policy and actions. It then adheres to those beliefs. If an organization is to meet the challenges of a changing world, it must be prepared to change everything about itself, except those beliefs as it moves through corporate life.

Labour Practices

Though India's labour is very cost effective, it has been exploited by child labour, bonded labour, exploitative wages and so on. Saying that poverty, unemployment, traditional family crafts is a reason for such explorative practices is an excuse. We have to attain labour standards set by WTO. To revamp the existing labour scenario, it would cost us US $ 15 billion (65,000 crores). India can afford to pay this amount in instalments with in the next 20 years. If the West insists that we need to change the labour scenario by 2005 or 2010, its high time that India carries on investment in the same.

SUGGESTIONS TO MEET THE CHALLENGES

Have a Global Mind Set?

Globalization does not mean inviting foreign companies to do business in India but it also involves Indian companies penetrating global markets. If the Indian companies have to seize the new opportunities created by the changing world economy, they have to think and compete globally. This requires more than a good product or service. It demands strategic thinking, ability to position their companies in a global context, capacity to satisfy most demanding customers and a long-term commitment to innovating productivity and customer service. Indian businesses should be more aggressive in their approach and not given to foreign competition. We should also identify markets in countries psychologically not close.

Aiming at Market Share and not Margins

The success of a business does not depend on profits alone. It is the market share that is the success to the business. This can be achieved through economies of scale and by decreasing the cost of a product. Using local staff, advertising agencies and running advertisements in local media can increase the gross profit of the business. The customer needs have to be properly identified and taken care of.

Create Added Value to the Product

The product has to be given appropriate dressing. We have

to project our product as a bundle of utilities. Various discounts, free gifts, offers, incentives etc., should be given. Provide proper after sales service. The business has to be a custodian of customer's interest. Put effort on dissemination of information about product features.

Core Competencies

Core competence is something, which the competitors cannot simply imitate. It enables a company to gain a leading position in its chosen market segments, despite stiff competition. Firms will have to develop their core competencies in certain selected areas and build sustained competitive advantage in order to successfully compete in foreign markets. Korean steel and semi-conductor producers, for example, have successfully attacked world markets using low cost strategy. On the other hand, German machine tool producers compete with differentiated strategies involving high product performance, reliability and responsive service.

Customer Driven Philosophy

For too long Indian companies have been producing what is easy to sell rather than to produce what the customers want. But this has to be changed. The proper penetration of foreign markets requires a deeper understanding of consumer behaviour. Management and marketing policies of our business firms should be customer driven instead of production driven or sales driven.

Quality Standards

In the context of global marketing, quality standards have assumed a new significance. Even though our products are exported only on meeting ISO 14000 standards, not much has been achieved in regard to quality standards. The most urgent need is, therefore, to bring about a 'quality revolution' in Indian business and industry which will enable them to meet the international quality standards and specifications and also gear up to face global competition. For this purpose they can use techniques like TQM, ERP, BPR, JIT and so on.

Innovation

Innovation should become a mind set and not a process, there is intense pressure for innovation from the markets. With the technology and customers changing rapidly there is no other way to be alive to these changes but continuous innovation. Innovation is a creative process and is one of the most significant parameters that encourages creative thinking in the organization. The successful firms are ones that tolerate failure and are willing to invest in discovering the unknown future.

Considering Macro-economic Variables

Firms should select markets that have potential to grow than the saturated. They should make assessment of demography, government policy, political stability, customer orientations, technology, etc. before penetrating a particular foreign market. How much we export is more important than to the countries we export. Government should provide supporting measures to achieve global competitiveness and should soften the impact of import liberalization and balance of payments. One move is to devalue rupee by 10%. It will ensure surging exports to grow despite, weakening our economy. We have to bring domestic production cost in line with international ones. We have to decrease the shift from domestic production to imports.

Have Correct Advertising and Promotion Policy

There are different markets, segmented consumers, diverse strategies, good, effective advertising is the result of understanding individual preferences rather than treating consumers as a moronic mass. Firm should have proper ethical standards and should look at the long-run perspective. The success of a brand will depend on what the firm projects about the product in the media channel. They should suggest unique selling proposition and should create a strong brand appeal. They should screen out advertisement which viewers don't want to see but rather pay attention to the viewers' interest. In this redefined communication environment, the intelligent human being will be the ultimate beneficiary.

Simultaneous Loose-tight Principles

Organizations that live by loose-tight principle are on one hand rigidly controlled, yet at the same time (indeed, insist on) autonomy, entrepreneurship and innovation from rank to file.

They do this literally through faith and value systems. They do it through taking attention to detail, to getting the "itty-bitty, teeny-tiny things" right. The smart firms are ones who shift direction all the time, based upon the latest output from the expected value equation, the ones who juggle hundred-variable models with facility; the ones who design complicated incentive systems; the ones who wire up matrix structures.

Industrial Restructuring

In this dynamic era it expects some adjustments interms of restructuring the economy and industry in particular. Product upgradation, capital restructuring, etc. are need of the hour. Labours rationalization interms of human face has to be taken care of. Some sort of social security network needs to be evolved. At the same time, it is not to be forgotten that organized industrial labour in the country represents a mere 9 percent of the entire labour force. Thus the marketing is still beyond the pale of economic guarantee.

Indian firms have to strengthen their alliances with foreign manufactures and form tie-ups making investment and technology in order to make their presence felt in the global market place. The Indian companies have to penetrate into global market using their state-of-art technology. India has to follow sustainable competitive advantage by beating the competition.

CONCLUSION

The new economic policy initiated in June 1999 has two main objectives: domestic economic liberalization and integration of Indian economy into global economy in a phased manner. In the current international economic environment, globalization is a good option. Globalization can confer the following benefits. First, India can get foreign direct investment of US$ 12-15 billion per annum. It can supplement our domestic saving and bring new technology and managerial skills in infrastructure industries and export-oriented industries. Second, India has signed various multilateral treaties and it must play a proactive role in order to reap benefits from the treaties. Liberalization of agricultural trade, phasing out of multi-fiber agreement and rule-based trading regime provide ample opportunities for India to exploit its comparative advantage in agricultural product like rice, cotton and fruits and vegetables, agro-based products and computer software. Third, international competitiveness can result in dynamic efficiency gains to Indian economy. But India must undertake legal, administrative and procedural reforms to reduce transaction cost of doing business and government must play catalytic role in export promotion. India should adopt a concrete program of action by the review of business portfolio, restructuring of balance sheet, asset management, improving quality, productivity and cost structure.

References

1. Sankar, U., "Beyond Hindu Rate," *Charted Financial Analyst*, Jan. 2000.
2. Neelamegham, S., *Competing Globally*, Allied Publishers Limited.
3. Rajan Saxena, "Global Competitiveness of Indian Enterprises," *Charted Secretary*, Vol. 21, November 2001.
4. Srikanth, R., "FDI-Perception for Growth", *Charted Finance Analyst*, Oct. 2000.
5. Thomas J. Peters & Robert H. Watermann, *in Search of Excellence*, Warner Brothers.
6. J.T.K. Daniel & R. Gopalan, *A Vision for India Tomorrow*; MCC Publications.
7. "New Initiatives to Boost Inflows", *The Hindu*, March 30, 2002.
8. Prem Shankar Jha, "Why India's Globalization has Failed", *The Hindu*, March 26, 2002.
9. Subramaniam Swamy, *WTO—Challenges and Strategies for Indian Economy*.
10. Pradeep S. Mehta & Purnima Purohit, *Globalization and India—Myths and Realities*, CUTS.
11. Sanjeev Dubey, "EPZs an Evaluation" in *Yojana*, March 2002
12. Jean Pierre Jeannet & Herbert D. Hannessey, *Global Marketing Strategies*.
13. Vandana Dangi, "Managing Globalization, What India must do," *JIMS*, July-Sept. 2001.
14. S. Guruswamy, "Managing Global Competitiveness an Agenda for Action" in *JIMS*, July-Sept. 2001.
15. Lester Thurow, "Economic Forces," *Executive Excellence*, June 2000.
16. Douglas N. Daft, "Connecting with Global Consumers", *Executive Excellence*, Dec. 2000.

7

Conflicts and Dilemmas of Decentralization in India

A. MEENAKSHISUNDARARAJAN

INTRODUCTION

Political decentralization has been the norm in industrial democracies for decades. Now, increasingly, Eastern European countries and developing countries are following this lead and decentralizing their public sectors. As recently observed, "the twentieth century is ending, as it began, with great aspirations for extending the benefits of democratic self-government to even numbers of men and women."

Decentralised planning can be defined as 'planning at different levels' or 'multi-level planning'. This may consist of planning at national level, state level, district level, block level, panchayat level or it could be planning for a region. Decentralised planning also means, an overall institutional effort undertaken to decentralize decision-making according to a process defined throughout the country.

Decentralization can be achieved in a number of ways. Fiscal and political federalism is probably the most common form, but the new wave of decentralization has adopted other strategies as well. In many countries decentralization is achieved through the transfer of power to local units (deconcentration), coupled with revenue sharing or other forms of transfers from the center to regional and local governments. Other countries achieve decentralization by transferring power to sub-national political institutions above the local level (devolution), or to decentralized entities (delegation). In countries where privatization programs have been implemented, decentralization has transferred power and responsibilities to the private sector.[1] But in India, eventhough Gandhiji suggested for Decentralization of power to the local authorities, till date, is a dream.

WHY DECENTRALIZATION IN INDIA?

The centralized government in India has failed in its duty to deliver services to the communities effectively. Moreover, the local government in India is not able to solve the problem of societies till date. The Government of India as well as State Governments in allocating the resources it raised through a centralized tax system is day-by-day increased, while local Governments' role in influencing the distribution of government services to the local Governments have been diminished for the last 52 years.

So however, local bosses still depended on the state for resources, and their influence had to be exercised through complex negotiations involving political commitments and pledges of congressional support for government programs. Their next move, therefore, was to secure a greater degree of financial independence. This was achieved by promoting legislation and constitutional amendments that increased the share of central government funds earmarked to regional and local governments for general investment. The political bosses of India pushed to increase the resources earmarked to local and regional governments but never for the popular election of regional and local authorities. Nor did local barons encourage a clear transfer of responsibilities from the center to lower levels of government. Rather, those initiatives were advanced by progressive members of the executive and national party leadership.

Some of the progressives' reforms in India have not been in the best interest of the local political barons. The popular election of mayors and regional governors, for example has undermined the influence of party congressional bosses, e.g. Chennai Mayorship. The public in India has demonstrated considerable independence through local body elections, electing several civic and independent candidates not linked to the party machinery or to the local barons. But in India in other cases the experience has not been positive, since the political bosses have taken over local governments, the level and quality of community participation has been almost nil. Even in the economic point of view, these political has improved significantly and bosses have failed to get adequate funds from their respective state governments for providing basic services to the people.

Decentralization is associated with the greater participation of local citizens in government decision-making. Communities perceive that, they are obtaining a larger share of public resources, and decentralization is regarded as an entitlement in local and regional public opinion. For these reasons the recent reforms seem irreversible as long as the more participatory forms of government prevail. The public in India does not favour centralization because it has traditionally failed to deliver and because the public attaches value to the election of local and regional officials, to the possibility of public oversight of local authorities, and to the proximity of the decision-making process.[3] In short, the public supports decentralization.

North (1990, p. 140) states that, the greatest obstacle to efficient decentralization in India is the cultural conservation of local communities and the tradition within central and state governments of monopolizing resources and initiatives. Communities are accustomed to obtaining services and favours from their central and state governments, and local administrators have long depended on the center for resources, and their respective state initiatives, and ideas. For their part, national-level and state level politicians traditionally have stunted the civic development of the communities by imposing informal but hierarchical structures such as those derived from political patronage.

A pervasive problem in the decentralization process is the

overlap of responsibilities among different levels of government stemming from constitutions, laws, or the structure of government bureaucracy. The overlap of functions and the lack of clarity in inter-governmental transfers create conflict between the different authorities that may discredit the system. Such overlap can also impede the delivery of social services because each level expects the others to perform.

Even when a decentralized system is adopted, the rules and constraints imposed by the constitution, the law, or the central bureaucracy may preserve a bias that favours the pre-existing tradition of centralism. In such cases programs and priorities are determined by the centre, state and local governments are simply expected to carry them out (*Ahmed and others*, 1995). Although this outcome is undesirable, it is equally undesirable for local administrations to take revenues from the centre and the state and use them, for example, to increase the bureaucracy or to fund programs that have a lower priority than the provision of basic education and health services.

DECENTRALIZATION AND LOCAL GOVERNMENT AUTONOMY

In order to achieve efficient decision-making in a decentralized system and effective political interactions between the government and its constituencies, local government units must have a high degree of autonomy. At the same time, local governments should be protected from being captured by special interest groups, by the political bosses of the old order or by any other force that is "bent on capturing the state apparatus for (its) own purposes. The state then is in danger of dissipating its own special contribution, which lies in its ability to operate on the basis of a more general and inclusive vision than is feasible for private actors embedded in the market. If decentralization destroys the ability of the state to act coherently . . ., then the unique character of its contribution is lost" (*Rueschemeyer and Evans*, 1985, p. 56)

When local Government get autonomy it would tend to become more area-specific i.e., it would be possible to establish close complementarity between development schemes and local potentials, problems and priorities.

The need for local autonomy is felt to tackle the problem of poverty because centralized planning has failed to eliminate poverty and the benefit of growth has not percolated down to the people.

Active participation, involvement and support of local people in the process of development and utilization of local resources are possible only if the local Government get autonomy.

The effective use of local resources, to satisfy local needs and aspirations of people in given areas, resource generation and the effective participation of the people is possible only if local Government get autonomy. Autonomy for local Government would allow the planning to be of manageable size.

Local governments may be more susceptible to capture by divergent forces unless there is also a strong and cohesive civic society that provides political support and a dependable national government that protects opposing economic interests.

These conditions do not exist in India. Thus India must develop strong bureaucratic institutions at all levels of government to foster discipline, cooperation, and relative autonomy among civil servants (*Rueschemeyer* and *Evans*, 1985). Strong institutions can also be a shield against outside influence unless managers at the local level become vulnerable to external pressure through their association with local elites or guerrillas.

PROBLEMS OF DECENTRALIZATION IN INDIA

(A) Political Challenges and Credibility

The weakness of the central state, the newness of decentralization, and the cultural attachment to the formal and informal institutions of centralism may conspire to create a political and social environment in which decentralized institutions are discredited. Decentralization can also be hindered by inexperienced local administrations, disaffected congressional or political bosses, inadequate civic organizations, and an unresponsive populace.

In practice, local governments in India are assigned two types of functions: those that involve strictly local activities (tax collection, road maintenance, drinking water distribution, and so on) and those that cross-jurisdictional boundaries and for which there is central or state government interest. In addition, a number of functions that would be more effectively performed by the central government—such as poverty reduction or other income distribution programs—are often assigned to local governments. In other instances poorly defined functions overlap the various levels of government, causing gaps and duplication in service provisions. In these cases decentralization requires a strong central and state administration that can clearly assign responsibilities, assist weak sub-national entities, and ensure compliance with central and state government objectives such as poverty reduction, income distribution, and environmental protection (*Campbell, Paterson* and *Brakarz,* 1991). The Central and the state Governments in India should set the stage for the activities of the decentralized, lower levels of government and should be responsible for coordination when there are conflicts and overlapping functions.

(B) Agency Problems

Agency problems derive from the nature of Central and state administration responsibility. The Centre and the state can delegate, deconcentrate, or devolve functions and power, but it cannot shake the ultimate responsibility for the quality of basic services like education, health, and crime prevention. A state-central government cannot watch impassively when local governments fail to provide these basic services because the long-run costs of these failures will be enormous.

Those problems are minimized when functions are well defined for all levels of government, either through legal or constitutional provisions or through contracts between different levels of government. Still, because contracts and legislation cannot foresee all possible outcomes, the Central and state governments must use performance measures and provide an adequate set of incentives to induce the desired behaviour and to extract information about performance and about local capacity to deliver delegated and devolved services.

In a decentralized system the public should hold local governments accountable for the provision of services financed by the Central and the State governments. Accountability requires systematic disclosure of government activities and an institutional setting that facilitates community involvement and control. It also requires that the government create citizen supervisory boards or lay the legal foundation for community entities that are involved in decision-making, such as school supervisory boards. Citizens belonging to these entities must receive proper training and support in financial management and administration. The government must provide them with timely information about the resources being disbursed, quality standards, and coverage targets. The best way to induce community participation is to demand that programs financed with government grants be confinanced with local tax revenues. By linking performance and taxation, this creates a strong incentive for community involvement (*Winkler*, 1994). Even though 73rd and 74th amendment of India's constitution stressed to have Gram Sabhas in rural areas, it has failed to give any supervisory and other powers mentioned above.

A complementary solution would be to pass laws imposing a strict code of behaviour and rigid due process on local administrators, making them personally responsible—and legally liable—when they fail to perform in the best interests of the community. In this sense public administrators would hold trust of the community with a mandate to pursue its welfare, much as the head of a family would zealously pursue the well-being of his or her dependents.

Such laws can act as a powerful deterrent to corruption and political clientelism if civic institutions are in place to initiate court actions against local officials, when required. Alternatively, a superintendency of local administrators could be made responsible for initiating the same actions.[4] If these types of mechanisms would be implemented, a code of behaviour call an "esprit local officials would definitely serve for the benefit of the society in semi-urban and rural area."

(C) Political Dilemmas

Decentralization entails loss of power by the central and state governments, by political parties, and by local political bosses. These three groups constituted the governance capacity under centralized systems. Through a complex network of favours and patronage, the center maintained the loyalty of the local elites while exercising both formal and informal authority in the regions. The lack of political will is the main reason for the non-implementation Decentralization in India.

(D) Governance and Power

Decentalization breaks some of the links on which centralized governance was based: resources flow to the regions and municipalities automatically, through constitutionally and legally mandated channels; the allocation of resources is increasingly a local responsibility, with a considerable degree of independence from the central government; and the authority of local elites can be effectively challenged by civic or dissident groups, who through elections can gain access to resources that are in turn a source of power in the community.

Under decentralization the states no longer has any means of manipulating local authorities when it seeks cooperation for problems of governance. For all practical purposes, once the revenue-sharing mechanisms are defined and the communities are able to raise taxes, local authorities do not have to fully cooperate with the state in a voluntary manner.

DECENTRALIZATION AND ITS ECONOMIC IMPACT

(A) Macro-Economic Stability

The fiscal behaviour of lower levels of government therefore has a significant macro-economic impact on aggregate fiscal accounts. During the transition from centralized to decentralized government, this impact has been largely negative. Decentralization measures in a broad spectrum of countries have had adverse impacts on macro-economic stability, at least in the short-run. At the same time central governments are often uncertain,how far to extend local autonomy (*Campbell, Paterson,* and *Brakarz,* 1991). The problem does not lie so much with decentralization as with the absence of budget institutions for and effective controls on local government spending and debt, and with the source of the funds that are financing the process.

When state and local budget institutions and controls are weak, the autonomous spending and indebtedness of lower levels of government may contribute to greater deficit spending.

It is unlikely that strong budget institutions will develop during the early stages of the transition to decentralized forms of government. The absence of institutions may create a lack of fiscal discipline at the lower levels of government that increases macro-economic instability by generating large deficits in the aggregate public sector budget. This is an undesirable but not improbable result of decentralization that must be corrected when it occurs.[5] In these cases it may be appropriate to subordinate local autonomy to centrally determined budgetary controls until the local governments develop institutions and rules that foster fiscal discipline.

Of paramount importance are rules that limit the indebtedness of all levels of government, and in this case the lower levels. When borrowing by the sub-national governments within a monetary union creates negative externalities, it must be restrained, local governments' access to credit should be limited so that they do not have free rein to create budget deficits and finance them through debt, much less to obtain foreign credit without the authorization of the central government (*Wilesner* and *Munohy*, 1994).

(B) Fiscal Problems

The other issue connected with the impact of decentralization on fiscal results is the local government's source of funds. Decentralization should include an increased local tax effort to raise resources for the provision of services. This local tax effort provides the price discipline that is required to efficiently produce and deliver local services and allows consumers to express their preferences. When local governments have relative budget autonomy but do not have to raise taxes to support their spending, they tend to overspend. Furthermore, the political system may induce greater fiscal irresponsibility.

When funds are centrally raised and spending is decentralized, spending is higher. In addition, centralized taxes and decentralized spending are likely to become permanent because of voter preferences. This preference may be caused in part by democratic institutions—because voters prefer centralized taxes when there is capital mobility—and in part by patronage and corruption.[6]

Financing decentralization through local taxation is an effective check against the Leviathan tendency of government to increase its size and its tax resources monotonically. Cross-country evidence indicates that the simultaneous decentralization of the national government's taxing and spending powers exerts a negative influence on the overall size of the public sector. Thus revenue sharing and taxing decisions should be made at the center in order to eliminate the negative influence of decentralization of the spending power[7] (*Ehdaie,* 1994).

Despite these clear conclusions, "there has been much less action to grant new revenue-raising authority to local governments than there has been to increase centrally financed resource transfers" (*Camgbell, Paterson* and *Brakarz,* 1991, p. 13). One reason for this neglect, as already discussed, is the desire of regional barons and voters to acquire a share of the central government boundry. Another reason is the existing organization of taxes. In India income tax is monopolized by the Central government.[8]

In these cases, the lower-level governments must rely on property taxes, a few minor taxes, and their share of central government revenues. Quite often, these governments are not allowed to establish their own income and sales tax, nor can they impose surcharges to be collected with broadly based and more buoyant national taxes.

(C) Problems of Revenue Sharing

As discussed earlier, revenue sharing mechanism are linked to the delegation or devolution of new functions and responsibilities to local governments. If these new responsibilities do not impose additional financial burdens on the local governments, decentralization does not introduce any new or additional fiscal problems to those of the centralized system. The same services will be supplied and financed, but, the hope is, at a higher level of productive and allocative efficiency.[9]

But that is not the whole story. When resources and responsibilities are transferred from one level of government to another, there is also a shift of power—and there is no guarantee that a new political equilibrium will be achieved automatically. These situations lead to political and budgetary gamesmanship and may have a negative bearing on the overall fiscal picture.

CONCLUSION

Decentralization is therefore not a trivial development but an institutional change that has the potential to induce a true social revolution along the path to a more dynamic and self-reliant society—a society that promotes progress and technical change and plays down the traditional symbols and sources of power that typified the centralist state.

The paradox of decentralization is that it demands more central government and more sophisticated political skills at the national level. This problem is more political than economic. If decentralization is to develop as an institutional change that enhances the economic and social progress of the countries that are experimenting with it, central governments must be able—and willing—to steer the institutional change in the direction of a more democratic and efficient society. Because this is a new function for most national governments, they are at the beginning of a long learning curve.

References

1. Ahmed Etisham, and Charles Vehorm, Giorgio Brosio, and Bernd Spahn (1995), *Colombia: "Reforming Territorial Taxation and Transfers,"* International Monetary Fund, Fiscal Affairs Department, Washington, D.C.
2. Alesina, Alberto, and Roberto Perotti (1994a), *"Budget Deficits and Institutions,"* Harvard University and Columbia Univesity, Department of Economics, Cambridge, Mass., and New york.
3. —— (1994b), *"The Political Economy of Budget Deficits,"* NBER working Paper 4637, National Bureau of Economic Research, Cambridge, Mass.
4. Bomfim, Antulio, and Anwar Shah (1994), "Macro-economic Management and the Division of Powers in Brazil: Perspectives for the 1990s". Background paper prepared for World Development Report, 1994: Infrastructure for Develcpment, World Bank, Washington, D.C.
5. Campbell, Tim (1994), *"Decentralization and Reform of the State in Latin America and the Caribbean,"* World Bank, Washington, D.C.
6. Cambell, Tim, George Paterson, and Jose Brakarz (1991), *"Decentralization to Local Government in Latin America and the Caribbean: National Strategies and Local Response in Planning, Spending, and Management,"* World Bank, Washington, D.C.
7. Cremer, Jacques Antonio Estache, and Paul Seabright (1994), *"The*

Decentralization of Public Services: Lessons from the Theory of the Firm," Policy Research Working Paper 1345, World Bank, Washington, D.C.

8. Dillinger, Williams (1994), *"Decentralization and its Implications for Urban Service Delivery,"* World Bank, Washington, D.C.
9. Ehdaie, Jaher (1994), *"Fiscal Decentralization and the Size of Government: An Extension with Evidence from Cross Country Data,"* Policy Research Working Paper 1387, World Bank, Washington, D.C.

8

Globalization and Indian Economy—Impact and Evaluation

P.N. Rao

India after independence started planned economic development. The main objective of our five year plans was, to increase the rate of Economic growth, which enable us to increase the employment and reduce inequalities in all spears. So, for nine five year plans, the annual plans were designed and got implemented. In all these plans, large investments was made in key sectors to increase the peace of development and expected that the benefits of growth would spread to all sections of the people. But five decades of planned development have not made any significant effect in spreading the benefits to different sections of the community. The objective of planning in India is to rise the per capita income and to ensure that the benefits are evenly distributed between regions and people.

However, after four decades of planning, the levels of development achieved is far from satisfactory by the year 1990, more than 40 percent of the population was living below poverty line. The economy was suffering with very low growth rate of high levels unemployment, low levels of exports, high levels of imports and crisis in balance of payments.

To solve the problem of low economic growth rate and balance of payment crisis Government of India has initiated the policy reform measures like structural adjustment program, liberalization and globalization. These measures are aimed at efficient allocation of Productive resources and to eliminate market distortions. These measures lead to market economy where market regulates the economy and role of state is reduced. These reforms are based on the belief that once macro-economic stabilization is achieved, it will alter the structural characteristics of the economy and lead to sustainable economic growth.

Champions of policy of Economic liberalization and globalization viewed that the poor growth rate of Economy is due to the extensive bureaucratic controls over production, investments and trade. The highly protected Indian industries become inefficient and uncompetitive in the international market and could not develop productive capabilities.

The policy measures like SAP, liberalization and globalization are claimed as unavoidable measures from the angle of resource-use efficiency and competitiveness of the economy with high growth rate. However, these policy measures have created a lot of controversy among social scientists of the country. Some economists express doubt about such strategy of development which will reduce, socio-economic inequalities between people and regions. In spite of planned and regulated development under state intervention, the country has failed to reduce socio-economic inequalities between people and regions. Some other economists argue that for India it is not possible to dispense with reforms but they should be introduced with a human face. India cannot continue with system where vast majority of people are deprived of the gains from the economic development. Given the on going process of development in the Indian economy, it is viewed that if the economic growth of the country is left to market forces and the role of the state is minimized, the economic development is expected to take higher path. Though it may not be correct and scientific to make sweeping conclusions, since these reforms are less than 10 years old, but regular assessment and timely correction of the policy reforms help us to make them success. In this backdrop, the present paper makes an attempt to compare the development process during the planning period of strong state intervention and public investments—with the recent development process under market forces.

The key dimensions of Economic performance are gross national and domestic product, national investment, savings, imports and exports and balance of payments. GDP growth rate is the principal yardstick of Economic performance. Between 1950-51 to 1980-81 the average growth of GDP per year is 3.6 percent. The GDP growth has accelerated to 5.6 percent in eighties and stayed at that level up to 2000-01, since 1990-91. The growth performance of eighties can be attributed to the emergence of unsustainable fiscal deficits and balance of payment crisis that may be due to the government policy of anti-export bios in trade policy and growing reliance on external borrowing to fund, the current account deficit in the balance of payments. The reforms helped the country to come out of the balance of payment crisis and the external sector is more manageable. The average growth rate was stayed at 5.6 percent between 1990-91 to 2000-01, during the reform period. When we look at per capita GDP growth, it looks better, which accelerated from 0.3 percent in seventies to 4.0 percent in late nineties. The per capita GDP is an indicator of average living standards of the people.

While comparing the economic performance in the post-reform period to pre-reform period, it is evident that high growth rate of GDP in post-reform period can be attributed to service sector where growth rate is 7.8 percent, the average growth of agriculture between 1991-2001 is 2.7 percent while it is 3.6 percent between 1981-91. Average growth of Industrial sector also shows lower growth in the post-reform period that is 5.7 percent when compared to pre-reform period that is between 1980-82 to 1991-92 which is 7.1 percent.

Now looking at the past-reform Quinquennium the growth rate of GDP increased to 6.7 percent from pre-crisis decadal average of 5.6 percent, which is impressive. It clearly indicates that on going reform process is on the right path. Agriculture, industries and service sectors growth rate is high in post-crisis quinquennium then pre-crisis decade. If we look at the average growth of last four years the overall GDP growth fells to 5.4 percent. Much more disturbing is that agricultural growth collapsed to 1.2 percent. But industrial growth drops to 4.8 percent. Service sector grew at an average of 8.1 percent, in these four years, otherwise GDP growth could have been very low.

TABLE 1

Average Growth of GDP

(*Percentage*)

	1950-52 1960-61	*1961-62 1970-71*	*1971-72 1980-81*	*1980-81 1990-91*	*1990-91 2000-01*	*1992-93 2000-01*	*1992-93 1996-97*	*1997-98 2000-01*
Agriculture, Allied sector	3.1	2.5	1.8	3.6	2.7	3.7	4.7	1.2
Industry	6.3	5.5	4.1	7.1	5.7	6.4	7.6	4.8
Services	4.3	4.8	4.4	6.7	7.5	7.8	7.6	8.1
GDP (Fact of Cost)	3.9	3.7	3.2	5.6	5.6	6.1	6.7	5.4
Per Capital GDP	2.0	1.5	0.8	3.4	3.6	4.0		

Source: CSO.

The pattern of growth in service sector in post-reforms period is quite different from that of the pre-reform period. The changing pattern of service sector in Indian economic growth is given in Table 2. Nearly, half of GDP growth is accounted to service sector in both pre-reform decade and post-reform Quinquennium. In the post-reform decade the service sector contribution to GDP growth is 60 percent. In the last four years the contribution of service sector to GDP is 70 percent, which is remarkable. This rise in service sector contribution may be due to increased expenditure on defense and high pay scales due to the implementation of fifth pay commission.

AGRICULTURAL SECTOR

The process of economic liberalization as a policy reform at the all India level, and state level has generated no doubt a series of socio-economic transformations in the agrarian sector, through changes in the crop production in past reform period. The average growth of agricultural crop production has fallen for various crops. This is evident from the Table 3.

TABLE 2

Sectorial Contribution to Growth

(*Percent*)

	1991-81	*2000-01/ 1991-92*	*1996-97/ 1991-92*	*2000-01/ 1996-97*
Agriculture	21.9	14.1	21.1	5.9
Industry	32.0	28.2	36.8	25.0
Services	46.1	57.7	48.1	69.1
GDP (fact of Cost)	100.0	100.0	100.0	100.0

Source: CSO.

TABLE 3

Average Growth Rates of Agriculture Products

Year	*All Crops*	*Foodgrains*	*Non-foodgrains*
1981-91	3.5	2.9	4.8
1991-2000	2.6	2.6	2.5

Source: *Economic Survey*, 2000-01.

The fall in the growth rate of crop production means fall in the incomes of the population livng on the agriculture sector. The agricultural output growth declined to 2.7 percent per annum during the period 1991-2000 as against the growth rate of 3.6 percent during the period 1981-91. That is output growth rate is declaimed by 1 percent in post-reform period when compared to pre-reform decade.

The fall in the agricultural production growth in post-reform period is due to the fall in the non-food grain production. The growth rate of non-food grain production is 4.8 percent in pre-reform decade and it has decreased to 2.5 percent in post-reform period. The average growth rate in food grain production has decreased marginally in post-reform period when compare to pre-reform decade. This growth rate reveals that agricultural production pattern changed substantially in favour of food grains in post-reform period. Another important structural change that took place in post-reform period is that, the share of Rabi and Karif production of food grains. The Rabi production has become as important as Karif production in the post-reform period, that is

Rabi production accounts for half of the total production of food grains.

This clearly shows that decline in Agricultural growth rate in post-reform period is partly may be due to the withdrawal of the subsidies on inputs like fertilizer's power, irrigation, etc. and partly due to the decline in the public and private investments in agricultural sector.

INDUSTRIAL SECTOR

To study the impact of policy reforms like liberalization and globalization on industrial sector, we have to compare the performance of industrial sector before and after the reform period. For this the growth rate of industrial production is given in Table 4. From the table it can be observed that growth performance of industrial sector during post-reform period does not appear to be better than performance during pre-reform period.

TABLE 4

Industry-wise Average Growth Rate in Industrial Production

(In percent)

Period	*Mines and Quarries*	*Manufacturers*	*Electrical*	*General*
1980-90	6.6	6.8	3.0	6.9
1990-2000	3.6	6.9	6.4	6.5

Source: *Economic Survey*, 2000-01.

The trends in growth rate of industrial production shows that the index of average growth rate of industrial production has declined in post-reform period, when compared to pre-reform decade. It has fallen to 3.6 percent in post-reform period from 6.6 percent in pre-reform period. In case of mines and quarries, to 3.6 percent in the post-reform period from 6.6 in pre-reform period. In case of Electricity production there is a considerable increase in the growth rate in post-reform period. Overall trend in all the sectors taken together is that growth rate has declined about 0.4 percent in post-refonn period when compared to the pre-reform period. The decline in the growth of manufacturing as well as mining and quarrying is a matter of serious concern and causes infrastructural bottlenecks. These bottlenecks reduce the growth efficiency of overall investments.

In recent years the structure of industrial production has undergone radical changes. In the pre-reform period capital goods sector led the process of growth. But in post-reform period composition of manufacturing sector has changed. This can be observed from the Table 5. The decline in the growth rate of capital goods sector during post-reform period may be due to sluggish investment demand in the economy or partly may be due to import liberalization. But import of capital goods has declined in post-reform period. The manufacturing growth in post-reform period is cleanly led by intermediate goods. The average annual growth rate of consumer goods marginally increased to 6.5 per cent in post-reform period from 6.0 percent in pre-reform period.

TABLE 5

Average Annual Growth Rates of Industrial Production

	1980-91	*1991-2000*
Basic Goods	7.4	5.9
Capital Goods	9.4	5.4
Intermediate Goods	4.9	8.6
Consumer Goods	6.0	6.5
Consumer Durables	10.8	10.2
Consumer Non-durables	5.3	4.7

Source: *Economic Survey*, 2000-01.

One of the growth is the key measure of Economic performance, inflation is considered to be the measures of economic stability. The period between 1950-51 to 1960-61 is the best period as far as the inflation is concerned. In 1970's the average annual inflation rate reached to double digits, because of oil shock. In 1980's the inflation on an average varied between 7 to 8 percent. In post-reform period on an average per annum is around 7.8 percent. But in pre-reform period on an average inflation is 7.2 percent.

The Table 6 gives the inflation rate in WPI on an average per annum. The noteworthy point is that, inflation is in double digit in the first half of the post-reform period. The rate of inflation declined in the second half of the post-reform period. The decline was to 3 percent in 1990-2000. The inflation has its adverse effects on living conditions of people at all levels till 1995-96. It has its demoralizing effects on common people to have belief in the efficiency of these economic measures, despite the fact that this may be justified in transit period.

TABLE 6

Average Annual Inflation (Wpi)

1951-52 to 1960-61	1.8
1960-62 to 1970-71	6.3
1970-72 to 1980-81	10.3
1981-82 to 1990-91	7.2
1991-92 to 2000-01	7.8
1991-92 to 1995-96	10.6
1992-93 to 1995-96	9.8
1996-97 to 2000-01	5.0

Source: RBI Reports.

The most important objective of the development planning is to raise the employment opportunities. The strategy was not only to provide employment but also to plan for new additions to the labour force. The Economic growth will bring about structural changes in the job market. Economic reforms are aimed at employment-orientated growth. Abolishing quantitative restrictions, reducing tariffs changes in the labour laws, liberalizing FDI are aimed at more acceleration of economic growth along with creation of more employment opportunities. The growth of employment during the periods 1983 to 1994 and 1994-2000 is given in Table 7.

The average annual growth rate of employment was 2.04 per annum in the period from 1983 to 1994. But declined to 0.98 per cent per annum in 1994 to 2000. The sector-wise growth of overall employment indicate that the employment growth rate declined between the periods 1983-94 to 1994-2000 due to the negative growth of employment in Agriculture, Mines and Quarrying and Electricity. This is the first time that growth rate in agricultural employment has declined since the planning era.

Employment in sectors like trade, construction, financial services, transport, storage and communication has grown rapidly in post-reform period when compared to pre-reform period. The share of these sectors in total employment has increased in post-reform period which reflect that the structural changes in product market in post-reform period. The low employment growth may be attributed to low rate of growlh of the economy.

TABLE 7

Growth of Employment for Sectors

S. No.	*Industry*	*1983-94*	*1994-2000*
1.	Agricultural	1.51	-0.34
2.	Mines and Quarrying	4.16	-2.85
3.	Manufacturing	2.14	2.05
4.	Electrical	4.50	-0.88
5.	Construction	5.32	7.09
6.	Trade	3.57	5.04
7.	Transport Storage & Communications	3.24	6.04
8.	Financial Policies	7.18	6.20
9.	Communities, Social & Personal Services	2.90	0.55
	Total Employment	2.04	0.98

Source: CSO.

Another major component of Economic reforms is fiscal policy, which aims at to reduce the high fiscal deficits and strengthen the fiscal health of the economy. Several policy measures were initiated to achieve this objective. The question now is that how far these objectives are achieved and what is its impact on growth of the economy. The major parameters that detumine the fiscal strength of the economy are, total expenditure, revenue expenditure, capital expenditure, fiscal deficit and revenue deficit. These fiscal parameters as percentage of GDP for pre-reform and post-reform periods are given in Table 8.

The total expenditure of the government as a proportion of GDP declined to 14.6 percent of GDP in post-reform period from 17.8 percent of GDP in pre-reform period. The total expenditure has dropped by 2.1 percentage points in post-reform period. This decline is consistent with the objectives of the reform process. The revenue expenditure increased to 12.3 percent of GDP in post-reform period an average from 11.7 percent of GDP during pre-reform period. Capital expenditure declined to 3.5 percent of GDP in post-reform period from 6 per cent in pre-reform period.

TABLE 8

Fiscal Parameters of the Central Government

(as percentage of GDP)

	1998-91	*1991-2000*
Total Expenditure	17.8	15.6
Revenue Expenditure	11.7	12.3
Interest Payments	2.7	4.3
Subsidies	1.7	1.4
Capital Expenditure	6.0	3.3
Total tax revenues	10.0	9.1
Non-tax revenues	2.4	2.5
Gross fiscal deficits	6.8	5.6
Gross Primary deficits	3.9	1.3
Revenue deficit	1.8	3.2
Amentized deficit	2.0	0.5

Source: RBI Reports.

The large fiscal and revenue deficits is detrimental to the macro-economic performance. These deficits erase out private investments, increase inflationary potential, disrupt the balance of payment, and impose a serious burden on feature generations. To come out of these high fiscal deficits, reform process was initiated from 1991 onwards. The main objective of reform process is to bring down the fiscal deficit to a sustainable level within five years. Otherwise prolonged fiscal deficit at an unsustainable level lead to economic instabilities. The gross fiscal deficit has dropped to 5.7 percent of GDP in post-reform period form 6.8 percent of GDP in pre-reform period. Even, after the ten years of reforms, one percentage decrease in fiscal deficit cannot be treated as the success of the Economic reforms. The expenditure on subsidies has been reduced by 0.3 percentage points. The burden of interest payments has increased to 4.3 percent of GDP in post-reform period from 2.7 percent of GDP in pre-reform decade. The burden of interest payment raises the revenue deficit. A rising revenue deficit leads to forced borrowings. The fiscal deficit dropped by 1 percentage of the GDP in post-reform period compared to the pre-reform period inspite of the rise in 1.3 percentage of revenue deficit rise in post-reform period compared to pre-reform period. This may be due to the fact that capital expenditure has declined to 3.4 percent of GDP in post-reform period. This trend is bad for the economy. If this is not checked, economy may get trapped in debts. The only positive impact of the reform is that monetized deficit is contained and brought to lowest level.

The large fiscal and revenue deficits will have adverse impact on private investments and capital formation. The changes in fiscal position influence the savings and investments and are shown in Table 9 for the period before and after reform. Public savings before reforms decade reached an average 3 percentage of GDP. The revenue deficit was 1.8 percent of GDP during the same period. But after reform period revenue deficit rose to 3.2 of percent GDP on an average and the public savings fall to 1.4 percent of GDP, in post-reform period, the failure of the government in reducing revenue deficit during reform period adversely effected the public savings and investment. The rate of growth of ratio of gross domestic savings in GDP declined drastically in later part of reforms period. This is an evidence of the failure on the part of reform process in reducing fiscal deficit. The growth rate of gross domestic capital formation has a declining trend in later part of reform period when compared to pre-reform period. The gross domestic capital formation has been

TABLE 9

Average Savings and Investments as a percent of GDP at Current Market

	Household Savings	*Private Savings*	*Public Savings*	*GDS*	*GDCF*
1980-81 to 1984-85	13.16	1.56	3.6	18.4	19.0
1985-86 to 1989-90	12.70	1.96	2.4	20.2	21.4
1990-91 to 1994-95	18.34	3.1	1.4	22.8	22.1
1995-96 to 1999-2000	22.58	4.2	1.4	23.3	22.3

Source: Economic Survey, 2002-02.

TABLE 10

Growth in External Sector

Period	*Exports*	*Imports*
1980-81 to 1990-91	16.2	14.9
1990-91 to 1999-2000	22.2	20.1

Source: Economic Survey, 2002-02.

lower than gross domestic savings by 1 percent of GDP between 1995-96 to 2000-01. This investment and savings gap reflects that, the private savings are going to unproductive government expenditure.

The focal point of reform process was in external sector. The reform initiation started from balance of payment crisis of 1991. The international trade was at the centre stage of the reform process. The Indian economy was integrated with the global economy. The share of exports and imports in GDP has increased in post-reform period considerably. The trade deficit has been considerably reduced.

CONCLUSION

This paper reviews the policy reforms like structural adjustment, liberalization and globalization that are initiated since 1991. For this economic performance of post-reform period is compared to pre-reform decade that is 1980-81 to 1990-91. Although acceleration in GDP shows the increased economic activity in post-reform period it has not raised the income levels of the rural poor. The growth rate of GDP is driven by service sector. The buoyancy in service sector is due to the increased expenditure by government. The stagnation or decline in the growth rates of the industries and agriculture sectors reveals that the growth has not changed the economic position of the majority people. The trends in industrial production reveal that the rate of industrial production has declined. The agricultural growth rate has been declined by 1 percent per annum in post-reform period when compared to pre-reform period, which has reflected in the declining growth rate of employment in post-reform period.

Another failure of the reform process has been that the fiscal deficit did not decline even after 10 years. The government expenditure and interest payments have not declined. On the other hand they have swelled in such a way that erosion took place in government savings and capital formation and led to large revenue deficits. This finally contributed to a fall in private and public savings and investments in the Economy. There is a failure in the fiscal management by government, which is a key parameter that will help to step up savings and investments and further accelerate the economic growth.

The major success of this reform process, is that some sort of stability is achieved in the external sector. Globalization and liberalization policy reforms provided the economy with stability and also liquidity in external sector. The external financial sector has well managed in post-reform period. The later part of reform process, inflation has been remained low, which is an indication of stability in the economy. This has to be verified in the ionger.

Finally, it may be concluded that there is an urgent need of policy measures that will take to the growth movements to 10 percent and above. The growth movement should come from all sectors of the economy. The main objectives of our growth should be societal transformation, which lead to a just and equitable social order to aim to alleviate poverty. The most important policy initiation necessary to achieve these objectives is reforms in agricultural sector, health, education and governance. For the success of these policy initiatives, successful fiscal consolidation is a pre-requisite.

References

Government of India (2001), *Economic Survey, 2000-01*, Ministry of Finance, New Delhi.

Gulati, Ashok and Seema Bathal (2001), 'Capital Formation in Indian Agriculture', *Economic and Political Weekly*, Vol. 36, No. 20, pp. 1697-1708.

Pandit, V.K. Krishnamurty and G. Mohanty (2000), 'India: Economic Outlook, 2000-03', Paper presented in the fall Meeting of the World Project Link, Oslo, Norway.

Uchikawa, Shuji (ed.) (2001), *Economic Reforms and Industrial Structure in India*, Institute of Developing Economies and Japan External Trade Organization, China, Japan.

Acharya, Shankar (1995), 'The Economic Consequences of Economic Reforms', Sir Puroshotamdas Thakurdas Memorial Lecture, delivered in Mumbai, November 1996, reprinted in *Indian Economy: Update*, Volume I, edited by Raj and Uma Kapila, Academic Foundation, Delhi, 1996.

—— (1999), 'Managing External Economic Challenges in the Nineties: Lessons for the Future', 18th Anniversary Lecture of the Centre for Banking Studies, Central Bank of Sri Lanka Occasional Paper No. 33, September, also available on the website www.icrter.org

Rao, M. Govind and H.K. Amar Nath (2000): 'Fiscal Correction: Illusion and Reality, *Economic and Political Weekly*, August 5.

Reserve Bank of India (1995): Annual Report, 1994-95 September.

9

Decentralised Development Experience: A Post-Reform Perspective

DEBASIS CHAKRABORTY AND ARUP GUHA

INTRODUCTION

Decentralisation has two major advantages, first it enables better information collection, and second it also imparts greater ability to process and utilise the information. Upto the British period, panchayats were the most prevalent governments in India. The reason was the lack of ability to collect information at village levels and also an absence of inclination to do so. The British replaced this system with a more centralised set-up, which served their objective of exploitation better. Post-independence, both due to the shortage of resources and the prevalence of the philosophy of balanced growth, we adopted and maintained the centralised system. However, today when the concept of balanced growth is no longer in vogue and our principal aim is to attract more and more foreign investment through better infrastructure development, we must go back to the panchayat system and avail of the twin advantages mentioned above.

The paper is organised along the following lines. We first describe the policies undertaken in the nineties to promote globalization in the Indian economy. However, the major focus of the paper is on the decentralisation of Indian economy over the past decade. The impact of decentralisation is viewed from two angles, first from the state level and then at the panchayat level. Finally, the study concludes with a policy prescription on the future course of decentralised development exercises.

GLOBALIZATION IN THE NINETIES

The change in attitude towards globalization was noticed in India since 1991. The economic crisis in the early years of the nineties urged the government to draw huge loans from international organization like the IMF and the World Bank. As a precondition for obtaining the loans, the government had to undertake a structural adjustment programme, where the role of the market was given a high priority. On the domestic front, the minimal role played by the state enhanced the decentralization exercise. On the other hand, on the external front, the government policies resulted in a closer association of the Indian economy with the global scenario, which in other words, could be termed as globalization. The withdrawal of the self-reliance doctrine pushed forward the need to pursue an active trade policy. The necessity to initiate an export growth strategy was further fuelled by the high import growth rate. In addition, the economy embraced the global economic set up more closely by allowing foreign capital inflow with simpler procedures. As a result, the Foreign Direct and Institutional Investment have increased manifold over the period. The openness indicator, which expresses total trade as a percentage of GDP, has gone up from 13 percent in 1991-92 to 31 percent in 1999-2000. The scenario is illustrated with the help of Table 1.

STATE LEVEL DECENTRALIZATION

We shall consider the decentralization exercise at two political levels: the State level, and the Panchayat level. The exercise is undertaken because the reforms have given rise to certain issues that make the progress of decentralization at the two

TABLE 1

The Time-series Trend in India's Export and Import

(Rs. Crore)

Year	*Export (X)*	*Export Growth (%)*	*Import (M)*	*Import Growth (%)*	*Trade Balance*	*TB Growth (%)*	*GDP at Factor Cost*	*TB as % of GDP*	*X+M as % of GDP*
1	2	3	4	5	6	7	8	9	10
Pre-Reform period									
1977-78	5408		6020		-612		374267	-0.16	3.05
1978-79	5726	5.88	6811	13.14	-1085	77.29	394861	-0.27	3.13}
1979-80	6418	12.09	9143	34.24	-2725	151.15	374323	-0.73	4.16
1980-81	6711	4.57	12549	37.25	-5838	114.24	401152	-1.46	4.80
1981-82	7806	16.32	13608	8.44	-5802	-0.62	425111	-1.36	5.04
1982-83	8803	12.77	14293	5.03	-5490	-5,38	437638	-1.25	5.28
1983-84	9771	11.00	15831	10.76	-6060	10.38	471191	-1.29	5.43
1984-85	11744	20.19	17134	8.23	-5390	-11.06	490027	-1.10	5.89
1985-86	10895	-7.23	19658	14.73	-8763	62.58	514059	-1.70	5.94
1986-87	12452	14.29	20096	2.23	-7644	-12.77	536337	-1.43	6.07
1987-88	15674	25.88	22244	10.69	-6570	-14.05	556874	-1.18	6.81
1988-89	20232	29.08	28235	26.93	-8003	21.81	615206	-1.30	7.88
1989-90	27658	36.70	35328	25.12	-7670	-4.16	656469	-1.17	9.59
1990-91	32553	17.70	43198	22.28	-10645	38.79	693051	-1.54	10.93

(*Contd.*)

TABLE 1 (*Contd.*)

1	*2*	*3*	*4*	*5*	*6*	*7*	*8*	*9*	*10*
Post-Reform Period									
1991-92	44041	35.29	47851	10.77	-3810	-64.21	702067	-0.54	13.09
1992-93	53688	21.90	63375	32.44	-9687	154.25	738003	-1.31	15.86
1993-94	69751	29.92	73101	15.35	-3350	-65.42	781345	-0.43	18.28
1994-95	82674	18.53	89971	23.08	-7297	117.82	888031	-0.82	19.44
1995-96	106353	28.64	122678	36.35	-16325	123.72	899563	-1.81	25.46
1996-97	118817	11.72	138920	13.24	-20103	23.14	970083	-2.07	25.57
1997-98	130101	9.50	154176	10.98	-24075	19.76	1016266	-2.37	27.97
1998-99	139753	7.42	178332	15.67	-38579	60.25	1083047	-3.56	29.37
1999-2000	162925	16.58	204583	. 14.72	-41658	7.98	1151991	-3.62	31.90

Source: Export, Import and GDP figures obtained from Economic Survey, 2000-01.

levels sometimes conflicting and at other times mutually beneficial. In this section, we examine certain phenomena concerning the progress of state level decentralization. The questions we are concerned with are as follows:

- Whether a particular state has increased or decreased its share in the GDP?
- Post-reform, what is the status of the issue of the convergence of the State Domestic Product (henceforth SDP) growth rates? How can we explain the prevailing scenario? How can the states that have fallen out recover themselves?
- What is the relation between State level decentralization and that at the Panchayat level?

Post-1991 reforms, the policy objective of balanced growth is no longer in fashion. Moreover, fewer central government controls and the arrival of the era of coalition governments at the Centre have increased the power of state level parties. Powerful regional satraps like Chandrababu Naidu can use their Lok Sabha MPs as bargaining pawns both to wrest more grants from the Centre and also to gain permission to receive funds and to attract investment from external agencies. Infact, sanction to foreign investment is largely devoid of political colour. So, there is ample opportunity for states with enterprising governments to strike their own growth curves. It is this post-reform freedom for states to not only generate their own resources but to also choose their own development expenditure heads (for instance IT for Andhra Pradesh) that we refer to as State level decentralization. Our objective is to isolate the effects of this decentralization.

We do not run any formal regressions, but that is hardly necessary since our objective is not to find formal indices of states' share in the national GDP but to explain why a particular state's share is rising or falling. Therefore, an informal analysis will serve our purpose pretty well. A careful examination of the data[1] allow us to draw the following broad conclusions:

First, the share of Eastern and North-Eastern Indian states in the national GDP has been falling in the 90's. However, most of the northern states, notably Rajasthan and Madhya

Pradesh have improved their shares. Uttar Pradesh is a notable exception. Therefore, it seems that in the 90's, Assam, Orissa and West Bengal have replaced the BIMARU states of the 80's.

Second, among the hinterlands of metropolises, the contributions of those surrounding Delhi, Mumbai. Bangalore, Hyderabad and Pune have increased while the share of Kolkata, Ahmedabad and Chennai have fallen.

Third, all the states in the south and the west have increased their shares of the economy.

We have isolated the following six broad phenomena from the above trends:

First, all the non-oil natural resource-based economies have shown a fall. UP, Bihar, West Bengal, the newly formed states of Chhattisgarh, Uttarakhand and Jharkhand have all recorded decreasing shares of the GDP exhibiting this trend. These regions are marked by mineral production and processing units and industries directly based on minerals, like the steel industry. In contrast, growth in states like Karnataka and Maharashtra, which have improved their share in the GDP, is driven by non-resource-based industries like infotech, textiles, chemicals, etc.

Second, states with agriculture based on natural inputs like high quality soil, rain and manure have experienced a reduced share in the GDP compared to the states where agriculture is dependent on artificial irrigation, chemical fertilizers, HYV seeds, etc. Another notable trend is that, states having a production bias in favour of foodgrains have reduced their share compared to cash crop biased states. Notable examples of states of the first kind are Assam, Orissa and West Bengal while Punjab and Haryana belong to the second category.

Third, states with Higher shares of SDPs in the national GDP are also the ones with better fiscal performances. This affects the distribution of central funds. Still the Finance Commissions give greater importance to population and area while disbursing central taxes. However, if the poor fiscal performance continues, how long this will last is debatable which will further worsen the condition of these states. Table 2 illustrates the fiscal self-reliance of the states.

TABLE 2

Index of Fiscal Self-Reliance of Indian States

States	*Own Revenue/Revenue Expenditure*		*Improvement Index*
	Average (90-91 to 92-93)	*Average (96-97 to 97-98)*	
Andhra Pradesh	0.5965	0.5611	97.40
Assam	0.3784	0.3142	85.97
Bihar	0.3429	0.3537	106.82
Gujarat	0.8297	0.7850	97.97
Karnataka	0.7273	0.7418	105.61
Kerala	0.5710	0.6042	109.56
Maharashtra	0.8359	0.8013	99.26
Manipur	0.0855	0.0862	104.37
Orissa	0.3808	0.3418	92.95
Tripura	0.0813	0.0966	123.08
Uttar Pradesh	0.3985	0.3781	98.22
West Bengal	0.4997	0.4241	87.88
All States	0.5617	0.5424	100.00

Source: Eleventh Finance Commission Recommendations.

Fourth, political clout has also had a role to play in this divergence. The states governed by parties having some clout with any of the two post-1990 stable central governments have improved their share. Orissa is a notable exception in this regard. Inspite of its ruling party, the Biju Janata Dal being a part of the ruling coalition at the Centre, the state's share has fallen.

Fifth, the above trends have also highlighted the importance of cities in the country's development. Cities serve two major functions: they are both the most important trading centres and the biggest sources of consumers for their hinterlands. Therefore, circumstantial evidence suggests that cities, whose surroundings have experienced a fall in their share of the GDP either have low per capita incomes (Kolkata), or require a significant improvement in trading infrastructure and incentives (Ahmedabad, Chennai).

Sixth, reforms have made trade freer and so exports are easier to make. States, which specialise in commodities that are in global demand, especially services, have in general improved their share compared to states with industries experiencing falling global demand. For instance, most of the IT output of Indian companies is of the nature of generic software, which mainly consists of IT solutions for official activities. Textile in Maharashtra and Gujarat and in Andhra and Karnataka fall in the first category while coal and steel in Bihar and West Bengal belong to the second.

Last, governance, law and order, institutes for technical education, the extent of corruption, etc. are also issues which determine both the competence of existing industries and the potential to attract further investment. Hence, they affect growth.

It must be fairly obvious from the above analysis that post-reform, the SDPs are not converging. However, we take a more formal look at this issue in the following lines.

The theoretical base of the concept of convergence lies in the neoclassical growth theory. In this model, the principal force ensuring convergence is diminishing returns to reproducible capital. So, economies with lower initial capital-labour ratios will have higher marginal productivity of capital and so tend to grow at higher rates. Assuming that, households maximise their utility and firms maximise their profit, a general equilibrium for the growth rates of income, capital and consumption can be calculated from which the steady state levels of these variables can be derived. Then, the issue is, whether the economy is converging to this steady state and if yes, then at what speed.

In the Indian context, K.P. Kalirajan, R.T. Shand and S. Bhide (2000) have dealt with these two questions in the greatest detail. Studying the data on 14 major Indian states they failed to find any evidence of absolute or conditional convergence of interstate per capita incomes. In fact, they found that states with high per capita SDPs tended to grow faster than those with low per capita SDPs. Concerning the agricultural growth rates, they find, that post-reform, the states with initially lower agricultural growth rates landed to grow at a faster rate than those with initially higher agricultural growth rates. Therefore, the agricultural growth rates seem to be converging at a lower rate of growth. This may ex-plain our earlier finding of the decreasing share of the natural resource-based eastern states in the national GDP.

The above findings indicate that, the post-reform growth rates of Indian SDPs seem to be diverging due to divergent industrial growth rates. The industrial growth rates are thus flouting the predictions of the neo-classical growth theory. One explanation that can be provided is that, the capitalization of Indian industries is so low that even the states with comparatively higher capital output ratios haven't yet reached the stage of diminishing marginal productivity of capital. Another possible explanation is through imperfect mobility of factors. In the presence of perfect factor mobility, states with higher growth rates of per capita income will instantaneously attract factors from technologically similar states with slower growth rates of per capita income and there will be instantaneous convergence even if we rule out diminishing returns to capital. Therefore, the fact that per capita income growth rates which are diverging may also indicate imperfect factor mobility across Indian states. A result reported by *Kalirajan et al (2000)* might support our explanation. While they found the inter-state per-capita incomes to be diverging, the speed of divergence was lesser than in the pre-reform period. This may be the result of increased capital imports in the freer trading regimes of the post-reform period. Similarly, this may be the preliminary sign of increased factor mobility ensured through the reforms process. The agricultural growth rates meanwhile seem to be obeying the neo-classical model. The only way to avoid the approaching low level steady state in agricultural growth rates and set it at a higher level is technology infusion. However, given that farmers have been traditionally suspicious of newer technology, there may be a case for using a more centralised network for introducing technology. This is contrary to the view that promotes decentralization as the panacea for all evils.

Another relevant study worth mentioning is by Dasgupta *et al* (2000). Apart from confirming the finding of increasing divergence of state per capita incomes in the post-reform period, they also report another very interesting result. They find that the structural characteristics of Indian states where structure is defined as the shares enjoyed by the three sub-sectors, i.e. primary, secondary and tertiary was tending over time to the all India structure. Therefore, structurally, the states seem to be converging although in terms of per capita income they are diverging. As the states become structurally more and more similar and manufacturing becomes more and more important compared to agriculture in all states, none of them can do without opening up its economy and attempting to attract increasing amounts of capital. It could clearly be seen from Table 3 that states with higher growth rates also enjoy higher investor confidence, measured by the number of industrial investment proposals. That should open up the route to convergence in the long-run. As for the states (especially eastern) with falling relative industrial growth rates, how they can recover is anybody's guess. However, from our earlier findings we can only say that anything, which achieves greater infusion of capital, will help.

TABLE 3

The Industrial Investment Proposals Across States

(Inv. in Rs. Crore)

States	*1992-96*		*1999*		*2000*		*2001*	
	No.	*Inv.*	*No.*	*Inv.*	*No.*	*Inv.*	*No.*	*Inv.*
Andhra Pradesh	145	5852	36	1692	44	450	51	1605
Assam	3	4	5	2	3	2	12	967
Bihar	4	50	0	0	0	0	1	14
Gujarat	465	13642	46	2816	4	1308	85	4409
Haryana	184	7425	13	451	14	233	29	158
Karnataka	88	7086	6	13	7	377	20	211
Maharashtra	487	1 8394	38	1956	21	406	104	2038
Orissa	1 1	1474	1	5	0	0	6	33
Punjab	140	1575	15	228	20	731	22	449
Tamil Nadu	237	6287	12	839	17	225	57	767
Tripura	0	0	0	0	0	0	0	0
West Bengal	76	2750	23	21080	33	967	54	581

Source: *SIA Newsletter*, April 2002.

To construct the most important requirement for development: improved infrastructure, decentralization at an even more elementary level than the stale level that is the panchayat level may help. Through increased decentralization, both better collection of information and implementation of projects more suited to local needs can be ensured. This is where we entertain our third and last question: Does decentralization at the state level and at the panchayat level aid each other, or are they in conflict?

To discuss this point we must first understand what decentralization really means. Very simply, it means giving more power to some kind of authority at the level you want to decentralise. However, this also means taking away the same power from the levels above the one at which you want to decentralise and that is not what the authorities at the centre relish. If greater autonomy to states means taking away some of the powers of the Centre then giving more powers to the panchayats would involve stripping off the same from the states and the latter would not relish that. In short, decentralization may have the cure for a lot of evils but the more we decentralise at the state level the harder it will become to implement the same reforms at the panchayat level. As evidence, we may consider the progress of panchayat reforms in the country. Bihar has managed to hold its panchayat elections after a gap of 20 years. West Bengal holds regular elections but do not give much power to its panchayats. Haryana, Rajasthan and Himachal Pradesh have created so many parallel bodies that their panchayats are left with no meaningful powers. Finally, no state has yet taken any meaningful step to achieve that ultimate landmark of decentralization: strengthening the gram sabha, the village parliament.

Another danger is of latent centralization. Even if we achieve full decentralization both at the state and the panchayat levels, panchayats, which are essentially political units, may be controlled through the party mechanism. So, a form of hidden centralization through the party mechanism may be exercised in which the top leaders use the panchayats to dish out doles to their followers in the villages while the truly poor get bypassed, like what happened in case of the loan melas where members of a particular party got all the loans. States like West Bengal, where the panchayats are otherwise functional should be checked for this phenomenon. The final hurdle to panchayat level reforms from the state level is due to the resource crunch. The precarious fiscal situations of the states may have two adverse effects on the panchayats. First, the funds given by the Centre to the states meant for distribution to the panchayats are unlikely to be used as such. This explains the creation of the bodies parallel to the panchayats under the guise of expert committees, development monitors, etc. in almost all states. Through these, the state can maintain control over the funds meant for panchayats. The second danger is that, the panchayats are never likely to be given meaningful taxing powers. This is where the central bureaucracy still has a role to play. Collectors and other officers can ensure that, due importance is given to the gram sabhas while the central government can ensure that resources meant for the panchayat actually get to them. They can also make sure that state level laws giving more powers to the panchayats actually do get passed. This is pressure from above. However, pressure from below is more important. Panchayats should be more vocal and demanding about the rights promised to them in the 73rd amendment. NGOs can play a big role in their mobilization.

We consider these issues more in the next section, which is on panchayats.

THE OBJECTIVE OF DECENTRALIZATION AT THE PANCHAYAT LEVEL

The decentralization exercise was further fuelled by the introduction of panchayati raj system, brought into force by the 73rd and 74th amendments of the constitution, where the primary objective was to empower people. The first and foremost conception about decentralization is that, the governing body will be closer to people in all senses. On one hand, decentralization is supposed to enhance people's participation in the decision-making process, and on the other, weaker sections are supposed to receive greater rights under the new administration. To put it in another way, local governments are more sensitive to local problems. Again, corruption is markedly less under the decentralised administration, due to the close interaction of the governing body and the governed. Almost ten years have passed since the introduction of the panchayat raj institutions (henceforth PRIs) in India. Hence, there is ample reason to investigate whether the decentralization exercise has achieved its desired objective.

THE ACHIEVEMENTS

The basic idea of introducing PRIs was to empower people at micro level. At present, we see that PRIs have been formed at three levels, village, intermediate and district levels. In terms of coverage, almost in all the states PRIs have come into existence. Eléctions are held in time and the eagerness of people in choosing their representatives is enormous. The upliftment of the weaker sections has always been a major driving force behind amending the constitution. After 10 years of the introduction of the PR system, the situation on the face of it shows a very promising picture. To ensure the participation of women, a mandatory reservation of 33% of the total seats was enacted on a rotational basis. This measure was instrumental in ensuring more participation from the womenfolk and creating an atmosphere of truly participatory local governance. As seen from Table 4, the recent status of women's and backward castes' participation in PRIs reveals an impressive trend.

TABLE 4

Number of Elected Women and Dalit Representatives in PRIs

PRI Tier	*Women*		*SC*		*ST*	
	Number	*Percent*	*Number*	*Percent*	*Number*	*Percent*
Zilla Parishad	4030	31.8	1904	15.0	1247	0.1
Panchayat Samiti	38582	20.7	18867	14.5	8442	0.07
Gram Panchayat	768582	31.3	343792	14.0	240178	0.1
Total	811194	31.3	364563	14.1	249867	0.1

Source: PRIA (2000).

THE PROBLEMS

Although the achievement of the PRIs cannot be undermined, the problems in their proper functioning should be identified and suitable actions should be taken to eliminate them. A close view of the ongoing scenario reveals that a number of shortcomings are the system and in future might pose serious problems. A brief account of the potential concern areas are discussed below:

The participation of common people, especially the weaker sections, had been the driving force in implementing the PR system. However, a PRIA study (2000) reveals that, in a number of instances, the quorum is not fulfilled. In addition, the actual power is confined to the elite sections of the society. The main target group of the decentralization exercise, are the poor classes who have not benefited much from the reforms.

The representation of women and the weaker sections in the decision-making process were guaranteed through reservation of seats. Although, in principle, the measure seems sufficiently pragmatic, in practice, it has hardly yielded the desired outcome. For instance, 33% of the panchayat seats are reserved for women on a rotational basis. Now, in most cases, the woman member of the panchayat replace a male member of the family and is 'guided' (or dictated) by him in all matters. Finally, at the end of five years, when she is gaining confidence, the reservation is taken off.[2] Thus, all her hard work does not give her dividends and the so-called empowerment turns into a fruitless exercise.

In theory, the PRIs are the lowest decision-making units of the three-tier governance structure in India. However, existences of several parallel bodies act as a major hindrance in smooth functioning of the PR system. A few parallel bodies like Joint Forest Management (JFM), Water User Groups (WUGs), etc. existed from pre-73rd amendment period. However, a number of PBs like Expert Committees in Kerala, Janmabhoomi in Andhra Pradesh, Vigilance Committee in Himachal Pradesh. Gram Vikas Samiti in Haryana, etc. have been established in the post-reform period. In principle, the PRIs and the PBs are expected to compliment each other, the resultant effect of which is expected to facilitate decentralization. However, the actual experience suggests that the functions of these two bodies are often in conflict. For example, in Gujarat there is a major conflict between PRIs and PBs over the possession of minor forest produce.[3]

Finally, the 73rd amendment speculated that the PRIs would have sufficient power generate own resources, thus enhancing their autonomy and authority. Moreover, observation suggests that states dictate most of the financial powers of these PRIs. The experience of tax sharing between the PRIs and state authorities

TABLE 5

Panchayat Finances (all tiers)

(*Rs. Lakh*)

States	*1991-92*			*1994-95*			*1997-98*		
	TR	*TE*	*Balance*	*TR*	*TE*	*Balance*	*TR*	*TE*	*Balance*
Andhra Pradesh	115805	115763	41.72	158151	160403	-2251.82	251159	250359	800
Assam	307.11	826.95	-519.84	370.64	3990.68	-3620.04	1550.31	4056.91	-2506.6
Bihar	565.13	15087.4	-14522.3	59164.2	92655.7	-33491.5	36596.1	66039.7	-29443.7
Gujarat	111822	122836	-11013.7	149445	150919	-1473.57	223254	226881	-3627.14
Karnataka	161146	149955	11190.5	245746	199249	46496.4	376807	369641	7165.65
Kerala	10362.5	10557.4	-194.9	19352.7	19452.8	-100.14	98276.6	73056.1	25220.5
Madhya Pradesh	23584.3	23369.2	215.02	30233.8	30265.7	-31.83	177901	178530	-628.13
Maharashtra	118569	188330	-69761.2	204688	319695	-115007	330747	458538	-127791
Punjab	10975.3	11253.7	-278.39	16616.3	15829.5	786.78	13541	15953.1	-2412.07
Tamil Nadu	31173.1	19208.7	1 1964.4	32604.7	26134.4	6470.36	42216.4	49061.9	-6845.46
West Bengal	20312.1	32178.2	-1 1866.1	48770.5	53587.4	-4816.82	48775.5	55487.9	-6712.45

IR = Total Revenue; TE = Total Expenditure.

Source: The Eleventh Finance Commission Recommendations.

shows that buoyant taxes are never shared. To make the situation worse, a PRIA study revealed that the share of own revenue of PRIs in total income is declining at all levels. It clearly shows that the revenue generation efficiency of PRIs is declining, and their increasing dependence on governmental grants. From Table 5, it could be seen that PRIs at the state level are experiencing deficit. However, given the erosion in the fiscal position of the states, illustrated in Table 6, it is highly unlikely that the grant from state governments to PRIs is likely to increase in the near future. Unless the local bodies attain financial self-sufficiency, they will never achieve sovereignty.

TABLE 6

The Financial Position of the States

States	*1991-92*		*1994-95*		*1997-98*		*1999-2000*	
	RD	*FD*	*RD*	*FD*	*RD*	*FD*	*RD*	*FD*
Andhra Pradesh	-0.41	-2.70	-1.17	-3.76	-0.80	-2.75	-1.10	-3.76
Assam	2.27	-2.15	-1.87	-4.30	1.35	-0.67	-4.42	-7.88
Bihar	-1.74	-3.87	-3.04	-3.97	-1.89	-4.03	-4.55	-7.22
Gujarat	-0.74	-4.70	0.44	-2.19	-1.18	-3.47	-1.26	-4.06
Karnataka	-0.59	-3.05	-0.65	-3.33	-0.42	-2.46	-1.67	-3.91
Kerala	-2.08	-4.58	-1.48	-4.11	-2.59	-5.54	-3.74	-5.22
Madhya Pradesh	-0.13	-3.02	-0.38	-2.84	-0.17	-2.07	-1.99	-3.41
Maharashtra	-0.38	-2.26	0.22	-2.28	-1.42	-3.53	-3.40	-5.00
Punjab	-2.11	-5.04	-2.09	-5.02	-2.95	-4.92	-2.88	-4.42
Tamil Nadu	-5.15	-3.52	-0.68	-2.46	-1.56	-2.43	-2.36	-3.81
West Bengal	-1.60	-2.83	-1.29	-3.29	-2.56	-4.48	-6.48	-9.34

RD = Revenue Deficit expressed as a percentage of Gross State Domestic Product.

FD = Fiscal Deficit expressed as a percentage of Gross State Domestic Product.

Source: The Eleventh Finance Commission Recommendations. (Figures for 1999-2000 in estimated form).

One point should be borne in mind. In recent years, the flow of funds from government to the PRIs has increased considerably. The central funds to the PRIs generally consists of Jawahar Rojgar Yojana (JRY), Indira Awas Yojana (IAY) and

Million Wells Scheme (MWS), and certain other projects on rural development. The assistance from the state government comes either through Grants-in-aid or state sponsored projects. However, most of these funds are tied in nature. Often, the state funds are insufficient.[4] Hie ratios of the untied grants/transfers to total income of gram panchayats vary between 0 to 12% across the states.[5] In addition, there is no clear regulation for distribution of governmental funds to the PRIs.

The empowerment of the local bodies is also not complete. For instance, Gram Sabha decisions are not binding in nature and constrained in several other ways.[6] Apart from this, the legislatures across the states often constrain the financial and decision-making capability of the PRIs.[7]

POLICY PRESCRIPTION

Measures, which may serve to increase the capital inflow to loser states and thus achieve convergence, include increased urbanization, better governance, encouragement to non-natural resource-based industries, export-oriented production and improved infrastructure.

As for panchayats, two issues must be borne in mind. First, people's participation must be ensured and second, the PRIs should get precedence over any institutions, which are not constitutionally mandated. This objective could be fulfilled by imparting education to village masses, removal of parallel bodies when they are in conflict with the PRIs, and, granting them control over local resources.

Notes and References

1. Economic Survey 2000-01 and report of the Eleventh Finance Commission.
2. Although women are not legally debarred from contesting these elections from a general seat, socio-economic conditions prevent them from doing so.
3. Gujarat Panchayat Act bestows the minor forest produce of forest land falling outside National Parks and Sanctuaries to village panchayats, and the sales proceedings of these products go to panchayat fund. However, Gujarat Minor Forest Produces Nationalization Act lists 13 categories of 6 minor forest produce and these products are properties of Gujarat State Forest Development Corporation. As a result, the PRIs

are clearly worse off. Several likewise examples could be cited, where the PBs are getting preference over the PRIs. In addition, the funds available to PBs are often far more than the same to the PRIs.

4. For instance, the District Level Panchayats in most cases does not receive any state assistance. In addition, the state assistance to intermediate and village panchayats are considerably lower than the corresponding central fund. The problem is further compounded by the inordinate delays made by the state in releasing its own funds.
5. Only in the case of Kerala, the provision of funds to PRIs is somewhat generous in comparison to other states, PRIA, 2000.
6. Gram Sabha has not been enabled to consider subjects of general interest. In addition, no proper follow up of the Gram Sabha decisions are seriously performed. All this reduces these meetings to mere formalities.
7. In this connection, the panchayat acts present in Andhra Pradesh, Bihar, Himachal Pradesh, Karnataka, Rajasthan and Madhya Pradesh could be mentioned which constrain the PRIs both functionally and financially.

References

Barua, A. and Das, S.K., "Economic Growth, Regional Inequality and Inefficiency: The Indian Experience" in Agarwal, Barua, Das and Pant (Ed.), "Indian Economy in Transition: Environmental and Development Issues", Har-Anand Publications Pvt. Ltd., New Delhi, 1998.

Dasgupta, D., Maiti, P. Mukherjee, R., Sarkar, S., Chakrabarti, S., "Growth and Interstate Disparities in India," *Economic and Political Weekly*, July 1-7, 2000, pp. 2413-22.

Debroy, B., Bhandari, L., Banik, N., "How are the States Doing?", *Confederation of Indian Industry*, 2000.

Kalirajan, K.P., Shand, R.T. and Bhide, S., "Economic Reforms and Convergence of Incomes across Indian States: Benefits for the Poor", in Shubhashis Gangopadhyay and Wilima Wadhwa (Ed.) "Economic Reforms for the Poor", Konark Publishers Pvt. Ltd., New Delhi, 2000, pp. 47-77.

Mathias, Edward, "Panchayati Raj Institutions and Role of NGOs: The Experience in Mysore and Tumkur Districts of Karnataka," *Indian Social Institute*, New Delhi, 2000.

Pinto, Ambrose and Reifeld, Helmut, "Women in Panchayati Raj", *Indian Social Institute*, New Delhi, 2001.

Prasuna, D.G., Mallik, D., Singh, R.K., "A Tale of Two States", *Chartered Financial Analyst*, July 2002.

PRIA, "Panchayati Raj Institutions: A Balance Sheet", February 2000.

PRIA, "Parallel Bodies and Panchayati Raj Institutions: Experience from the States," December 2001.

Proceedings of the D.T. Lakdawala Memorial Symposium, "Decentralised Planning and Panchayati Raj," *Institute of Social Sciences*, New Delhi, 1994.

Rajiv Gandhi Foundation, Task Force on Panchayati Raj, "Revitalization of Panchayati Raj in India: Problems and Prospects", New Delhi, 1997. Recommendation submitted by 11th Finance Commission.

SECTION II

SECTORAL, REGION-SPECIFIC AND GOODS-SPECIFIC ISSUES OF GLOBALIZATION

10

Rural Non-farm Activities as an Alternative Path Towards Economic Development

SUCHISMITA MONDAL AND PINAKI CHAKRABORTI

I

The present paper is an analytical investigation in the conditions of development with decentralization in the environment of globalization. In the 21st century, most of the LDC's have been subjected to diminishing returns stage. The scenario from 1991 implies that, the previous processes were not sustainable. The situation is one of the continuously rising government deficit which can be traced out from stagnation or deceleration in the conventional economic activities. Moreover, if we look at the World Bank Report, Asian Development Outlook for the last two years, we will find that agriculture has also been overburdened with the pressure of activities. In fact, in the third world, the rural economy has until recently been equated with the agricultural economy. Agriculture has reached a saturation point in terms of its labour absorption capacities—especially within the given technological options. There has been a considerable amount of literature arguing that during the period of New Economic Policy reforms (NEP) major displacement of labour has taken place.

There has been a considerable amount of literature arguing that during the period of New Economic Policy reform (NEP) major displacement of labour has taken place. This process with its simultaneity with the recent crises in debt and balance of payments have created a very stringent situation for the LDCs, including India. It is necessary that exports increase which is impossible in traditional sectors. And only hope perhaps is from the rural non-agricultural activities. This period is characterized by capital drying of LDC's, mainly because of accumulated debt and balance of payments crisis. Inflow of aid and soft loans have dried up over the last two decades. Hence, foreign supply of capital, through trade, payments and borrowing at feasible terms have decreased. Besides, the internal savings and capital formation have slowed down.

Hence, there is involved a trade-off in the new developments over use of factors. That is why one needs an analytical framework of general interdependence that we visualize in our model. We develop a dynamic general equilibrium model of three sectors and workout the conditions on steady growth. Non-farm development appears to be a feasible way out in the age of globalization of decentralization.

Moreover, technology in use are being constantly replaced by eco-friendly type which are not much in use in the LDC's and are mostly capital-intensive—a fact against the existing factor supply advantage of the LDC's. Hence, it is extremely necessary that we workout our own alternative that will be supported by the new era of globalization and decentralization. Hence, the targets at hand are three-fold; increase foreign exchange earnings, increase employment fast enough to absorb the outgoing unemployed labour force; and look out for new less capital-intensive diversification replacing increase in stagnating traditional agriculture and industry.

Globalization at the international level is a move towards this end through marketization, unleashing the latent forces towards incentives available in a market driven economy. This is being led the World Bank and WTO. In this process all economies are to be integrated into the one world economy and there will be no obstruction for resources and goods to move freely across all national boundaries. This process with its simultaneity with the recent crisis in debt and balance of payments have created a very stringent situation for the LDCs, including India. It is necessary that exports increase which is impossible in traditional sectors. And only hope perhaps is from the rural non-agricultural activities.

This period is characterized by capital drying of LDCs, mainly because of accumulated debt and balance of payments crisis. Inflow of aid and soft loans have dried up over the last two decades. Hence, foreign supply of capital, through trade, payments and borrowing at feasible terms have decreased. Besides, the internal savings and capital formation have slowed down. Surplus generation in the public sector industries have been very low, even negative in many cases. Hence, it is worthwhile to ask what is the way out in this seeming impasses. This is the question we address in this paper.

In the next section, we describe the motivation and context of the problem. In the third section we develop a three sector dynamic general equilibrium model to work out the condition that have to be fulfilled for a self-sustaining growth, generally captured by a steady state in some determining essential space governing all other sectors. In our paper, we take savings to be such a variable. We analyze conditions of general equilibrium of positive growth supported by a steady state in savings.

II

Savings assumes this extremely high significance because, the present crises driven reaction and development since then fundamentally resulted from low domestic savings given rising volume of investment. The situation aggravated through the shackles of red tapes and imperfect or dictionary controls of acentally governed economy with badly performing public heavy industry sector.

The NEP aimed at unshackling the Indian economy from the cobwebs of the unnecessary bureaucratic controls, induce liberalization with a view to integrate the economy with the world economy. But the adverse economic environment in the LDCs have been aggravated because of ruthless pressure of markets through LPG which has out competed many LDC products in even in their domestic market. The rate at which the NEP reforms have been dislocating labour would not be outweighed or neutralized by a growing employment is either of the rural agricultural sector or urban industrial sector. NEP reforms imply new competitive strength, which has to be, sought from new activities which does not come from traditional agriculture or from traditional industries. This naturally points out to new economic activities those will be self-sustaining with low capital requirement and relatively high market and demand potential.

In the context of saturated agriculture, financial short supply, less surplus from existing industries and trade with pressure of liberalization, the promising choice is Non-Farm Development (NFD) in the rural-urban interfaces, with international attention remaining strongly for capacity and infrastructure development forthcoming from World Bank, IMF set-up. This interface is likely to vibrate with economic vitality as there has been external support for developing the transport and social overheads in large scale in recent times for the leaders of Globalization.

Some newly industrialized countries such as Taiwan, Korea or countries like Vietnam and China have shown unimpressive growth and employment potential in such activities known as Township and Village Enterprise (TVE's). The idea is close to the concept of rural industrialization. TVE's have been emerging as a dependable alternative choice to get rid of less development, as is pertinent from the logical empirical study of some related issue. (Saith, 1992).

However, one must note that in the newly emerging state of affairs, TVEs and NFDs will require factors and resources which will not be allocated in the traditional sector. Hence, there is involved a trade off in the new developments over use of factors. That is why one needs an analytical framework of general interdependence that we visualize in our model constructed in the next section.

The process pre-requires inroads of markets and freedom from central control. Decision to undertake new economic activities being local information and comparative advantage dependent, decision-making has to be decentralized. Decentralization relatively recently emerged as a popular approach to development in LDCs and elsewhere, strongly advocated by the World Bank is an attempt to bring about market orientation by dividing decision-making into smaller units than centralized collective bodies. Development programmes involves large number of human beings in possession of given size of fragmented and agriculturally stagnating land. The interplay, between markets are expected to take place and apart from major labour displacement, the new developments are likely to involve other factors in a process of emerging markets in this orientation. The trade off between equity and efficiency in decentralized approach to development has been under controversy for some time (*Bardhan* and *Mookherjee* (2001). In a poor economic region as argued by economists in favour of market driven development through local decision variety, actions through collective organization of local governments would promote distributional equity at the cost of efficiency as the shift is not likely to be Pareto optimal. Efficiency on the other hand is a strong point of markets. In the recent literature Bardhan (1996), Bardhan and Mukherjee (2001), this trade off has been reexamined and found to be either non-existent or less effective in poverty alleviation activities through decentralized development. The intuition that is not found in their work is the fact that move to markets from nearly non-existence of them, will organize resource allocation for the better which initiating at least makes things more equitable. Introduction of markets in NFDs and TVEs are necessary at the micro unit level of decision-making. The efficacy of the market can be ensured by increasing its outreach that is what is done by decentralization. Let us suppose that local government induced decision-making at the stakeholder group is capable of developing to markets in the NEP context.

III

We have a three sector economy agriculture, industry and non-farm sector apart from the other two, finally clubbed into two —traditional and non-traditional. All produce both consumption and production goods, agricultural, industrial and new. The goods enter in the utility and production functions which are assumed to be homothetic and CRS.

The representative consumer's problem may be stated as follows:

$$\underset{\{C_a, C_n, C_i\}}{\text{Max}} \int_0^{\alpha} e^{-\alpha} U(C_a, C_n, C_i)\, dt$$

$$\text{S.t. } S = Y - WL_T - iS - wL_T - wL_N$$

where S is the supply of saving (finance capital) by the consumers and is the increment in finance, w, i, are price of the associated resources/factors of production L (labour), S (finance), S though is not a direct physical factor of production, is the exogenous presence of quality of environment in generating the level of utility.

The present value Hamiltonian under this problem will be given by

$$H = e^{-\beta t} U(C_a, C_n, C_i) + q(\hat{w} L_T + iS + \hat{w} L_N - C_a - pn\, Cn - pi\, Ci)$$

With $q = \Phi e^{-\beta t}$

The first order conditions yield

$$U_a - \Phi = 0 \qquad (1)$$

$$U_n - \Phi = 0 \qquad (2)$$

$$U_i - \Phi = 0$$

And $-\delta H/\delta S = \Phi' - \beta \Phi = -i \Phi \qquad (3)$

It follows from conditions (1) and (2) that the amount demanded of the two final commodities coming from the consumers

$$C^d_a = C_a(\Phi_a P_i, P_n) \qquad (1^*)$$

$$C^d_i = C_i(\Phi_a P_i, P_n) \qquad (2^*)$$

$$C^d_n = C_a(\Phi_a P_i, P_n) \qquad (3^{*1*})$$

The information in the box says that labour used in traditional and non-traditional sectors takes the total labour supply, which may not be full employment but an adjusted market clearance condition

Production Structure

$X_a = X_a (L_{Ta}, I_{Ta}, N_a)$
$X_I = X_I (L_{Ti}, I_T, N_I)$
$X_N = X_a (L_N, I_N, N_N)$

Agricultural good is the numariare Equilibrium in the production

$$M P_{LT} = \hat{w}$$

$$P_n M P_{LN} = \hat{w}$$

$\hat{w}$ being the institutionally given wage rate.

$\Rightarrow M P_{LT} = P_N MP_{LN}$ marginal productivities of labour must be equal in value in the three sectors.

$$\frac{M P_{LT}}{M P_{IT}} = \frac{w}{P_i^0} = \frac{M P_{LN}}{M P_{IT}}$$

Market Clearance

Demand for and supply of all goods and factors must be equal

$C_a^d = X_a^S$
$(I_N + I_{Ta} + I_T + L_I^d)\ p_I = p_I = p_I X_{oi}^S;$
$p_a (N_N + N_I + C_N) = p_a X_n^S$ Commodities Market Equilibrium
$L_a + L_I + L_N = L$ Factor Market Equilibrium

Inter-temporal zero profit condition

$$= \frac{\delta X_j}{\delta S} \rightarrow j = i, N$$

The solution to these equations determine the values of the variables equal in number with that of independent equations. The values represent moving equilibrium at each point of time.

The fundamental dynamic equation is given by two differential equations.

$$\dot{S} = Y - WL_T - iS - WL_T - wL_N$$

$$\text{And } -\sigma H / \sigma S = \Phi - \beta\Phi = -i\Phi$$

These two define the laws of motion in the $S - \Phi$ plane. The system is highly unstable, though has a steady state. It is nteresting to note that the space is of savings and its shadow price vhich is its opportunity cost. The dynamics is controlled by avings and its uses. Setting both $\dot{s}$ and $\dot{\Phi}$ equal to zero gives us he values of S and F in steady state.

IV
IMPLICATION OF GROWING A GENERAL EQUILIBRIUM

The growth equation can be written as

$$G_Y = \eta_T G_T + \eta_N G_N$$

vhere, G_K represents growth in the Kth sector and η_i being the hare of the j the sector in the economy.

In a steady state G_Y is constant.

Hence $\eta_T G_T = G - \eta_N G_N$ and there if $n_T G_T$ falls, $n_N G_N$ must ise.

Also in a positive non-steady state $G_y > 0 \Rightarrow$ (a) $n_T G_T$ and $_N G_N$ are both positive but slow.

(b) $n_T G_T$ is positive but slow with $n_N G_N$ rising.

(c) $n_T G_T$ is zero or negative but $n_N G_N$ is increasingly rising.

ropositions

(a) For a positive and fast growth in stagnant traditional sectors a necessary condition is fast growth of non-traditional sectors.

(b) For a positive and fast growth in a growing economy, a sufficient but not necessary condition is a growing non-traditional sector.

(c) The equilibrium requires fall in pn, which is possible if and only if new growth is relatively intensive in abundant factor.

V

CONCLUSION

The conclusions that follow are evident from the proposition. It only suggests that in the midst of economic laws of motion, unemployment is not supported. The steady state requires that if there is a falling sector (the traditional one) it has to be exactly neutralized by the other (non-traditional—NFD).

The Non-Farm Activities in rural and non-urban areas can be promoted successfully through decentralized development. The empirical surveys so far vindicate our result as reported very briefly below.

The non-farm sector, as evident from the study of J. Lanjouw and P. Lanjouw, has played an important role in absorbing a growing labour force, in slow rural-urban migration, as a contributor to national income growth and in promoting more equitable distribution of income.

One of the important roles of Non-farm activities is no provide work in the slack periods of agricultural cycle. Some surveys of African farm households suggest that about 15 to 65% of farmers have secondary employment in the non-farm and 15 to 40% to total family labour hours are devoted in income generation in non-farm activities. The NFA's are substantial in many countries—both in terms of income and employment and has in aggregate been growing over time. In rural China NFA's has grown from 11% in 1980 to 20% in 1986. TVE's increased real output and employment at annual rates of 23.4% and 12.7% respectively in 1978-86 with employment in manufacturing increasing at 7.7%. In fact, TVE's has proved to be "engines of growth" for the Chinese economy.

References

Lanjouw, O. Jean & Lanjouw O. Peter: "Rural Non-farm Employment", *A Survey Background Paper for World Bank.*

Singh, Sukhpal, Prabhakar, R.: "Determinants and Dynamics of Rural non-farm Activities: A Study from Rajasthan.

Dev, Mahendra S.: "Non-Agricultural Employment in Rural India".

Jeemol, Unni: "Diversification of Economic Activities and Non-Agricultural Employment in Rural Gujarat".

Jeemol, Unni: "Regional variations in Rural Non-Agricultural Employment", An Explanatory Analysis.

Basu, N.D. & Kashyap, S.P.: "Rural Non-Agricultural Employment in India—Role of Development process and Rural-Urban Employment Linkages".

Eapen, Mridul: "Rural Non-Agricultural Employment in Kerala—Some Emerging Tendecies".

Bardhan, Pranab: "Decentralized Development".

Saith, Ashwani: "The Rural Non-farm Economy: Process and Policies".

Han Jun: "Experiences of Rural Industrialization and its New Trends in China".

11

Globalization: A Myth of the Indian States

MD. ABDUS SALAM

1. INTRODUCTION

India with the total population of 1027015247 persons as on March 1st 2001 (Census of India 2001) residing in 29 states and 6 union territories is the second largest country in the world after China to cross the 1 billion mark. India accounts for 2.42 per cent of the world surface area and it sustains a 16 percent of world total population. India is rich in managerial skills, technical manpower and abundant of natural resources, but all these resources have not been efficiently utilized. India with the plenty of skilled manpower, and other natural resources is in a good position to benefit from globalization. According to Eduardo Aninat (2002), "globalization—the process through which an increasingly free flow of ideas, people, goods, services and capital leads to the integration of economies and societies—has brought rising prosperity to the countries that have participated". Anne Krueger, the IMFs first deputy managing director has also highlighted the significance of globalization by saying that "Thanks to globalization, parts of the world have broken out of poverty and improve their living standards, but that more needs to be done for those who have left behind. She emphasized that globalization will continue to be a vehicle for closing the gap between the industrial countries and the rest of world". Like many countries of the world India too has welcomed globalization. "Since 1991, India has embarked on a programme of wide ranging economic liberalization and reforms with the objective of globalization of the Indian economy. To that extent, the sweeping reforms launched in 1991 have been carded through by successive governments, which is an indication of the all round political consensus in India about the need for economic dynamism and growth. The country has now embarked upon the second round of reforms. Reforms are continuous in policies relating to virtually every sector of the economy like capital, money, real estate and labour markets, debureaucratization, privatization of state enterprises, maintaining fiscal discipline and curbing deficits, cutting subsidies and financial sector reform, including opening the insurance sector". Indian economy is now on the path of Global integration, accelerating growth, improving productivity, innovation and international competitiveness.

In an age of globalization, the infrastructure sector is the backbone of any economy. Growth of this sector is a prerequisite for a sustainable growth and development of the economy. In a broader sense, infrastructure can be physical, social or financial in nature. Basic infrastructure services like energy, transportation, telecommunication, water, education, health, etc. play a crucial role in supporting economic growth and development. In the World Development Report of 1994, it has been highlighted that good infrastructure raises productivity and lowers production costs. The kind of infrastructure put in place also determines whether growth does all that it can to reduce poverty. Most of the poor are in rural areas, and the growth of farm productivity and non-farm rural employment is linked closely to infrastructure provision. An important ingredient in China's success with rural enterprise has been a minimum package of transport telecommunications, and power at the village level. Rural enterprises in China now employ more than 100 million people

(18 percent of the labourforce) and produce more than a third of national output. Lewis T. Preston in his foreword note for World Development Report 1994 has mentioned that in recent decades, developing countries have made substantial investment in infrastructure, achieving dramatic gains for households and produces by expanding their access to services such as safe water, sanitation, electric power, telecommunications, and transport. Even more infrastructure investment and expansion are needed in order to extend the reach of the services—especially to people living in rural areas and to the poor. He has further emphasized that infrastructure is an area in which government policy and finance have an important role to play because of its pervasive impact on economic development and human welfare.

2. OBJECTIVES OF THE STUDY

This paper while focusing on globalization seeks to examine how Indian states can reposition themselves to take full advantage of globalization to accelerate economic growth. In order to take full advantage of globalization, economists suggest that "most countries probably need to implement stronger domestic policies and reforms designed to consolidate macro-economic stability, enhance human resource development, improve basic infrastructure and spur agricultural development, accelerate trade liberalization and regional economic integration, promote a sound banking system, foster private investment, and ensure good governance. Nirumpam Bajpai and Jeffrey D. Sachs (2000) observed that central government of India has undertaken a series of reform measures but at the state level it is slow-moving because of the following reasons. First, limited decentralization of decision-making has meant that the States lack the authority to formulate and implement policies which are under the control of the Centre. Second, unlike the Centre, the State Governments do not have sufficient institutional back-up. Third, due to short-terms of office that the State Governments have been holding, they are governed by short-term political considerations. Fourth, populist policies have always been preferred to harsh reform measures. Subsidies on rice, urban transport water, electricity and so on are persisted with to advance the political interests of the party in power. Economists have rightly observed that India's overall growth rates can be substantially stepped up. Should the Centre decentralize economic policy-making and allow the States to take crucial economic decisions on their own? Crucial fiscal, infrastructure and regulatory decisions on economic management remains at the Central level. Essentially what this centralized system of governance implies is that the States have very little jurisdiction in, or control over, policy and regutatory decisions which would make them more attractive to prospective foreign investors. A gradual process of decentralization has begun because regional political parties have been lending support in the formation and running of the government at the Centre. This is the sign of healthy development. It is assumed that greater decentralization of decision-making will lead to greater competition among the States and therefore to higher efficiency, productivity and overall economic development in these regions. There are considerable evidences that States and region with better physical infrastructure and good human capital attract more international and private investment. In the light of the above discussions and keeping in view the nature of infrastructural facilities required in a country like India and a wide variation among Indian States in regard to culture, availability of natural resources, population density, availability of institutional finance, etc. and the availability of published data the objectives of this paper are to:

- Focus essentially on few major infrastructural facilities like energy, transport and communication.
- Analyse the variation in the Net State Domestic Product across the States and compute the Compound Rate of Growth in Net State Domestic Product.
- Analyse the pattern of expenditure made by different States of India on Energy, Transport and Communication for the period of 1996-97 to 2001-02.

3. METHODOLOGY OF THE STUDY

A simple and basic statistical analysis like Maximum value (Max.) Minimum value (Min.), Mean, Standard deviation (STND), Coefficient of variation (C.V.) and Correlation Coefficient (r) is carried out primarily with the help of secondary data available from the Economic Survey, 2001-02, Govt. of India and Economic Times.

Growth rates of various states in regard to Net State Domestic Product expenditure made on Energy and Transport and Communication have also been calculated by taking time as independent variable and rest of the variables (NSDP, expenditure on Energy and expenditure on Transport and Communication) as dependent variables.

The equation used for calculating the growth rates is the well-known compound interest formula as:

$$X = \alpha\,(1 + r)^t \qquad \ldots (1)$$

Taking the natural logarithm of equation (1), we get

$$\mathrm{Ln}X = \mathrm{Ln}\,\alpha + t\,\mathrm{Ln}\,(1 + r) \qquad \ldots (2)$$

Putting $\beta_1 = \mathrm{Ln}\,\alpha$ & $\beta_2, = \mathrm{Ln}\,(1 + r)$ Equation (2) now can be written as,

$$\mathrm{Ln}\,X = \beta_1 + \beta_2 t \qquad \ldots (3)$$

Equation (3) shows that regressand is the logarithm of X and the regressor is "time". The percentage compound growth rate is calculated by taking antilog of regression coefficient, subtracting 1 from it and multiplying the difference by 100. All the results are presented in Regression results Tables 1(a), 3(a) and 4(a) respectively.

4. RESULTS OF THE STUDY

We have analysed the data of 23 Indian States for which comparable data is available. The variation across the States is enormous in regard to various indicators. It can be observed from Table 1 that over the period from 1995-96 to 1999-2000 the average Net State Domestic Product varies from the top five States—Maharashtra with Rs. 172889 Crore, U.P. with Rs. 133939.2 Crore, West Bengal with Rs. 91932 Crore, Tamil Nadu with Rs. 93604.4 Crore and Andhra Pradesh with Rs. 90518.8 Crore to the poorest five States, Sikkim with Rs. 582.2 Crore, Arunachal Pradesh with Rs. 1231.2 Crore, Manipur with Rs. 1978.2 Crore, Meghalaya with Rs. 2206.2 Crore and Tripura with Rs. 2974.8 Crore. It can also be observed from Table 1 (a) that during the period 1995-96 to 1999-2000 the Compound Rate of Growth of Net State Domestic Product was highest among top five States—Delhi, West Bengal Tripura, Manipur and Jammu & Kashmir at the rate of 18.29 per cental, 16.88 per cent, 16.77 per cent, 16.30 per cent and 15.72 per cent per year respectively. Arunachal Pradesh, Assam, Gujarat, Orissa and Maharashtra registered the lowest Compound Rate of Growth, at the rate of 9.42 per cent, 9.52 per cent, 9.53 per cent, 10.29 percent and 10.41 per cent per year respectively. It is important to note that relatively smaller States (Delhi, West Bengal, Tripura, Manipur and Jammu & Kashmir) had higher growth rates in Net State Domestic Product (Table 1(a)) and simultaneously they had highest coefficient of variation (at 35.63 per cent, 28.81 per cent, 25.93 per cent, 24.65 per cent and 23.72 per cent respectively) in Net State Domestic Product. It seems that almost all the top five smaller States who had registered highest compound rate of growth in Net State Domestic Product have better infrastructural facilities to attract more private and foreign investment which act as catalyst in generating income at the higher rate. Much of the reason for lower compound rate of growth in Net State Domestic Product is poor infrastructural facilities.

In order to verify the above arguments, it is essential to know the position of different States with respect to the investment in infrastructure. Trend in Central Government Plan Outlay on infrastructure can be observed from Table 2. Trend in expenditure made by different States on infrastructure can be observed from Tables 3 and 4. It is evident from Table 3 that there is a significant positive Correlation between Central Government Plan Outlay on Energy and expenditure made by top five States—Sikkim, Delhi, U.P., Karnataka and Gujarat with the values 0.96, 0.93, 0.87, 0.83 and 0.79 respectively on energy during the period from 1996-97 to 2001-02. States like M.P., Orissa, Punjab, West Bengal and Tamil Nadu exhibit relatively highest negative correlation with the values –0.67, –0.57, –0.35, –0.31 and –0.26 respectively. Negative values suggest that States are not giving priority to the energy sector. Here, West Bengal is the exception, which had higher per annum growth rate in Net State Domestic Product. Compound Rate of Growth in expenditure on energy by different States can be observed from Table 3(a). Results shows that during 1996-97 to 2001-02 Assam, Gujarat, Delhi, Andhra Pradesh and Karnataka have registered highest growth rates at the rate of 133.03 per cent, 29.3 per cent, 19.36 per cent, 18.65 per cent and 17.59 per cent per annum respectively. Orissa, Bihar, M.P., West Bengal, Kerala and Rajasthan have registered negative Compound Rate of Growth at the rate of –29.95 per cent, –26.21 per cent, –20.47 per cent, –9.97 per cent, –5.16 per cent and 2.47 per cent per annum respectively. It is significant to note that almost all the so-called BIMARU States, Bihar, M.P. and Rajasthan have negative growth rates in expenditure on energy. U.P. data is not sufficient for finding the growth rate for the said period.

Table 4 shows that West Bengal, Andhra Pradesh, Punjab, Assam and Karnataka have registered highest degree of positive correlation (0.994, 0.993, 0.974, 0.938 and 0.926 respectively) between Central Government Plan Outlay for Transport and communication and the expenditure made by the said States during the period from 1996-97 to 2001-02. During the same period Manipur, Maharashtra and Tamil Nadu have registered negative correlation (–0.870, –.0713 and –0.185 respectively). In terms of Compound Rate of Growth in expenditure on Transport and Communication [Table 4 (a)] West Bengal, Andhra Pradesh, Delhi, Assam and Karnataka have highest at 36.89 per cent, 28.27 per cent, 22.02 per cent and 21.23 per cent respectively. Three states—Manipur, Maharashtra, and Tamil Nadu have registered negative growth rates at –20.15 per cent, –8.61 per cent and –0.079 per cent respectively.

5. CONCLUSIONS

On the basis of regression, results as well as general observations we can conclude that relatively smaller states are spending more on infrastructure sector. Better infrastructural facilities attracted more private and foreign investment which is attributed to the higher Compound Rate of Growth in Net State Domestic Product. It may be said that smaller states are beneficiary of globalization. This study further revealed that from the ongoing economic reforms since 1991 with stabilization, deregulation and significant role of private investment the poor states like Bihar, Orissa, M.P. and Rajasthan have not been benefited. Because none of the above states is in the list of top rank states who have good indicators like higher average Net State Domestic Product or Higher Compound Rate of Growth in Net State Domestic Product. One of the reasons may be the poor infrastructural development in the said states. It is confirmed with the lower value of Compound Rate of Growth in expenditure on Energy, Transport and Communication. In summary, our analysis suggests that in order to produce efficiently, to export competitively, to use available resources effectively, to accelerate the process of urbanization in the country and above all to maximize the gain from globalization, it is must for all the Indian states to improve the infrastructure sector immediately.

REFERENCES

Dutta, Roy, Choudhury, U. (1993); Inter-State and Intra-State Variations in Economic Development and Standard of Living, *Economic and Political Weekly*, Vol. 27, Nos. 49 & 50.

Eduardo, Aninat (2002); "Surmounting the Challenges of Globalization", *Finance & Development*, IMF, March, Vol. 39, No. 1.

Gustafsson, H.L. (1979) ; "Electricity for Development," Problems and Prospects in Equipment Acquisition, *Economic and Political Weekly*, July 7.

Bajpai, Nirupam and Jeffrey, D. Sachs (2000) ; "Reforms in the States-I," *The Hindu*, January 24.

Parikh, Jyoti, *et al.* (1997); "Energy System: Need for New Momentum" Parikh, Krit S. (ed.) *India Development Report*, 1997, Oxford University Press, New Delhi.

World Bank (1994); *World Development Report*, Washington, D.C.

World Bank (1996); *India: Five Years of Stabilization and Reform and the Challenges Ahead*, Washington D.C.

APPENDIX

TABLE 1

National Income: Net State Domestic Product at Current Prices (New Series)

S. No.	State	1995-96	1996-97	1997-98	1998-99	1999-2000	Max.	Min.	Mean	STND	C.V.
1.	Andhra Pradesh	71796	81517	85791	102295	110525	110525	71796	90518.8	15883	17.547
2.	Arunachal Pradesh	1067	1078	1192	1286	1533	1533	1067	1231.2	191.086	15.52
3.	Assam	17170	18465	20211	21597	25051	25051	17170	20498.8	3050.76	14.883
4.	Bihar	38423	46671	52680	57688	62759	62759	38423	51644.2	9495.68	18 3S7
5.	Delhi	25240	30161	37075	43020	49040	49040	25240	36907.2	956.62	25.926
6.	Gujarat	62017	74802	79011	89486	89317	89486	62017	78926.6	11428.2	14.48
7.	Haryana	25672	30871	33371	37852	41627	41627	25672	33878.6	6174.08	18.224
8.	Himachal Pradesh	5719	6534	7432	8689	9971	9971	5719	7669	1694.59	22.097
9.	Jammu & Kashmir	6963	7851	8858	11128	12148	12148	6973	9391.6	218636	23.28
10	Karnataka	50055	58580	63460	76263	84686	84686	50055	66608.8	13860	20 808
11.	Kerala	JB38	40699	44883	51053	58704	58704	35330	461.33	908139	19.689
12.	Madhya Pradesh	5663	65166	70546	79052	86385	86385	56631	71556	11626.4	16.248
13.	Maharashtra	140730	155680	170700	185119	212216	212216	140730	172889	2752S.8	15.923
14.	Manipur	1410	1671	1945	2311	2554	2554	1410	1978.2	46185	23.448
15.	Maghalaya	1689	1853	2149	2534	2806	2806	1689	2206.2	464417	21.05
16.	Orissa	3277	22189	27437	29850	32729	32729	22189	27096.4	4418.57	16.307
17.	Punjab	34275	39323	42865	47900	54960	54960	34275	43864.6	7952.64	18.13
18.	Rajasthan	41824	51166	57064	64980	66645	66645	41824	56335.8	10323.9	18.104
19.	Sikkim	426	491	583	675	736	736	426	582.2	127.459	21.893
20.	Tamil Nadu	70329	80062	92850	106956	117825	117825	70329	93604.4	19304.2	20623
21.	Tripura	2073	2500	3015	3473	3813	3813	2073	2974.8	705 528	23.717
22.	Uttar Pradesh	102341	122643	130370	149712	164630	164630	102341	133939.2	24132.4	18017
23.	West Bengal	67136	74422	89595	106174	122333	122333	67136	91932	22660.3	24.649

Source: Economic Survey, 2001-02, Govt. of India.

TABLE 1(A)

Compound Rate of Growth (CRG) in Net State Domestic Product

S. No.	*State*	*Dept. Var*	*Intercept*	*Reg. Coeff.*	*R.-Square*	*CRG (%) per yr.*
1.	Andhra Pradesh	In (AP)	11.072 (347.25)	0.109 (10.96)	0.975	11.52
2.	Arunachal Pradesh	In (ARP)	6.36 (136.72)	0.090 (5.63)	0.915	9.42
3.	Assam	In (ASM)	9.646 (358.84)	0.091 (11.38)	0.978	9.52
4.	Bihar	In (BR)	10.479 (255.59)	0.119 (9.15)	0.966	12.64
5.	Delhi	In (DL)	9.983 (383.85)	0.168 (21.00)	0.993	18 29
6.	Gujarat	In (GUJ)	10.995 (199.82)	0.091 (5.29)	0.901	9.53
7.	Haryana	In (HR)	10.066 (343.89)	0.117 (1.26)	0.981	12.41
8.	Himachal Pradesh	In (HP)	8.506 (1038.63)	0.139 (53.93)	0.999	14.91
9.	Jammu & Kashmir	In (JK)	8.688 (241.33)	0.146 (13.27)	0.981	15.72
10.	Karnataka	In (KAR)	10.695 (427.6)	0.132 (16.38)	0.989	14.11
11.	Kerala	In (KER)	10.351 (796.15)	0.124 (31.00)	0.997	13.20
12.	Madhya Pradesh	In (MP)	10.856 (678.5)	0.104 (20.6)	0.993	10.96
13.	Maharashtra	In (MAH)	11.752 (734.38)	0.099 (19.8)	0.993	10.41
14.	Manipur	In (MAN)	7.114 (309.13)	0.151 (21.57)	0.993	16.30
15.	Maghalaya	In (MEG)	7.282 (330.91)	0.133 (19.0)	0.991	14.22
16.	Orissa	In (OR)	9.903 (157.14)	0.098 (5.16)	0.889	10.29
17.	Punjab	In (PUN)	10.333 (645.63)	0.114 (22.8)	0.994	12.08
18.	Rajasthan	In (RAJ)	10.574 (195.74)	0.117 (6.88)	0.940	12.41
19.	Sikkim	In (SIK)	5.923 (160.00)	0.141 (17.63)	0.989	15.14
20.	Tamil Nadu	In (TN)	11.033 (689 38)	0.132 (26.4)	0.995	14.11
21.	Tripura	In (TRI)	7.509 (202 97)	0.155 (12.83)	0.983	16.77
22.	Uttar Pradesh	In (UP)	11.447 (384.23)	0.115 (12.78)	0.980	12.19
23.	West Bengal	In (WB)	10.938 (475.65)	0.156 (22.14)	0.993	16.88

Source: Figures in parenthesis show t-value.

TABLE 2

Central Plan Outlay (Rs. Crore)

Year	*1996-97*	*1997-98*	*1998-99*	*1999-2000*	*2000-01*	*2001-02 (BE)*	*Total*	*Max.*	*Min.*	*Mean*	*STND*	*C.V.*
1. Energy	19601.4	21129	23979	26183	26095.5	33787.6	150775	33787.6	19601.4	25129.1	4597.9	19.9
of which Power	6596.3	7423	3822	9367	10064.8	12374.7	54648	12374.7	6596.3	9107.9	2043.7	22.4
Petroleum	10528.3	10915	11938	12318	12418.9	16935.7	75054	16935.7	10528.3	12509.0	2299.2	18.4
Coal and lignite	1932.1	2329	2625	3683	2753.4	3438.3	16761	3683.1	1932.1	2793.4	662.6	23.7
Non-conventional energy Source	544.8	4626	594	8144	858.5	1039	4313.3	1039.0	462.6	718.9	220.3	30.6
2. Transport	1438.7	12985	14398	17156	20847.7	22570	102340	22570.0	1438.7	17056.6	3887.7	22.8
of which Power	8300.0	8403	8755	8965	11249.0	10040	55712	11249.0	8300.0	9285.3	1145.3	12.3
Ports and lighthouses	768.0	879.3	1002	1543	1347 7	1092.8	6632.9	1542.9	768.0	1105.5	291.9	26.4
Shippings	1933.4	308.9	1121	645	740.5	976.9	5725.6	1933.4	308.9	954.3	555.8	58.2
Civil aviation	2237.5	1594	1302	1681	1885.4	16413	10841	2237.5	1594.2	1806.8	236.7	13.1
Roads & bridges	1092.9	1735	1643	4264	5548.2	8745.3	23033	8745.3	1092.9	3838.9	2964.5	77.2
Road transport	13.5	9.2	7.1	0	0.0	0	29.8	13.5	0.0	5.0	5.8	117.2
Inland water transport	23.4	34.4	41.2	37.8	55.5	52.2	244.5	55.5	23.4	40.8	11.8	29.0
Other transport services	15.0	21.6	20.9	20.5	21.5	21.5	12.1	21.6	15.0	20.2	2.6	12.7
3. Communication	10074.6	11137	13467	114900	20317.3	20288.7	90185	20317.3	10074.6	15030.9	4422.2	29.4
of which Postal services	85.0	80	84	96	120.0	135	600.1	135.0	80.0	100.0	22.4	22.4
Telecommunication	9387.0	10050	12185	13885	18165.3	18174	81846	18174.0	9387.0	13641.0	2852.0	28.2
Other communication service	602.6	1007	1198	9194	2032.0	1979.7	7739	2032.0	602.6	1289.8	587.3	455
4. =2+3	24458.3	24123	27864	32056	41165.0	42858.7						

TABLE 3

Expenditure of Energy by Different States (Rs. Crore)

	State	*1996-97*	*1997-98*	*1998-99*	*1999-20*	*2000-01*	*2001-02*	*r*	*Max.*	*Min.*	*Mean*	*STND*	*C.V.*
1.	Andhra Pradesh	1345.50	1269.70	76.90	343.00	2297.50	2316.00	0.43	2316.00	76.90	1274.77	942.15	73.91
2.	Arunachal Pradesh	100.50	93.30	77 40	104.40	124.70	99.80	0.17	124.70	77.40	100.02	15.40	15.10
3.	Assam	0.10	0.50	0.10	3.10	97100	0.20	0.10	971.00	0.10	162.50	396.08	243.74
4.	Bihar	2.90	158.50	18.20	98.70	2.60	2.90	0 33	158.50	2.60	47.30	66.02	139.58
5.	Delhi	1.50	1.80	2.40	2.21	2.10	4.80	0.93	4.80	1.50	2.47	1.19	48.15
6.	Gujarat	994.30	1340.30	1582.50	1391.90	3489.90	3471.40	0.79	3489.90	994.30	2045.05	1128.13	55.16
7.	Haryana	632.80	681.10	1172.80	763.60	880.70	1147.10	0.69	1172.80	632.80	879.68	232.93	26.48
8.	Himachal Pradesh	116.00	263.20	211.40	98.50	253.30	237 00	0.26	283.30	98.50	201.57	77.17	38.28
9.	Jammu & Kashmir	500.90	378.70	1126.00	1544.50	474.30	514 40	0.08	1544.50	378.70	756.47	469.85	62.11
10.	Karnataka	975.60	614.40	688.60	788.40	895.40	2360.40	0.83	2360.40	614.40	1053.80	653.50	62.01
11.	Kerala	16.80	26.50	22.00	1.30	23.10	22.10	0.40	26.50	1.30	18.63	9.04	48.54
12.	Madhya Pradesh	1374.80	1227.00	534.70	1325.60	464.40	413.10	0.67	1374.80	413.30	889.97	463.24	52.05
13.	Maharashtra	1320.60	370.00	317.20	231.70	5455.40	811.90	0.07	5435.40	231.70	1414.47	2011.65	142.22
14.	Manipur	92.40	119.70	92.20	21.20	100.80	119.10	0.22	217.20	92.20	123.57	47.49	38.43
15.	Meghalaya	8.90	3.90	16.30	9.90	11.50	12 00	0.41	16.30	3.90	10.42	4.08	39.19
16.	Orissa	208.80	8.10	77.70	15.90	1770	14.80	-0.57	208.80	8.10	57.17	78.58	137.46
17.	Punjab	1.338.70	874.50	0.80	404.10	452.30	702.30	-0.35	1338.70	0.80	628.78	457.33	72.73
18.	Rajasthan	564.60	1024.50	299.30	483.80	519.70	648 50	-0.15	1024.50	299.30	590.07	242.32	41.07
19.	Sikkim	46.30	49.00	56.10	54.20	62.10	71 40	0.96	71.40	46.30	56.52	9.16	16.20
20.	Tamil Nadu	136.30	575.50	-56.31	-723.70	-216.50	135.70	-0.26	575.50	-723.70	24.83	4.33.19	1744.40
21.	Tripura	183.70	632.40	-3.20	-643.50	-103 60	198.40	-0.25	632.40	-643.50	44.03	421.01	956.11
22.	Uttar Pradesh	0.00	0.00	120.00	100.00	770.30	1086.30	0.87	1086.30	0.00	346.10	464.56	134.2.3
23.	West Bengal	978.50	91.40	52.20	63.20	157.30	326.80	-0.31	978.50	52.20	278.23	357.66	128.55

Note: Where r = Correlation Coefficient between Central Government Plan Qutlay on Energy and Expenditure made different States on Energy.

TABLE 3 (A)

Compound Rate of Growth (CRG) In Expenditure on Energy

	State	Dept. Var	Intercept	Reg. Coeff.	R.-Square	CRG (%) per year
1.	Andhra Pradesh	In (AP)	6.071 (4.496)	0.171 (0.494)	0.057	18.65
2.	Arunachal Pradesh	In (ARP)	4.497 (30.233)	0.0297 (0.778)	0.131	3.01
3.	Assam	In (ASM)	(-) 2.778 (0.848)	0.846 (1.006)	0.202	133.03
4.	Bihar	In (BR)	3.671 (1.976)	(-)0.304 (0.367)	0.092	-26.21
5.	Delhi	In (DL)	0.209 (0.900)	0.177 (2.969)	0.688	19.36
6	Gujarat	In (GUJ)	6.604 (29.223)	0.257 (4.429)	0.831	29.30
7.	Haryana	In (HR)	6.419 (32.054)	0.095 (1.843)	0.459	9.96
8.	Himachal Pradesh	In (HP)	4.928 (11.360)	0.087 (0.777)	0.131	9.09
9.	Jammu & Kashmir	In (JK)	6.375 (11.016)	0.032 (0.216)	0.011	3.25
10.	Karnataka	In (KAR)	6.277 (16.133)	0.162 (1.625)	0.398	17.59
11.	Kerala	In (KER)	2.802 (2.325)	(-)0.053 (0.173)	0.007	-5.16
12.	Madhya Pradesh	In (MP)	7.464 (17.813)	(-)0.229 (2.280)	0.566	-20.47
13.	Maharashtra	In (MAH)	6.069 (4.775)	0.152 (0.500)	0.059	16.42
14.	Manipur	In (MAN)	4.607 (13.277)	0.046 (0.554)	0.072	4.71
15.	Meghalaya	In (MEG)	1.836 (3.817)	0.121 (1.052)	0.217	12.86
16.	Orissa	In (OR)	4.601 (3.986)	(-)0.356 (1.289)	0.294	-29.95
17.	Punjab	In (PUN)	5.301 (1.699)	0.029 (0.039)	0.0004	2.94
18.	Rajasthan	In (RAJ)	6.399 (14.379)	(-)0.025 (0.236)	0.013	-2.47
19.	Sikkim	In (SIK)	3.739 (77.895)	0.081 (7.364)	0.925	8.44
20.	Tamil Nadu	In (TM)	—	—	—	—
21.	Tripura	In (TRI)	—	—	—	—
22.	Uttar Pradesh	In (UP)	—	—	—	—
23.	West Bengal	In (WB)	5.425 (4.421)	(-)0.105 (0.358)	0.031	-9.97

Note: Figures in parenthesis are t-values. —: Data are not sufficient.

TABLE 4

Expenditure of Transport and Communication by Different States (Rs. Crore)

	State	*1996-97*	*1997-98*	*1998-99*	*1999-20*	*2000-01*	*2001-02*	*r*	*Max.*	*Min.*	*Mean*	*STND*	*C.V.*
1.	Andhra Pradesh	466.20	429.70	628.90	832.60	1166.90	1391.40	0.993	1391.40	429.70	819.28	455.74	55.63
2.	Arunachal Pradesh	144.50	150.90	149.20	131.70	151.50	156.50	0.346	156.50	0.35	126.38	47.09	31.95
3.	Assam	211.90	226.20	302.20	375.20	592.20	464.90	0.938	592.20	0.94	310.79	184.21	50.82
4.	Bihar	235.10	115.30	310.30	575.90	380.30	309.00	0.433	575.90	0.43	275.19	188.90	58.85
5.	Delhi	323.00	474.70	326.90	439.20	685.50	982.50	0.876	982.50	0.88	461.81	506.78	56.95
6.	Gujarat	541.70	654.40	849.60	923.70	897.10	1019.10	0.833	1019.10	0.83	698.06	309.51	38.01
7.	Haryana	456.70	490.40	598.60	607.50	706.50	917.30	0.926	917.30	0.93	539.70	262.64	41.72
8.	Himachal Pradesh	241.40	322.50	399.20	457.10	451.00	461.20	0.803	461.20	0.80	333.31	147.59	37.97
9.	Jammu & Kashmir	52.00	55.30	128.40	117.10	86.60	117.70	0.488	128.40	0.49	79.66	42.29	45.55
10.	Karnataka	311.70	364.50	416.80	522.30	594.60	860.90	0.926	860.90	0.93	440.25	260.01	50.64
11.	Kerala	306.90	413.70	399.30	488.50	513.50	489.80	0.814	513.50	0.81	73.22	155.65	35.76
12.	Madhya Pradesh	448.60	465.00	493.20	388.30	509.20	634.20	0.660	634.20	0.66	419.88	177.74	36.29
13.	Maharashtra	1327.10	1558.70	1011.50	946.90	804.50	1063.90	-0.713	1558.70	-0.71	958.87	450.51	40.27
14.	Manipur	85.30	72.70	59.70	82.70	32.60	26.70	-0.870	85.30	-0.87	51.26	30.09	50.21
15.	Meghalaya	87.60	93.70	99.60	112.10	118.70	131.20	0.963	131.20	0.96	91.98	57.36	34.86
16.	Orissa	286.90	260.70	239.00	275.40	279.70	360.80	0.671	360.80	0.67	243.31	100.19	35.11
17.	Punjab	376.60	409.60	481.20	519.40	599.80	674.20	0.974	674.20	0.97	43.40	195.76	38.37
18.	Rajasthan	330.60	367.60	389.40	269.50	426.80	379.70	0.385	426.80	0.39	309.14	125.80	34.89
19.	Sikkim	50.40	63.60	50.50	51.10	114.10	97.10	0.857	114.10	0.86	61.09	34.67	48.74
20.	Tamil Nadu	738.90	781.40	779.60	786.20	648.40	820.30	-0.185	820.30	-0.19	650.66	246.13	32.42
21.	Tripura	49.40	65.70	51.10	72.40	69.00	88.50	0.773	88.50	0.77	56.70	25.25	38.25
22.	Uttar Pradesh	676.20	642.10	1035.20	978.50	1378.30	1201.00	0.908	1378.30	0.91	844.60	417.75	42.40
23.	West Bengal	366.00	413.40	488.30	804.70	1308.90	1497.70	0.994	1497.70	0.99	697.14	524.39	64.49

Note: Where r = Correlation Coefficient between Central Government Plan Outlay on Transport and Communication and Expenditure made different States on Transport and Communication.

TABLE 4 (A)

Compound Rate of Growth (CRG) in Expenditure of Transport and Communication

	State	*Dept. Var*	*Intercept*	*Reg. Coeff.*	*R.-Square*	*CRG (%) per year*
1.	Andhra Pradesh	In (AP)	5.738 (45.904)	0.249 (8.586)	0.946	28.27
2.	Arunachal Pradesh	In (ARP)	4.963 (76.354)	0.008 (0.533)	0.065	0.80
3.	Assam	In (ASM)	5.127 (30.52)	0.199 (4.975)	0.860	22.02
4.	Bihar	In (BR)	5.106 (10.19)	0.159 (1.33)	0.305	17.23
5.	Delhi	In (DL)	5.509 (21.86)	0.199 (3.32)	0.731	22.02
6.	Gujarat	In (GUJ)	6.260 (65.22)	0.119 (5.17)	0.870	12.64
7.	Haryana	In (HR)	5.957 (88.95)	0.131 (8.18)	0.944	13.99
8.	Himachal Pradesh	In (HP)	5.499 (44.35)	0.125 (4.31)	0.815	13.31
9.	Jammu & Kashmir	In (JK)	3.934 (12.56)	0.152 (2.03)	0.508	16.42
10.	Karnataka	In (KAR)	5.509 (79.83)	0.193 (12.06)	0.972	21.23
11.	Kerala	In (KER)	5.742 (57.4)	0.091 (3.96)	0.783	9.53
12.	Madhya Pradesh	In (MP)	6.006 (40.82)	0.050 (1.67)	0.337	5.13
13.	Maharashtra	In (MAH)	7.311 (38.57)	(-)0.090 (2.25)	0.499	-8.61
14.	Manipur	In (MAN)	4.789 (16.18)	(-)0.225 (3.21)	0.717	-20.15
15.	Meghalaya	In (MEG)	4.379 (273.68)	0.081 (27.00)	0.991	8.40
16.	Orissa	In (OR)	5.489 (43.57)	0.04 (1.40)	0.337	4.08
17.	Punjab	In (PUN)	5.801 (305.26)	0.118 (23.6)	0.994	12.52
18.	Rajasthan	In (RAJ)	5.800 (33.52)	0.022 (0.55)	0.066	2.22
19.	Sikkim	In (SIK)	3.702 (13.70)	0.144 (2.25)	0.552	15.49
20.	Tamil Nadu	In (TN)	6.632 (71.29)	(-)0.0008 (0.036)	0.000	-0.08
21.	Tripura	In (TRI)	3.828 (27.36)	0.097 (2.94)	0.682	10.19
22.	Uttar Pradesh	In (UP)	6.344 (40.64)	0.146 (3.92)	0.792	15.72
23.	West Bengal	In (WB)	5.449 (36.76)	0.314 (8.97)	0.952	36.89

Note: Figures in parenthesis are t-values.

12

Border Trade with Bangladesh: Opportunities for Economic Development in Assam

SAUNDARJYA BORBORA AND RATUL MAHANTA

I. INTRODUCTION

The North Eastern Region (NER) also known as seven sisters comprises of Arunachal Pradesh, Assam, Meghalaya, Nagaland, Manipur and Tripura. Geographically two-third of the region consists of hilly terrain. Economically; the plain areas are more active than the hilly terrain areas. Out of all states, only in Assam the percentage of plain areas is more than hilly areas. In Assam only two districts, namely, Karbi Anglong and N.C. Hills are hilly terrain. While the country is trying to integrate with the global economy, the state has not integrated fully with the national economy. However, due to special constitutional arrangements, historical background as well as geographical locations, the Central Government has formulated various schemes for development of infrastructure and economy. In addition, the state has been declared special category state, which got central assistant on the basis of 90 per cent and 10 per cent loan.

The state provides vast scope for enhancing transport and communication facility in terms of rail, road and waterways but remains underdeveloped. Geographical isolation of this land locked region with the rest of the country and low utilization of international border in terms of trade opportunities have resulted in downsizing scope and vision of market oriented economic development of the state though there are lots of scope for develop this region by using systematically, the border trade. India's effort in trying to globalize itself with the global economy has opened new vistas for the state. As the NER is very close to the vibrant economies of South East and East Asian countries, this has led to a new hope in the development horizon of the state with more and more softening of the geographical rigidities with neighbouring countries especially with Bangladesh.

The liberalization of trade and normalization of India's relationship with the neighbouring countries, particularly with Bangladesh, has brought forth a new challenge to the state of Assam. The challenge is in terms of utilization of border trade. The earlier development of the state centers around national resources like tea, oil was basically pre-industrial in nature and hence failed to provide the growth impetus. The far away distance of the main market centers of the country crippled the regional market to spread up to a reasonable size thereby denying the manufacturing activities to attain the economics of scale. Therefore, it is quite likely that the increasing export through cross-border in new being viewed as potential vents for expansion of market size which will help for the economic development of the state.

II. OBJECTIVES OF THE STUDY

The following are the main basic objectives of our study:

(i) to assess the present level of resource potentials of the state of Assam,
(ii) to study the extent of export from Assam to Bangladesh,
(iii) to study the target market for export of goods and commodities domestic and international,

(iv) to identify investment opportunities based on demand potential of the neighbouring country and evolve development strategy, and

(v) to prepare action plans—both short-term and long-term plans for the promotion of export from Assam.

III. A BRIEF SCENARIO OF RESOURCE POTENTIAL OF ASSAM

The cropping pattern in Assam is more or less similar to that in other states of the country. Food crops occupy the highest percentage of total cultivated area. Rice is the principal crop in Assam. In the production of rice, the state is not yet self-sufficient. But there is immense potential to increase production by using scientific cultivation which has not happened much in the state. The important spices grown are chilies and turmeric. Characterized by the prevalence of tropical, sub-tropical and temperate climate and supplemented with high rainfall and favourable soil conditions, the state is highly conductive for the cultivation of diverse and exotic horticultural products. Assam having 43 per cent of the horticultural land, in the North-Eastern Region accounts for the highest production of fruit crops. 79 per cent of the banana produced in the NER comes from Assam while the state accounts for 69 per cent of the land under banana production. Similarly in citrus fruits and pineapples, Assam accounts for 26 per cent are 30 per cent of the production respectively. Fruit nut, areas nut and coconut are mostly grown in Assam. Assam is one of the leading producers of good quality jute in the world. This industry enjoys a competitive advantage because of the availability of superior fiber and in-expensive, semi-skilled labour. Assam also provides scope for Ramie cultivation, which is the stronger natural fiber in the world. This is grown in the tropical region of the upper Assam.

Assam's economy is predominantly a tea economy. The state alone produces more than half of all India production of tea. In 1990, the production of tea in Assam was 18439 thousand kg. Out of 760825000 kg in the country Assam alone producers 399344000 kg in 1994. In non-agricultural sector, the dominant activities is rural areas in Assam is handloom, weaving, sericulture and handicrafts.

The following table shows the production of coal, crude oil, natural gas and limestone in Assam, which depicts its potential also.

TABLE 1

Production of Coal, Crude Oil, Natural Gas and Limestones in Assam

Year	*Coal ('000 MT)*	*Crude Oil ('000 M.T.)*	*Natural Gas (M.Cu.M.)*	*Limestone ('000 M.T.)*
1992	1069	4703	1030	243
1993	1249	4737	838	284
1994	1292	4861	893	338
1995	1036	4790	1024	416
1996	858	4553	1232	441
1997	726	4801	1316	—
1998	575	5251	1257	488
1999	921	5001	1333	379

Source: Statistical Hand Book 2000, Government of Assam.

IV. EXPORT TO BANGLADESH

The bilateral trade between India and Bangladesh has increased rapidly during nineties but the balance of trade is significantly in favour of India. It can be observed from the Table 2 that the trade surplus has increased rapidly, since 1993.

India's export to Bangladesh consisted of diversified products and varies from primary commodities to manufacturing products. The Table 3 shows that cotton yarn, fabrics and made ups constitute the most important product group in India's export followed by rice (other than basmati) and machinery and instrument.

India's border with Bangladesh in 4096.70 km out of which 263 km border is shared by the state of Assam. Out of 263 km 160 km is land border and remaining 103 km is riverine. In order to facilitate border trade with Bangladesh and movement of passenger of the both countries, customs department has set-up

TABLE 2

India's Trade with Bangladesh

(*Rs. crores*)

Year	*1991-92*	*1992-93*	*1993-94*	*1994-95*	*1995-96*	*1996-97*	*1997-98*	*1998-99*	*1999-00*
Export	789.49	1030.6	1349.69	2024.13	3509.09	2912.4	2922.87	4168.03	2789.02
Import	14.06	35.96	56.09	152.2	287.22	210.42	188.84	267.65	345.54
Trade Surplus	784.3	994.87	1293.6	1898.93	3221.87	2701.98	2734.03	3900.38	2443.48

Source: DGCI & S, Kolkata.

13 number of land customs station along Assam and Bangladesh border. Out of 13 LCS only 2 are now functioning. The following Table 4, gives the details about it.

TABLE 3

Commodity-wise Trend of Indian Export to Bangladesh from 1994-95 to 1999-2000

(*in %*)

Principal Commodities	*1994-95*	*1995-96*	*1996-97*	*1997-98*	*1998-99*	*1999-00*
Cotton yarn and fabrics made ups	39.44	26.4	40.95	34.74	53.03	24.79
Rice other than basmati	4.38	27.07	4.48	12.23	12.5	13.07
Machinery and instruments	6.01	4.34	6.45	6	4.01	7.72
Transport and equipments	8.4	8.25	8.12	4.4	2.51	6.23
Glass and glassware/ cetamics/	5.55	2.85	1.96	5.25	2.46	3.58
regractory/cement	3.12	3.02	4.66	4.37	1.54	5.07
Primary and semi finished iron	3.03	2.41	2.61	1.39	0.8	1.61
and steel Paper and wood product						
Coal	3.48	2.17	1.61	2.4	2.65	3.16
Rubber manufactured products	1.59	2.17	2.89	2.38	1.5	1.67
Other ores and minerals	0	1.52	2.32	1.15	0.59	1.73
Total (Rs. crores)	2024.1	3509	2912.4	2922.8	4168.03	2789.02

Source: DGCI&S.

The National Council of Applied Economic Research, New Delhi, had made a study on cross border trade between India and Bangladesh and viewed that by this two LCS both official and unofficial export are going to Bangladesh from Assam. The unofficial export through Assam is more than double the volume of its official exports as can be seen from the following Table 5.

TABLE 4

Land Customs Station along the Assam—Bangladesh Border

States	*No. of LC*	*Functioning*	*Non-Functioning*
Assam	13	1. Karimganj ferry station 2. Sutarkandi	1. Karimganj Steamerghat, 2. Mahisasan Rly. Station, 3. Silchar RMS office* 4. Dhubri Steamerghat 5. Mankachar 6. Guwahati Steamerghat 7. Karimganj Rly Station 8. Latu Bazar* 9. Silchar Steamerghat 10. Tezpur Steamerghat* 11. Golakganj Rly. Station*

* Denotified.
Source: Customs Department.

TABLE 5

Value of Official and Unofficial Exports of Assam with Bangladesh

State	*Official Exports*		*Unofficial Exports*		*Total*
	Value (Rs. in Lakhs)	*% of Total*	*Value (Rs. in Lakhs)*	*% of Total*	
Assam	1742.22	32.92	3550	67.08	5292.22

Source: Office of the Commissioner, Shillong and N.C.E.A.R., New Delhi.

Sutarkandi Land Custom Station

The main commodities exported through Sutarkandi Land Custom Station include coal, paper, onion, non-basmati rice, ginger and fruits such as oranges, grapes, pears, citrus fruits. Total value of export during 1996-2001 was Rs. 135.05 crores. The following Table 6, gives the details of the export of commodities, quality and value in Rs. Lakhs to Bangladesh through Sutarkandi border.

Ferryghat Station

Main commodities exported from Ferryghat station include coal, ginger, onion, paper, rice, fish and different fruits such as

TABLE 6

Export through Sutarkandi Border

Name of the Commodity	Quantity					Value in Rs. in Lakhs				
	1996-97	1997-98	1998-99	1999-00	2000-01	1996-97	1997-98	1998-99	1999-00	2000-01
Coal	102475.97 MT	102475.97 MT	106895.80 MT	202342.40 MT	105744.00 MT	1469.27	1469.27	1809.12	3496.09	1936.90
Non-basmati Rice	4938.95MT	18950.03 MT	960494 MT	90.00 MT	N.A.	79.50	1799.20	979.32	9.80	N.A.
Fresh ginger	1722.27 MT	984.55 MT	664.23 MT	195.61 MT	31.68 MT	94.97	51.16	43.17	19.14	2.87
Onion	91.51 MT	N.A.	N.A.	13 MT	N.A.	5.38	N.A.	N.A.	1.44	N.A.
Dry Chilli	42.70 MT	N.A.	15.50 MT	N.A.	N.A.	14.70	N.A.	6.33	N.A.	N.A.
Grapes	1.77 MT	0.71 MT	N.A.	N.A.	N.A.	0.44	0.01	N.A.	N.A.	N.A.
Apple	3.29 MT	N.A.	N.A.	N.A.	N.A.	0.59	N.A.	N.A.	N.A.	N.A.
Methi	10.80 MT	N.A.	N.A.	N.A.	N.A.	0.91	N.A.	N.A.	N.A.	N.A.
Cement	N.A.	17112.50 MT	N.A.	N.A.	N.A.	N.A.	37.40	N.A.	N.A.	N.A.
Citrus Fruit	33056 Nos.	N.A.	88198 Nos	10400	N.A.	0.40	N.A.	1.01	0.16	N.A.
Tomato	3.30 MT	N.A.	N.A.	N.A.	N.A.	0.19	N.A.	N.A.	N.A.	N.A.
Motor Parts	N.A.	N.A.	965 Nos	1052 Nos	N.A.	N.A.	N.A.	0.48	1.24	N.A.
Others	N.A.	N.A.	N.A.	N.A.		26.68	15.36	22.06	13.12	97.64
Total						1693.03	3372.40	2861.49	3540.99	2037.40

N.A.: Not available.
Source: Data from land custom point.

TABLE 7

Export through Ferryghat Border

Name of the Commodity	*Quantity*					*Value in Rs. in Lakhs*				
	1996-97	*1997-98*	*1998-99*	*1999-00*	*2000-01*	*1996-97*	*1997-98*	*1998-99*	*1999-00*	*2000-01*
Coal	645.10 MT	N.A.	N.A.	N.A.	9705.MT	55.48	N.A.	N.A.	N.A.	177.69
Non-basmati Rice	N.A.	8371.5 MT	19765.90 MT	N.A.	N.A.	N.A.	7512.17	2071.90	N.A.	N.A.
Fresh ginger	N.A	1512.34 MT	1771.99 MT	1094.38 MT	696.64 mt	N.A.	79.81	114.11	135.39	56.36
Onion	714.49 MT	N.A.	52.89 MT	53.25 MT	5.52 mt	36.70	N.A.	3.09	3.70	0.24
Dry Chilli	35.61 MT	81.05 MT	N.A.	6.58 MT	N.A.	12.21	32.94	N.A.	0.21	N.A.
Grapes	6.20 MT	22.06 MT	6.31 MT	49.50 MT	N.A.	1.50	5.51	1.93	1.89	N.A.
Apple	1.10 MT	5.10 MT	N.A.	N.A.	N.A.	0.22	1.46	N.A.	N.A.	N.A.
Fresh Oranges	7860415.00 Nos.	8549748.00 Nos.	19260.98 Nos.	21955. Nos.	279725 Nos.	69.10	71.78	21.96	29.09	3.93
Pears	12.94 MT	N.A.	12.78	N.A.	4.81	0.39	N.A.	.032	N.A.	0.20
Cirrus Fruit	25157.70 Nos.	196461.00 Nos.	7247.80 Nos.	76014.42 Nos.	N.A.	20.11	20.01	7.24	10.73	N.A.
Soya Bean	N.A.	3.00 MT	N.A.	N.A.	4.00 MT	N.A.	0.49	N.A.	N.A.	0.78
Motor Parts	N.A.	19 items	6 items	460 items	192 items	N.A.	0.42	71.58	15.92	36.24
Paper	3057.85 MT	49.99 MT	N.A.	N.A.	N.A.	240.60	13.44	N.A.	N.A.	N.A.
Others	N.A.	N.A.	N.A.	N.A.	N.A.	2.27	2.79	37.69	3.21	3.05
Total						439.49	7710.82	23298	200.14	278.50

TABLE 8

Trend of Import Demand by Groups of Commodities

(value is in US Dm)

Commodity	*1996*		*1997*		*1998*	
	Quantity	*Value*	*Quantity*	*Value*	*Quantity*	*Value*
Rice	1238755	258.6	194544.0	41.0	1186173.0	246.2
Vegetables and fruit	N.A.	48.0	145679.0	30.7	96639.0	200.5
Milk and cream	23396	52.5	25673.0	68.4	21504.0	57.4
Wheat etc. unmilled	1199270	171.5	1411680.0	206.6	1040304.0	150.3
Coffee and Tea	N.A.	23.4	N.A.	13.6	N.A.	12.6
Spices	20230	22.3	10033.0	12.0	8746.0	11.0
Crude petroleum	1441197	158.9	1505082.0	186.8	1445065.0	177.1
Petroleum Products refn.	1415628	263.1	1652692.0	384.1	1453550.0	133.6
Lime, bidg. prods.	2982856	133.0	N.A.	210.1	N.A.	242.3
Cement	2957948	192.2	3316452.0	209.4	6779493.0	241.0
Gasoline, other light oils	84516	14.2	105894.0	24.0	74677.0	16.7
Kerosene incl. Jet oils	203848	40.0	268597.0	60.9	262152.0	58.6
Coal coke and briquettes	N.A.	20.0	N.A.	30.5	N.A.	9.4
Minerals fuels etc.	N.A.	448.1	N.A.	612.8	N.A.	529.1

Note: N.A. = Not Available.
Source: UN Trade Directory.

orange, mango, apple, grapes and citrus fruits. The annual export figures from 1996 to 2001 are 439.49 lakhs, 7710.12 lakhs, 2329.82 lakhs, 200.14 lakhs, 278.5 lakhs respectively. The foregoing Table 7 gives the details of the export of commodities, quantity and value in Rs. Lakhs to Bangladesh through Ferryghat border.

V. ASSESSMENT OF DEMAND POTENTIALITIES OF GOODS

(A) Information related to trend of import by Bangladesh for 1996-98 is presented in the Table 8.

(B) Demand-Global Import: Bangladesh

The annual import demand of goods has been listed below. The commodities are classified in three groups—A, B and C in order of their import intensity. The A group of commodities are less than 12 per cent of the total items but command 54 per cent of the total import bill of Bangladesh. The B group of items is 21 per cent of the item and command 25 per cent of the total import bill. The C class items though constitute 63 per cent of the total commodities but the total value it covers is only 21 per cent of the total import bill.

TABLE 9

Commodities Classified According to Categories of Preference—Bangladesh

Sl. No.	*Description*	*Import during 1998 (in USM$)*	*Category*
1.	Milk and Cream	51.4	B
2.	Wheat un-milled	150.3	A
3.	Rice	246.2	A
4.	Vegetables	71.9	B
5.	Sugar, Molasses	48.2	B
6.	Tea Coffee	1.6	C
7.	Spices	11.0	C
8.	Petroleum oil, crude	177.1	A
9.	Paper and Paper board	104.4	B
10.	Textile Yarn	411.3	A
11.	Lime, Cement and fabricated construction materials	242.3	A

Source: U.N. Trade Directory.

VI. INVESTMENT OPPORTUNITIES: BASED ON IMPORT DEMAND AND RESOURCE AVAILABILITY

The annual export of goods from India to Bangladesh for the year 1997-98 and 1998-99 has been listed in the Table 10 below.

TABLE 10

Bangladesh's Import from India

Sl. No.	*Items*	*Bangladesh import from India*	
		1997-98 (Lakhs)	*1998-99 (Lakhs)*
1.	Rice non-Basmati	35992.69	221022.2
2.	Coal	7029.89	11089.58
3.	Glass/glassware/ceramics/refractories/ cement	15350.31	10274.19
4.	Machinery equipments	17552.76	16749.07
5.	Cotton yarn, fabrics, made ups	101559.3	52135.93
6.	Spices	982.35	1960.06
7.	Fresh vegetables	2623.57	1650.55
8.	Drugs, pharmaceuticals and fine chemicals	7989.97	9776.03
9.	Rubber mfd. products except footwear	6968.38	6258.37
10.	Paper and wood products	4060.32	3348.87
11.	Other commodities	7695.06	9976.71

Source: U.N. Trade Directory.

The commodity-wise demand pattern of Bangladesh, import from India shows prospect for further investment in certain key areas. However, a cross matching with potential resource-base on Assam reveals that all the commodities do not possess compatibility. The compatible areas have been listed in the Table 11 given below.

From the above Table 11, it is observed that coal, fresh vegetable, spices, lime and cement, paper and paper products and Ayurvedic products has compatibility with the resource potential of the state. Although Rice and Petroleum oil has high demand in Bangladesh, there is no exportable surplus from Assam now. With the potentiality to increase rice production and setting up of Numaligarh refinery may occur well in these commodities also in near future.

TABLE 11

Demand Vs. Resource Compatibility—Bangladesh

	Product	Import from India	Resources Compatibility
1.	Rice	A	No exportable surplus
2.	Cotton fabrics woven	A	More emphasis on handloom
3.	Petroleum oil	A	No exportable surplus
4.	Coal	A	Compatibility exit
5.	Natural Gas	B	Production possibility exit
6.	Fresh vegetables	B	Compatibility exit
7.	Spices	B	Compatibility exit
8.	Lime, cement	C	Compatibility exit
9.	Paper and Paper products	B	Production possibility exit
10.	Tea	C	Low demand, resource exit
11.	Medical and pharmaceutical product	B	Resources compatibility for Ayurvedic products only

VII. INVESTMENT POTENTIAL IN ASSAM— A SUGGESTED ACTION PLAN

The state of Assam is endowed with large resource of high-grade limestone. The production of limestone is 399000 MT in 1999 which was 448000 MT in 1998. Cement/Clinker Plants may be set-up in the state of Assam. The demand of cement in Bangladesh is quite high and it shows a rising trend. Based on the availability of cement grade limestone and to cater the demand of cement in Bangladesh and also the regional demand, it is suggested to extablish units in Assam or the N.E. Region in a phase manner. Location of the plant would be more feasible in and around Lumshnong area in Jaintia hills district and the area is approximately 100 Km from Karimganj in Assam (nearest Land Custom Station for export to Bangladesh) and 80 Kms from the nearest railway head at Badarpur situated in Assam. If we can produce quality product at a competitive cost, the state has the advantage of nearness to market thereby reducing transport cost. Lime is one of the most widely used chemicals. Present industrial demand for Lime in Bangladesh is worth 242 MUSD. Lime plants can be set-up to meet 100 per cent requirement of paper and sugar industries in Bangladesh and in the North Eastern Region. As far as paper industry is concerned, unsatisfied demand for paper and paper products in Bangladesh, and in the country necessitates setting-up new plants. Other raw materials required for paper industry like bamboo/wood, etc. are available in Assam. It is observed that during the year 1998-99 Bangladesh imported paper and paper products to the tune of Rs. 3348.97 lakhs. The Ashok Paper Mill at Joghighopa is now in running mood under private sector after years remained closed. By using the modern technique, minimizing the cost of production of paper can be increased, as there are enough raw materials for the finished goods.

The demand for coal in Bangladesh is also very high. It is observed that the total value of coal was to the tune of Rs. 11089.58 lakhs during the year 1998-99. The most important coalfield in N.E. Region is Makum coalfield in Assam. Crude oil and Natural gas are also heavily demandable in Bangladesh. The production of crude oil and Natural gas in 1999 in Assam are 5001000 MT and 1333 M Cu M, respectively. By investing more and producing more Assam can increase its export to Bangladesh in near future.

The demand for spices in Bangladesh is quite high. At present, raw form of spices mainly ginger, turmeric are exported to Bangladesh. There is much scope for value addition by setting up few units of spice processing.

It is observed that Bangladesh has huge demand for non-basmati rice. Bangladesh in imports value worth about 246 USD of non-basmati rice. Based on demand potential and also the potentiality to increase rice production in the state, we may look positively to enter into export of rice in near future. Rice flakes are also known as flaked rice. It is suggested to set-up few rice flake-manufacturing units in the state of Assam particularly in Barak valley region and in Dhubri and Goalpara district of Assam because of the locational advantage of nearness to Bangladesh market.

Vanaspati is a product, which is obtained by controlled hydrogenation of edible oils and its hardness, consistency and grainy appearance, resembles natured ghee. The main raw materials for vanaspati are mustard, sesamum, safflower, castor and linseeds. Considering the availability of raw materials and the demand of Bangladesh as well as of regional demand it is suggested to set-up a Vanaspati plant in Assam.

VIII. STATE LEVEL POLICY INCENTIVES

For the growth of export, the Government of Assam announced its latest industrial policy in the year 1997. The policy includes a number of incentives for export-oriented units:

(a) Additional State Capital Investment subsidy of 10 percent subject to a ceiling of Rs. 10 lakhs.
(b) Additional 20 percent subsidy on phase of testing equipments for obtaining ISO 9000/BIS-14000 series registration, subject to a ceiling of Rs. 2 lakhs.

Special incentives for units other than 100 percent Export Oriented Units with an export effort of a minimum of 25 percent of the value of the turnover will be as below:

Subsidy on purchase of testing equipments for obtaining ISO 9000/BIS-14000 series registration @ 30 per cent of the cost of the equipments subject to a ceiling of Rs. 5 lakhs. This is proposed to support quality improvement efforts.

In addition to the incentives mentioned above the Government of Assam has created the following facilities for boosting up of export.

Export Promotion Industrial Park

The State Government with the assistant of the Government of India has set-up an Export Promotion Industrial Park (EPIP) at Amingaon (Guwahati). The park is built on an area of 68.10 acres with 168 separate plots. The park offers facilities like wide approach road, uninterrupted power supply, water supply, modern means of communication central effluent treatment plant, etc. There are also facilities like customs and central excise offices, banks, etc.

Software Technology Park

The State Government has set-up a Software Technology Park near the airport at Borjhar (Guwahati).

Inland Container Depot (ICD)

An Inland Container Depot has been set-up at Amingaon, outskirts of the Guwahati city. The ICD mainly handle the export of tea and few other items to different destinations of the world.

Land Custom Station (LCS)

The Customs Department has set-up 4 land custom stations in the state. Such LCS helps the exporters of Assam with Bangladesh to export various commodities through the LCS.

Export House Status to AIDC

With a view to encourage participation of State Government in export promotion. The AIDC has given the status of Export House, even though the criterion for giving the recognisation as an Export House is not full-filled by AIDC.

IX. CONCLUSION

It is true that Assam will be most benefited state in the region from the new trade regime because of her strategic Locational and relatively better infrastructural facilities compared to other states of the N.E. region. Being, the gateway to the N.E. region and having direct rail and road links with the rest of the country as well as with the rest of the N.E. region, Assam has a definite Locational advantage, which will offer relatively better prospects of economic activities and their linkages. Opportunities are there but it needs capital investment and necessary environment to develop. There is an urgent need to change the work culture and make the policies investor friendly without any red tapism. Then only investment climate will brighten-up and the state will be able to harvest benefits from border trade with Bangladesh. Also in order to increase the export of commodities, the entire border trading districts of Assam must take adequate steps to improve the provision of infrastructural facilities like transport and communication system.

References

Industrial Development and Export Potential of the North Eastern Region (Main Report), Vols. I, II & III by Indian Institute of Foreign Trade.

Project on: "Prospect of Border Trade with Myanmar and Bangladesh Pre-Investment Feasibility Study," by Indian Institute of Entrepreneurship, Guwahati, prepared for North Eastern Development Finance Corporation Ltd.

Export Potential of North Eastern States, March by FEIO, 2000.

Statistical Handbook of Assam, 2000, Published by Directorate of Economics and Statistics of Assam.

Country Report Bangladesh, Economic Intelligence Unit.

India's formal Trade with Bangladesh and Nepal: A Quantitative Assessment, Purohit, Sanjib and Taneja, Nisha: July 2000.

Report on Issues Related to Indo-Bangladesh Trade and Investment Trade and Investment by Indian Chambers of Commerce, Calcutta.

Bangladesh Economic Report, Ministry of Finance, Government of Bangladesh, 2000.

13

Impact of Globalization on Expert Performance of Manufactured Goods in India

R. ANNAPOORANI AND K. NIRMALADEVI

Exports are of vital importance to spur the country's programme of economic development, to attain the objective of self-reliance and to reduce the dependence on foreign aid. According to Kindleberger (1961) expanded export contains in its embryo the scope for additional investment opportunity, capacity to embark upon cost reducing innovations and the benefits from economies of large-scale production. Kaldor (1971) has postulated that, exports potentially have the strength to trigger industrial growth with significant level of scale economies which in turn will contribute for economic growth. Researchers like Kavousni (1985), Singer and Cray (1988), Tyler (1981), Dodaro (1991) and Michaely (1997) have found that association between export growth and economic growth is stronger for lower income countries like, India than for high income countries.

In Indian economic development, specifically export promotion has a notable effect since an increase in exports contributed doubly to economic growth by providing foreign exchange. Between 1980-81 to 1999-2000, the overall exports increased from Rs. 6740.17 crores to Rs. 1,62,924.42 crores. Indian exports are classified in to three categories: (i) Food, beverages and tobacco group include tea, coffee, black pepper, tobacco, cashew kernel oil cake etc., (ii) Raw materials group includes raw hides and skins, wool and other animal hairs, raw cotton and waste mice, iron ore, manganese ore, lac, minerals and fuels, and (iii) Manufactured goods include jute manufactures, leather manufacture, woolen carpets and rugs, chemicals, cereals and vegetable oils, fats and silk manufacture, etc., machinery and transport equipment, iron and steel and engineering goods.

Of the different items of exports of manufactured goods have greater impact on economic growth because manufacture exports has greater value addition. The manufacturer sector has greater linkage with the rest of the economy and hence the downstream effect of exports from these sectors is likely to be greater than primary exports (*Nidugala*, 2000). The manufactured goods emerged as single largest export item in India, since they accounted for more than 76.6 per cent of the total exports in 1999-2000 (*Economic Survey*, 2000). Further the growth of exports of manufacturing goods was higher than total exports. Between 1992-93 to 1999-2000 while total exports increased by only 10.1 percent, the exports of manufactured goods increased by 10.6 percent. The manufactured goods include textile fabric and manufacture cotton yarn and fabrics made ups, readymade garments of all textile materials, coir yarn and nurtures, jute manufactures including twist and yarn, leather and leather manufacturers, handicrafts—gems and jewellery, transport and machinery equipments including iron and steel and engineering goods.

The policy of globalization introduced in 1991 has created significant effect on export performance. Globalization, a term first used in 1985 by Theodore Levitt connotes pervasiveness, inclusiveness and sweepingness, with significant implication in international trade and financial relations. The 'double' part of globalization signifies that it widens the frontiers of economic activities across political boundaries of nations and helps the process to increase economic integration and growing economic interdependence between countries onto the World economy

(*Jagdish Gandhi*, 2001). According to the U.N. Secretary General, Mr. Kofi Annan, 'Globalization is perfect the most profound source of transformation since the industrial revolution began to turn external trade into a routine feature of international life. Globalization and the liberalization that produced, it have generated a sustained period of economic expansion and a rapid configuration of international geography.

As a part of globalization to overcome the crisis of acute foreign exchange crisis, the Government of India attempted 22 percent of devaluation of the Indian rupee to increase the price competitiveness of India's exports. Further cash assistance to exporters was abolished. The REP incense scheme was replaced by Export-Import script which entitled all exporters to import license worth 30 percent of the free on board (f.o.b.) value of exports.

Due to globalization, many export measures were introduced. Attention was paid to the setting-up of export promotion councils, state trading houses, rationalize export incentive scheme, laying emphasis on measuring foreign exchange earnings and relax quantitative restrictions. The cash compensatory scheme was abolished in July 1991. The replenishment (REP) import licensing was replaced by EXIM scrips? Further globalization boost trade in existing and new products, enhance competitiveness in market, stimulate production and foster technology transfer (*World Development Report*, 1999-2000).

In India, the various export promotion measures introduced in 1991 has helped to increase exports. Between 1991 to 1998 exports increased from Rs. 4,40,400 million to Rs. 14,16,040 million. Similarly, the percentage share of India in total World exports increased from 0.50 percent in 1991 to 0.63 percent in 1997. Exports as a ratio of imports increased from 74.1 percent in 1990-91 to 83.4 percent in 1998-99 (*Economic Survey*, 2000). India has registered 21 percent export growth in 2000-01 and the manufacturing sector's share significantly had gone up to 83 percent from 76 percent in 1999-2000.

However, the export performance of India is poor as compared to other developing countries. In 2000, while the export from China was US $ 182.3 billion, from Singapore it was US 5113.4 billion, from Malaysia it was US $ 81.7 billion, from Thailand it was US $ 63 billion, India had exported only US $ 35.1

billion. As such, the new EXIM Policy, 2002-07 envisages that India should capture 1 percent of global share of trade by 2007 and the absolute value of exports should increase to US $ 80 billion during Tenth Five Year Plan requiring a compound growth rate of 11.9 percent in dollar terms. This goal can be achieved through the exports of manufacturing goods occupy a prominent place in total Indian exports.

The impact of globalization on export of manufactured goods is expected to be important since they occupy a prominent place in total India's export. In India there have been any studies analyzing the export performance of manufacturing, Kareem (2000), Kumar and Singhal (1998) have analyzed determinant of India's manufacturing exports. However, there has been little attempt to study the impact of globalization on India's manufactured exports by comparing the export performance of manufacturing in pre and post-globalization period.

Hence, a research study on 'Impact of globalization on export performance of manufacturing goods in India is undertaken with the following objectives:

(i) To study the trends in the pattern of exports of commodities in pre and post-globalization period.
(ii) To study the trends in the direction of exports of manufactured goods in pre and post-globalization period, and
(iii) To analyze the determinants of India's manufactured exports.

METHODOLOGY

The current study is based on the data relating to pattern and direction of manufactured exports from India. The data on item-wise value of manufactured goods was complied from the published reports of Economic Survey, Industrial Database, Foreign Trade and Balance of Payment published by CME (Center for Monitoring India Economy) and Reserve Bank of India, Reports on Currency and Finance. The value of manufactured exports directed to various countries like Australia, China, Canada, Netherlands, Egypt, Bangladesh Commonwealth of Independent States, Germany, Hong Kong, Japan, Italy, Belgium,

UAE, UK, USA, USSR, were also complied from various issues of Reserve Bank of India Reports on Currency and Finance.

Following Part (1993), to adjust for inflation, the value of exports of various manufactured commodities directed to various countries was indicated in US 5 million. The study covers the time period 1980-81 to 1999-2000. The period 1980-81 to 1990-91 is termed as pre-globalization period and 1991-92 to 1999-2000 is treated as post-globalization period. The study used the following quantitative tools.

(i) Compound Growth Rate

The current study tries to estimate annual compound growth rate in the value of exports of various manufactured goods in pre and post-globalization period. The compound growth rate is Mailated by using the following regression equation.

$$Yi = a\ (b)^t$$

Transforming this into log form

$$\text{Log } Yi = \log a + \text{to } t \log (b)$$

where Yi = the value of exports of different manufactured goods; and t = the time variable.

Based on the above formula the annual compound growth rate (t) is calculated as

$$r = (\text{antilog } b - 1)^{*}\ 100$$

To identify the nature of significance of the compound growth rate, t values are calculated. Similarly, the current study estimates compound growth rate value of exports of manufactured goods directed to various countries.

(ii) Instability Index

To find out the extent of instability in the value of exports of various manufactured goods Koppack's Instability Index is applied.

The formula used is

$$V \log = \frac{\sum \left(\frac{X_{t-1}}{X_t} - M\right)^2}{N}$$

The Instability Index (I – T) = (anti-log) V log–1)* 100

where X_t = The value of export of commodities in year t;
N = The number of years minus one;
M = The arithmetic mean of the differences between the logs of X_t, X_t, + 1, X_{t+1}, X_{t+2}, etc; and
V log = the log arithmetic variance of the series.

Similarly, the current study estimated Instability Index of value of exports of manufactured goods directed to various countries.

(iii) Multiple Regression Model

The current study applied multiple regression analysis to find out the major factors influencing the export performance of manufactured goods. Following Das and Sharma (1999), the current study fitted multiple regression equation of the following form:

$$Y = \beta0 + \beta1X1 + \beta2X2 + \beta3X3 + \beta4X4 + \beta5X5 + \beta6X6 + D + E$$

where Y denotes the value of exports of manufactured goods from India, denoted in US $ million;

X1 denotes the value of Gross National Product in US $ million. The overall growth of the economy decides the volume and nature of exports of the country and Gross National Product best reflects economic growth of the economy. As the economy growth total output increases by widening the country's industrial base and this development encourages the exports;

X2 denotes the value of total production of manufacturing goods in India measured US $ million;

X3 represents World exports measured in US $ million;

X4 represents domestic demand of manufactured goods expressed in US $ million. Domestic demand for manufactured goods is derived by adding industrial production of manufacturing goods and subtracting this total figure from exports;

X5 represents the value of imports measured in US $ million. Exports are affected by imports since many export products contain imported inputs;

X6 represents the wholesale price index of manufacturing goods (base 1981-82=100). The data obtained from Economic Survey was related to wholesale price index containing base 1980-81 = 100 and 1993-94 = 100. By the method of splicing price index the base was converted into 1981-82 = 100. Domestic inflation increases the price of exported goods and hence high inflation rate adversely affects exports; and

D is the dummy variable. In pre-globalization period the dummy variable was assumed to be zero and in post-globalization period dummy variable was assumed to be one. The theoretical understanding is that with the inclusion of dummy variable (globalization), the exports of manufactured goods is expected to increase.

FINDINGS OF THE STUDY

Globalization by widening-up the market and by the provision of export incentives has created a change in the pattern of export of manufactured goods. The impact of globalization on the pattern of export of manufactured goods is analyzed under the following heads:

(a) Trends in item-wise value of exports of manufactured goods in pre and post-globalization period;
(b) Estimated compound growth rate of item-wise value of exports of manufactured goods in pre- and post-globalization period; and
(c) Estimated instability index of item-wise value of exports of manufactured goods in pre and post-globalization.

(a) Trends in Item-wise Value of Exports of Manufactured Goods in pre- and Post-globalization Period

Table 1 reveals that, in pre-globalization period between 1980-81 to 1990-91, the value of exports of total manufactured goods

TABLE 1

Trends in Item-wise Value of Exports of Manufactured Goods in Pre-Globalization Period

Sl. No.	Commodity	1980-81	1981-82	1982-83	1983-84	1984-85	1985-86	1986-87	1987-88	1988-89	1989-90	1990-91	Average Exports
1.	Textile fabric and manufacture (excl. Carpet hand made) of which	1179	1167	1609	1432	1445	1467	1705	2540	2570	3232	3807	2014
		(20.50)	(19.20)	(26.37)	(25.10)	(24.02)	(24.90)	(25.10)	(29.10)	(23.64)	(26.10)	(26.30)	
2.	Cotton yarn, fabric made-ups	516	502	434	415	521	469	498	781	798	913	1170	638
		(8.98)	(8.50)	(7.10)	(7.30)	(8.66)	(7.90)	(7.30)	(8.90)	(7.34)	(7.40)	(8.10)	
3.	Readymade garments of all textile materials	696	536	611	702	802	872	1041	1402	1451	1938	2216	1117
		(12.12)	(9.10)	(10.02)	(12.30)	(13.33)	(14.80)	(15.40)	(16.10)	(13.35)	(15.70)	(15.50)	
4.	Coir yarn and manufacture	22	31	27	25	24	28	27	23	22	25	27	26
		(0.40)	(0.50)	(0.40)	(0.40)	(0.40)	(0.50)	(0.40)	(0.30)	(0.20)	(0.20)	(0.20)	
5.	Jute manufacture incl. Twist and yarn	417	288	212	160	287	214	191	186	161	175	166	223
		(7.30)	(4.90)	(3.50)	(2.80)	(4.77)	(3.60)	(2.80)	(2.10)	(1.48)	(1.40)	(1.10)	
6.	Leather and leather manufacture incl. Leather foodwear, travel goods and garments	793	450	429	477	609	629	721	965	1051	1213	1449	771
		(8.58)	(7.60)	(7.00)	(8.40)	(10.12)	(10.70)	(10.60)	(11.10)	(9.67)	(9.80)	(10.00)	
7.	Handicrafts (incl. carpet handmade) of which	1204	1338	1358	1546	1473	1538	1994	2503	3524	3071	3437	2090
		(2096)	(22.60)	(22.26)	(27.10)	(24.48)	(26.20)	(29.40)	(28.70)	(32.40)	(24.80)	(23.80)	

8.	Gems and jewellery	782 (13.60)	932 (15.80)	1050 (17.20)	1251 (21.90)	1040 (17.29)	1228 (20.90)	1623 (23.90)	2015 (23.10)	3033 (37.89)	3177 (25.70)	2924 (20.20)	595
9.	Chemicals and allied products	284 (4.94)	406 (6.90)	146 (5.67)	269 (4.70)	406 (6.75)	407 (6.90)	456 (6.70)	618 (7.10)	889 (8.18)	1288 (10.40)	1176 (8.10)	1732
10.	Machinery, transport equipments and metal manufacture incl. Iron and steel	1045 (18.19)	1047 (17.70)	826 (13.50)	668 (11.70)	804 (11.17)	480 (13.30)	787 (11.60)	1034 (11.90)	1558 (14.33)	1968 (15.90)	2158 (14.90)	1152
11.	Engineering goods	1100 (19.20)	1182 (20.00)	1293 (21.20)	1132 (19.83)	967 (16.08)	817 (13.90)	900 (13.30)	852 (9.80)	1097 (10.09)	1411 (11.40)	2240 (15.49)	1181
	Total	5744	5909	6100	5709	6015	5880	6781	8721	10872	12383	14460	8052

Figures in parenthesis indicate percentage share and they are calculated based on the data compiled from Economic Survey.
Source: *Economic Survey*, various issues, 1981-82 to 1991-92.

increased from US $ 5,744 million to US $ 14,460 million Export of textile fabric and manufacture (including carpet hand made) increased from US $ 1,179 million in 1980-81 to US $ 3,807 million in 1990-91. The value of exports of coir yarn and manufactures increased from US $ 22 million in 1980-81 to US $ 27 million in 1990-91. The export of leather, leather manufacture including leather footwear, leather travel goods and ferments from US $ 493 million to US $ 1,449 million.

Handicrafts were the major item of exports in pre-globalization period. The value of exports of handicrafts increased from US $ 1,204 million in 1980-81 to US $ 3,347 million in 1990-91. Gems and jewellery was an important component of handicrafts and the value of exports of gems and jewellery increased from US $ 782 million in 1980-81 to US $ 2,924 million in 1990-91. Between 1980-81 to 1990-91, the value of exports of chemical and allied products increased from US $ 1,176 million.

Globalization has created a significant change in the commodity composition of Indian exports. The policy of globalization has reduced the share of traditional commodities and increased the share of non-traditional commodities. Further new commodities have entered into India's export basket. Table 2 helps to analyse the trends in item-wise value of export of manufactured goods in post-globalization period.

Table 2 implies that, in post-globalization period between 1991-92 to 1999-2000 the value of exports of manufactured goods recorded a nearly two-fold increase from US $ 14,954 million in 1991-92 to US $ 25,736 million in 1999-2000. Between 1991-92 to 1999-2000 the value of exports of textile fabric more than doubled from US $ 4,024 million to US $ 9,351 million. Globalization had given a severe blow to the export of handicrafts. Between 1991-92 to 1999-2000 the export of handicrafts decreased from US $ 3,387 million to US $ 1.277 million. However, gems and jewellery, an important component of handicrafts have got better export prospect. Between 1991-92 to 1999-2000, the value of exports of gems and jewellery increased from US $ 2,738 million to US $ 7,636 million.

The current study tried to compare the percentage share of various manufactured items in total manufactured exports in pre- and post-globalization period. Table 3 presents the information on

TABLE 2

Trends in Item-wise Value of Exports of Manufactured Goods in Post-Globalization Period

Sl. No.	*Commodity*	*1991-92*	*1992-93*	*1993-94*	*1994-95*	*1995-96*	*1996-97*	*1997-98*	*1998-99*	*1999-2000*	*Average Exports*
1.	Textile fabric and manufacture (excl. Carpet hand made) of which	4024 (26.91)	4315 (27.47)	4739 (25.46)	6352 (28.32)	7220 (26.71)	7829 (27.57)	8640 (34.03)	8457 (36.43)	9351 (36.33)	6770
2.	Cotton yarn, fabric made-ups	1300 (8.69)	1350 (8.60)	1537 (8.26)	2234 (9.96)	2577 (9.50)	3122 (10.99)	3264 (12.86)	2772 (11.90)	3139 (12.20)	2366
3.	Readymade garments of all textile materials	2199 (14.71)	2392 (15.24)	2586 (13.89)	3282 (14.63)	3676 (13.60)	3253 (13.22)	3876 (15.27)	4365 (18.80)	4802 (18.66)	3437
4.	Coir yarn and manufacture	28 (0.20)	31 (0.20)	41 (0.20)	55 (0.20)	63 (0.20)	61 (0.20)	69 (0.30)	75 (0.30)	44 (0.20)	52
5.	Jute manufacture incl. Twist and yarn	159 (1.96)	123 (0.80)	124 (0.70)	151 (0.70)	186 (0.70)	155 (0.50)	187 (0.70)	138 (0.60)	119 (0.50)	149
6.	Leather and leather manufacture incl. Leather foodwear, travel goods and garments	1269 (8.49)	1277 (8.10)	1300 (6.99)	1611 (7.20)	1731 (6.40)	1580 (5.60)	1631 (6.40)	1580 (6.81)	1502 (5.80)	1498
7.	Handicrafts (incl. carpet handmade) of which	3387 (22.65)	3781 (24.09)	4768 (25.62)	5323 (23.73)	6129 (22.70)	5665 (19.95)	936 (3.69)	1177 (5.07)	1277 (4.96)	3605

(*Contd.*)

TABLE 2 (*Contd.*)

Sl. No.	*Commodity*	*1991-92*	*1992-93*	*1993-94*	*1994-95*	*1995-96*	*1996-97*	*1997-98*	*1998-99*	*1999-2000*	*Average Exports*
8.	Gems and jewellery	2738 (18.31)	3072 (19.56)	3996 (21.47)	4501 (20.07)	5275 (19.50)	4753 (1674)	5346 (21.06)	5929 (25.54)	7636 (29.671)	4805
9.	Chemicals and allied products	1583 (10.59)	1378 (8.22)	1813 (9.70)	2434 (10.85)	2945 (10.90)	3229 (11.37)	3684 (14.51)	3378 (14.55)	3810 (14.80)	2695
10.	Machinery, transport equipments and metal manufacture incl. Iron and steel	2234 (14.94)	2458 (5.65)	3024 (16.25)	3486 (15.54)	4358 (16.12)	49.10 (17.29)	5254 (20.69)	4393 (18.92)	4947 (19.22)	3896
11.	Engineering goods	2270 (15.18)	2341 (14.91)	2801 (15.05)	3020 (13.46)	4398 (16.27)	4967 (17.49)	4988 (19.65)	4016 (17.30)	4686 (18.20)	3721
	Total	14954	15706	18610	22432	27030	28396	25389	23214	25736	19382

Figures in parenthesis indicate percentage share and they are calculated based on the data compiled from Economic Survey.
Source: *Economic Survey*, various issues, 1992-93 to 2000-2001.

commodity-wise percentage share of manufactured exports in pre- and post-globalization period.

TABLE 3

Commodity-wise Percentage share of Manufactured Exports in Pre- and Post-Globalization Period

Sl. No.	*Commodity*	*Pre-globalization period*	*Post-globalization period*
1.	Textile fabric and manufacture (excl. Carpet hand made) of which	24.6	29.9
1.1.	Cotton yarn, fabric made-ups	7.9	10.33
1.2.	Readymade garments of all textile materials	13.4	15.34
2.	Coir yarn and manufacture	0.4	0.2
3.	Jute manufacture incl. Twist and yarn	3.2	0.7
4.	Leather and leather manufacture incl. Leather footwear, travel goods and garments	9.4	6.8
5.	Handicrafts (incl. carpet handmade) of which	25.7	16.9
5.1.	Gems and Jewellery	20.68	21.3
6.	Chemicals and allied products	6.94	21.3
7.	Machinery, transport equipments and metal manufacture incl. Iron and steel	14.22	17.18
8.	Engineering goods	15.4	16.4

Source: Values are calculated based on data compiled from Economic Survey.

Prior to globalization the major item of export of manufactured goods was handicrafts since it accounted for 25.7 percent of total manufactured goods. The lowest share was by coir yarn since it accounted for 0.4 percentage of total manufactured goods. In post-globalization period the exports of textile fabric and manufacture excluding carpet hand-made was the major item of exports since it accounted for 29.9 percentage of total manufactured exports.

(b) Estimated Compound Growth Rate of Item-wise Value of Exports of Manufactured Goods in Pre- and Post-Globalization Period

Table 4 presents the estimated growth rate of item-wise value of exports of manufactured foods in pre- and post-globalization period.

Table 4 also explains that globalization had given a boost to the export of cotton yarn and fabric made-ups, jute manufactures, machinery, transport equipment and manufactures and engineering goods. The estimated growth rate of export of these commodities in post-globalization period was higher as compared to pre-globalization period.

TABLE 4

Estimated Compound Growth Rate of Item-wise Value of Manufactured Goods in Pre- and Post-Globalization

Sl. No.	*Commodity*	*Pre-globalization period*	*Post-globalization period*
1.	Textile fabric and manufacture (exc.. Carpet hand made) of which	54.88 (2.55)**	31.38 (3.32)**
1.1.	Cotton yarn, fabric made-ups	45.45 (1.47)	54.68 (2.05)*
1.2.	Readymade garments of all textile materials	60.66 (3.09)**	45.45 (3.04)**
2.	Coir yarn and manufacture	45.45 (0.45)	42.93 (0.82)
3.	Jute manufacture incl. Twist and yarn	1.91 (0.02)	16.39 (0.28)
4.	Leather and leather manufacture incl. Leather footwear, travel goods and garments	57.8 (3.43)**	24.27 (0.79)
5.	Handicrafts (incl. carpet handmade) of which	58.38 (2.99)**	-24.54 -(0.37)
5.1.	Gems and Jewellery	66.65 (3.84)**	49.85 (0.19)
6.	Chemicals and allied products	67.65 (2.24)*	56.9 (2.59)**
7.	Machinery, transport equipments and metal manufacture incl. Iron and steel	44.64 (1.05)	47.84 (1.83)
8.	Engineering goods	27.03 (0.49)	46.99 (1.40)

Figures in parenthesis indicate t-values.
* Significant at 5 percent level.
** Significant at 1 percent level.
Source: Values are calculated based on the data compiled from Economic Survey.

(c) Estimated Instability Index of Item-wise Value of Exports of Manufactured Goods in Pre- and Post-Globalization Period

Table 5 reveals the estimated instability index of item-wise value of exports of manufactured goods in pre- and post-globalization period.

TABLE 5

Estimated Instability Index of Item-wise Value of Exports of Manufactured Goods in Pre- and Post-Globalization

Sl. No.	*Commodity*	*Pre-globalization period*	*Post-globalization period*
1.	Textile fabric and manufacture (excl. Carpet handmade) of which	61.41	15.68
1.1.	Cotton yarn, fabric made-ups	60.74	22.43
1.2.	Readymade garments of all textile materials	31.71	18.21
2.	Coir yarn and manufacture	51.12	79.14
3.	Jute manufacture incl. Twist and yarn	93.23	48.04
4.	Leather and leather manufacture incl. Leather footwear, travel goods and garments	30.58	21.87
5.	Handicrafts (incl. carpet handmade) of which	34.36	45.92
5.1.	Gems and Jewellery	63.52	31.39
6.	Chemicals and allied products	83.89	29.29
7.	Machinery, transport equipments and metal manufacture incl. Iron and steel	54.64	28.55
8.	Engineering goods	63.16	39.49

Source: Values are calculated based on the data compiled from Economic Survey.

Table 5 makes it clear that, in post-globalization period there had been low instability in the value of exports of all the manufactured goods except coir yarn. The estimated instability index for all these commodities in post-globalization period was lower as compared to pre-globalization period. This implies that globalization has helped India in securing stable export earnings which in turn might be due to the reputation of our products in the global market.

The impact of globalization on the direction of export of manufactured goods is analyzed through the comparison of percentage share of various items of manufactured goods directed to various countries in pre- and post-globalization period.

Table 6 presents the information on the percentage share of various items of manufactured goods directed to various countries in pre- and post-globalization period.

Table 6 reveals that, in pre-globalization period USA was the major buyer of our manufactured products since 83.69 per cent of our manufactured exports were directed to USA. Next to USA, USSR accounted for 60.46 per cent of our manufactured exports. However, the lowest percentage of our export of manufactured goods was directed to Mauritius (1.3). Table 6 implies that, in post-globalization period USA was the major buyer of our manufactured products since 90 per cent of our manufactured exports were directed to USA. Next to USA, UK accounted for 75 percent of our exports. However, the lowest percentage of our exports of manufactured goods was directed to Indonesia (0.52).

Table 7 helps to explain the growth hue of country-wise exports of manufactured goods in pre- and post-globalization period.

Table 7 implies that globalization had created a favourable impact on the export of manufactured goods directed to Australia, Belgium, Hong Kong and Italy since the estimated growth rate of export of manufactured goods to these countries in post-globalization period was higher as compared to pre-globalization period. However, in port-globalization period India has been losing market of export of manufactured goods in Japan, USSR, CIS, Egypt, Hong Kong, Italy, Netherlands, UAE, USA, Germany and UK as the estimated growth rate of exports to these countries were low in post-globalization period.

Table 8 represent the estimated instability index of country-wise value of exports of manufactured goods in pre- and post-globalization.

TABLE 6

Percentage Share of Various Items of Manufacturing Goods Directed to Various Countries in Pre- and Post-Globalization

Countries	*Cotton Yarn*		*Readymade Garments*		*Jute Manufacture*		*Leather & Leather Manufacture*		*Gems & Jewellery*		*Chemicals & Allied Products*		*Engineering Goods*	
	Pre	*Post*	*Pre*	*Post*	*Pre*	*Post*	*Pre*	*Post*	*Pre*	*Post*	*Pre*	*Post*	*Pre*	*Post*
1	*2*	*3*	*4*	*5*	*6*	*7*	*8*	*9*	*10*	*11*	*12*	*13*	*14*	*15*
Australia	0.47	—	—	—	2.17	2.54	0.87	—	—	—	—	—	—	—
Bangladesh	4.87	8.89	—	—	—	—	—	—	—	—	0.63	—	4.78	3.57
Belgium	—	—	—	—	5.59	18.77	—	—	16.83	13.75	—	—	—	—
Benin	1.85	—	—	—	—	—	—	—	—	—	—	—	—	—
Canada	—	—	2.86	3.58	1.71	—	—	—	—	—	—	—	—	—
China	—	—	—	—	—	—	—	—	—	—	1.11	2.51	—	—
CIS	—	—	10.3	3.44	13.32	11.02	8.51	4.2	—	—	19.5	6.47	—	—
Czechoslovakia	—	—	—	—	3.86	—	0.33	—	—	—	—	—	—	—
Egypt	—	—	—	—	1.89	3.75	—	—	—	—	—	—	—	—
France	0.76	—	6.14	6.96	—	—	4.27	5	—	—	1.16	—	—	—
Germany	5.37	5.64	14.8	10.6	1.87	2.43	18.8	22.6	—	—	5.17	6.17	3.51	4.36
Hong Kong	1.3	5.43	—	—	—	—	2.86	3.41	13.26	22.05	1.65	3.07	—	—
Hungary	—	—	—	—	—	—	0.21	—	—	—	—	—	—	—
Indonesia	—	—	—	—	—	—	—	—	—	—	0.31	—	—	—

(Contd.)

TABLE 6 (*Contd.*)

1	2	3	4	5	6	7	8	9	10	11	12	13	14	15
Iran	—	—	—	—	1.33	—	0.42	—	—	—	—	—	—	—
Israel	—	—	—	—	—	—	—	—	2.03	3.09	—	—	—	—
Italy	3.16	4.56	3.84	3.23	—	—	11.9	11.5	—	—	1.42	2.45	1.28	2.48
Japan	3.03	3.61	2.96	2.64	4.22	4.45	0.92	—	18.36	1.0.1	1.53	1.68	4.57	3.23
Kenya	—	—	—	—	0.2	—	—	—	—	—	—	—	—	—
Korea	—	3.62	—	—	—	—	—	—	—	—	—	—	—	—
Kuwait	1.05	—	—	—	—	—	—	—	—	—	0.17	—	—	—
Malaysia	—	—	—	—	—	—	—	—	—	—	—	—	2.08	3.13
Mauritius	0.61	2.74	—	—	—	—	—	—	—	—	—	—	—	—
Netherlands	—	—	4.15	3.77	—	—	0.89	2.35	—	—	3.23	3.44	—	—
Nigeria	1.02	—	—	—	—	—	—	—	—	—	—	—	—	—
Poland	0.25	—	—	—	—	—	—	—	—	—	—	—	—	—
Portugal	—	—	—	—	—	—	0.68	1.5	3.22	—	—	—	—	—
Romania	—	—	—	—	—	—	0.26	—	—	—	—	—	—	—
Saudi Arabia	—	—	—	—	0.42	3.14	—	—	—	—	0.65	—	—	—
Singapore	0.94	—	—	—	—	—	—	—	1.02	1.65	—	—	6.4	5.57
Spain	—	—	—	—	—	—	0.75	3.04	—	—	—	—	—	—
Sri Lanka	—	—	—	—	—	—	—	—	—	—	0.09	—	2.76	3.63
Sudan	—	—	—	—	—	—	—	—	—	—	—	—	—	—
Switzerland	—	—	—	—	—	—	—	—	2.28	1.55	0.46	—	—	—
Thailand	—	—	—	—	—	—	—	—	—	2.87	—	—	—	—
Turkey	—	—	—	—	—	6.89	—	—	—	—	—	—	—	—

UAE	2.68	3.47	2.57	5.75	—	—	—	—	1.27	3.02	1.32	2.71	2.92	6.61
UK	8.87	8.57	11.1	8.98	5.14	8.69	9	12.9	2.27	1.99	3.6	4.39	5.96	6.82
USA	9.81	13.3	27.3	31.4	11.94	17.88	10.9	16.7	34.31	35.51	9.41	10.12	12.33	16.39
USSR	7.7	—	—	—	25.59	—	9.26	—	—	—	17.9	—	—	—
Yemen	—	—	—	—	—	—	—	—	—	—	0.15	—	—	—
Yugoslavia	—	—	—	—	—	—	0.33	—	—	—	—	—	—	—
Other Countries	46.24	40.2	13.9	19.6	20.73	21.26	18.7	16.9	5.14	4.44	28.9	56.98	53.42	44.2

Source: Values are calculated based on the data compiled from Reserve Bank of Currency and Finance.

TABLE 7

Estimated Compound Growth Rate of Country-wise Exports of Manufactured Goods in Pre- and Post-Globalization Period

Sl. No.	*Countries*	*Pre-globalization*	*Post-globalization*
1.	Australia	-22-55 (5.07)**	5.38 (1.07)**
2.	Belgium	-6.32 (4.84)**	8.44 (12.71)**
3.	CIS	39.11 (11.34)**	-1.75 (3.29)**
4.	Egypt	15.85 (3.90)**	2.71 (3.53)**
5.	France	6.75 (4.90)**	9.56 (16.26)**
6.	Hong Kong	66.09 (11.07)**	17.56 (10.86)**
7.	Italy	17.91 (8.17)**	9.85 (8.97)**
8.	Japan	8.34 (4.89)**	-2.55 (3.35)**
9.	Netherlands	21.45 (4.42)**	11.93 (10.75)**
10.	UAE	18.6 (7.76)**	15.52 (11.09)**
11.	USA	16.75 (9.04)**	13.43 (16.04)**
12.	USSR	-3.18 (3.64)**	—
13.	Germany	23.22 (11.41)**	4.43 (4.97)**
14.	UK	19.77 (9.28)	9.61 (11.45)**

Figures in parenthesis indicates t-values.
* Significant at 5 per cent level.
** Significant at 1 per cent level.
Source: Values are calculated based data compiled from Reserve Bank of India Reports on Currency and Finance.

In pre-globalization period, the instability index was the highest for exports directed to Netherlands (146.61), followed by Hong Kong (93.3) and it was the lowest for the UAE (46.26). However, in post-globalization period, the export of manufactured goods directed to CIS (60.18) exhibited highest instability index.

Hence the globalization had affected our trade with CIS countries. The value of exports of manufactured goods directed to France (39.54) exhibited the lowest instability index. A careful perusal of Table 8 indicates that in post-globalization period for all countries except CIS, there had been lower instability index as compared to pre-globalization period.

TABLE 8

Estimated Instability Index of Direction of Exports of Manufactured Goods in Pre- and Post-Globalization Period

Sl. No.	Countries	Pre-globalization	Post-globalization
1.	Australia	65.18	49.29
2.	Belgium	46.77	39.94
3.	CIS	48.47	60.18
4.	Egypt	71.56	49.3
5.	France	52.08	39.54
6.	Hong Kong	93.3	42.9
7.	Italy	51.93	44.07
8.	Japan	52.94	52.94
9.	Netherlands	146.26	40.24
10.	UAE	46.26	44.76
11.	USA	48.32	42.69
12.	USSR	47.25	—
13.	Germany	49.97	41.93
14.	UK	53.05	40.89

Source: Values are calculated based on data compiled from Reserve Bank of India Reports in Currency and Finance.

The estimated multiple regression equation of value of exports of manufactured goods in relation to selected variables is as follows:

$$Y = -30824.7514 + 37.1003\ X1 - 0.0102\ X2 + 0.2465\ X3 -$$
$$(-3.602) \quad (2.49)^{*} \quad (-1.19) \quad (1.43)$$
$$0.0088\ X4 + 0.2689\ X5 + 138.5635\ X6 + 2468.5788 \quad (1)$$
$$(-1.24) \quad (0.89) \quad (3.05)^{*} \quad (1.235)$$

$X^2 = .99$

Adjusted $R^2 = .98$

F = 178.63

Durbin-Watson test =2.44

Number of cases = 20.

The estimated equation implies that, Gross National Product has got a positive impact on the export of manufactured goods. An increase in Gross National Product by 1 percent is expected to increase the exports of manufactured goods by 37.1 per cent.

However, the estimated multiple regression coefficient of exports in relation to industrial production of manufactured goods was negative. This might be due to the fact that though industrial production is increasing, the producers are willing to sell in domestic market rather than in foreign market as they are not willing to face risk and uncertainties involved in export trade.

The estimated multiple regression coefficient of exports of manufactured goods in relation to World export implies that an increase in value of owns by 1 percent is expected to increase export of manufactured goods by 0.25 per cent.

Equation (1) makes it evident that there is a negative association between domestic demand for manufactured goods and exports of manufactured goods since estimated multiple regression coefficient of exports in relation to domestic demand was negative. As increase in domestic demand by 1 per cent will bring out decrease in export of manufactured goods by 0.0088 percent.

However, in accordance with the theoretical postulate the study found the positive impact of imports on exports of manufactured goods. An increase in imports of manufactured goods by 1 per cent will increase exports by 0.27 per cent. An increase in wholesale price index by 1 percent will bring about 138.56 per cent in value of exports of manufactured goods.

From equation (1) it can be observed that the impact of dummy variable, i.e. globalization, on the exports of manufactured goods is more. With the introduction of globalization the total value of exports of manufactured goods is expected to increase by 2468.58 per cent. Hence globalization had got favourable impact on the value of exports of manufactured goods is expected to increase by 2468.58 per cent. Hence globalization had got favourable impact on increasing the value of exports of manufactured goods.

The estimated multiple regression equation was, statistically valid since the estimated R2 value was 0.99, the variables Gross National Product, industrial production, World exports, domestic demand, imports and wholesale price index as a whole explained

99 per cent of total variation in exports. The statistical validity of fitted equation is confirmed by F value (178.63) and Durbin Watson value (2.44).

CONCLUSION

(1) Globalization has created a change in the pattern of export manufactured goods. It has encouraged the exports of textile fabrics and manufactures, cotton yarn and fabrics nude-ups, leather and leather manufactures machinery, transport equipment and manufactures and engineering goods. But it has affected the export of handicrafts, readymade garments, etc.

(2) Globalization has created a change in the direction of exports of manufactured goods. With the introduction of globalization, new countries like Netherlands, Spain and Portugal, etc. have entered into the group of buyers of our manufactured goods.

(3) Exports of manufactured goods are favourably affected by the trade reforms in the period of globalization.

REFERENCES

Ray, Amit Shovan, "Liberalization and India's export Competitiveness" in *Liberalization its Impact on the Indian Economy*. Edited by Gupta, S.P., Macmillan India Ltd., Lucknow, 1993, pp. 182-200.

Gandhi, Jagdish, (2001); "Dynamics of Global Economy", *Southern Economist*, May, pp. 11-14.

Kaldor, (1971); "Conflicts in National Economic Objectives", *The Economic Journal*, Vol. 81.

Kindleberger, (1985); "Direction of India's Foreign Trade: Some Emerging Trends", *Southern Economist*, Vol. 24, No. 3, pp. 72-77.

Mehar, K.S., "Liberalization and Recent Policy Reforms: Their impact on the Indian economy, edited by Gupta, S.P., Macmillan India Ltd., Lucknow, 1993, pp. 147-66.

Jain, Neelam, (2001); "Globalization the Indian Business Scenario", *Southern Economist*, May, pp. 15-18.

Streeton, Paul (2001); "Integration, Interdependence and Globalization", *Sourthern Economist*, Vol. 40, No. 6, pp. 17-19.

Vasudevan, A., (2001); "Generation of Reforms for a Brave New World", *The Indian Economic Journal*, Vol. 48, No. 3, Jan.-March, pp. 39-49.

Web sites

www.onlineindia.com

www.rbi.org.in
www.eximpolicy.com
www.workingpapers.com
Redelet, (1997); "Manufactured Exports, Export Platforms and Economic Growth", CARF November.
Marconi, (1997); "On Export and Economic Growth: The Case of Italy," CARE discussion paper No. 2.

14

Local Area Development for Export Promotion under Globalization—A State Level Study

Paramjit Nanda and P.S. Raikhy

It is widely believed that globalization or increased international economic integration promotes economic growth and reduce poverty by changing country's sources of comparative and competitive advantage. Today, comparative advantage of a country is not only determined by host country's natural and created assets, but also by access to MNC's and related services. Various empirical studies (*Emery*, 1967, *Balassa*, 1978, *Attri*, 1996, *Gonclaves*, 1987) show that sustained export growth or increased openness is good for economic growth.

In an effort to achieve high economic growth and to integrate with world economy, India embarked upon export promotion strategy since 1976. But the strategy at central level could not succeed in achieving even one percent share in world exports, narrowing of trade deficit and achieving sustainable export growth. India also lost comparative advantage in main commodities (textiles, leather and agricultural commodities) during era of globalization (after 1980s). Failure of export promotion strategy at central level calls for adoption of export promotion strategy at state or local level. Government may have to adopt regionally differentiated export promotion strategy which takes into account agro-climatic and, environment conditions of that region so that, export potential of that region is fully exploited and as a result, export competitiveness of that region is increased. Thus, there is need to exploit State/district level export potential. In this context, local level policies may become part of broader process of liberalization, privatization and other market reforms.

Realising this, present study has been undertaken at the level of agriculturally glittering state of Punjab so as to realise its export potential at local (district) level. The paper has been divided into four sections. Section I studies extent of India's trade integration with world economy and comparative advantage in exports of different commodities of India, Section II provides details of techno-economic survey of Punjab, Section III discusses commodity-wise and area (district)-wise export performance, and conclusions and implications have been given in Section IV.

To study trade integration in different commodities, 'revealed comparative advantage' in exports, developed by Balassa (1965), has been calculated for India as well as for Punjab as follows:

$$RCA_X = (X_i^k/X_i) / (X_w^k/X_w)$$

RCA_X = The revealed comparative advantage for exports for commodity X,

X_i^k = India/State exports of product k,

X_w^k = World/India exports of product k,

X_i = India/State's total exports, and

X_w = World/India's total exports.

II

The process of globalization defined as the integration of production, distribution and use of goods and services among the economies of the world, has been under way for over a century. Globalization occurs at factor level through increased flow of capital, and labour and at product level through growth of world trade being greater than growth of world output (World Bank, 2002). First wave of globalization (1870-1914) (extensive globalization) led to linking of entire world economically by trade and capital. As a result, there was substantial growth of these flows due to reduction in transport costs and tariff barriers. Period between 1914-45 was period of growing nationalism. Various events like world wars and depression led to increased trade barriers. As a result of beggar the neighbour trade policy, trade as well as capital flows decreased. By 1950, trade again reached the 1870 level. Second wave of globalization (1945-80) was marked by partial reductions in trade barriers. These reductions again led to doubling of trade relative to world income and trade reached the level of 1914. But second wave of liberalization did not led to movements of capital and labour and as a result, developing, countries suffered. Trading system was of Intra-North type. Trade between developed countries was not determined by comparative advantage but by cost savings from agglomerations and scale. Period since 1980 is called new wave of globalization or deepening or intensive globalization. In the new wave, there were tremendous changes in trading system, quantitatively, qualitatively and technologically. New wave of globalization is marked by increasing flow of foreign direct investment, intra-firm trade among MNCs, portfolio investment, mergers and acquisitions, internationalization of money market with instant computer-based satellite communications, increase in electronics and growth of consumerism (Shahid Usuf, Weiping Wu Simon Evenett, 2000).

The extent of globalization measured in terms of growth of world GDP and world trade since 1720 has been depicted in Table 1. Table shows that trade has increased at faster pace than output in all periods except 1913-50.

To meet challenges of increasing India's share lit world trade, the country adopted export Promotion strategy since 1976. During 1976-90, efforts were made to increase exports by providing various incentives (fiscal as well as monetary), setting up various organizations, councils and adopting export-oriented import policy. Since 1991, Government introduced major changes in export policy in the form of exchange rate changes, removal of quantitative restrictions and reductions of tariff barriers in imports. The effect of all these measures, as reflected in export performance of India is given in Table 2.

TABLE 1

Growth in World GDP and Merchandise Exports in Real Terms

(percent)

Period	*Real GDP*	*Export Volume*	*Export Growth/GDP Growth Ratio*
1720-1820	0.8	1.4	1.7
1820-1870	1.9	4.5	2.4
1870-1913	2.5	3.9	1.6
1913-1950	1.8	0.5	0.3
1950-1973	5.4	9.8	1.8
1973-1990	2.7	4.0	1.5
1990-1996	2.9	5.9	2.1

Source: WTO (World Trade Organization), Annual Report, 1998, p. 34.

TABLE 2

India's Export Performance

Period	*Exports as Percent of GDP*	*Ratio of Exports to Imports (percent)*	*Compound Annual Growth Rate*	*India's Share in World Exports*
1980-81 to 1990-91	5.58	65.09	16.14	0.51
1992-93 to 2000-01*	9.31	86.07	16.31	0.60

* Year 1991-92 has been excluded due to devaluation of Indian rupee.
Source: Government of India, *Economic Survey* (Various Issues).

Table 2 shows that, foreign trade performance has been impressive in terms of ratio of exports to imports and ratio of exports to GDP during nineties as compared to eighties. But performance has been poor in terms of share of India's export in world exports. Country has not been able to achieve even one percent share in world exports. Exports have increased at slightly higher rate in nineties as compared to eighties.

Commodity-wise analysis of comparative advantage given in Table 3 shows that India has comparative advantage in all agricultural commodities (except meat and meat preparations, sugar, sugar preparations and honey, manufactured tobacco and oil seeds and oleaginous fruits), iron ores and concentrates, dyeing, tanning and colouring materials, medicinal and pharmaceutical products, essential oils and perfume materials, soap cleansing, etc., leather, leather manufactures and dressed fur skins, textile yarn fabrics, made up articles, articles of apparel and clothing accessories, and pearls—precious and semi-precious stones. During new wave of globalization, India has lost comparative advantage in commodities namely fish crustaceans and molluses and preparations, vegetables and fruits, coffee, tea, cocoa, spices (loss in tea and mate and in spices being the maximum), unmanufactured tobacco and effuse, iron ore and concentrates, medicinal and pharmaceutical products, essential oils and perfume materials, soap cleansing, etc., leather, leather manufactures and dressed for skin (loss is, greatest), woven cotton fabrics, as well as other than of cotton, while revealed comparative advantage has increased in cereals and cereal preparations, rice (gain is maximum), feeding stuff for animals, oil seeds and oleaginous fruits, dyeing, tanning and colouring materials, and pearls, precious and semi-precious stones.

TABLE 3

India's Comparative Advantage in Exports (Revealed Comparative Advantage Index)

Sl. No.	*Code Group*	*Commodity/Division Group*	*Year*			
			1980	*1985*	*1990*	*1998*
1	2	3	4	5	6	7
01		Meat and meat preparations	0.87	0.83	0.40	0.70
03		Fish, crustaceans and molluses & prep. thereof	4.67	5.10	2.89	3.98
04		Cereals and cereal preparations	1.12	1.39	1.14	2.49
	042	Rice	8.95	12.06	11.58	16.81
05		Vegetable and fruits	2.54	3.04	1.44	1.57
06		Sugar, Sugar preparations and honey	0.66	0.00	0.25	6.47
07		Coffee, tea, cocoa, spices and manuf. thereof	9.40	10.18	7.36	5.31
	072	Coffee and coffee substitutes	4.98	4.21	3.11	4.35
	074	Tea and Mate	66.50	58.00	40.25	29.40
	075	Spices	36.60	42.83	15.00	21.00

(Contd.)

TABLE 3 (*Contd.*)

1	*2*	*3*	*4*	*5*	*6*	*7*
08		Feeding stuff for animals	3.78	3.22	3.93	6.82
12		Tobacco and Tobacco manufactured	10.41	3.92	1.46	1.52
	121	Tobacco unmanufactured, tobacco refuse	10.41	6.63	3.86	6.08
	122	Tobacco manufactured	—	1.50	0.55	0.00
22		Oilseeds and oleaginous fruit	0.74	0.55	1.45	2.58
28		Metalliferous ores and metal scrap	3.62	5.25	3.84	2.21
	281	Iron ore and concentrates	15.12	17.29	13.82	7.42
51		Organic chemicals	0.12	0.14	0.59	1.42
52		Inorganic chemicals	0.38	0.28	0.41	0.56
53		Dying, Tanning and colouring materials	1.94	1.68	2.13	2.12
54		Medicinal and pharmaceutical products	1.85	1.78	2.18	1.51
55		Essential oils and perfume, materials, toilets, polishing and cleaning preparations	2.65	1.47	2.09	0.58
57		Explosives and pytotechnic products	0.33	0.00	0.25	1.00
58		Artificial resins & plastic materials & cellulose esters and ethers	0.02	0.03	0.07	0.16
59		Chemical materials and products n.e.s.	0.11	0.36	0.40	0.92
61		Leather, Leather mfrs. n.e.s. & dressed fur skins	16.44	18.15	16.35	4.70
	611	Leather	23.70	17.66	8.78	3.25
	612	Mfrs. of leather or of compositions leathers n.e.s.	18.25	37.66	26.5	9.54
	613	Fur skins, tanned or dressed etc.	0.14	0	0	0
65		Textile yarn, fabrics, made up articles	5.52	4.67	3.77	5.29
	652	Cotton fabrics woven	12.51	10.48	6.68	6.88
	653	Fabrics woven of man made fibres	1.10	0.44	1.28	2.53
	654	Textile fabrics woven, other than of cotton or man made fibres.	16	11	4.28	4.38
66	667	Pearls, precious and semi-precious stones	7.41	21.09	17.98	17.08
67		Iron and steel	0.29	0.15	0.48	1.32
69		Manufactures of metals n.e.s.	1.41	0.82	0.93	0.91
71		Power generating machinery and equipment	0.57	0.33	0.27	0.24

72	Machinery specialised for particular industries	0.26	0.38	0.36	0.31
73	Metal working machinery	0.47	0.93	0.33	0.31
74	General industrial machinery & equipment n.e.s. and machine parts thereof	0.26	0.24	0.18	0.17
75	Office machinery and ADP equipment	0.01	0.11	0.15	0.14
76	Telecommunication and sound recording and reproducing apparatus and equipment	0.08	.01	0.05	0.03
77	Electrical mach., apparatus and appliances n.e.s.	0.43	0.34	0.23	0.14
78	Road vehicles (including air cushion vehicles)	0.38	0.17	0.19	0.22
79	Other transport equipment	0.17	0.11	0.02	0.06
84	Articles of apparel and clothing accessories	4.29	4.98	4.25	3.60
	Other Export	0.43	0.31	0.45	0.48

Source: Calculated from data given in Economic Survey, Government of India (various issues).

Agriculturally glittering Punjab is considered 'Food Basket' of country with 85 percent net area sown, high cropping intensity (185 as against 131 in India), rice-wheat cropping pattern, and Punjab contributing 42.1 percent of rice and 55 percent of wheat to central pool in 1999-2000. Punjab has higher productivity in crops like rice, maize, wheat, barley than those for the country as a whole (Table 4).

At district level, Bhatinda and Hoshiarpur were considered to be backward districts, while Ludhiana, Ferozepur and Faridkot districts were considered as developed districts in agricultural productivity as well as in most of variables affecting agricultural productivity.

In Punjab, only 0.59 percent area was covered under fruits and 2.43 percent area was under vegetables in 1999-2000. Fruits, namely kinnows, mangoes, oranges and malta are grown in Hoshiarpur and Ferozepur, while gauva is grown in Sangrur and Amritsar. Potato is main vegetable, which is grown in Jalandhar, Kapurthala and Hoshiarpur.

Punjab produced 9.14 percent of India's production of milk in 1994-95. Milk production in the state increased from 5142 thousand tons in 1990-91 to 6215 thousand tons in 1994-95 and as a result, per capita availability of milk increased from 682 grams per day in 1990-91 to 788 grams per day in 1994-95.

TABLE 4

Yield per Hectare of Principal Crops in India and Punjab (1998-99)

Crops	*India*	*Punjab*	*Punjab as percentage of India*
Rice	1928	3152	163
Maize	1755	2286	130
Wheat	2583	4332	168
Barley	1882	3226	171
Gram	794	788	99
Sugarcane	72560	59515	82
Potato	17571	18726	107
Cotton	223	180	80

Source: Government of Punjab, Statistical Abstract of Punjab, 2000.

The contribution of forestry and logging, fishing and mining and quarrying in net state domestic product is negligible.

Punjab cannot be considered as industrialized state as share of secondary sector in NSDP is very small (20.66 percent in 1999-00 as compared to 31 percent for India as a whole). In secondary sector, manufacturing takes lead by contributing 12.6 percent to NSDP, while construction sector contributed 6.51 percent to NSDP in 1990-00. Punjab's industrial sector is dominated by small scale sector (99 percent units are in small scale). These units provided employment to 79 percent workers and produced 36 percent output in 1998-99. Most of the small scale units have been set-up in Ludhiana, Jalandhar and Amritsar, while large scale units have been set in Ludhiana, Patiala and Ropar. Mansa, Faridkot and Fatehgarh Sahib lagged behind in small scale units, while Muktsar, Moga and Faridkot in large scale units. Most of workers in the State (about 55 percent) are absorbed in textile-based products industry, food products, transport equipment and metal products (Table 5). Food products constitute highest share in production (about 17 percent) followed by chemicals and chemical products (12.24 percent) and alloy products (11.10 percent transport equipment 11.00 percent), woollen textiles (0.65), and cotton textile indicating that Punjab has potential to promote exports in these industries.

TABLE 5

Composition of Manufacturing Industries in Punjab (1998-99)

(*percent*)

Sl. No.	*Industry*	*Production Share*	*Employment Share*
1.	Food products	17.30	12.68
2.	Beverages, tobacco and tobacco products	2.75	0.68
3.	Cotton textiles	9.29	5.52
4.	Woollen textiles, silk synthetic including art silk hosiery	9.65	18.11
5.	Wooden/wood products furniture and fixtures	0.64	3.55
6.	Paper and paper products, printing, publishing and allied industries	1.78	2.05
7.	Leather and fur products (except repair)	0.82	3.52
8.	Rubber, plastic, petroleum and coal products	4.18	3.73
9.	Chemicals and chemical products (except products of petroleum)	12.24	3.34
10.	Non-metallic mineral products	1.91	2.85
11.	Basic metal and alloy industry	11.10	6.30
12.	Metal products	3.42	9.31
13.	Machinery except electric machinery	6.77	6.27
14.	Electrical machine apparatus appliances supplies and parts	5.12	3.01
15.	Transport equipment and parts	11.00	9.38
16.	Other industries	1.01	2.07
17.	Repair and personal services	0.93	7.57

Source: Calculated from data given in Statistical Abstract of Punjab, Government of Punjab, 2000.

III

Table 6 shows that exports of Punjab increased from Rs. 162.13 crore in 1980-81 to Rs. 4014.96 crore in 2000-01, registering growth rate of 20.57 percent during this period. Exports of Punjab increased at higher rate in nineties as compared to in eighties. Openness of economy as measured by ratio of exports to GDP, increased from 3.22 percent in 1980-81 to 5.86 percent in 1990-00 (increase was rapid after 1992-93 and reached at highest level in 1997-98) (8.68 percent). Despite increased openness, Punjab export constituted very low share of India's exports. The share has remained virtually constant during the study period. Export share only improved in 1997-98 (when share increased to 3.32 from 2.54 percent in 1996-97) and reached at low level of 1.97 percent in 2000-01.

TABLE 6

Export Performance of Punjab

Year	*Exports (Rs. Cr.)*	*GDP (Rs. Cr.)*	*Exports as percent of GDP*	*India's Exports (Rs. Cr.)*	*Punjab Exports as percent of India's Exports*
1	2	3	4	5	6
1980-81	162.13	5024	3.22	6711	2.41
1981-82	224.72	5991.4	3.75	7806	2.87
1982-83	228.61	6643.5	3.44	8803	2.59
1983-84	197.19	7350.2	2.68	9771	2.01
1984-85	203.57	8303.1	2.45	11744	1.73
1985-86	245.2	9540.9	2.56	10895	2.25
1986-87	274.9	10444	2.63	12452	2.2
1987-88	341.66	12308	2.77	15674	2.17
1988-89	466	14158	3.29	20232	1.3
1989-90	647.65	16980	3.81	27658	2.34
1990-91	769.2	188881	4.09	32553	2.36
1991-92	900.81	22300	4.03	44041	2.04
1992-93	1214.5	26275	4.62	53688	2.26
1993-94	1815.5	34095	6	69751	2.6
1994-95	2082.3	34095	6.1	82674	2.51
1995-96	2564.6	38514	6.65	106353	2.41
1996-97	3024.8	44163	6.84	118817	2.54
1997-98	4204.8	48388	8.68	130700	3.32
1998-99	3629.1	54414	6.66	139752	2.56
1999-00	3676.4	62700	5.86	159561	2.3
2000-01	4015	—	—	203571	1.9

1	2	3	4	5	6
Compound Annual Growth Rate					
1980-81 to 2000-01	20.57 (21.84)	—	—	—	—
1980-81 to 1990-91	15.18 (7.03)	—	—	—	—
1991-92 to 2000-01	17.73 (7.51)	—	—	—	—

Source: Government of Punjab, Statistical Abstract of Punjab and Government of India, *Economic Survey* (Various Issues)

Commodity-wise analysis of comparative advantage of Punjab given in Table 7 shows that, Punjab bias comparative advantage in textiles and textile articles (readymade garments), rubber products, drugs and pharmaceuticals, engineering goods (transport equipment and electrical machinery and apparatus). Punjab has been continuously losing comparative advantage in rubber products during period 1980-81 to 2000-01. Punjab, after suffering loss in comparative advantage in textiles (readymade garments) and in engineering goods during nineties, gained in these commodities in 2000-01 and in food products (1995-96) indicating that potential exist in these products, comparative advantage in drugs and pharmaceutically transport equipment and in electrical machinery and apparatus has been widely fluctuating during the study period.

District-wise analysis given in Table 8 shows that three districts, namely, Ludhiana; Jalandhar and Amritsar accounted for major share in exports (i.e. ranging between 52 percent to 90 percent) during the period 1980-81 to 2000-01. Ludhiana always remained at top position in exports during these years. Other districts with major share in exports included Patiala, Faridkot, Kapurthala and Ropar, Patiala accounted for major share in exports in 1981-82, Faridkot during 1980-81 to 1983-84, Kapurthala during 1983-84 to 1990-91 (except 1988-89) and Ropar during 1988-89 to 1995-96 (except 1991-92).

As compared to 1980-81, Ludhiana and Amritsar experienced an increase in export share, while 4 districts, namely, Patiala, Faridkot, Ropar and Kapurthala experienced decrease in export share in 2000-01. Position of Jalandhar remained at same level in 2000-01 as in 1980-81. Export share of Amritsar district increased after 1990-91 and of Ludhiana increased after 1995-96. Position of Jalandhar did not improve due to decline in export share from 1984-85 to 1995-96. Export share of Kapurthala decreased after 1992-93, while of Ropar decreased after 1995-96.

TABLE 7

Comparative Advantage in Exports from Punjab (Revealed Comparative Advantage Index)

Sl. No.	*Commodity*	*1980-81*	*1985-86*	*1990-91*	*1995-96*	*2000-01*
1.	Food products	0.41	0.23	0.52	1.11	—
2.	Textiles and textile articles	2.29	4.21	1.63	0.97	1.56
2.a	Cotton textiles	0.19	0.56	0.79	—	
2.b	Readymade garments	3.4	4.38	3.06	1.42	1.04
3.	Leather and leather products	0.34	0.42	0.48	0.37	0.67
4.	Rubber products	4.76	2.73	1.39	0.77	—
5.	Drugs and pharmaceuticals	1.97	0.71	2.77	7.39	—
6.	Engineering goods	2.15	2.51	1.96	1.96	2.02
6.a	Transport equipment	5.81	6.33	4.5	7	5.85
6.b	Electrical machinery and apparatus	1.84	2.11	2.67	2.3	—

Source: Calculated from data given in Statistical Abstract of Punjab, Government of Punjab, *Economic Survey*, Government of India, Report on Currency and Finance, RBI and Foreign Trade and Balance of Payments, CMIE (Various Issues).

TABLE 8

District-wise Export Share in Punjab

Sl. No.	*District*	*1980-81*	*1985-86*	*1990-91*	*1995-96*	*2000-01*
1	*2*	*3*	*4*	*5*	*6*	*7*
1.	Amritsar	9.48	5.14	10.26	14.97	18.48
2.	Bhatinda	1.25	—	2.00	2.32	0.36
3.	Fatehgarh Sahib	—	—	—	1.39	0.20
4.	Faridkot	8.31	3.78	1.19	—	0.30
5.	Ferozepur	—	—	0.13	0.08	—
6.	Gurdaspur	0.20	0.05	0.07	0.13	0.45
7.	Hoshiarpur	0.08	0.17	2.76	0.21	0.68
8.	Jalandhar	23.78	16.40	11.18	11.89	22.51
9.	Kapurthala	3.26	6.83	7.98	4.56	4.11
10.	Ludhiana	45.63	56.96	47.37	34.61	50.43

1	2	3	4	5	6	7
11.	Manisa	—	—	—	—	0.28
12.	Moga	—	—	—	5.35	0.07
13.	Muktsar	—	—	—	0.03	0.07
14.	Nawanshaher	—	—	—	1.89	0.05
15.	Patiala	5.99	5.41	3.37	5.34	1.35
16.	Ropar	1.97	5.12	13.61	13.70	0.35
17.	Sangrur	0.00	0.10	0.00	3.42	0.21
	Total	100	100	100	100	100

Source: Calculated from data given in Statistical Abstract of Punjab, Government of Punjab (Various Issues).

IV

The study reveals that, India has lost comparative advantage in consumer-oriented agriculture products (fish and fish preparations, vegetables and fruits, and manufactured tobacco), medicinal and pharmaceuticals and in essential oils and perfume materials, toilets, polishing and cleaning preparations as indicated, by slow increase in country's exports as compared to world exports in these commodities. The loss in comparative advantage in these commodities is due to various internal and external factors. At domestic level, supply constraints in the form of infrastructural bottlenecks, labour inflexibility, inefficient banking system, SSI reservations, low capacity, utilization, lack of timely and regular supplies of raw materials and delays (acting as drag on production) exist, (*Nanda*, 2001). Lack of marketing facilities in the form of lack of information about health and sanitary regulations act as drag on exports. Comparative advantage is further eroded by external factors like imposition of non-tariff barriers in developed countries in form of labour standards, stiff sanitary and phyto-sanitary conditions environmental concerns, increased access to subsidies under blue green box categories.

To realise potential to increase exports in commodities, now comparative advantage should not be determined by country's natural resources but by marketing skill, discovery product differentiation building brand image, getting international inputs at competitive prices, least time consuming transactions and world class infrastructural facilities (*Roul Chhabilendra*, 2001). While world class infrastructural facilities be made available by encouraging private sector in investment, adhocism in export policy should also come to an end.

India is a vast country with wide inter-state variations in levels of development. Punjab has potential to increase exports of sports goods, light engineering industries (auto parts, bicycle and bicycle parts, hand tools and machine tools), carpets, electrical machinery and apparatus. It can further develop potentials in drugs and pharmaceuticals, food products, electronics and ill biotechnology. Efforts be made to increase exports of engineering goods (from Roopnagar, Gurdaspur, Jalandhar and Patiala), wooden goods (Hoshiarpur), food products (Faridkot and Amritsar), rubber goods and processed fruits (Ferozepur), readymade garments (Sangrur) and leather goods (Jalandhar).

In agricultural sector, Punjab has potential to increase exports of wheat and rice especially, Basmati (Amritsar), cotton and fresh fruits (kinnows) (Ferozepur), fresh vegetables (Jalandhar), processed fruits and vegetables (Jalandhar and Hoshiarpur), milk and milk products and meat and meat preparations (Amritsar). Punjab is basically cereal-based agro-economy. High handling costs along with transportation cost, shipment costs makes market price of wheat and rice uncompetitive in the world market. Despite this State intervention in production of wheat, sugarcane and rice, erratic supply, uncertain and stop-go kind of *adhocism* policy of Central Government to boost agricultural exports, lack of timely delivery, lack of modern techniques, lack of bio-technological labs and tissue culture. Frame and lack of agro-processing industries are main hurdles in agricultural exports from Punjab. (*Roul Chhabilendra*, 2001). To realise Punjab's potential in dynamic agricultural commodities, State should embark upon a 'mission approach'. For this purpose, State should play promotional and selective policy intervention role. Promotional role can be in form of public-private partnership in infrastructure as well as in agro-processing industries. Central Government has sanctioned 2 Agro Export Zones for Punjab which should be implemented at the earliest. The role of Agro Export Zones will encourage linkages between farmers, processors so as to encourage crop diversification and increase productivity through technological break-through in biotechnology and tissue culture, green house technology, proper grading, packaging, pre-cooling, refringerated transportation, chartered freight, etc. in increasing exports of fresh vegetables. To increase exports of processed fruits and vegetables, organic farming and environment friendly and post-harvest infrastructural facilities are required. To Increase exports of meat and meat preparations, there is need for strict quality control by controlling various live stock diseases, encouraging refrigerated transportation, cargo facilities and establishing modern slaughter houses. MNC's can be invited in areas like floriculture products.

In manufacturing sector, exports from Punjab suffer from problems of low productivity in small scale sector, lack of minerals, and raw materials, increased transportation costs due to remoteness of the State from ports, inadequate credit and power shortage. In case of hand tools and machine tools, due to concentration of production on simple technology small tools, exports are limited to few simple items. Exports of sports goods are based on leather and wood-based items and consists of low price-low technology items (*Nanda and Raikhy*, 2000), in era or liberalization and globalization, manufacture exports from Punjab will depend on productivity, efficiency quality and cost competitiveness. For this purpose, the quality should play role of facilitation through decentralization components and raw materials to be used in production for exports. To provide world class infrastructure to new industrial areas, infrastructure wing of PSIEC should be upgraded. SSIs must adopt new management techniques for quality improvement and cost reduction. Government should disseminate knowledge about emerging technologies to SSIs. Trade fairs should be encouraged. To promote R&D, private industries be encouraged by making use of patents and other rights, in readymade garments and leather manufactures, there is need to adopt specific product techniques to comply with new environmental regulations introduced in target markets. Textile industry has to adopt the—'cradle to gravel' approach, i.e. industry must start applying eco-prescriptions right from the stage of cultivation to clothing. For developing competitive advantage ill Information Technology and electronics industry, efforts should be made to set-up Hardware Technology Parks along with Software Technology Parks of India (STPI). Market promotion efforts are required in exports of bicycle parts, auto parts, hosiery and readymade garments, leather products while product diversification and technology upgradation is required in sports goods and hand tools. There should be shift in production from traditional sports goods to non-traditional goods due to growing concerns for ecological considerations and reduction in availability of wood in case of hand tools and machine tools, there should be production of high and professional tools.

In a liberalized and globalized era, radical measures are needed to expand exports through strengthening of infrastructure by foreign participation marketing arrangements and by taking conducive policy initiatives in the regions having export potentials. Thus policies of globalization and decentralized developed have to be combined to reap maximum benefits from the emerging scenario.

References

Attri, N.V., (1996); "Export Led Growth in Developing Countries," 1960-80, *The Indian Economic Journal*, Vol. 43, No. 3, Jan.-March, pp. 19-35.

Balassa, B. (1965); "Tariff Protection in Industrial Countries: An Evaluation", *Journal of Political Economy*, LXXIII, pp. 579-94.

Balassa, Bela, (1978), "Exports and Economic Growth", *Journal of Development Economics*, Vol. 5, No. 2.

CMIE, *Foreign Trade and Balance of Payments*, July 2000.

Emery, F. Robert, (1967); The Relation of Exports and Economic Growth," *Koklos*, Vol. 20, Fasc. 2, pp. 483-84.

Gonclaves, Renialdo (1987); "Inter-Country Comparison of Export Performance and Output Growth", *The Developing Economics*, Vol. XXV, No. 1, pp. 3-11.

Government of India, *Economic Survey*, (Various Issues).

Government of Punjab, *Statistical Abstract of Punjab*, (Various Issues).

Nanda, Paramjit, (2001); "Impact of Trade Liberalization on India's External Sector", *Unpublished UGC Minor Research Project Report*.

Nanda, Paramjit and Raikhy, P.S., (2000); "Exports from Punjab: Performance and Potentials" in R.S. Bawa and P.S. Raikhy (ed.) *Punjab Economy: Emerging Issues"*, Guru Nanak Dev University, Amritsar.

RBI, *Report on Currency and Finance* (various issues).

Roul, Chhabilendra, (2001), "Agro Exports from Punjab," *Bitter to Better Harvest*, Northern Book Centre, New Delhi.

Shahid, Yusuf, Weiping Wu, Simon, Evenett, (2000); " Local Dynamics in an Era of Globalization", *The World Bank*, Washington D.C., USA.

World Bank, (2002); "Globalization, Growth and Poverty", *The World Bank Policy Research Report*, Washington D.C., USA.

WTO (World Trade Organization, 1998); *Annual Report*, Geneva.

15

Globalization and Exports

K. Sai Haragopal

1. INTRODUCTION

India initiated economic reforms in 1991 due to unprecedented balance of payments crisis coupled with the emergence of globalization. India undertook macro-stabilization and adjustment programme to get over the crisis created by the Balance of Payments. One of the basic premises of economic reforms is the stress on outward-oriented policy. Since modern economies are open economies, the importance of outward-oriented policy cannot be ignored. Today's world is an interdependent world. Internal economic stability and better quality of life are woven around external economic environment. International cooperation and understanding are pre-requisite to sustain economic growth and development. Hence, India opened up the economy with less controls and external sector reforms assumed greater significance. External sector was liberalized through relaxing the restrictions on international flow of goods and services, technology and capital. Government of India has announced several measures from time to time in order to be in tune with the globalization and liberalization process. It introduced liberal exchange rates to promote exports. Five-year exim policies were announced to liberalize trade sector and allow several tax benefits. Export promotion became the key word and trade reforms basically concentrated on exports.

2. THEORETICAL FRAME

2.1. Theoretical Base—Dominance of Private Sector

Post-seventies saw the emergence of petro-dollars. One of the major changes occurred in international capital movements are, that of excess current account surpluses generated by oil exporting nations since 1974. International capital movements undergone a change and oil exporting nations are advancing their surpluses to deficit nations through Euro-dollar market. This led the way for a private dominance in the economic affairs of many countries. In due course major changes have occurred in the world economies with declining role for the public lending and an increasing role to private lending. This allowed the private capital to play significant role to shape the world economy particularly the economies of under developed countries. The changes in the capital movements had an impact on the growing economies.

2.2. Trade Reform in the Framework of Globalization

Trade under the guise of globalization is the result of the emergence of MNCs. Foreign direct investment which comes through MNCs are controlled by private entrepreneurs seeking huge profits. MNCs are an offshoot of Vernon's product cycle and Posner's technology dominance coupled with intra-firm trade. Theoretically speaking liberalized external sector reforms seeks shelter in export promotion by raising investments through Foreign Direct Investment inflows. Foreign Direct Investment (FDI) and Multinational Corporations (MNCs) are the two sides of the same coin. Modern trade under imperfect market conditions is dominated by ever changing technologies. Even though FDI/MNCs emerged in seventies and spread its wings, it gained currency only after late eighties and early nineties due to trade liberalization and economic reforms taken up by many countries. In fact international capital moved with an increasing speed after seventies oil crisis. Seventies, eighties and later on nineties saw major changes in the flow of international capital movements. Of the private capital flows FDI has assumed greater importance due to its wider base package of technology, management, expertise, etc. As an important source of foreign capital many countries invited foreign direct investment to augment their investments. Globalization and liberalization process saw the opening up of the economy to be invaded by foreign capital. The paucity of resources forced UDCs to invite FDIs in order to boost investments in their economies. It is assumed that the inflow of FDI will supplement the investment in the export-oriented sectors, so as to increase exports of the home country. India's trade reforms mainly concentrated to boost exports with less controls on international flows of goods, services, technology and capital. Hence one can conveniently draw the inference that the growth of private sector, which is the backbone of globalization, is linked with the growth of MNCs and the resultant inflows of FDIs.

Against this theoretical framework of globalization, i.e., the dominance of private sector through FDI inflows and the resultant increase in exports an attempt is made in this paper to examine the behavioural pattern of different external variables. Basically the analysis was carried out from two major aspects of Globalization, i.e. growth of exports and inflow of FDI.

3. OBJECTIVES OF THE STUDY

The basic objectives of the study are as follows:

1. To examine the trends in the growth of external variables.
2. To examine the trends in inflow of FDI and the relationship between FDI and manufacturing exports.

4. PERFORMANCE INDICATORS

1. Ratio values of E/M, E/GDP, E/GFD, CAD/GDP, E/EA, Ex/FDI, MEx/FDI,
2. Incremental Ratio Values of dX, dM, dCAD, dGFD, dEA, dGDP,
3. Marginal Effects of dX/dM, dX/dCAI), dXIdGFD, d/IdEA, dMEx/dFDI,
4. Compound and Exponential growth of X, M, CAD, GFD, EA, GDP.

5. DATA BASE AND METHODOLOGY

Basic data was collected from Economic Surveys, Government of India and then computed. Data was collected at two levels. Firstly, data for the period 1980-81 to 1999-00 was collected for exports, imports, trade deficit, current account deficit, gross fiscal deficit, and gross domestic product in current prices. The period was further divided into two sub-periods namely pie reform period covering 1980-81 to 1991-92 and post-reform period covering 1992-93 to 1999-2000. Secondly, since the FDI inflows gained currency in the post-reform period due to the emergence of globalization, sector-wise data for FDI inflows and manufacturing exports were collected for the period 1992-93 to 1997-98 for an in-depth analysis. Ratio analysis was employed to construct different ratios to study the inter-relationship between different variables. Incremental ratios were constructed to study the marginal effects of important variables. The study also analyses the growth of external variables in terms of compound growth rates and semi-log/exponential growth. Exponential growth is computed using the formula log Y=a+bt, where Y is the independent variable and 'a' is the constant and 'b' is the slope.

6. EMPIRICAL RESULTS

6.1. Impact of Reforms on the Performance of External Sector Variables

Trends in the performance of external sector variables have been analysed through ratio values, incremental values, incremental ratios, compound growth rates, and exponential growth rates.

Ratio Values: Table 1 presents five important ratio values for the pre- and post-reform periods. They are export to import, export to GDP, current account deficit to GDP, export to GFD, and export to external assistance.

Export to import ratios indicate the extent of imports being financed by export earnings. Over a period the ratio has shown a marked improvement indicating improved performance of exports particularly in the post-reform period. However, the ratio has never recorded unity which means imports are always greater than exports. In the pre-reform period the ratio values varied between 53% to 75% during 1980-81 to 1990-91. In 1991-92 the ratio suddenly jumped to 95%. In the post-reform period the ratio maintained a higher percentage when compared to pre-reform period. This shows reform process resulted in increased export earnings.

Export to GDP ratio was almost constant at 5% in the pre-reform period. From 1988-89 it has raised more than 5%, i.e. 6, 7 and 8 per cent. In the post-reform the ratio rose to 9% and continued at that level up to 1999-00 except in the year 1995-96 where the ratio was 10%. It shows that exports as a proportion of GDP is not increasing but became stagnant in the post-reform period indicating not so good performance on the part of exports.

One of the important indicators of better performance on external front is the ratio of current account deficit to GDP, lesser the ratio better the performance on external front. The value of this ratio shows that in the pre-reform period external sector has not performed well. However in the post-reform period there is a decline in the values which indicates better performs of exports.

The ratio of Export to GFD indicates how export sector is performing against GFD that includes external borrowings. An increasing higher value can be interrupted as a positive sign since higher export earnings decrease the trade gap, which in turn can reduce external borrowing. On the other hand, declining values of the ratio can mean less support from external front to reduce external borrowings. The table reveals that the performance of external sector against GFD was far better in the post-reform period than in the pre-reform period. In the pre-reform period the ratio was less than unity in all the years except in the year 1991-92. However in the post-reform period the ratio was more than unity all the years indicating an improved performance on the part of exports.

The ratio of exports to external assistance has a fluctuating trend during the pre-reform period. The value of the ratio was varied between 3.10 to 4.98. However in the post-reform period the ratio values has risen continuously in all the years except in the year 1998-99. The values have increased to 11.31 by 1999-00.

TABLE 1

Rational Values
A. Pre-Reform Period

Year	E/M	E/GDP	CAD/GFD	E/GFD	E/EA
1980-81	0.53	6.05	0.02	0.76	3.10
1981-82	0.57	0.05	0.02	0.90	4.19
1982-83	0.62	0.06	0.02	0.82	3.91
1984-85	0.69	0.06	0.02	0.67	4.98
1985-86	0.55	0.05	0.03	0.50	3.71
1986-87	0.62	0.05	0.02	0.47	3.45
1987-88	0.70	0.05	0.02	0.58	3.10
1988-89	0.72	0.06	0.03	0.65	3.81
1989-90	0.78	0.07	0.03	0.78	4.77
1990-91	0.75	0.07	0.04	0.73	4.86
1991-92	0.92	0.08	0.00	1.21	3.79

B. Post-Reform Period

Year	E/M	E/GDP	CAD/GFD	E/GFD	E/EA
1992-93	0.85	0.09	0.02	1.34	4.89
1993-94	0.95	0.09	0.00	1.16	5.92
1994-95	0.92	0.09	0.01	1.43	7.60
1995-96	0.87	0.10	0.02	1.77	9.65
1996-97	0.86	0.09	0.01	1.78	9.92
1997-98	0.83	0.09	0.01	1.42	10.75
1998-99	0.78	0.09	0.01	1.23	10.56
1999-00	0.80	0.09	0.01	1.50	11.31

Marginal Values: Table 2 presents data related to incremental values of Exports (dX), Imports (dM), Current Account Deficit (dCAD), Gross Fiscal Deficit (dGFD), External Assistance (dEA), and Gross Domestic Product (dGDP). The Table reveals a fluctuating trend in incremental values for almost all variables. In some of the cases the variables has recorded negative values. This indicates inconsistent growth of the variables.

Marginal Effects: Table 3 presents data related to incremental ratios related to exports on the one side and imports, current account deficits, gross fiscal deficits, and external assistance on the other side. Marginal effects or in other words incremental ratios shows how incremental value of one variable can influence the incremental value of other variable.

TABLE 2

Marginal Values
A. Pre-Reform Period

	dX	*dM*	*dCAD*	*dGFD*	*dEA*	*dGDP*
1980-81						
1981-82	1095	1059	600	-220	-297	20449
1982-83	997	685	-72	2099	387	15975
1983-84	968	1538	-52	2264	14	27555
1984-85	1973	1303	766	4386	93	20316
1985-86	-849	2524	2999	4441	577	26583
1986-87	1557	438	-629	4485	669	27279
1987-88	3222	2148	463	702	1447	34267
1988-89	4558	5991	5287	3879	252	57855
1989-90	7426	7093	-192	4709	498	55956
1990-91	4895	7870	5981	9000	902-	69152
1991-92	11488	4653	15132	-8307	4911	74954

B. Post-Reform Period

	dX	*dM*	*dCAD*	*dGFD*	*dEA*	*dGDP*
1992-93	9647	15524	10527	3848	-633	78004
1993-94	16063	9726	-9128	20084	799	168305
1994-95	12923	16870	6947	-2554	-901	144331
1995-96	23679	32707	9062	2540	142	159830
1996-97	12464	16242	-3364	6490	957	182021
1997-98	7469	12633	4604	22204	-234	141411
1998-99	13466	26779	-4097	24412	1494	185713
1999-2000	23173	26251	1211	-4451	1166	174076

The ratio of incremental exports to incremental imports can reveal how far incremental export earnings are able to meet at least the incremental import bill.

This ratio presents a better picture in the pre-reform period than in the post-reform period. In the post-reform period the ratios were more than unity in many years indicating incremental import bill is being taken care by incremental export earnings. However, in the post-reform period the ratios were less than unity in all the years except in the year 1993-94. This clearly shows import bill is growing faster than export earnings particularly in the post-reform period. With regard to other variables of incremental ratios, the values have fluctuating and declining trend. This clearly shows that the growth of exports could not influence much to reduce CAD, GFD and EA.

TABLE 3

Marginal Effects

A. Pre-Reform Period

	dX/dM	*dX/dCAD*	*dX/dGFD*	*dX/dEA*
1980-81				
1981-82	1.03	1.83	-4.98	-3.69
1982-83	1.46	-13.85	0.47	2.58
1983-84	0.63	-18.62	0.43	69.14
1984-85	1.51	2.58	0.45	21.22
1985-86	-0.34	-0.28	-0.19	-1.47
1986-87	3.55	-2.48	0.35	2.33
1987-88	1.5	6.96	4.59	2.23
1988-89	0.76	0.86	1.18	18.09
1989-90	1.05	-38.68	1.58	14.91
1990-91	0.62	0.82	0.54	5.43
1991-92	2.47	-0.76	-1.38	2.34

B. Post-Refrom Period

	dX/dM	*dX/dCAD*	*dX/dGFD*	*dX/dEA*
1992-93	0.62	0.92	2.51	-15.24
1993-94	1.65	-1.76	0.8	20.1
1994-95	0.77	1.86	-5.06	-14.34
1995-96	0.72	2.61	9.32	166.75
1996-97	0.77	-3.71	1.92	13.02
1997-98	0.59	1.62	0.34	-31.92
1998-99	0.5	-3.29	0.55	9.01
1999-2000	0.88	19.14	-5.21	19.87

Growth Rates: Table 4 presents data pertaining to compound growth rates for the pre and post-reform period. The Table reveals that, external front has not performed well in the post-reform period. In the post-reform period while the export growth has fallen the growth of imports has risen. The other important variables, i.e. CAD and GFD has grown at a higher rate in the post-reform period. Only the growth of external assistance has recorded a lower growth indicating somewhat improved performance on the external front.

TABLE 4

Compound Growth

Period	*Exports*	*Imports*	*CAD*	*GFD*	*EA*	*GDP*
Pre-Reform	16.94	11.79	0.07	12.43	15.02	13.38
Post-Reform	14.86	15.77	4.39	13.26	3.44	13.89

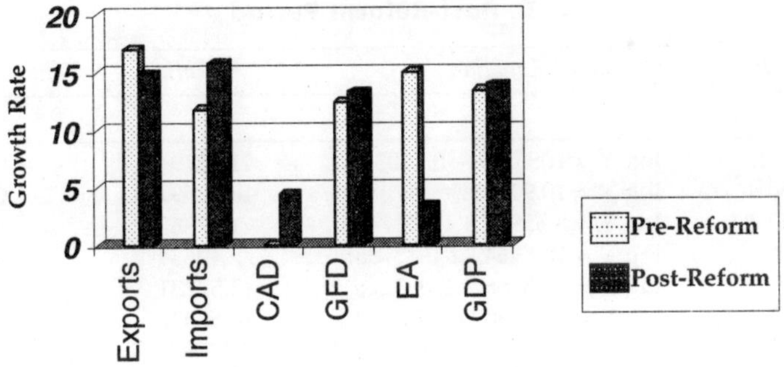

Exponential Growth

Using regression technique we have computed exponential growth with the help of semi-log method for Exports, Imports, CAD, GFD, External Assistance and GDP for the two sub-periods. The regression results of these variables are presented in Table 5.

The Table reveals that the growth of exports has fallen in the post-reform period from 16% to 15% in the pre-reform period. 94% of variation in the pre-reform period and 95% in the post-reform period were attributed to time factor through the value of R^2, and 't' ratios are significant.

Imports have recorded a higher growth in the post-reform period than in the pre-reform period. While it records 12% growth in the pre form period, the post-reform period saw a higher growth rate of 17%. The R^2 explains 95% of variation in imports during the pre-reform period and 98% of variation in post-reform period to time factor. The 't' ratios are significant in both the periods.

TABLE 5

Regression Results

A. Pre-Reform Period

Variable	*Estimated Equation*	*'t' Ratio*	*Value of R^2*
Export	log Y = 8.53559 + 0.16154t	12.96714	0.94
Import	log Y = 9.19413 + 0.12291t	14.09131	0.95
CAD	log Y = 7.69355 + 0.12378t	2.54095	0.39
GFD	log Y = 8.91384 + 0.15539t	13.69897	0.95
EA	log Y = 7.2254 + 0.15166t	10.41572	0.92
GDP	log Y = 11.57288 + 0.13435t	54.27775	0.99

B. Post-Reform Period

Variable	*Estimated Equation*	*'t' Ratio*	*Value of R^2*
Export	log Y = 1085119 + 0.15032t	11.88794	0.95
Import	log Y = 10.91513 + 0.17084t	16.43597	0.98
CAD	log Y = 8.85924 + 0.14174t	1.87867	0.37
GFD	log Y = 10.54642 + 0.13738t	7.49634	0.90
EA	log Y = 9.23886 + 0.03327t	3.57231	0.68
GDP	log Y = 13.28982+ 0.14513t	18.57932	0.98

CAD has grown faster in the post-reform period than in the pre-reform period. It has recorded an annual growth of 14.17% in the post-reform period against 12.37% growth in the pre-reform period. However the value of R^2 is very low in both the periods indicating other than time has more influence.

GFD has shown an improvement with a decline in its growth rate from 15% in the pre-reform period to 13% in the post-reform period. In the pre-reform period 95% of variation and in the post-reform period 90% of variation is attributed to the time factor through the values of R^2.

The growth of EA has drastically reduced in the post-reform period to 3% from 15% in the pre-reform period. However only 68% of variation in the post-reform period could be attributed to time factor through the value of R^2 GDP has recorded slightly higher growth in the post-reform period than in the pre-reform period. The value of R^2 explains 99% of variation in the pre-reform period and 98% of variation in the post-reform period are to time factor.

6.2 POST-REFORM TRENDS IN THE PERFORMANCE OF FDI

In a globalization framework, theoretically speaking, export is a function of FDI inflows. A positive correlation exists between the inflow of FDI and the growth of exports. Since the FDI is general, it is linked to MNCs and MNCs are industrialized giants. We can also assume that growth of manufacturing exports depends on the inflow of FDI. Hence, in this section an attempt is made firstly, to analyse the growth of exports in relation to FDI inflows and secondly, the growth of manufacturing exports in relation to FDI inflows.

TABLE 6

Exports to FDI Ratios

Period	*Exports*	*M. Exports*	*FDI*	*Exp./FDI*	*M. Exp./FDI*
1992-93	53688	40340	858	62.57	47.25
1993-94	69751	52240	1157	60.29	45.15
1994-95	82674	63991	2738	30.2	23.37
1995-96	106353	79433	4743	22.42	16.75
1996-97	118817	87377	7312	16.25	11.95
1997-98	126286	94511	10986	11.5	8.6

Table 6 presents data related to exports, manufacturing exports and FDI in flows along with two important ratios. The two ratios are exports to FDI inflows and manufacturing exports to FDI inflows. It is needless to say that a rising ratio indicate a better performance on the export front with a strong positive correlation. A glance through the Table reveals not so good performance on the export front in relation to FDI inflows. The ratio of export to FDI inflows declined during the post-reform period indicating no strong positive correlation between growth of exports and FDI inflows. Same is the case with the ratio of manufacturing exports to FDI inflows. Here also the ratios have declined suggesting that FDI inflows are not able to influence the manufacturing exports.

Since the two important ratios could not reveal strong positive correlation, we have attempted to analyze incremental ratio of manufacturing exports to FDI inflows. Such data is presented in Table 7. The Table reveals that the incremental ratio

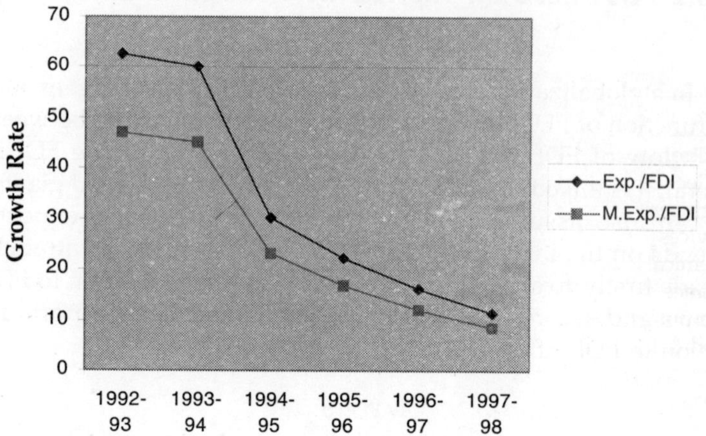

of manufacturing exports to FDI has shown a drastic decline over a period. Hence we can infer that inflows of FDI is not influencing export sector.

TABIE 7

Marginal Values and Effects

	dM.Exp.	*dFDI*	*dM.Ex/dFDI*
1992-93			
1993-94	11700	299	39.13
1994-95	11751	1581	7.43
1995-96	15442	2005	7.70
1996-97	7944	2569	3.09
1997-98	7134	3674	1.94

Table 8 presents data pertaining to the inflow of FDI into several sectors for the period 1992-93 to 1997-98. Over a period the share of Electronic & Elec. Equipments, Service sector have fluctuated in their shares in inflows. The share of FDI inflows to Engineering sector, Chemical & Allied sector, Finance, Domestic Appliances in general have shown a declining trend. The Table reveals the FDI inflows into different sectors do not exhibit any consistent trend.

TABLE 8

Sector-wise Inflow of FDI in Percentages

Year	*1992-93*	*1993-94*	*1994-95*	*1995-96*	*1996-97*	*1997-98*
Electronics & Elec. Equip.	11.71	15.48	6.47	9.14	7.45	21.8
Engineering	24.93	8.90	15.09	17.76	35.45	19.6
Services	0.87	5.46	10.7	7.08	0.73	10.86
Chemical & Allied	16.79	10.15	16.2	9.00	14.75	8.70
Finance	1.31	11.43	11.2	19.04	10.53	5.00
Computer	2.94	2.07	1.17	3.67	2.85	4.70
Food & Dairy	9.96	11.79	7.00	6.00	11.53	3.80
Domestic Appliance	9.96	0.63	12.42	0 03	0.73	2.02
Pharmaceuticals	5.65	13.41	1.16	3.86	2.31	1.14
Others	1.11	20.63	18.6	24.46	13.64	22.31
Total	100	100	100	100	100	100

Table 9 presents data related to sectoral share of manufacturing exports. The Table exhibits reasonably a consistent record in sectoral proportions of manufacturing exports. The export share of manufacturing goods for Electronic goods and Chemicals have improved.

TABLE 9

Sectoral Share of Manufacturing Exports

Year	*1992-93*	*1993-94*	*1994-95*	*1995-96*	*1996-97*	*1997-98*
Electronic Goods	1.52	1.82	2.02	2.82	3.18	2.75
Engineering	16.00	16.20	14.77	15.18	16.53	16.50
Chemical & Allied	5.50	5.62	6.28	16.15	6.56	7.33
Computer Software	0.07	0.13	0.27	0.34	0.30	0.18
Drug & Pharmaceuticals	3.80	3.85	3.92	4.30	4.96	5.53
Others	73.12	72.38	72.72	71.20	68.45	67.70
Total	100	100	100	100	100	100

Table 10 presents data related to the ratio of manufacturing exports to FDI inflows. A glance through the Table reveals that the ratios are on the decline. The ratios for all the sectors have drastically declined indicating that the FDI inflows into these sectors could not influence their exports.

TABLE 10

Ratio of Manufacturing Exports to FDI Inflows

Year	*1992-93*	*1993-94*	*1994-95*	*1995-96*	*1996-97*	*1997-98*
Electronic Goods	6.12	5.31	7.31	5.17	5.10	1.09
Engineering	30.30	82.02	22.88	14.32	5.57	7.24
Chemical & Allied	15.49	25.00	9.07	11.56	5.32	7.25
Computer Software	1.07	2.97	5.41	1.56	1.21	0.33
Drug & Pharmaceuticals	159.69	12.94	79.24	18.61	25.69	41.62

7. SUMMARY OF ANALYSIS

The study when looked from the angle of two major aspects of globalization, i.e export performance and inflow of FDI and resultant exports has brought out the following:

1. Export to Import ratios has shown a marked improvement indicating better export performance.
2. Export to GDP ratios was higher in the post-reform period, again indicating a better export performance.
3. CAD to GDP ratios has fallen in the post-reform period which means exports are performing better.
4. The ratio of Exports to External Assistance also has shown an improvement in the post-reform period.
5. Post-reform period saw a lower compound growth rate of exports and higher growth rate of imports. CAD and GFD recorded a higher growth in the post-reform period.
6. The analysis of FDI revealed increasing FDI inflows
7. Aggregate ratios of exports to FDI inflows and manufacturing exports to FDI inflows have declined.
8. The ratios of manufacturing exports to FDI inflows at the disaggregate level for the selected sectors also shows a decline in their performance.

8. CONCLUSIONS

The study clearly brings out that even though exports has improved a lot during the post-reform period, imports are also growing at a faster pace thus nullifying to certain extent the better performance of exports. This can be seen through the performance of incremental ratios and through growth rates of various variables in the post-reform period. The study also establishes a weak link between FDI inflows and resultant exports particularly in the manufacturing sector. Hence, the policy-makers has to evolve suitable policies to boost exports since curtailing imports is a difficult task particularly against reforms in the framework of globalization. With regard to the FDI inflows and the resultant exports, follow-up measures are essential to see how and why the sectors, which are receiving FDI, are not able to increase their exports.

References

Neog, A.K., "Some Aspects of India's External Sector," in *Structural Reforms in Indian Economy*, Ed. D. Borali.

Jalan, Bimal, "Balance of Payments, 1956-91" in *Indian Economy—Problems and Prospects*, Ed. Bimal Jalan.

Kaur Narinder, *"India's Exports—Instability, Performance and Policy,"* Deep & Deep Publications, New Delhi, 1995.

Varma, M.L., *"International Trade,"* Vikas Publishing House (P) Ltd., New Delhi, 1995, p. 223.

Haragopal K. Sai, "Post Reform Trends" in International Capital Movements—In *International Institutions and Economic Development of Underdeveloped Countries* (ed.) M.R. Agarwal, Deep & Deep Publications Pvt. Ltd. New Delhi, January 2002.

Haragopal K. Sai, "Post-liberalization Trends in FDI inflows" presented at the National Seminar on Liberalization And Welfare Implications of Industrialization in India, held on 23rd Jan. 1999, at Hyderabad.

Haragopal K. Sai, "Impact of Trade Reforms on External Front" at the National Seminar on 'Economic Reforms in India: Retrospect and Prospect' held at the Department of Economics, O.U. Hyderabad on Feb. 15-18, 2001.

Haragopal K. Sai, "Performance of External Sector—A Review" in *The Indian Economic Journal*, Vol. 49, No. 3, January-March 2001-02.

Government of India, Various *Economic Surveys*.

Reserve Bank of India, Various *Annual Reports*.

Appendix

Table A1

External Variables in Rs. Crores—Current Prices

Pre-Reform Period

Year	*Exports*	*Imports*	*CAD*	*GFD*	*EA*	*GDP*
1980-81	6711	12549	2218	8887	2162	122427
1981-82	7806	13608	2818	8667	1865	142876
1982-83	8803	14293	2746	10766	2252	158851
1983-84	9771	15831	2694	13030	2266	186406
1984-85	11744	17134	3460	17416	2359	206722
1985-86	108953	19658	6459	21857	2936	23305
1986-87	12452	20096	5830	26342	3605	260584
1987-88	15674	22244	6293	27044	5052	294851
1988-89	20232	28235	11580	30923	5304	352706
1989-90	27658	35328	11388	35632	5804	408662
1990-91	32553	43198	17369	44632	6704	477814
1991-92	44041	47851	2237	36325	11615	552768

Post-Reform Period

Year	*Exports*	*Imports*	*CAD*	*GFD*	*EA*	*GDP*
1992-93	53688	63375	12764	40173	10982	630772
1993-94	69751	73101	3636	60257	11781	799077
1994-95	82674	89971	10583	57703	10880	943408
1995-96	106353	122678	19645	60243	11022	1103238
1996-97	118817	138920	16281	66733	11979	1285259
1997-98	126286	151553	20885	88937	11745	1426670
1998-99	139752	178332	16788	113349	13239	1612383
1999-00	162925	204583	17999	108898	14405	1786459

TABLE A2

Sector-wise inflow of FDI in Rs. Crores

Year	*1992-93*	*1993-94*	*1994-95*	*1995-96*	*1996-97*	*1997-98*
Electronics & Ele. Equip.	100.5	179.2	177.1	433.6	545.4	2395.6
Engineering	214.0	103.1	413.2	842.5	2592.2	2155.1
Services	7.3	63.3	293.2	336	53.9	1194.1
Chemical & Allied	144.1	117.5	443.3	423.8	1078.5	956.2
Finance	11.3	132.3	306.9	903.3	770.4	549.7
Computer	25.3	23.9	32.0	174.3	208.4	517.2
Food & Dairy	85.5	136.5	191.3	284.2	843.2	417.8
Domestic Appliance	40.5	7.4	340	1.6	53.5	222.8
Pharmaceuticals	9.6	155.3	31.7	183.2	169	125.6
Others	211.9	238.8	509.3	1160.5	997.5	2451.8
Total	858.2	1157.3	2738	4743	7312	10985.9

TABLE A3

Sectoral Distribution of Manufacturing Exports

Year	*1992-93*	*1993-94*	*1994-95*	*1995-96*	*1996-97*	*1997-98*
Engineering Goods	615	952	1294	2241	2782	2600
Engineering	6484	8456	9455	12062	14447	15596
Chemical & Allied	2232	2938	4020	4899	5733	16928
Computer Software	27	71	173	272	253	170
Drugs and Pharmaceuticals	1533	2010	2512	3409	4641	5228
Others	29649	37813	46537	56550	59816	63989
Total	40540	52240	63991	179433	87377	9451

16

The Impact of Globalization on India's Sea Food Exports

S. Perumalsamy and P. Krishna Thulasimani

Fisheries play an important role in India's economy augmenting food supply, generating employment, raising nutritional levels and earning foreign exchange. The marine fisheries sector of India has, over the years, grown to the level of a major industry, with a gross capital investment of around Rs. 3350 crores and gross annual income of about Rs. 8000 crores. The income through marine products export has grown to the level of Rs. 5096 crores during 1999-2000 accounting for 7 per cent of the country's net foreign exchange earnings. About 3 million people in the country are dependent on sea-fishing directly or indirectly and the demand for sea-fish is growing steadily year after year. At present, about 56 percent of the population in India eats fish and present per capita availability of fish in the country is 9.85 kg.

The annual world trade in fish is estimated at $ 55 billion. At present, the developing countries are the major exporters and the developed countries accounted for the major importers of fish.

At present just 6 developed countries accounted for about 60 percent of the world imports of fish.

After globalization, however, the growth rate in exports of developing countries has started failing due to non-tariff barriers of developed economies by setting quality parameters, eco-labeling, sanitary conditions, etc., with this background, an attempt has been made to analyse the impact of globalization on Indian marine products export.

OBJECTIVES

1. To study the impact of globalization on marine export of India.
2. To explore the relationship between marine exports and total marine production of India.

METHODOLOGY

This study is based on the secondary data, collected from "The Marine Products Export Review" published by Marine Products Export Development Authority (MPEDA), Cochin, India. The study covers the period of 20 years from 1981-82 to 1999-2000. In this analysis, the statistical tools like correlation and multiple regression methods have been employed.

RECENT TRENDS IN MARINE EXPORTS

Seafood exports from India is mainly to two types of countries: (i) developed countries like Japan, USA and the East European countries who buy for their own consumption, and (ii) developing countries like Taiwan, Thailand and Indonesia who process the raw material imported from India and then export these as value added products to the developed countries and making huge profits. Till the globalization, Indian seafood industries were mainly producing shrimp in block frozen form for export, which was re-processed in the importing countries. The importers were re-processing/repacking these products for sale to institutions and retail trading under their brand names. As a result of this, the Indian seafood products could not establish an image of their own in the importing countries.

After the globalization, the industry has been in the process of modernization and technology upgradation. Attempts are made to introduce advanced technology in the production of diversified value added products. As a result, the processing industry is presently changing from being primarily a frozen fish exporter to become a modern industry, that is more competitive in the market of protein base value-added products and convenience food. Value added fishery products are those products in which addition of ingredients adds value to the low priced and uneconomical varieties of fish to get good recognition as high quality products in the market. A number of value added products are being developed from shrimp, squid, cuttle fish and minced meat of low priced fish. .

The Indian seafood industry mainly depends for its raw material for export 'production on the traditional and non-traditional fishing sectors, which together contribute about 86 per cent of the total exports. The deep sea fishing sector contributes only about 7 per cent of the overall marine product exports and remaining 7 per cent is provided by traditional and scientific shrimp farming.

Today, the Government is keen on extending technical assistance for transfer of know-how in the modern production line. It organized training for seafood industry personnel in India and abroad to familiarize them with the advanced production technology. The Indo-EEC projection technical assistance to the Indian shellfish industry would contribute considerably in our efforts of modernization and upgradation of the Indian seafood processing industry.

In March 1991, the Government announced a new policy, which focused on three new schemes, namely, leasing of foreign fishing vessels for operation in Indian Exclusive Economic Zones (EEZ), test fishing was allowed by engaging foreign fishing vessels and promotion of joint ventures in Deep Sea Fishing (DSF), processing and marketing. The new DSF policy of the Government has generated considerable enthusiasm among both the domestic and foreign entrepreneurs. Under the liberalized policy relating to DSF sector, the percentage of foreign equity has been increased and clearances are expedited.

Government of India has introduced a 100 percent export-oriented units, it has to export the entire output except permitted quantities of non-exportable and rejects. The main features of the 100% EOU schemes are no custom and exercise duty is levied on capital goods, profit exempted from corporate income tax, liberal foreign equity is allowed, third party exports is permitted, purchases are exempted from central sales tax, etc. The marine products sector deserves very encouragement, as it is an important source of foreign exchange earnings with insignificant import content.

Though the value added products are moving today, the Indian exporters are not getting the price, brand image and recognition. When an exporter from a developing country gets into the process of value addition, the resistance builds up in importing countries, especially among the re-processors. They discourage the export of value added products through tariff and non-tariff barriers. The consumers in developed world go by established brand name, which is a very expensive affair for an exporter in the developing country.

In 1996, the US banned the imports of sea-caught shrimps from countries including India, which do not use turtle excluder devices in their crafts/boats/trawlers that prevent the endangered sea turtles from drowing and dying. In addition to that Hazard Analysis Critical Control Point (HACCP) which is a quality control measure formulated by the US Food and Drug Administration (USFDA) to ensure safety and quality in seafood being imported into the US. The regulation comes into effect by December 01, 1997, after which any seafood exporter to the US will have to set-up quality control measures based on the principles of HACCP in the processing unit. Japan's imports of shrimp delivered in the same year also due to lower demand and also because of high international prices and poor economic situations.

The EU ban on India was imposed on August 1, and lifted on December 23, 1997. The EU regulations require each industry to have its own portable water system, continuous power supply, and effluent treatment plant, flake ice machines, chill room and laboratory. Despite a ban imposed by the EU in 1997-98, India could maintain its exports at the same level as in the previous year because of increased demand from Japan, South East Asia and the US. However, after the lifting of EU ban, India's exporters to EU was not showing any improvement because only a fewer numbers of Indian exporters was eligible for exports.

Over the last few years significant changes in policy and quality criteria have been observed in the international seafood trade. The governments of major market countries have increasingly become aware of the necessity of protecting the health of their citizens.

RESULTS AND DISCUSSION

The Influence of Trade Openness and Total Marine Production on Marine Exports of India.

The Marine Exports of India is being influenced by many factors. It is also generally held that the Trade openness, Total Marine Production are also responsible for rising marine exports. So the researcher has analyzed the marine exports with the help of these two variables. This analysis is based on multiple regression model and fitted for the time series data for the period of 1981-82 to 2000. The sign of the co-efficient of the Trade Openness (B_1) is expected to be positive in its character. It is based on the reason that a unit increase in trade openness will exert a positive influence on marine exports of India.

Similarly, in theory, the sign of the coefficient of the variable total marine production (B_2) is to be a positive value. It shows that a unit increase in total marine production would tend to increase in marine export of India. The coefficient of multiple determination (R^2) of the model is 0.87 i.e., it explains nearly 87 per cent of the variations in marine exports of India are explained by the variables viz., Trade openness and total marine production. The estimated value of the parameter (B_1) reveals that one unit change in trade openness or globalization, the marine export increases by 0.309 units during the study period. This variable emerges statistically significant at 90 per cent. For one unit change in production the marine exports increased by 2.052 E-07 units. However this variable is not statistically significant. The constant term of the model is –1.694. As the calculated F value is greater than the table value, the whole model is significant at 5 per cent as well as one per cent level.

INFLUENCE OF TOTAL MARINE PRODUCTION OF MARINE EXPORTS

The estimated function shows good fit as the value of coefficient of determination (R^2) exceeds 80 per cent. In other words, keeping other variables affecting the marine exports as constant, the 80 per cent variation in marine exports is explained by the changes in total marine production. The estimated parameter (B) reveals that one unit change in total marine production, the marine exports increases by 1.244 E-06 units. This variable emerges statistically significant. Further, the computed value of F is greater than the table value at 1 per cent level. This meant that the marine export of India was considerably influenced by total marine production of India. In order to find out the presence of any auto-correlation the Durbin Watson Statistic was computed. Since the value of D.W. is nearer to 2, it can be inferred that the estimated model does not show the presence of auto-correlation.

As far as Indian marine products industry is concerned, the above results proved that, globalization and total production of marine product exerts a positive impact on marine exports and protectionism by developed countries has a relatively low impact.

CONCLUSION

As the Indian seafood industry as a whole is upgrading their production facilities to keep pace with the quality requirements of the importing markets especially USA and Europe, the importers confidence have changed to a certain extent recently. This would help the Indian seafood industry to go in for a larger production and marketing of value added products. On the other hand, the increasing cost of raw materials and labour would attract the Japanese importers into India for more value added products coupled with the growing demand for specific value added products from the catering and retail sectors. Thus the future of the seafood exports from India can be improved with more stress in value added products and their marketing strategy based on consumer-oriented processing and packing.

TABLE 1

Model 1	*Regression Constant* α	*Coefficient of Parameter* β_1	*Coefficient of Parameter* β_2	*Coefficient Determination* R^2	*Adjusted* R^2	*F Ratio*	*D.W. Test*
$Y=\alpha+\beta_1X_1+\beta_1X_1+U$	-1.694 (0.698)	0.309 (0.11)	2.052E-07 (0.001)	0.871	0.854	53.854	1.518
t		*2.778	*0.521				

Note: Figures in paraenthesis denotes standard error.
*Not significant at 5 percent as well as 1 per cent level.
Y = Marine Exports of India.
X_1 = Trade Openness.
X_2 = Total Marine Production of India.

TABLE 2

Model 2	*Regression Constant* α	*Coefficient of Parameter* β	*Coefficient Determination* R^2	*Adjusted* R^2	*F Ratio*
$Y=\alpha+\beta$	–0.355 (0.595)	1.244E-06 (0.01)	0.808	0.797	71.670
	**–0.596	**–8.466			

Note: Figures in parenthesis denotes standard error.
*Not significant at 5 per cent as well as 1 per cent level.
Y = Marine Exports of India.
β = Total Marine Production of India.

REFERENCES

Ceusep D. Attokaren, (1983), "Export Prospects for Indian Marine Products to East European Countries," *Foreign Trade Review*, April-June, Vol. XVIII, No. 1, pp. 35-41.

Krishanan, M. *et. al.*, (1999), "HACCP Guidelines and the Economics of Seafood Processing—An Impact Analysis," *Indian Journal of Agriculture Marketing*, 13(2), pp. 122-27.

The Hindu: "US gets 13 months to lift ban on Indian Shrimps," 16.2.99.
Industry News (1999), "Quality Processing Improves Seafood Exports," *Indian Food Industry*, July-Aug., Vol. 18(4), p. 208.

MPEDA: Statistics of Marine Products Export, 1999, Cochin.

17

Utilization of Labour in Maharashtra with Reference to Backward Areas

U.B. KONDEWAR

INTRODUCTION

Labour utilization is the most important factor of development not only in the state of Maharashtra but also in India. Government of India and Maharashtra have been taking efforts to create opportunities for the better utilization of labour force. Indian economy has witnessed a series of reforms since 1991.[1] The first economic reform took place during the period 1991-98, while second economic reform has been working since 1998. W.T.O. has started it's working since 1995. India is a member of W.T.O. India has relaxed quantity restrictions as per the agreement under W.T.O. All these factors have impact on labour utilization. Attempt is made to study the impact of above factors on labour utilization in the state of Maharashtra.

Impact of above factors is not identical in all the areas. Therefore, attempt is made to study the impact of all these factors in rural and urban areas and comparisons is also made between backward area and forward areas. Paper is divided into four parts. Part one deals with introduction and objectives. Methodology of the paper is explained in part two of the paper. Main theme of the paper is explained in part three. Part fourth of the paper is devoted for general conclusions and suggestions.

I. OBJECTIVES

1. Main aim of the paper is to measure the impact of reforms and W.T.O. agreements on labour utilization in the State of Maharashtra.
2. To compare the impact of reforms and W.T.O. agreements pertaining to labour utilization in rural and urban areas.
3. To compare the impact of reforms and W.T.O. agreements on labour utilization in forward and backward areas of the state of Maharashtra.
4. To suggest measures to raise the level of labour utilization and suggest policy measures to tackle the problem of unemployed youths.

II. METHODOLOGY OF THE PAPER

Comprehensive labour utilization data is not available in consolidated form at the district level. Government has taken surveys to collect data pertaining to utilization of labour. Second reliable source to collect information pertaining to utilization is, data collected by employment exchange on district level and same is consolidated and has been published on state level. It is difficult to paint accurate picture of labour utilization, however the trend of the labour utilization can be guessed in the shade of the available data.

The published data of employment exchange of offices has been presented in the form of index. The index method is the best method to compare and assess the impact of various factors on the labours utilization.[1] Year 1990 is taken as a base year in order to measure the impact of reforms and W.T.O. agreements on labour utilization, Marathwada is the highest backward region of state of Maharashtra[2]. Hence, it is selected for comparison of impact of reforms and W.T.O. agreements of labour utilization in backward area and rest of Maharashtra is considered as a forward area. Beed district is the highest backward district not only in Marathwada region but also in the state of Maharashtra and even in India[3].

III. MAIN THEME

The index of the labour utilization shows that the position of labour utilization during direct economic reform and during second economic reform period was not constant. There are several ups and downs. The labour utilization position is worse during first and second reform period compared to period earlier to reforms on all levels, i.e. on Beed district, Marathwada region and on Maharashtra state level. The labour utilization index during the period 1991 to 1996 has constantly increase but during later years it is decreased, baring few exception at Beed district level. The labour utilization position at Marathwada level is worse when compared with labour utilization position at Beed district level. The index pertaining to labour utilization in the Marathwada region shows ups and downs. The picture of labour utilization is disappointing. The picture of labour utilization on Maharashtra level during reform periods is not satisfactory, however, labour utilization position at Maharashtra state level is better than the labour utilization position at backward area. In short, comparatively the backward area is hitted worse compared to the forward area.[4]

Index of the candidates on the live register at the end of year shows the position of unemployment. The index of unemployed candidates shows the constant increase in unemployment on Beed district, Marathwada region and on Maharashtra level during reform periods. The position of unemployment is worse during economic reform periods compared to the period earlier to reform process. The position of unemployment in Beed district and in the Marathwada region is more serious than the position of unemployment in state of Maharashtra. The economic reforms proved unfavourable for backward area compared to forward area.[5]

The candidates who are in need of employment use to register their names in employment exchanges. The index of the candidates registration shows constant increase at Beed district, Marathwada region and Maharashtra level during economic reforms period. The index of the candidates registered their names shows higher increase at the Beed district and the Marathwada region level compared to registration of unemployed candidates at Maharashtra level.

This is sufficient to prove that the backward areas are hitted worse compared to the forward area.

Attempt is made to take review of labour force participation rate in the state of Maharashtra. The labour participation rate of rural male during 1983 in state of Maharashtra was 56.6, but it reduced to 54.2 during 1999-2000. In case of rural female, the rate of rural labour participation is reduced from 47.4 to 43.7 during period 1983 to 1999-2000. The labour participation rate of rural person is reduced from 52 to 49.

In short, rural labour participation rate is declined during economic periods. On the contrary, the rate of urban labour force participation has increased during the period 1983 to 1999-00.

The rate of urban female labour force participation during the decade (i.e. 1983 to 1993-94) has increased, but in later years the direction of labour participation rate is reversed. The rate of labour force participation of urban persons remain constant.

The urban female labour force participation rate is adversely affected at the end of first economic reform period and in the period of second economic reform period. It can be guessed that there is shifting of rural labour to urban areas.

Sector-wise labour participation position of rural and urban workers are also considered. It is observed that the percentage of rural persons as well as urban persons, considerably reduced in agricultural sector, during the period of 1983 to 1993-94 in state of Maharashtra.

The percentage of rural persons and urban persons engaged in manufacture sector has enhanced barring few exceptions, in the state of Maharashtra.

The percentage of rural and urban persons working in non-agricultural sector during 1983 to 1993-94 has enhanced in state of Maharashtra.

In short, the role of Manufacturing sector and non-agricultural sector compared to agricultural sector is more vital in regard to labour participation rate in the state of Maharashtra during reform period.

The percentage of self-employed rural persons and the percentage of rural regular persons have come down in state of Maharashtra during economic reform periods but the direction of trend pertaining to percentage of casual labour has gone up during reform periods. In short, the life of rural people is depended upon other's efforts or in other words their self-confidence is on declining stage.

The percentage of self-employed persons and regular salaried persons of urban areas are enhanced during a decade (i.e. 1983 to 1993-94) but direction of the trend changed in later years. The percentage of casual labour has declined in the decade of 1983 to 1993-94 but direction changed in opposite direction. It can be concluded that the effect of reforms was positive for a decade but position changed later on. This clearly means that, the reforms are not proved in favour of urban persons also.

Efforts are taken to study the labour utilization in vital sectors pertaining to rural and urban areas. It is quite clear that in rural areas the comparative growth rate of labour utilization has declined in almost all sector barring utilities sector, in regard to State of Maharashtra during the period 1983 to 1993 and 1993-94 to 1999-2000. The picture pertaining to labour utilization in various vital sectors of urban areas of state of Maharashtra is quite different. The rate of growth has gone up in trade, transport, storage, communication, community social and personal service, manufacturing and in construction sector pertaining to urban areas of state of Maharashtra. But direction of trend is in opposite direction in regard to agriculture, mining and quarrying utilities, finance, insurance and real estate and in non-agricultural sector during the period of first economic and second economic reform period. The comparative picture of labour utilization in regard to rural and urban areas of Maharashtra state is dismal during the period 1983, 1993-94, 1993-94—1999-2000.

In short, labour utilization position is deteriorated during the period 1983 to 1994 and 1993-94 to 2000, pertaining to rural and urban areas in the state of Maharashtra.

In short, the first and second economic reforms are proved unfavourable, in creation of employment opportunities.

IV. GENERAL CONCLUSIONS AND SUGGESTIONS

1. It is clear that the problem of unemployment turned bad to worse during economic reform periods. The reforms have proved more unfavourable backward areas compared to forward areas. It does not mean that the employment position in forward areas is satisfactory. More attention is required for creation of employment opportunities in the backward areas.

2. Accurate figures pertaining to the unemployment is not available in consolidated form at district level. It is necessary to know exact figure of unemployed person at any moment along with the nature of unemployed persons. It should be made compulsory for every employer that they should give employment to those who have obtain number from government agencies. The Sarpanch should be authorised to issue the number to the persons who are in need of job. Sarpanch has to maintain the record at village level. The farmers and others who are in need of man-power will note their demand in the register in own handwriting or by taking help of the any office bearer at village level. Sarpanch should send the detail information pertaining to job-seekers to Tahsildar at the end of every month.

This method is very useful to know exact number of unemployed persons along with the nature of the unemployed persons. District employment office has to collect data at the end of every month. Tahsildar along with village people a teacher has to formulate projects to provide job to needy persons. Adequate training should be given to village persons to satisfy the need of the villagers.

Employment officer, collector, member of legislative assembly and other district level dignities have to make plans to create job opportunities for the unemployed persons on district level. At city level Tahsildar has to maintain the record of job-seekers and job-suppliers.

State Government has to make programmes for those who cannot absorb village or district level. State Government has to make review of unemployed persons and make projects to create atmosphere to absorb the unemployed persons.

The projects should be formulated on the basis of needs of native foreigners. This policy will prove to provide jobs to needy persons. Persons should be punished if they violate the rule. The system should be implemented in such a manner that persons should not be harassed.

3. Modernization of agriculture is the need of the time. Agriculture department has to provide training camps for farmers and agricultural labour to suit them for modernization of agriculture sector. Farmers are advised and guided to take two more crops per year.

Water supply assurance is necessary for modernization of agricultural sector. State Government has to encourage farmers to adopt water saving; methods and link of rivers to avoid flood and famine situation. Central government has to provide financial and technical aids to the state governments. Master plan of linkage of Indian rivers is essential and only central government can prepare master plan. The role of private sector and foreign investors can not be neglected to enhance the speed of the project. India has manpower, Technical knowledge but central government has not accepted the plan of linkages of all Indian river. This is essential for modernization of agriculture sector. Agricultural production will prove helpful to instal agro-based industries. Infrastructure facilities at village level will prove useful to encourage small scale. Rural earning will increase demand for goods prepared in urban areas. This structure will solve the problem of unemployment.

4. Training centres should be provided at every revenue circle level. Those who have interest to run own business, will get training from such centres. The period of training is of duration of four years. The trainee will get minimum wages plus the 25% of the total profit earned by him in training period during the period of first year. The percentage of minimum wages should be reduced and share in profit should be enhanced. After four years of training the trainee has to start his own business, such person will not get any benefit from such centres. This method will create confidence among youths to start their own business.

5. There is scope to develop tourism centres.

6. Training to produce export goods and guidelines for marketing the goods will be useful to create additional employment creation. Constant market survey in native and foreign markets is essential.

7. Private agencies, foreign agencies and government agencies should be given free hand in development activities.

Manpower planning, efficient implementation of projects can

solve the problem of unemployment. The conclusions and suggestions are not only applicable to the state of Maharashtra but it is also applicable to India and other developing nations of the world.

Notes and References

1. Chadha, G.K., Sahu, P.P., "Post-Reform Setbacks in Rural Employment," *E.P.W.*, May 25, 2002.
2. *Commerce*, Vol. 151, No. 3892, Dec. 28th 2001, Vol. xxxvi, No. 21.
3. Kondewar, U.B., "*The Perspective of the Rural Health Programme of the Beed District*", Paper presented at Dr. Babasaheb Ambedkar Marathwada University, Nov. 1988.
4. Employment and self-employment in Maharashtra State, during 1991-92 to 2000-01.
5. G.O.I. *Sarvekshan* for 1990, 1997 and 2001. (through *E.P.W.*, May 25-31, 2002).

APPENDIX
TABLE A-1

The Table Shows Index of the Candidates Placed in an Employment during Years Shown Below

Sl. No.	Location/Yr.	1989	1990	1991	1992	1993	1994	1995	1996	1997	1998	1999	2000
1.	Beed Dist.	83.33	100	110.28	114.59	119.78	118.26	129.41	143.23	151.70	161.03	159.21	156.60
2.	Marathwada Region	86.46	100	119.69	110.49	116.65	120.35	131.74	146.19	154.91	162.10	163.94	165.86
3.	Maharashtra State	90.71	100	103.53	107.55	113.02	114.01	117.06	123.70	128.90	133.87	139.88	142.40

Source: *4—Index is prepared on the basis of the data published by Director Employment and Self-employment Directorate, Maharashtra State.

TABLE A-2

The Table Shows Index of Candidates on the Live Register at the End of Year

Sl. No.	*Location/Yr.*	*1989*	*1990*	*1991*	*1992*	*1993*	*1994*	*1995*	*1996*	*1997*	*1998*	*1999*	*2000*
1.	Beed Dist.	90.67	100	103.91	108.61	107.23	117.34	129.87	137.55	146.01	144.36	14.1.99	144.89
2.	Marathwada Region	94.94	100	104.90	110.75	114.27	125.08	138.01	147.08	153.90	156.90	157.49	160.46
3.	Maharashtra State .	96.58	100	103.87	109.16	110.11	112.93	119.47	124.50	129.30	135.10	137.54	140.04

Source: Ibid.

TABLE A-3

The Statement Shows Index of Candidates Registered their Names during Years Shown Below

Sl. No.	*Location/Yr.*	*1989*	*1990*	*1991*	*1992*	*1993*	*1994*	*1995*	*1996*	*1997*	*1998*	*1999*	*2000*
1.	Beed Dist.	94.08	100	76.42	88.08	93.39	105.70	110.48	124.34	112.54	112.48	132.92	145.42
2.	Marathwada Region	88.58	100	77.70	96.26	95.92	112.34	124.30	117.68	107.20	107.20	138.01	144.70
3.	Maharashtra State	96.05	100	92.06	92.81	93.29	98.91	112.02	107.13	107.78	113.46	113.46	137.33

Source: *Ibid*.

TABLE A-4

Labour Force and Participation Rate by Place of Residence and Person's in State of Mahrashtra during 1983/1999-2000

Year	*Labour Force Participation Rate*					
	Rural Male	*Rural Female*	*Rural Person*	*Urban Male*	*Urban Female*	*Urban Person*
1983	56.6	47.4	52.0	54.2	15.7	36.1
1993-94	55.8	47.8	51.8	54.9	17.7	37.3
1999-2000	54.2	43.7	49.0	56.3	14.6	36.7

Source: *5—GOI—*Survekshan* for 1990, 1997 and 2001 (Through *E.P.W.*, May 25-31, June 2002).

TABLE A-5

Sectoral Distribution of Usual Status Workers in Maharashtra State 1983/1999-2000

Year	Agriculture			Manufacturing			Non-Agriculture		
	Rural Person	*Urban Person*	*Total Person*	*Rural Person*	*Urban Person*	*Total Person*	*Rural Person*	*Urban Person*	*Total Person*
1983	85.8	12.6	66.2	5.0	31.7	12.1	14.2	87.4	33.8
1993-94	82.6	9.2	59.4	5.3	27.5	12.3	17.4	90.8	40.6
1999-2001	82.7	5.7	56.4	5.2	28.1	13.1	17.3	94.3	43.6

Source: *Ibid*.

TABLE A-6

Composition of Rural Usual Status Workers in Maharashtra N.S.S. Data 1983/1999-2000

Year	Rural Persons			Urban Persons			Non-Agriculture		
	Self-Empioyed	Regular Salaried	Causal Labour	Self-Employed	Regular Salaried	Causal Labour	Rural Person	Urban Person	Total Person
1983	517.39	87.02	40.50	31.14	49.02	17.52	46.52	19.21	34.20
1993-94	48.70	7.60	43.70	36.60	49.60	13.80	44.95	20.84	34.21
1999-2000	44.30	7.30	48.40	33.80	51.50	14.70	40.69	22.44	36.87

Source: Ibid.

TABLE A-7

Growth of Employment for Usual Status Workers in Maharashtra State by Rural-Urban Location and Motor Sectors (1983/1999-2000) for State of Mahrashtra

Location Sector	Agriculture Year		Mining and Quarrying		Utilities		Trade		Transport Storage and Communication		Finance Insurance Real estimate		Community Social and Personal Service		Manufac-turing		Construc-tion		Non-Agriculture		All Sector	
	83 93	93.94 99-00	83 93	93-94 99-00	83 93	93-94 99-00	83 93	93-94 99-00	83 93	93-94 99-00	83 93	93-94 99-00	83 93	93-94 99-00	83 93	93-94 99-00	83 93	93-94 99-00	83 93	93-94 99-00	83 93	93-94 99-00
Rural	1.26	0.41	6.86	-18.42	-0.57	5.24	4.48	0.46	5.33	9.93	10.27	-2.53	-2.04	3.61	2.27	-0.04	1.40	0.66	3.61	0.20	1.63	0.37
Urban	0.76	-.5.41	13.33	-3.76	3.54	-1.61	4.82	5.46	3.09	5.72	7.42	5.01	-2.33	4.10	12.34	2.82	6.05	8.33	4.10	3.08	3.73	2.43

Source: *Ibid*.

18

Globalization and Labour Utilization in India

KAPILDEO SINGH

I
INTRODUCTION

In the beginning of 1991, the country faced severe crisis of balance of payments and very higher rate of inflation. This forced the government to take some corrective steps to reduce fiscal deficit, tighten money supply and control increasing inflation. In view of these developments and compulsion in July 1991, the government reformulated its economic strategy, which is popularly known as the new economic policy. The new economic policy is grouped into three broad categories, i.e., liberalization, privatization and globalisation of Indian economies. Sustained close interrelation, combination and integration of trade and investment in the world economy at a higher stage of development is theorized as globalization. India decided to participate in the process of globalization. We have made weeping changes in our policies to reform our economy and reorient the policies to make them market friendly and outword looking India has now a decades experience of living under the 'Global Umbrella'. Hence, the objective of my paper is to analyse that what has been the situation about labour utilization in the period of globalization in India?

II
THEORETICAL ANALYSIS AND STRATEGIES OF GLOBALIZATION AND LABOUR MARKETS

Globalization means the global reach of capital to all the world's resources and markets. Globalization has become a magical word and is being projected as the road to paradise. Globalization is viewed as a two-way thing: (1) First, it envisages free competition, high productivity using state of the art technology and second, selling in one single marketplace of the whole world. Globalization of the economy meaning thereby to gradually abolish import control over all items including consumption goods. Globalization can be defined as the expansion of economic activities across political boundaries of nation states. It refers to a process of increasing economic integration and growing economic interdependence between countries in the world economy.[1] It is associated not only with an increasing cross-border movement of goods, services, capital, technology, information and people, but also with an organization of economic activities which straddles national boundaries. This process is driven by the lure of profit and the threat of competition in the market.[2]

When considering globalization related to labour utilization; it is essential to take a glance at the theoretical perspectives from which this issue has been viewed in the economic literature. The key element of the neo-classical framework hinged on a higher level of employment being dependent primarily upon free and unhindered operation of market forces in the labour market. Given this condition, it was envisaged that downward flexibility of the labour markets by making labour less costly, would induce employers to engage more labour and would generate higher levels of employment and output. The chief limitation of this mechanism was that, it overlooked the role of aggregate demand in the product market, without which a market economy cannot sustain higher levels of output and gainful absorption of available labour force. The Keynesian paradigm carved out macro-economic tools of analysis in terms of which employment was made a function of aggregate level of demand, which in turn was dependent upon the level of investment. In contrast to the above two paradigms, within the framework of the developmental paradigm, the key element holding back gainful absorption of available labour in the case of less developed economies is the limited stock of physical capital and the poor level of technology employed. Unless the stock of capital gets augmented and antiquated modes of inefficient technology get replaced by more productive techniques, the less developed countries will not go on the road to higher level of productive employment.[3]

The labour effects of economic reform and structural adjustment depend in the short-run on the stabilization effects of macro-economic policies and exchange rate policies.[4] Stabilization on involves a reduction in domestic final demand through restrictive monetary policies, budget deficit reduction and exchange rate policies the assumption is that, the labour market functions in such a way that it can absorb the decline in demand. According to neo-classical production theory, stabilization is expected to slow down increase in prices at the product market, which will lead to decline in production levels and decline in labour demand. The general assumption is that the price of labour (real product wage) will fall which will reduce production cost and maintaining levels of production at a lower product price level. It is often argued that if wages are flexible, the labour market is working well and therefore, rules and institutions which prohibit such wage flexibility in periods of stabilization and adjustment should be changed in order to increase flexibility. But this short-run supply side interpretation of the labour market shows some serious flaws. Despite uncertainties about the allocative function of the labour market policies to improve the allocative efficiency of the labour market dominate the reform process.[5] Yet in the long-run it is not the allocative efficiency of the labour market which will allow reform efforts to be translated into a renewal of growth but rather the dynamic efficiency of labour market policies. Policies under the aegis of structural adjustment are supposed to increase dynamic efficiency.

Distinguising between the short-term and long-term consequences of structural adjustment policies is especially important with respect to the role and the functioning of the labour market. If, in the opinion of policy-makers, the short-term allocative function of the labour market prevails, which is often the case, many labour market instruments are seen as not being macro-economically compatible.[6]

This leads, then, to recommendations abolishing minimum wage laws, contesting the practice of making wage settlements binding for the whole sectors, revoking dismissal laws, etc. and frequently viewing trade unions as a hindrance factor in achieving stabilization policies. Yet many of these labour market policies were not taken with a view to increasing the allocative function of the labour market but to increasing dynamic efficiency through building-up of social stability, through augmenting human capital by providing a minimum living wage, and achieving a certain amount of equity in the society. These contrasting views of the role and functioning of the labour market often give rise to contrasting policy recommendations between different parts in the government.[7]

III
IMPACT OF GLOBALIZATION OF LABOUR UTILIZATION

According to the world development Report, 1995[8] trade liberalization and global free competition could impart substantial benefits to working class in number of ways: first, free international trade and globalization enhance labour productivity and stimulate faster economic growth through sound investment in physical and human capital, including health and education. Secondly, increased integration between countries, including through migration can benefit workers in both poor as well as in rich countries provided of course the respective government to protect the interests of those workers who could be hurt by the process of change in trade patterns and capital flows in the form of retraining and provision of social safety nets. Third, the pressure of survival under intense international competition leads the respective governments to devise rational labour policies within the framework of cooperation with the workers/unions so that adequate safeguards against the exploitation of the poorest labour force at the informal sector are evolved. It is thus argued that workers are eventually benefited train globalization as states in general move from central planning to market-based systems and from protection to openness. But the negative effects are more than compensated by the positive ones, and those who are likely to be hurt because they are stuck in declining activities and lack the flexibility to change do not constitute a significant portion of the workforce exposed to the hazards of globalization in many developing countries. In the very poor developing countries globalisation may help by raising the demand for low skilled workers, whereas in the middle income and rich countries the negative effects of globalization induced employment shrinkage are expected to be more than counterbalanced by the effects of skill improvement which increases the demand for such labour services. World bank in its policy research bulletin has observed that the changes can be wrenching and it speaks of the more worsening condition of labour in free market-oriented reform in the words that it "can create opportunities for some workers but have wrenching effects on others," and that employment and wages very often decline as workers move from old to new jobs.[9]

The world Development report of 1995 entitled workers in an Integrating world documents, the fact that the world economy is integrating and the working conditions in the labour markets are changing everywhere in the world. These days most of the world's population lives in countries that are either integrated with world markets for goods and finance or rapidly becoming so. The participation of people in the labour markets varies from country to country. Their participation of people in the labour markets varies from country to country. Their participation in developing countries differs from that in developed countries. Most workers in developing countries work in the informal sector, and are found in agriculture or in small units in the service and manufacturing sector. In India, out of 286 million main workers only 27 millions or 9.4% work in the formal sector and 259 millions or 90.6% work in the informal sector. We can stratify workers in India into the following categories:[10]

(i) *Government Employees:* They work directly under the central government, state governments, local bodies and constitute about 4.5% of the total workforce.
(ii) *Public sector workers:* About 2.2% of all workers in the

public sector enterprises of the central and the state governments.

(iii) *Private sector workers in the formal sector:* They constitute about 2.7% of all workers, which includes workers in large and medium sized firms.

(iv) *Casual and contractor workers:* They work in the informal sector, but for the formal sector mentioned in (i), (ii) and (iii). There is no clear estimate about their number.

(v) *Workers in small and tiny units and establishments:* Contributing about 24% of all workers, they work both in manufacturing and service sectors and include self-employed workers.

(vi) *Agricultural workers:* They constitute a major proportion (66.7%) of the total workforce. Only a very few of these workers are in the formal sector—agricultural firms and plantation.

As a result of globalization, any worker lost their jobs due to closure of uneconomic units, shrinkage in public sector employment, and drastic reduction in expenditure in different activities of governments. Increased competition amongst the domestic industrial units and with units outside the country forced a restructuring of many units, which invariably involved labour restructuring with shrinkage in employment. All these factors contributed to the loss of jobs and increased unemployment in different forms, the structural adjustment programme had an adverse effect on workers. Infact, workers are the losers in the globalization process. The workers have been adversely affected by neo-liberal policies. Kapstein has rightly observed that globalization results in growing income inequality, job insecurity and unemployment.[11] Table 1 shows the picture of unemployment and other variables.

The Table 1 shows that total employment in the organised sector grew slower than output in each sub-period and the gap widened in the 1990s. Both public and private organised sector grew slower than output. While the public sector decelerated continuously, the private sector accelerated in the last two sub-periods. Organised sector employment grew slower than population. Work force (usual status principal and subsidiary workers taken together) and labour force which shows that either unorganised sector or unemployment, or probably both may have increased. Data from employment exchanges shows that unemployment is growing faster than total organised sector, labour force and workforce calculated with and without subsidiary workers. The growth of unemployment data slows wide fluctuations. The organised sector employment, workforce and labour force, all shrinked in 1993-94—1999-2000 to 0.7% and 1.3% respectively.

TABLE 1

Rates of Growth in Output, Organised Sector Employment, Labour Force, Workforce and Unemployment, 1977-78 to 1999-2000

Variable	*1977-78/ 1983*	*1983/ 1987-88*	*1987-88/ 1993-94*	*1993-94/ 1999-2000*
1	*2*	*3*	*4*	*5*
GDP as 1993-94 Prices	3.8	4.1	5.6	6.5
Organised Sector Empt. (Total)	2.0	1.1	1.0	0.7
Public Sector	2.6	1.5	1.0	0.1
Private Sector	0.6	0.1	1.2	2.2
Population	2.0	2.4	2.1	1.8
Workforce (P+S)	2.1	1.8	2.1	0.8
Labourforce (P+S)	2.0	2.0	2.2	1.9
Workforce (P)	2.6	2.0	2.3	1.3
Labourforce (P)	1.8	2.2	2.2	1.3
Unempt. in live (register)	10.3	6.1	3.3	1.9
Unempt. estimated from NSSO Data	11.8	9.1	2.7	1.2

Source: Vide Table 1 of L.K. Deshpande, *IJLE*: Vol. 44, No. 3, July-Sept. (2000).

In the age of globalization, the change in macro-economic policies are expected to make significant impact on the demand for labour. So, it is essential to sketch out in brief the contours of the changing winds which are blowing over the labour market.

The following Table 2 shows the Changing Mode of Employment between 1972-73 and 1997 in Rural and Urban area.

TABLE 2

Composition of Workers (Usual Staus) by Sex and R-U Residence: NSS Data 1972-73/1997: An India

Worker's Residence	*Worker Sex*	*Year*	*Mode of Employment*			*Index of Casualization*
			Self-Empld.	*Regular Employed*	*Casual Labour*	
1	*2*	*3*	*4*	*5*	*6*	*7*
Rural	Male	1972-73	65.9	12.1	22.0	182
		1977-78	62.8	10.6	26.6	251
		1983	60.5	10.3	29.2	283
		1987-88	58.6	10.0	31.4	314
		1993-94	57.9	8.3	33.8	407
		1997	59.5	7.3	33.2	455
Rural	Female	1972-73	64.5	4.1	31.4	766
		1977-78	62.1	2.8	35.1	1254
		1983	61.9	2.8	35.3	1261
		1987-88	60.8	3.7	35.5	959
		1993-94	58.5	2.8	38.7	1382
		1997	57.0	2.1	40.9	1948
Urban	Male	1972-73	39.2	50.7	10.1	20
		1977-78	40.4	46.4	13.2	28
		1983	40.9	43.7	15.4	35
		1987-88	41.7	43.7	14.6	33
		1993-94	41.7	42.1	16.2	38
		1997	40.7	41.5	18.5	45
Urban	Female	1972-73	48.4	27.9	23.7	85
		1977-78	49.5	24.9	25.6	103
		1983	45.8	25.8	28.4	110
		1987-88	47.1	27.5	25.4	92
		1993-94	45.8	28.6	26.0	91
		1997	39.7	313	29.0	93

Source: Vide Table 2 of G.K. Chadha, IEA Conf., Vol. 1999.

The above table shows that in rural India the incidence of self-employment has been consistently on relative decline, both for male and female workers. In urban India, it has been hovering around 40% between 1972-73 and 1997 for male workers. There is a decline of regular salaried jobs both for rural male and female and urban male workers. The incidence of employment under casual labour basis has increased for all the four categories of workers. The point of economic substance is that, casual wage employment is steadily rising at the cost of self-employment, in rural India, while in urban India, it is regular salaried jobs which are gradually yielding to casual wage labour. For rural areas, the switch over is a more worrisome matter since the declining incidence of self-employment may be throwing some people out of self-cultivation only to swell the ranks of the landless agricultural labourers. The recent years provide a disappointing employment scenario for the rural workers in general.[12]

Despite economic growth during globalization period, there is low labour absorption is the Indian economy. The declining trend in labour utilization particularly in the organised industrial sector of the economy is due to rise in the growth rate of population and labour force, use of more and more capital-intensive techniques of production and use of labour saving devices. The recession in the economy is also affecting adversely the labour utilization. The globalization of the industries is aggravating the worst situation on account of its bias against labour-intensive techniques. It is also inevitable to look for the labour utilization capacity of agricultural sector. Currently as high as 66% of the people depend on agricultural and it contribute 55% of the national income. At present even the agricultural sector is not utilising labour sufficiently due to use of labour saving capital-intensive techniques, lowering of agricultural output and lack of institutional reforms. During the globalization period rate of labour utilization is lower than the pre-globalization period and globalization did not contribute to utilise labour in significant way.

The basic problem with globalization is not to treat labour as an asset but as a mere instrument. A review of the post-globalization and impact on labour utilization reveals that workers are being pushed from the organised to the unorganised sector from secure to insecure employment. The following table shows the percentage distribution of total workforce in India.

The Table 3 shows that the proportion of casual labour in total employment has increased in the post-reform period. It may be pointed out that casual labour which stands to west in terms of average income as well as security has risen in proportion from 31.2% in 1988 to 37% in 1998. Growing casualization of labour adversely impacts on the income of the labour.[13]

TABLE 3

Percentage Distribution of Total Workforce

Years	*Self-Empld.*	*Wage Employed*	*Casual Labour*
1	*2*	*3*	*4*
1988	53.6	15.2	31.2
1994	51.9	14.7	33.5
1996	52.4	15.9	32.8
1997	52.6	14.5	32.9
1998	50.7	12.3	37.0

Source: Vide Table 8 of Ruddar Dutt and K.P.S. Sundharam, Indian Economy, 2001.

IV
NEED FOR CHANGE IN LABOUR POLICY

Labour policy essentially implies legislation or government action calculated to effect changes in the labour markets to attain specific objectives of social and economic policy. The changes in the economic policy have necessitated the change in the labour policy of India. In the debate, one side has called for an exit policy for labour and the removal of protection that restrict downsizing and labour adjustment, maintaining that, this is essential that if Indian firms have to be competitive in the global market. Others, on the other hand, favour protection of workers in the changing environment through social safety nets, poverty alleviation programmes and measures for reduction of inequality. The policy must, therefore, be acceptable to the parties concerned representing the different viewpoints and should be developed through political compromises and consensus between capital and labour. The government can intervene directly through enactment and enforcement of labour legislation achieve particular social goals and indirectly through the creation of independent institutions that can regulate different aspects of labour markets. Direct intervention involves enactment or amendments of labour laws, which generally takes a long time and the implementation can not be very flexible. By contrast indirect intervention through institutions of business and labour can be more flexible in adapting the changes.

In the current climate it is unlikely that any trade-linked international regime of labour standards would be successfully negotiated and implemented. It is recognised fact that there are limits to what can be achieved by insisting on trade-linked labour standards lesson that can be learned from past experience is to focus international efforts on process standards rather substantive standards. Process standards allow the parties to work out rules by mutual agreement as the need arises. It allows flexibility in developing solutions as conditions change. Substantive standards are much less flexible although they would need to be changed as the economic, technological and economic contexts for labour change. If multiple parties are involved changing the standards would be a cumbersome and difficult task. For many reasons it would be important to resist any attempt to develop and impose international substantive standards. Process standards would give every country greater control over their own labour standards, process standards would allow an indigenous, internal process within each country to develop, implement, monitor and enforce labour standards.[14]

Labour policy reform should be viewed as integral components of economic reforms in India. The basic objective of labour policy reforms should be to increase labour market flexibility. Labour market flexibility can minimise job losses in the short-run because speedy wage adjustment is possible and can facilitate industrial restructuring in the medium-term because, labour reallocation is relatively smooth. But in the India context, labour market flexibility cannot prevent economic contraction or job losses in the organised sector induced by stabilization measures. Careful management of the reform process and strengthening of safety net programmes therefore, assume great significance in the short-run. On the other hand, labour market flexibility can indeed facilitate structural adjustment in the medium-term.

Labour laws in India are fairly rigorous. In practice, however, there is significant dilution. One sees a major change in the attitude of politicians, bureaucracy and judiciary towards the claims of organised labour. There is need to reform labour laws to ensure that core minimum standards apply universally to all working people and checks and balances against abuse of power by any party are more precisely defined with time bound procedures for their disposal and accountability on the part of those vested with authority. The union structures and their recognition should be predictable to make it easy for employers to find which union they deal with. What is needed is a renewed focus on the labour policy that views developments as a sustainable process of expanding the capabilities of people and seeks to mobilise the human resource with the changing economic environment. The occupation and skills profiles of workers are also changing. This requires flexibility of the workforce to acquire new skill. The unorganised sector is the mainstay for a majority of the workforce and therefore, the role of skill development is crucial for enhancing productivity and income levels in this sector. Hence, the changing economic environment in the world; in the wake of globalization and the resultants fast pace of technological development also necessitates the formulation of an appropriate labour policy.

V
CONCLUDING OBSERVATIONS

Globalization means many things to many people. It is essentially about the movement of capital, products, technology and peoples. Globalization has its passionate protagonists and antagonists. Presently, regionalization is growing stronger than globalization. Debt, poverty, unemployment and inequality have been on the rise in most parts of the world and have thus become truly global. Social disintegration has become the price of economic globalization and the labour is made to bear the major brunt of globalization. Many of the workers are the losers from global Ration. In India, implementation of adjustment programmes has lead to deterioration of labour conditions and there has been decline in real wages for the unskilled workers.

Globalization programmes call for changes in the labour market in order to make it more effective. Guy Standing has rightly observed that the labour market can be regarded as a means of assisting in the allocative process of the means of production and as means of realising human development, through facilitating work as creative and social activity. What is encompassed by the labour market is not just the means of raising income in order to consume goods, services and to afford leisure.

In assessing a labour market, one should also be concerned with notions of social justice.

Thus, for India's successful march towards globalization, the government will have to pay serious attention to reformulate labour policy and the dynamic function of the labour market. Labour market policies, especially the dynamic, equity and social cohersion elements of such policies, are an important element of a permanent set of redistribute and growth policies.

Notes and References

1. Mody, Russi (1992), "Globalization Effort with Accent on Exports," *The Economic Times*, April 21.
2. Nayyar, Deepak (1995), "Globalization: The Past in Our Present," *IEJ*, 1995.
3. Mathur, Ashok (1999), *"Economic Reforms, Employment and Non-Employment," Theory, Evidence and Policy*, IEA Conf. Volume.
4. Hortons, R. Kanbur and D. Majumdar (1994), *"Labour Markets in an Era of Adjustment"*, World Bank, Washington.
5. Taylor, L. (1993), *"The Rocky Road to Reform"*, MIT Press, Cambridge.
6. Toye, J.C. (1995); *"Structural Adjustment and Employment Policy"*, ILO Geneva.
7. Van Per Hoeven, Rolph (2001), "Labour Markets and Economic Reform under the Washington Consensus": What Happened to Income Inequality? *IJLE*, Vol. 44, Nov. 3.
8. World Bank (1995), *"World Development Report,"* Oxford University Press.
9. *World Bank Policy Research Bulletin*, Washington, August-Oct. 1995.
10. Das, Subendu (2001), "Globalization and Workers in Developing Countries": Can Social Partnership Become a Model for Industrial Relations? *IJLE*, Vol. 44, No. 3.
11. Kapstein, E. (1996), "Workers and the World Economy," *Foreign Affairs*, Vol. 75, No. 3.
12. Dutt, Ruddar and Sundharam, K.P.M. (2001), "Indian Economy," S. Chand and Company, New Delhi.
13. Verma, Anil and Gunderson, Morley, (2001), "Labouring for Advantage: Worker Stakes in a Globalising Economy," *IJLE*, Vol. 44, No. 3.
14. Standing, Guy (1999); *"Global Labour Flexibility Seeking Distributive Justice"*, Mcmillan Press Ltd., London.

19

Globalization and Labour Utilization in Rural India: An Inter State Analysis

P.K. Pal

Economic Reforms in India has started on July 24, 1991 to correct the problems of macro-imbalances in the economy. Since then a period of 11 years has passed and the economy has witnessed changes in different economic fields. The purpose of this paper is to examine the changes in the field of rural labour in the context of globalization and decentralised development in India.

Economic Reforms was not designed for rural economy (i.e., primary sector) in India. The GDP growth rate of the primary sector has declined in the reform period, though the overall growth rate has risen. On the other hand, the overall economy has experienced lower employment growth rate and the employment growth rate in the primary sector has declined drastically to arrive at a state of retrogression: 1.13% in 1991 to –0.21% in 1997. Employment in both agriculture and mining has decreased (–0.25% and –0.16%). Agriculture being almost saturated, off-farm jobs are to be created in the rural and semi-urban region through creation of new production centers (food processing, ancilliary industry, repairing based on transport and construction works, etc). New agro-industry linkages are to be grown; otherwise the goal of more jobs in the long-run will be a cry (*Pal & Pal*, 2000).

In the decentralised development of the rural India, rural labour is utilised in alternative sectoral activities: (a) Primary sector (PS) consisting of cultivation and agricultural activities, livestock, forestry, fishing, mining and quarrying; (b) Secondary sector (SS) including manufacturing, servicing and repairing in both household and non-household industries and construction; (c) Tertiary sector (TS) consisting of transport, trade and commerce, storage and communications and services. The last two sectors jointly we call the Non-Farm Sector (NFS) while the former is the Farm Sector (FS). Therefore, total rural labour force is utilised in these two sectors. Inter-sector or inter-farm sector shifting of labour force is utilised in these two sectors. Inter-sector or inter-farm sector shifting of labour occurs with the development of the rural economy. More the non-farm activities, more the growth of SS and TS. And expectedly, more the rate of utilization of rural labour in the non-farm activities. It is, thus expected that with the development of the rural economy, the percentage share of the FS in total rural labour would decline, resulting in a rise in the percentage share of the NFS (SS & TS combined) during the reform periods.

In the context of the decentralised development of the Indian economy an attempt has been made to examine the utilization of rural labour across the states and the sectors. The changing scenario of inter-state rural labour (male-female differentials) is discussed in section I. Section II contains the mode of rural labour. Section III discusses the occupational distribution of rural labour. The determining factors (causes) of rural labour are discussed in section IV. Section V contains the concluding remarks. The NSS data for 1987-88, 1993-94 and 1999-2000; and census data for 1991 and 2001 are used in the analysis.

I. CHANGING SCENARIO OF RURAL LABOUR IN INDIA: AN INTER STATE ANALYSIS

With the structural transformation of the rural economy in

the context of decentralised development employment of rural labour is expected to decline over time. Employment of male and female has declined during the reform period 1993-99. But male employment has been more than female employment.

Indian states have exhibited wide variations in rural labour. It is expected that more and more a state is economically and educationally backward, more and more is the utilization of rural labour in the the state. The Worker-Population Ratio (WPR) for person defined as number of persons employed per 1000 persons was more in relatively backward rural Indian than in urban India in both 1993-94 and 1999-2000. Sex-wise analysis reveals (Table 1) that rural male WPR is more than rural female WPR in India and in all the constituent states during 1993-99. This is persumably due to the fact that, with decentralised development of the rural economy, various types of activities particularly non-farm activities are generated, which has resulted in an increasing demand for male labour during the globalization period.

Time Trend Analysis Reveals

(i) Rural male WPR has declined in India and in almost all the states expecting Assam, Gujarat, Haryana, Karnataka, Kerela and Tamil Nadu during the reform period 1993-99.

(ii) Rural female WPR has also declined in India and in almost all the states expecting Assam, Bihar, Gujarat, Karnataka, Kerala, Madhya Pradesh, Punjab and West Bengal during 1993-99.

Rural male WPR was lowest in Haryana in 1993-94 and in Uttar Pradesh in 1999-2000. Andhra Pradesh was ranked highest in both 1993-94 and 1999-2000. On the other hand, rural female WPR was lowest in Punjab in 1993-94 and in Haryana in 1999-2000. Thus, among the states only Andhra Pradesh has utilised more rural labour irrespective of sex in the globalization era.

It thus follows from the above discussion that WPR of rural labour had not been uniform in Indian States. It had been relatively low in some states while it had been relatively high in some other states. All these clearly indicate the existence of inter-state disparity in WPR of rural labour. Such inter-state disparity in WPR of rural labour is clearly revealed by the Disparity Index

(DI) of WPR as:

$$DI = 100 \left[\sum_{i=1}^{n} (e_i - \bar{e})^2/(n-1)\right]^{1/2} / \bar{e}$$

where e_i: WPR of rural labour in the state i, i = 1, . . . , n.

$\bar{e}$: WPR of rural labour in India as a whole, and

n : Number of states in India.

Estimates (Table 1) reveal that DI of WPR for rural female has risen over time while the reverse has happened in case of rural male. DI of female WPR has been relatively more than that of male WPR. This indicates that, inter-state disparity has widened more for rural female labour than for rural male one in the decentralised development of the economy.

II. RURAL LABOUR IN INDIA: MODE OF EMPLOYMENT

Rural labour is utilised in different types of activities. Activities are agricultural and non-agricultural. Labour is classifed as self-employed and wage (regular plus casual) labour. Mode of employment of rural labour has been expectedly changing over time in context of decentralised development of the economy. Estimates (Tables 2 and 3) reveal that the incidence of self-employment has been consistently declining in India and in almost all the states both for male and female labour over time. It has declined from 65.9% in 1972-73 to 59.5% in 1983 and 56.7% in 1993-94 and 54.4% m 1999-2000 in case of male labour. The respective figures are 65.5%, 51.3% and 50% in case of female labour. Regular-salaried employment has also been declining both for male (12.1% in 1972-73 to 9% in 1999-2000) and female (4.1% in 1972-73 to 3.9% in 1999-2000) labour. But the incidence of casual labour gives a noticeable picture. It has increased gradually from 22% in 1972-73 to 45.2% in 1993-94 and to 46.1% in 1999-2000 for female labour at the cost of self-employment in the context of the globalization of the rural India.

Indian states have exhibited wide variations in the utilization of rural labour during the globalization era. The incidence of self-employment for male has declined over time in almost all the states excepting Rajasthan while that for female has also declined in almost all the states excepting Assam, Gujarat, Punjab,

Rajasthan and West Bengal. It has varied from 39.2% in Kerala to 71.7% in Uttar Pradesh in 1993-94 and from 35.5% in Tamil Nadu to 73.1% in Rajasthan in 1999-2000. Kerala (34.6%) and Himachal Pradesh (95.6%) have ranked respectively lowest and highest in 1993-94 in respect of the rural female self-employment. In 1999-2000 the respective states are Assam (26.8%) and Himachal Pradesh (93.4%). On the other hand in most of the states the incidence of casual labour for both male nad female has increased at the cost of self-employment.

The incidence of casualization in measured by index of casualization which is defined as the number of casual wage labour for every one hundered of regular salaried wage labour. Estimates (Tables 2 and 3) reveal that, in rural India the index has gradually increased from 182 in 1972-73 to 455 in 1997 and then decline to 406 in 1999-2000 for male; and from 766 in 1972-73 to 1948 in 1997 then declined to 1182 in 1999-2000 for female. Irrespective of sex, the index has varied across the sates over time. The index is lowest in Himachal Pradesh (104 in 1993-94 and 121 in 1999-2000) and highest in Bihar (840 in 1993-94 and 1007 in 1999-2000) for male; lowest in Himachal Pradesh (76 in 1993-94 and 37 in 1999-2000). And highest in Bihar (3973 in 1993-94) and Orissa (3365 in 1999-2000) for female. So, Rural labour is casually employed more in Bihar and less in Himachal Pradesh during the reform periods. Also, sex-wise analysis reveals that the casualization of female labour is more than that of male ones in India and its constituent states of Andhra Pradesh, Bihar, Gujarat, Haryana, Karnataka, Madhya Pradesh, Maharashtra, Orissa, Rajasthan, Tamil Nadu and Uttar Pradesh during the period under study. That is female labour finds jobs of casual and/or contractual nature or on a daily basis more relative to ones at a low wage rate.

Several hypothesis are tested by several studies (*Minhas & Majumdar*, 1987, *Jayadevan*, 1996) in respect of the rate of casualization and other variables. In their study Minhas & Majumdar found that the higher the rate of unemployment, the higher the rate of casualization of labour. This means that if there is a larger surplus of labour, from the demand side, the employer can demand the service of labour at lower cost. Jayadevan also found that, there is a positive correlation between the magnitude of casualization and poverty level in the rural areas. This is due to the fact that the labourers from the supply side, instead of waiting for long to get a better job, accept and job at any wage rate and under any kind of work situations.

The incidence of casualization is not uniform across different levels of education in rural India. Estimates (Table 4) reveal that, the incidence of casualization is found to be quite high among illiterate women as compared to men. A larger proportion of illiterate women as compared to illiterate men is found to be casually employed both in the agricultural and non-agricultural sectors during the reform periods under study. 46% of the illiterate rural men and 79% of the illiterate rural women are employed in agriculture in 1999-2000. Such workers have limited prospects for entering into off-farm jobs. On the other hand, at the secondary and above level of education the proportion of educated workers in agriculture is low: 12% for men and 2% for women. Therefore, we see that utilization labour (men/women) in non-agricultural activities has been increasing with the increasing level of education (6.7% in 1993-94 to 26.7% in 1999-2000 for and 2.2% in 1993-94 to 13% in 1999-2000 for women) during the globalization era.

III. RURAL LABOUR IN INDIA BY SECTORS

Apart from variations in mode of employment, variations in the activity status (occupation) of rural labour are also observed. Rural labour is utilised in alternative sectoral activities like primary sector known as farm sector (FS) and secondary and tertiary sectors jointly known as non-farm sector (NFS). The farm and non-farm sectors are to a great extent interdependent. Modernization of the farm sector (in the post-Green Revolution period) has brought about a series of changes in the rural economy. Villages are linked with the cities and towns through a wide net of transports, markets are develop and expanded, farm outputs are transported, agricultural machinery and reparing shops are opened small electrical units are set-up etc. All these necessitate increasing utilization of rural labour in non-farm activities in the contest of decentralised development of the rural India.

Estimates (Table 5) reveal that employment in NFS has increased all through in rural India at the cost of farm employment both for male and female during the period under study. For male it has increased from 24.8% in 1987-88 to 25.2% in 1993-94 and to 28.1% in 1999-2000, while for female it has decreased from 14.9% in 1987-88 to 13.6% in 1993-94 and increased to 15.6% in 1999-2000. However, male non-farm employment is more than female ones in the rural economy of India.

Inter-state analysis reveals that, Indian states have exhibited wide variations in rural non-farm employment. Extimates (Tables 6 and 7) that employment in NFS for male has increased overtime in almost all the states excepting West Bengal—while, that for female has increased in almost all the states excepting Andhra Pradesh, Gujarat, Karnataka, Maharashtra and West Bengal at the cost of farm employment. Thus, among the states, only in West Bengal utilization of labour (both male and female) has decreased in the non-farm activities in the rural area. Across the states, the non-farm employment has varied. It has varied from 13.4% and 15.4% in Madhya Pradesh to 45.7% and 56.6% in Kerala in 1993-94 and 1999-2000 respectively for male, from 4.8% in Orissa to 54.7% in West Bengal in 1993-94 and from 5.8% in Maharastra to 53.7% in Kerala. Thus, Kerela has ranked highest in respect of the utilization of rural male and female labour as the non-farm activities during the globalization era.

Sex-wise analysis reveals that, rural female employment in the NFS in more than male once in the states of Punjab and West Bengal during the period of 1993-99. This is persumably due to the fact that during the globalization era various types of activities mostly non-farm activities have been generated in favour of rural female so that they can utilise more relative to male at a low wage rate.

As to the structure of labour utilization we note the following:

(a) Among the 3 (three) constituent sectors, the share of PS has all through been the highest both for male and female in India and its constituent states (Tables 7 and 8). At the national level, its share has decreased marginally from 74.4% in 1993-94 to 71.8% in 1999-2000 for male; from 85.2% in 1993-94 to 84.5% in 1999-2000 for female. The share has also decreased in almost all the states excepting West Bengal for male; excepting Andhra Pradesh, Gujarat, Karnataka, Maharashtra and

West Bengal for female during the period of 1993-99. Also we note that, the female employment is more than the male ones in India and its almost all the constituent states excepting Kerala, Punjab and West Bengal in this sector.

(b) TS has the second largest share in India and its almost all the constituent states both for male and female followed by SS. At the national level, its share has risen from 14.7% in 1993-94 to 16.2% in 1999-2000 for male; from 6.2% in 1993-94 to 6.6% in 1999-2000 for female. The share has also risen in almost all the states excepting Haryana, Karnataka, Tamil Nadu and West Bengal for male; excepting Karnataka, Maharashtra, Orissa and West Bengal for female. Interesting we note that among the states we considered Punjab is the only state where TS has utilised more rural female labour than male ones due to the expansion of the service sector activities for female during the globalization period.

(c) Employment in SS has also risen in India and its almost all the constituent states. Its share has risen from 10.6% in 1993-94 to 12% in 1999-2000 at the national level for male. The respective figures for female are 8.6% and 8.9%. Sex-wise analysis reveals that SS has absorbed more rural female labour than male ones (i) in 1993-94 in the states of Assam, Karnataka, Kerala, Maharashtra and West Bengal, and (ii) in 1999-2000 in the states of Andhra Pradesh, Bihar, Haryana, Karnataka, Kerala, Madhya Pradesh, Orissa, Punjab, Rajasthan, Tamil Nadu, Uttar Pradesh and West Bengal. Thus the job opportunities for rural female relative to rural male have been expanded in these states due to rural industrialization during the globalization period.

Measure of Diversification

We have so far discussed the sectoral (occupational) distribution of rural employment for both sex. The occupational distribution has changed during the period. Employment has risen in some occupations (sectors) while it has declined in some others. We shall now measure the extent of variations in the occupational distribution of employment. For this, we have estimated the occupational diversification index (DI) based on Theil (1967) entropy measure defined as:

$$DI = E/\log n$$

where

$$E = \sum_{i=1}^{n} e\,(\log(1/e_i))$$

e_i : share of the i-th occupation in the total, and
n : number of occupations.

Here, (a) DI = 0 for E = 0. It means that a particular occupation captures all workers: employment is not diversified occupationally. (b) DI = 1, when E = log n, maximum value. This happens when all workers are employed equally by different occupations: employment is completely diversified occupationally. So $0 \leq DI \leq 1$. The higher (lower) the value of DI, the higher (lower) the degree of diversification of rural employment occupationally.

Estimates (Tables 5 and 6) reveal that in rural India DI for male has increased from 0.330 in 1972-73 to 0.476 in 1987-88 and 0.518 in 1999-00. The rising trend is also observed in case of female: 0.260, 0.329 and 0.333. DI for male exceeds that for female. Thus the occupational distribution of rural employment for male has been more and more diversified than that for female.

Across the states, we also observe (Tables 7 and 8) that DI for male has increased in all the states in India excepting Haryana, Madhya Pradesh and Uttra Pradesh during 1993-99.

The rising tendency is also observed in case of female excepting Gujarat, Karnataka, Maharashtra and West Bengal. DI for male is lowest in Madhya Pradesh (0.279 and 0.263) and highest in Kerala (0.709 and 0.782) during 1993-99. Also, DI for female is lowest in Himachal Pradesh (0.157 in 1993-94) and Maharashtra (0.172 in 1999-00) and highest in Kerala (0.609 and 0.685) during the period under study. Thus, among the states Kerala has occupied more and more occupational diversification in both rural male and female employment. But the diversification for male is more than that for female. This is also true in all the states excepting Punjab and West Bengal during the period under study.

IV. DETERMINING FACTORS

Decentralised development of the rural economy is brought about by many factors. Rural labour plays an important role in such development, no doubt. The fact that the non-farm sector has been increasingly absorbing rural labour has stimulated considerable interest among the researchers to identify the underlying factors (*Krishnamurty*, 1984; *Vaidyanathan*, 1984, 1986; 1994; *Papola*, 1987; *Sankarnarayan*, 1980; *Visaria and Basant*, 1994; *Parthasarathy et al*, 1998; *Unni*, 1997, etc.) Several explanatory hypotheses have been forwarded and tested in the context of Indian rural NF sector. The hypotheses of agricultural prosperity, increasing degree of commercialization, input-output linkages and distress diversification (the residual sector) have been widely discussed. But no hypothesis has turned out to be adequate to explain the full growth of the non-farm activities.

Researchers are curious to know whether utilization of rural labour in the NF sector is a distress diversification or a normal phenomenon of development. Is it due to the fact that the FS is surplus in labour? Is it due to the fact that the FS is not optimally operated? Or its operational holdings are not fully utilised? All these concerns us much.

Labour may flow to the NFS from the FS as a result of distress diversification. Over time, the number of marginal holdings rises, resulting in declines in the average size. Landless marginal labour grows and ultimately shifts to the NFS for absorption at a relatively lower wage rate. This is distress diversion. The average size of marginal holdings is then indirectly related to the NFS employment. Or it may so happen that the average size of large holdings rises resulting in more concentration of holdings in large holders who are now in a position to earn more agricultural surplus, which they subsequently invest in the NFS. Employment in the NFS rises. It is not distress diversion. It is natural absorption, an effect of development. Therefore, absorption of rural labour in the NFS is neither solely due to distress diversion nor solely due to natural absorption. It is stimulated by serveral factors like literacy rate, inter-sector as well as rural-urban linkages, urbanization, poverty level and above all prosperity of the FS.

We have statistically examined the role of the following determining factors in explaining inter-state variations of rural non-farm employment in India for the years of 1993-94 and 1999-2000. We have considered 11 (eleven) factors: population growth, rural literacy rate, sex ratio and urbanization for the years of 1991 and 2001; rural poverty level for the years of 1993-94 and 1999-2000; cropping intensity for the years of 1995-96 and 1996-97; degree of commercialization (non-food grains area as a percentage of total gross cropped area) for the years of 1996-97; index of agricultural propsperity (food-grains output per hec.) for the years of 1995-96 and 1999-2000; average land size cultivated by agricultural labourer for the year of 1993-94; average daily real agricultural wages (Rs./day) for the year of 1993-94 and Human Development Indiex (HDI) for the year of 1993. We have taken 16 large states in India: Andhra Pradesh, Assam, Bihar, Gujarat, Haryana, Himachal Pradesh, Karnataka, Kerala, Madhya Pradesh, Maharashtra, Orissa, Punjab, Rajasthan, Tamil Nadu, Uttar Pradesh and West Bengal.

States are ranked accordingly to those variables and rank correlation coefficient (r) between non-farm employment and each of those variables are estimated separately for male and female employment for the years of 1993-94 and 1999-2000. The coefficients are, in turn, statistically tested. The testing procedure is as follows:

Let, r and $\hat{r}$ be the population and sample rank correlation coefficient respectively. Then for r = 0, the sampling distribution of r may be approximated by Normal Distribution (*Koutsoyiannis*, 1979: *Pal*, 1994):

$$r \sim N\,[0,\ 1/(n-1)^{1/2}]$$

The testing hypotheses are

$$H_0 : r = 0$$
$$H_a : r \neq 0$$

The test statistic is here:

$$Z = \hat{r}\ (n-1)^{1/2}$$

The estimated Z is then computed with the tabulated value of Z at the chosen level of significance. For example, at 10% level of significance, Z = ± 1.645. Then the null hypothesis H_0 is rejected if Z > 1.645; i.e., the hypothesis of the presence of rank correlation is accepted. Otherwise, H_0 is accepted.

Estimates of rank correleation coefficient are presented in Table 9. Estimates reveal that among the variables, cropping intensity, degree of commercialization, index of agricultural prosperity, average land size cultivated by agricultural labourer, average daily real agricultural wages, rural literacy rate, urbanization, rural poverty, Human Development Index have turned out to be significant. But all these variables are not uniformly significant over time and across sex in India. Thus these variables are instrumental for the utilization of rural labour in non-farm activities skillfully and hence the decentralised development of the rural economy of India.

In our multiple regression analysis, we have considered the following hypotheses: Non-farm employment is directly related to: (i) the cropping intesity (CI), (ii) the degree of commercialization (COM), (iii) the index of agricultural prosperity (AP), (iv) average daily real agricultural wages (RAG), (v) rural literacy rate (LR), (vi) sex ratio (SR), (vii) urbanization (UR), (viii) rural poverty level (RP), and (ix) the population growth (PG). On the other hand, non-farm employment is indirectly related to the average land size cultivated by labourer (ALA).

Based on the above hypotheses, we have estimated the multiple regression in India using state-wise data for the two years of 1993-94 and 1999-2000 in the globalization period separately for rural male and female non-farm employment (MNFE & ENFE). The estimated multiple regression equations are the following:

1993-94

$$\underset{}{MNFE} = \underset{(-2.231)}{-265.567^*} \underset{(-0.881)}{-0.138\,CI} + \underset{(2.543)}{0.438^*\,COM} + \underset{(2.088)}{1.371\,AP} \underset{(-0.604)}{-8.511\,ALA} + \underset{(1.165)}{1.217\,RAG}$$

$$+ \underset{(2.662)}{0.742^*\,LR} + \underset{(2.037)}{0.108^*\,SR} \underset{(-1.309)}{-0.389\,UR} + \underset{(1.445)}{0.342\,RP} + \underset{(2.243)}{23.051^*\,PG}$$

$R^2 = 0.91$, Adjusted, $R^2 = 0.73$

$$FNFE = \underset{(-2.830)}{-599.869} + \underset{(0.772)}{0.229\,CI} + \underset{(1.257)}{0.482\,COM} + \underset{(0.436)}{0.589\,AP} \underset{(-2.399)}{-76.368^*\,ALA} + \underset{(1.697)}{5.792\,RAG}$$

$$-0.199\,LR + 0.433^*\,SR + 1.367^*\,UR + 0.943\,RP + 38.556^*\,PG$$
$$(-0.395) \quad (2.602) \quad (2.070) \quad (1.970) \quad (2.134)$$

$R^2 = 0.89$, Adjusted $R^2 = 0.68$

1999-2000:

$$MNFE = -197.329 - 0.368\,CI - 0.291\,COM + 2.064\,AP + 4.755\,ALR - 0.599\,RAG$$
$$(-1.301) \quad (-0.932) \quad (-1.062) \quad (1.607) \quad (0.179) \quad (-0.301)$$
$$+1.817\,LR + 0.126\,SR - 0.859\,UR - 0.417\,RP + 13.296\,PG$$
$$(2.581) \quad (1.008) \quad (-1.793) \quad (-1.453) \quad (1.540)$$

$R^2 = 0.88$, Adjusted $R^2 = 0.63$.

$$FNFE = 404.000^* + 0.858^*CI + 0.238^*\,COM - 0.457\,AP - 29.826^*\,ALA + 2.054\,^*RAG$$
$$(-8.187) \quad (3.730) \quad (2.288) \quad (-0.601) \quad (-2.081) \quad (2.167)$$
$$-0.235LR + 0.303^*\,SR + 0.691^*\,UR + 0.163\,RP + 5.798^*\,PG$$
$$(-0.786) \quad (7.214) \quad (2.383) \quad (1.314) \quad (1.866)$$

$R^2 = 0.99$, Adjusted $R^2 = 0.97$.

Note: Significant at 10% level of significance.
Fig. in () indicates t-values.

From the above two equations we observe that the explanatory variables are highly significant for explaining the rural non-farm employment in the decentralised development of the rural india. Estimates reveal that:

(i) The coefficient of cropping intensity is negative for male and positive for female non-farm employment in both 1993-94 and 1999-2000. But it is highly significant only for female in 1999-2000.

(ii) The coefficient of the degree commercialization is positive and significant for male in 1993-94 and female non-farm employment in 1999-2000.

(iii) The coefficient of the index of agricultural prosperity is positive for male in 1993-94 and 1999-2000 and female non-farm employment in 1993-94. But it is significant only for male in 1993-94.

(iv) The coefficient of the average land size cultivated by labourer is negative excepting male non-farm employment in 1999-2000. It is statistically significant for female in both 1993-94 and 1999-2000.

(v) The coefficient of average daily real agricultural wages is positive expecting for female non-farm employment in 1999-2000. It is statistically significant only for male non-farm employment in 1999-2000.

(vi) The coefficient of rural literacy rate is positive and statistically significant for male in both 1993-94 and 1999-2000. But it is negative and not statistically significant for female in both the years.

(vii) The coefficient of sex ratio is positive and statistically significant for male and female non-farm employment.

(viii) The coefficient of urbanization is positive and statistically significant for female non-farm employment in both 1993-94 and 1999-2000. The reverse has happened in case of male employment during the period under study.

(ix) The coefficient of rural poverty level is positive but not statistically significant excepting male non-farm employment in 1999-2000. The positive relationship may be due to better infrastructural facilities in the decentralized development of the rural economy.

(x) The coefficient of population growth is positive in both the years 1993-94 and 1999-2000 and statistically significant for male and female non-farm employment only in 1993-94.

Thus, among the explanatory variables considered cropping intensity, the degree of commercialization, the index of agricultural prosperity, average land size cultivated by agricultural labourer, average daily real agricultural wages, rural literacy rate, sex ratio, urbanization and population growth have turned out to significant. But all these variables are not uniformly significant over time and across sex in India. These variables are instrumental for the utilization of rural labour in non-farm activities skillfully and hence the decentralised development of the rural economy of India in the globalization era.

V. CONCLUDING REMARKS

In the context of the decentralised development of rural India, employment of male and female has declined during the globalization period, 1993/94 to 1999/2000. But male employment has been more than female employment in India and in all the constituent states. This is presumably due to the fact that with the decentralised development of the rural India various types of activities particularly non-farm activities are generated which has resulted in an increasing demand for male labour relative to female labour. Also, inter-state disparity arises in respect of the utilization of rural male and female labour.

But it has widened more for rural female labour than for rural male ones.

The mode of rural employment has been changing over time in India. The incidence of self-employment has been continuously declining in India and in almost all the states both for male and female labour over time. This is also in respect of the regular salaried employment. But irrespective of sex and incidence of casual labour has increased in India and in most of the states over time at the cost of self-employment. Irrespective of sex, the index of casualization has varied in India and across the states over time. It is lowest in Himachal Pradesh and highest in Bihar for male; lowest in Himachal Pradesh and highest in Orissa for female. Also, sex-wise analysis reveals that the casualization of female labour is more than that of male ones in India and its almost all the states during the globalization period. Thus female labour finds jobs of casual and/or contractual nature of on a daily basis more relative to male ones at a low wage rate.

The incidence of casualization is related to the level of education in rural India. Estimates reveal that it is found to be quite high among illiterate women as compared to men. A larger proportion of illiterate women as compared to illiterate men is found to be casually employed both in the agricultural and non-agricultural sectors during the period under study.

Apart from variations in the mode of employment, variations in the activity status (occupation) of rural labour are also observed in India in its constituent states. Employment in non-farm sector for male has increased over time in India and in almost all the states excepting West Bengal while for female has also increased in almost all the states excepting Andhra Pradesh, Gujarat, Karnataka, Maharashtra and West Bengal at the cost of farm employment. Thus among the states, only in West Bengal utilization of rural labour (both male and female) has decreased in the non-farm activities but female employment in the NFS is more than male ones during the globalization era.

Employment in secondary and tertiary sector has risen in India and in almost all the constituent states at the cost of primary sector, though its share has all through been the highest irrespective of sex. Also we note that the job opportunities for rural female relative to rural male have been expanded in most of the states due to rural industrialization during the globalization period.

In rural India the occupational distribution of rural employment for male has been more and more diversified than that for female. Among the states we also observe that Kerala has occupied more and more occupational diversification in both rural male and female employment. But the diversification for male is more that for female. This is also true in all the states excepting Punjab and West Bengal during the globalization period.

The growth of rural non-farm employment in the context of the decentralised development of the rural India has been determined by serveral factors. Among the factors cropping intensity, the degree of commercialization, the index of agricultural prosperity, average land size cultivated by agricultural labourer, average daily real agricultural wages, rural literacy rate, sex ratio, urbanization, and population growth have turned out to be significant. But all these factors are not uniformly significant over time and across sex in India. Thus these factors are instrumental for the utilization of rural labour in non-farm activities skillfully and hence, the decentralized development of the rural economy of India during the globalization era.

References

Jayadevan, C.M., (1996), "Capitalization of Workforce in India: An Analysis of Special Variation," *The Indian Journal of Labour Economics*, Vol. 39, No. 4.

Krishnamurty, J., (1984), "Changes in the Indian Workforce," *EPW*, Vol. 19, No. 50, December.

Koutsoyiannis, A. (1979), *Theory of Econometrics*, 2nd Edition.

Mondal, S., (1990), "*Dynamics of Transformation of the Rural Economy: India, 1961-81*," Ph.D. Thesis (unpublished), University of Kalyani, India.

Minhas, B.S. and Majumdar, G., (1987), "Unemployment and Casual Labour in India: An Analysis of Recent NSS Data", *Indian Journal of Industrial Relations*, Vol. 22, No. 3.

Pal, D.P. and Mondal, S.K. (1993), "Rural Assets in India: Composition and Diversification", 1971-81, *Artha Beekshan*, Vol. 2, No. 1.

Pal, P.K. (1994), "Women and Rural Economic Transformation: A Study in West Bengal", 14th Annual Conference, Bengal Economic Association.

Pal, D.P. and Pal, P.K., (2000), "Structural Reforms, Development and Employment Projection in India" in P.D. Hajela & M.P. Goswami (eds.): *Economic Reform and Employment*, Deep & Deep Publications Pvt. Ltd., New Delhi.

Pal, R., (1994), "Farming Cooperatives in India: Progress, Problems and Prospects", Ph.D. Thesis (Unpublished), University of Kalyani, India.

Parthasarathy, G. and *et al*, (1998), "Determinants of Rural Non-Agricultural Employment: The India Case," *IJAE*, Vol. 53, No. 2.

Papola, T.S., (1987), "Rural Industrialization and Agricultural Growth: A Case Study of India", in R. Islam (ed): *"Rural Industrialization and Employment in Asia"*, Asian Regional Team for Employment Promotion, I.L.O., New Delhi.

Sankarnarayan, V. (1980), *"Inter-State Variation in Rural Non-agricultural Employment—Some Tentative Results"*, Centre for Development Studies, Working Paper No. 104, Trivandrum.

Theil, H., (1967), *Economics and Information Theory*, North-Holand Pub. Co.

Unni, J., (1994), "Inter-Regional Variations in Non-Agricultural Employment" in Visaria & Basant (Eds.), *op. cit.*

Unni, J., (1997), "Employment and Wages among Rural Labourers: Some Recent Trends," *IJAE*, Vol. 52, No. 1.

Vaidyanathan, A. (1986), "Labour Use in Rural India: A Study of Spatial and Temporal Variations", *EPW*, Vol. 21, No. 52, Dec. 27.

Vaidyanathan, A., (1994), "Employment Situation: Some Emerging Perspective", *EPW*, Vol. 29, No. 50, Dec. 10.

Visaria, P., (1995), "Rural Non-Farm Employment in India: Trends and Issues for Research", *IJAE*, Vol. I, No. 3, (Conference Number).

Visaria, P. and Basant, R. (Eds.), (1994), *"Non-Agricultural Employment in India: Trends and Prospects,"* Sage Publications India Pvt. Ltd., New Delhi.

Govt. of India (1990), *Sarvekshana*, Special No. NSSO.

Govt. of India (1996), *Key Results on Employment and Unemployment*, NSSO.

Govt. of India (1997), *Employment and Unemployment in India*, 1993-94, NSSO.

Govt. of India, (2000), *Employment and Unemployment Situation in India*, 1999-2000, NSSO.

Economic Review, Govt. of West Bengal, various issues.

Census of India, Govt. of India.

Appendix

Table A-1

Sex-wise Rural Employment (WPR) in Indian States per 1000 Persons

S.No.	District	1993-94		1999-2000	
		Male	*Female*	*Male*	*Female*
1.	Madhya Pradesh	621	462	589	443
2.	Assam	493	86	506	87
3.	Bihar	502	131	486	132
4.	Gujarat	565	254	577	311
5.	Haryana	446	56	470	33
6.	Himachal Pradesh	510	363	504	281
7.	Karnataka	585	326	593	354
8.	Kerala	515	152	526	159
9.	M.P.	559	301	531	331
10.	Maharashtra	537	404	523	393
11.	Orissa	553	210	540	203
12.	Punjab	542	37	526	40
13.	Rajasthan	527	299	496	272
14.	Tamil Nadu	588	405	589	401
15.	Uttar Pradesh	506	131	469	122
16.	West Bengal	538	84	524	116
17.	India	538	238	522	231
18.	DI (%)	7.93	58.21	7.91	58.66

Notes: DI: Disparity Index, WPR: Worker-Population Ratio
Source: NSSO, Govt. of India.

TABLE A-2

Percentage Distribution of Rural Employment in India by Activity Status and by Sex

Year	*Sex*	*Activity Status*				*Index of Casualization (IC) = (C.L./R.E.) × 100*
		S.E.	*R.E.*	*C.L.*	*Total*	
1972-73	Male	65.9	12.1	20.0	100	182
1977-78	"	62.8	10.6	26.6	100	251
1983	"	59.5	10.6	29.9	100	282
1987-88	"	57.5	10.4	32.1	100	309
1993-94	"	56.7	8.7	34.6	100	398
1997	"	59.5	7.3	33.2	100	455
1999-00	"	54.4	9.0	36.6	100	406
1972-73	Female	65.5	4.1	31.4	100	766
1977-78	"	62.1	2.8	35.1	100	1253
1983	"	54.1	3.7	42.2	100	1140
1987-88	"	54.9	4.9	40.2	100	820
1993-94	"	51.3	3.4	45.3	100	1332
1997	"	57.0	2.1	10.9	100	1948
1999-00	"	50.0	3.9	16.1	100	1182

Notes: SE: Self-employed, RE: Regular-salaried, CL: Casual Labour.
Source: Same as in Table A-1.

TABLE A-3

Percentage Distribution of UPS Employment by Activity Status in Different Status in Rural India

States	*Male: 1999-00*				*Male: 1999-00*				*Male: 1999-00*				*Male: 1999-00*			
	SE	*RE*	*CL*	*IC*	*SE*	*RE*	*CL*	*IC*	*SE*	*RE*	*CL*	*IC*	*SE*	*RE*	*CL*	*IC*
A.P.	48.2	7.6	44.2	1582	40.4	3.9	55.7	1428	48.6	8.2	43.2	527	43.5	1.9	54.6	2874
Assam	57.6	16.4	26.01	158	26.8	34.3	38.9	113	58.3	14.0	27.7	198	17.4	33.7	48.9	145
Bihar	53.5	4.2	42.3	1007	44.9	1.8	53.3	2911	54.9	4.8	40.3	8401	38.9	1.5	59.6	13973
Gujarat	50.6	9.6	39.8	415	51.8	2.1	46.1	2195	46.9	9.7	43.4	447	44.5	2.0	53.5	2675
Haryana	58.6	16.71	24.7	148	57.2	8.7	34.1	392	61.6	14.0	24.4	174	62.5	5.4	132.1	594
H.P.	60.6	17.8	21.6	121	93.4	4.8	1.8	37	71.2	14.1	14.7	104	95.6	2.5	1.9	76
Karnataka	51.7	7.6	40-7	535	45.3	2.0	52.7	2635	56.8	6.7	36.5	545	48.0	3.1	48.9	1577
Kerala	36.1	13.6	50.3	370	33.3	22.4	44.3	198	39.2	12.8	48.0	375	34.6	15.o	50.4	336
Madhya Pradesh	57.8	4.9	37.3	761	52.0	1.6	46.4	12900	61.7	6.1	32.2	528	55.8	1.7	42.5	2500
Maharashtra	43.8	12.0	44.2	368	42.7	1.7	55.6	13270	48.3	12.6	39.5	324	44.3	2.8	52.9	1889
Orissa	47.9	5.8	46.3	798	4.1	1.7	57.2	3365	55.7	6.4	37.9	592	46.6	1.9	51.5	2710
Punjab	53.8	17.6	28.6	162	41.61	23.0	29.4	128	54.3	13.3	32.4	244	42.1	18.4	39.5	215
Rajasthan	70.1	7.6	19.Oi	162	88.3	1.4	10.3	736	71.2	7.6	21.2	279	86.3	1.3	12.4	954
Tamil Nadu	35.5	15.4	49.1	240	35.1	7.3	57.6	1789	140.7	12.8	46.5	363	38.0	6.2	55.8	900
Uttar Pradesh	70.1	7.3	22.6	319	170.01	2.3	27.7	1204	71.7	5.9	22.4	380	74.2	1.5	24.3	1620
West Bengal	48.8	7.6	43.6J	574	54.7	6.9	38.4	556	53.3	10.7	36.0	336	38.2	15.8	46.0	291
India	54.4	9.0	36.6	406	50.0	3.9	146.1	11182	56.7	8.7	34.6	398	51.3	3.4	45.3	1332

Notes: SE: Self-employed, RE: Regular-Salaried, CL: Casual Labour, IC: Index of equalization =(CURE) × 100.
Source: Same as in Table A-1.

TABLE A-4

Educational Level of Rural Labour in India by Sectors and by Sex

Level of Education	*1987-88*				*1993-94*				*1999-2000*			
	Male		*Female*		*Male*		*Female*		*Male*		*Female*	
	Agri.	*Non-Agri.*	*Agri.*	*Non-Agri.*	*Agri.*	*Non-Agri.*	*Agri.*	*Non-Agri.*	*Agri.*	*Non-Agri.*	*Agri.*	*Non-Agri.*
Not Literate	54.4	33.9	85	72 1	61.7	43.33	85.5	74.51	45.9	25.5	78.7	57
Primary	28.6	32.9	11.3	6.4	26.4	35.95	10.9	18.37	27.3	27.8	114.1	20.4
Middle	10.2	14.6	2.6	5.3	7.6	14.03	2.1	4.88	14.6	19.9	5.0	9.4
Secondary & Above	6.8	18.6	1	6	3.3	6.7	0.5	2.24	12.2	26.7	2.1	13
All levels	100	100	100	100	100	100	100	100	100	100	100	100

Source: Same as in Table A-1.

TABLE A-5

Percentage Distribution of Rural Female Employment in India by Occupations

Years	*1*	*2*	*FS*	*3*	*4*	*5*	*SS*	*6*	*7*	*8*	*TS*	*NFS (SS+TS)*	*Total*	*DI*
1972-73	83.2	0.4	83.6	5.7	0.1	1.6	7.8	3.1	1	4.8	8.9	16.4	100.0	0.330
1977-78	806	0.5	81.1	6.4	10.2	1.7	8.3	4	1.3	5.3	10.6	18.9	100.0	0.368
1983	77.5	0.7	78.2	7	0.3	2.2	9.5	14.4	1.7	6.2	12.3	21.8	100.0	0.439
1987-88	74.5	0.7	75.2	7.4	0.3	3.7	11.41	5.2	2	6.2	13.4	24.8	100.0	0.476
1993-94	74.1	0.7	74.8	7.4	0.3	3.2	10.5	5.5	2.2	7	14.7	25.2	100.0	0.481
1997	755	0.6	76.1	6.5	0.3	3.2	10.0	4.9	2	6.8	13.7	23.7	100.0	0.460
1999-00	71.3	0.6	71.9	7.3	0.2	4.5	12.0	6.8	3.2	6.1	16.1	28.1	100.0	10.518

Notes: Column heads: 1. Aggr., 2. Mining & Quarrying, 3. Manufacturing, 4. Electricity etc., 5. Construction, 6. Trade etc., 7. Transport etc., 8. Services etc.

FS: Farm-sector, NFS: Non-farm Sector, SS: Secondary Sector, TS: Tertiary Sector, DI: Diversification Index.

Source: Same as in Table A-1.

TABLE A-6

Percentage Distribution of UPS Employment by Occupation in different States in Rural India, 1993-94

Years	1	2	*PS*	3	4	5	*SS*	6	7	8	9	*TS*	*Total*	*DI*
1	*2*	*3*	*4*	*5*	*6*	*7*	*8*	*9*	*10*	*11*	*12*	*13*	*14*	*15*
A.P.	75.7	0.9	76.6	6.4	0.1	2.6	9.1	5.4	1.8	0.4	6.7	14.3	100.0	0.439
Assam	77.8	0.2	78	2.2	0.3	0.8	3.3	8.1	1.7	0.3	8.6	18.7	100.0	0.386
Bihar	81.9	0.5	82.3	3.4	0.3	1.6	5.3	5.4	1.3	0.3	5.4	12.4	100.0	0.352
Gujarat	71.2	0.7	71.9	12.5	0.2	3	15.7	4.2	2.2	0.6	5.4	12.4	100.0	0.482
Haryana	59.9	0.9	60.8	5.5	0.7	6.6	12.8	7.2	5.3	0.3	13.6	26.4	100.0	0.618
H.P.	61.1	0.3	61.4	5.5	1.5	13.7	20.7	5.7	1.9	0.4	10.1	17.9	100.0	0.594
Karnataka	78.8	1	79.8	5.3	0.3	2	7.6	4.8	1.4	0.3	6.1	12.6	100.0	0.397
Kerala	52.2	2.1	54.3	9.9	0.4	7.5	17	11.9	5.9	1.4	8.7	27.9	100.0	0.709
M.P.	87.1	1.5	88.6	3.3	0.2	1.2	4.7	2.2	0.8	0.1	3.6	6.7	100.0	0.279
Maharashtra	75	0.5	75.5	0.7	0.3	3.4	10.4	4.4	2	0.7	7	14.1	100.0	0.453
Orissa	78.4	1.2	79.6	5.9	0.2	2.3	18.4	5.2	1.1	0.1	5.6	12	100.0	0.402
Punjab	67.9	—	67.9	6.2	1.5	4.8	12.5	6.3	3.6	0.6	9	19.6	100.0	0.570
Rajasthan	69.1	2.5	71.6	5.5	0.3	10	16.5	3.8	1.9.1	0.3	5.9	11.9	100.0	0.522
T.N.	63.7	0.5	64.2	12.8	0.4	3.6	16.8	6.3	3.7	1.3	7.6	19.0	100.0	0.577
U.P.	75.7	0.2	75.9	7.2	0.2	2.7	10.1	5.2	12.1	0.3	6.4	14	100.0	0.504
W.B.	64.2	0.2	64.4	11.9	0.1	2.8	14.81	9.2	3.6	0.5	7.5	20.8	100.0	0.553
India	73.7	0.7	74.4	7	0.3	3.3	10.6	5.5	2.2	0.4	6.6	14.7	100.0	0.481

Notes: Same as in Table A-5.
Source: Same as in Table A-1.

(*Contd.*)

TABLE A-6 (*Contd.*)

Years	*1*	*2*	*PS*	*3*	*4*	*5*	*SS*	*6*	*7*	*8*	*9*	*TS*	*Total*	*DI*
1	*16*	*17*	*18*	*19*	*20*	*21*	*22*	*23*	*24*	*25*	*26*	*27*	*28*	*29*
A.P.	83.3	0.6	83.9	7.6	—	0.7	8.3	3.3	—	0.1	4.4	7.8	100.0	0.345
Assam	84.6	—	84,6	3.1	—	0.3	3.4	2.2	0.2	0.2	9.4	12	100.0	0.180
Bihar	90.8	0.4	91.2	4.3	—	0.2	4.5	2.4	—	—	1.9	4.3	100.0	0.233
Gujarat	88.2	0.2	88.4	5.4	0.1	2	7.5	0.7	—	—	3.4	4.1	100.0	0.267
Haryana	84.7	—	84.7	2.5	—	1.3	3.8	2.5	—	—	9	11.5	100.0	0.372
H.P.	94.7	—	94.7	1.8	0.3	0.6	2.7	0.7	—	—	1.9	2.6	100.0	0.157
Karnataka	83	0.5	83.5	9.9	—	0.7	10.6	2	—	0.2	3.7	5.9	100.0	0.335
Kerala	50.8	0.6	51.4	24.1	0.2	3.2	27.5	4.8	0.7	0.7	14.9	21.1	100.0	0.609
M.P.	93.3	0.9	94.2	3.6	—	0.4	4	0.9	—	—	0.9	1.8	100.0	0.184
Maharashtra	91.4	0.2	91.0	3.1	0.1	1.3	4.4	1.5	0.1	0.1	2.3	4	100.0	0.195
Orissa	83.9	1.3	85.21	6.7	—	1.4	8.1	3.4	—	—	3.3	6.7	100.0	0.375
Punjab	64.5	—	6.3		1.1	—	7.5	2.7	—	—	25.3	28	100.0	0.594
Rajasthan	91.3	1.3	92.6	1.4	—	3.3	4.7	0.8	—	—	1.9	2.7	100.0	0.238
T.N.	77.5	0.2	77.7	13.1	—	0.8	14.5	2.5	0.1	0.3	4.9	7.8	100.0	0.379
U.P.	89	—	89	4.7	—	0.3	5	2.3	—	0.3	3.4	6	100.0	0.264
W.B.	44.9	0.4	45.3	35.8	—	2.8	38.6	4	0.5	0.1	11.5	16.1	100.0	0.608
India	84.7	0.5	85.2	7.5	—	1.1	8.6	2.2	0.1	1.9	2	6.2	100.0	0.284

Notes: Same as in Table A-5.
Source: Same as in Table A-1.

TABLE A-7

Percentage Distribution of UPS Employment by Occupation in Different States in Rural India, 1999-2000

Years	1	2	PS	3	4	5	SS	6	7	8	9	TS	Total	DI
1	2	3	4	5	6	7	8	9	10	11	12	13	14	15
A.P.	74.4	1	75.4	5.3	0.1	3.4	8.8	15.8	3	0.4	6.6	15.8	100.0	0.511
Assam	63.7	0.3	64	3	0.1	2.3	5.4	10.2	3.2	0.3	16.9	30.6	100.0	0.531
Bihar	78.9	0.6	79.5	5.3	0.11	2.8	8.2	5.3	11.9	0.3	4.8	12.3	100.0	0.398
Gujarat	71.4	0.4	71.8	10.1	0.3	3.3	13.7J	5.5	3.9	0.5	4.6	14.5	100.0	0.489
Haryana	59.2	0.6	59.8	9.3	1.3	8.8	19.4	7.4	4.6	0.9	7.9	20.8	100.0	0.608
H.P.	51	—	51	7.1	2.1	18.3	27.5	6.4	4.5	0.8	9.8	21.5	100.0	0.724
Karnataka	78.5	0.9	79.4	5.2	0.1	2.1	7.4	5.6	2.4	0.6	4.5	13.1	100.0	0.408
Kerala	41.3	2.1	43.4	9.6	0.3	13	22.9	16.3	19.3	2.2	5.9	33.7	100.0	0.782
M.P.	84.2	0.4	84.6	3.9	0.1	2.3	6.3	3.9	1.1	0.2	3.9	9.1	100.0	0.263
Maharashtra	73.9	0.2	74.1	6.9	0.4	3.4	10.7	5.8	3.2	0.6	5.6	15.2	100.0	0.468
Orissa	77.2	0.6	77.8	5.6	0.2	3.8	9.6	6	1.7	0.3	4.6	12.6	100.0	0.419
Punjab	63.6	—	63.6	7.7	1.1	7.9	16.7	8.2	5.6	0.5	5.4	19.7	100.0	0.618
Rajasthan	67.2	1.9	69.1	5.4	0.3	12	17.7	5.5	3	0.5	4.2	13.2	100.0	0.543
T.N.	62.1	0.7	62.8	13.8	0.3	5.8	19.9	7.2	4.3	0.8	5	17.3	100.0	0.591
U.P.	71.3	0.2	71.5	8.4	0.2	4.5	13.11	6.8	3	0.4	5.2	15.4	100.0	0.490
W.B.	66.3	0.4	66.7	11	0.1	2.7	13.8	10.3	4.3	0.4	4.5	19.5	100.0	0.534
India	71.2	0.6	71.8	7.3	0.2	4.5	12.0	6.8	3.2	0.6	5.6	16.2	100.0	0.518

Notes: Same as in Table A-5.
Source: Same as in Table A-1.

TABLE A-7 (*Contd.*)

Years	*1*	*2*	*PS*	*3*	*4*	*5*	*SS*	*6*	*7*	*8*	*9*	*TS*	*Total*	*DI*
1	*16*	*17*	*18*	*19*	*20*	*21*	*22*	*23*	*24*	*25*	*26*	*27*	*28*	*29*
A.P.	84.2	0.7	84.9	5.9	—	0.8	6.7	3.1	—	—	5.3	8.4	100.0	0.362
Assam	75.5	—	75.5	6.2	—	—	6.2	1.8	0.6	0.4	15.5	18.3	100.0	0.443
Bihar	84.3	0.1	84.4	9.2	—	0.6	9.8	2	0.2	0.1	3.5	5.8	100.0	0.294
Gujarat	90.2	0.5	90.7	2.7	—	2.4	5.1	1.7	0.2	—	2.3	4.2	100.0	0.244
Haryana	71.2	—	71.2	3.4	—	5	8.4	6	—	—	14.4	20.4	100.0	0.594
H.P.	92.1	—	92.1	1.6	0.2	0.6	2.4	0.9	0.2	0.1	4.3	5.5	100.0	0.184
Karnataka	87.8	0.6	88.4	5.7	—	0.6	6.3	2.4	—	—	2.9	5.3	100.0	0.296
Kerala	45.2	1.1	46.3	25.1	—	3.8	28.9	5	0.3	1.7	17.8	24.8	100.0	0.685
M.P.	91.9	0.3	92.2	3.6	—	1.3	4.9	1	—	—	1.9	2.9	100.0	0.217
Maharashtra	94.1	0.1	94.2	1.8	—	1	2.8	1.3		—	1.7	3	100.0	0.172
Orissa	80.3	0.2	80.5	12.3	—	2.5	14.8	2.2	—	—	2.5	4.7	100.0	0.397
Punjab	49	—	49	10.8	1.1	0.8	12.7	6.7	—	—	31.6	38.3	100.0	0.683
Rajasthan	90.1	0.8	90.9	3.5	.	2.9	6.4	0.8	—	—	1.9	2.7	100.0	0.260
T.N.	75.2	0.3	75.5	14.5	—	1.7	16.2	3.5	0.2	0.2	14.4	8.3	100.0	0.414
U.P.	83.6	—	83.6	8.3	—	0.4	8.7	2.3	—	0.2	5.2	7.5	100.0	10.349
W.B.	57.2	—	57.2	30.5	—	0.6	31.1	3.4	—	0.1	8.2	11.6	100.0	0.581
India	84.1	0.4	84.5	7.7	—	1.2	8.9	2.2	0.1	0.1	4.2	6.6	100.0	0.333

Notes: Same as in Table A-5.
Source: Same as in Table A-1.

Variables	*Coefficient of Rank Correlation*	
	1993-94	*1999-2000*
Rural Male		
1. Cropping Intensity	0.276	0.435*
	(1.071)	(1.686)
2. Commercialization	0.497*	0.329
	(1.925)	(1.276)
3. Agricultural Prosperity	0.226	0.609*
	(0.877)	(2.358)
4. Average Land Size Cultivated by Agriculture	-0.450*	-0.582*
	(-1.743)	(-2.255)
5. Average Daily Real Agricultural Wages	0.841*	0.882*
	(3.257)	(3.417)
6. Rural Literacy Rate (%)	0 706*	0.465*
	(2.734)	(1.800)
7. Sex Ratio	0.185	0.200
	(0.718)	(0.775)
8. Urbanization	0.188	-0.029
	(0.729)	(-0.114)
9. Rural Poverty	-0.482*	-0.609*
	(-1.868)	(-2.338)
10. Population Growth	-0.200	-0.309
	(-0.775)	(-1.196)
11. Human Development Index (HDI)	0.706*	0.612*
	(2.733)	(2.369)
Rural Female		
1. Cropping Intensity	-0.018	0.474*
	(-0.068)	(1.834)
2. Commercialization	0.471*	0.168
	(1.823)	(0.649)
3. Agricultural Prosperity	0.376	0.691*
	(1.458)	(2.677)
4. Average Land Size Cultivated by Agriculture	-0.671*	-0.847*
	(-2.597)	(7.154)
5. Average Daily Real Agricultural Wages	0.497*	0.459*
	(1.925)	(1.777)
6. Rural Literacy Rate (%)	0.432*	0.194
	(1.674)	(0.752)
7. Sex Ratio	0.079	0.088
	(0.307)	(0.342)
8. Urbanization	0.491*	-0.076
	(1.902)	(0.296)
9. Rural Poverty	-0.376	-0.126
	(-1.458)	(-0.490)
10. Population Growth	-0.309	-0.318
	(-1.196)	(-1.230)
11. Human Development Index (HDI)	0.441*	0.241
	(1.704)	(-0.934)

20

Impact of Globalization on India's Export Performance

Pardeep Kumar

Since July 1991, new economic reforms were taken into consideration with the objective to move the economy to more liberalise and globalise. This package of new economic reforms is called the new economic policy which has three main aspects, i.e. privatization, liberalization and globalization. In this way globalization is an integral part of new economic policy. Globalization means to reduce the trade barriers and free flow of capital as well as technique. It increases the competitiveness on the one hand, and growth faster of the economy on the other. In fact, globalization accelerates the rate of growth of exports resulting higher rate of economic growth. No doubt, Government has taken several steps to boost up the exports from time to time but, even then the exports growth rates slowed down resulting lower share of Indian exports in world exports even in comparison with the developing countries also. Since July 1991, one decade has passed to follow the policy of globalization. Therefore, the objective is to analyse the impact of globalization on export performance. Specifically, the main objectives are to examine the

1. Growth of exports.
2. Changing Scenario of exports.
3. Percentage share of exports of selected countries in world exports.
4. Steps taken by Government.
5. Policy package for the future.

GROWTH OF EXPORTS

The trend of growth of exports has been shown in Table 1. This table reveals that, after the globalization the exports which were 17865 million dollars in 1991-92 increased to 44035 million dollars in 2001-02. It rose by 146.49 per cent during the same period. So far as the percentage change over the previous year is concerned, the export growth rate accelerated from 3.8 per cent to 20.8 per cent during the period 1992-93 to 1995-96. But as a percentage of GDP, it increased from 7.8 per cent to 9.7 per cent during the same period. After that the growth of exports decelerated continuously from 5.3 per cent in 1996-97 to –5.1 per cent in 1998-99. As a per cent of GDP it fell from 9.4 to 8.3 percent during the same period. The continuous sluggishness of exports growth rate as well as the percentage of exports as GDP is all due to the deceleration in the growth of world trade and export price of some manufactured goods. Exchange rate mismatch is also held responsible for the sluggishness. Appreciation of Indian rupee in comparison with the South-East Asian currencies also affected the price competitiveness of Indian exports in the international market resulting slowed down in Indian exports. But during the period 1999-2000 to 2000-01 the export growth rate accelerated from 10.8 per cent to 21 per cent. And as a percentage of GDP it rose from 8.4 to 9.8 per cent during the same period. It increased due to the increase in the volume of exports, global demand, improvement in world commodity prices and the revival of world trade. The exchange rate of the rupee was also stable is real effective terms for the retention of the competitiveness of India's exports in global market in 2000-01. Government also announced so many measures to boost up the exports. Consequently, industries like textiles, engineering goods, electronic goods, chemicals, leather and leather manufacturers, ores and minerals and petroleum products also contributed a lot to strengthen the exports. But during the period 2001-02 the growth of exports declined by –1.2 per cent in comparison with a sharp rise during 2000-01. Several factors like deceleration of global demand, downward information technology, falling of commodity prices and appreciation of the rupee in real effective terms are held responsible on the one hand, and deceleration of world output on the other. Moreover, the tragic event of September 11, 2001 in U.S.A. and in Afghanisthan also slowed down the global trade in general and Indian trade in particular.

TABLE 1

Growth of Exports in U.S. Million Dollars and as a Percentage of GDPmp

Year	*Million Dollars*	*Percentage Change over previous year*	*Growth of Exports as a percentage of GDPmp*
1991-92	17865	—	7.3
1992-93	18537	3.8	7.8
1993-94	22238	20.0	8.8
1994-95	26330	18.4	8.8
1995-96	31797	20.8	9.7
1996-97	33470	5.3	9.4
1997-98	35006	4.6	8.7
1998-99	33218	-5.1	8.3
1999-2000	36822	10.8	8.4
2000-01	44560	21.0	9.8
2001-02	44035	-1.2	—

Source: Government of India, *Economic Survey,* 2001-02 and *Economic and Political Weekly,* August 2002.

The observation in export growth rates fluctuated after the globalization. It was highest in 2000-01 and lowest in 2001-02. Several factors are held responsible for this fluctuation.

CHANGING SCENARIO OF INDIA'S EXPORTS

The volume of India's exports increased tremendously but in this total volume, the share of different commodities is entirely different and changing with the passage of time. The changing scenario of India's exports has been shown in Table 2 which indicates that the total volume of exports which was 18536 million dollars in 1992-93, increased to 44561 million dollars in 2000-01. It accelerated by 140.40 per cent during the same period. But in this total volume of exports the share of agricultural and allied products, ores and minerals, manufactured goods, minerals, fuels and lubricants and other commodities increased from 3265 to 6246, from 626 to 906, from 14099 to 35192, from 525 to 1931, from 21 to 286 million dollars during the period 1992-93 to 2000-01. So far as the percentage change is concerned, it accelerated by 91.30 per cent in agricultural and allied products, 44.27 percent in ores and minerals, 149.61 per cent in manufactured goods, 267.81 per cent in minerals, fuels & lubricants and 1261.90 percent in case of other commodities respectively during the same period. With respect to the percentage share in total exports, the picture is entirely different. The percentage share of agricultural and allied products and ores and minerals decreased from 17.61 and 3.38 per cent in 1992-93 to 14.01 and 2.03 per cent in 2000-01 whereas, the percentage share of manufactured goods, minerals, fuels and lubricants and other commodities rose from 76.06 to 78.97, 2.83 to 4.33, 0.11 to 0.64 per cent from the period 1992-93 to 2001-02 respectively.

TABLE 2

Changing Scenario of India's Exports

(in Million Dollars)

Commodity	*1992-93*	*2000-01*	*Percentage Change over 1992-93*
Agricultural & Allied Products	3265(17.61)	6246(14.01)	91.30
Ores & Minerals	626 (3.38)	906 (2.03)	44.73
Manufactured Goods	14099(76.06)	35192(78.97)	149.61
Minerals, Fuels & Lubricants	525 (2.83)	1931 (4.33)	267.81
Others	21 (0.11)	286 (0.64)	1261.90
Total	18536(100)	44561 (100)	140.40

Note: Figures in parenthesis show the percentage to total exports.
Source: Government of India, *Economic Survey*, 1997-98 and 2001-02.

The observation is so far as the volume of exports of different commodities is concerned, it is the highest in case of manufactured goods followed by agricultural and allied product, ores and minerals, minerals, fuels and lubricants and other commodities in 1992-93 but in 2000-01, it is the highest in case, of manufactured goods followed by agricultural and allied products, minerals, fuels and lubricants, ores and minerals and other commodities. But the highest share in total exports has been observed in case of manufactured goods and lowest in case of others commodities in both 1992-93 and 2000-01 years. Same case has been observed with respect to percentage share of various commodities in both the years. But in case of percentage change, the picture is somewhat different. It is the highest in other commodities and lowest in case of ores and minerals. In this way, in the per cent scenario the relative share of various commodities has undergone a drastic change.

PERCENTAGE SHARE OF EXPORTS OF SELECTED EAST ASIAN COUNTRIES IN WORLD EXPORTS

Table 3 shows the percentage share in world exports during the period 1992-2000. It increased from 2.28 per cent to 3.93 per cent in China, from 0.91 per cent to 0.98 per cent in Indonesia, 0.86 per cent to 1.09 per cent in Thailand and from 0.54 per cent to 0.66 per cent in case of India respectively. But the share of developing countries in world exports rose from 29 to 37 per cent during the same period. But so far as the percentage change is concerned, it accelerated by 192.4 per cent in China, 82.35 per cent in Indonesia, 115.63 per cent in Thailand and 110 per cent in India respectively during the period 1992 to 2000. But in case of developing countries and world, it increased by 115.97 per cent and 69.53 per cent during the same period.

The result is that, the highest percentage share in world exports has been observed in case of China and the lowest in case of India both in 1992 and 2000 years. So far as percentage change is concerned, it is the highest in case of China and the lowest in case of Indonesia during the period 1992 to 2000. So far as the comparison of percentage change of East Asian countries with the world during the period 1992-2000 is concerned, it is higher in case of all the four countries, i.e. China followed by Thailand, India and Indonesia than that of world. But in comparison with the developing countries, the percentage change is lower in all the countries except China. It shows that in case of China the highest percentage change of exports has been observed both at developing countries as well as world level. But in case of India, it is more than world but less than that of developing countries.

TABLE 3

Percentage Share of Exports of Selected East Asian Countries in World Exports (in US Billion Dollars)

Country	*1992*	*2000*	*Percentage Change over 1992*
China	85 (2.28)	249 (3.93)	192.94
Indonesia	34 (0.91)	62 (0.98)	82.35
Thailand	32 (0.86)	69 (1.09)	115.63
India	20 (0.54)	42 (0.66)	110.00
Developing Countries	1083 (29)	2339 (37)	115.97
World	3735	6332	69.53

Source: Government of India, *Economic Survey*, 1997-98, 2001-02.
Note: Figures in Parenthesis show the percentage to world exports.

STEPS TAKEN BY GOVERNMENT

The growth rates of exports fluctuated during the period 1991-92 to 2001-02. To boost up the exports, so many methods have been adopted from time to time. As a result, the highest growth rate of exports was observed in 2000-01 but in the next year in 2001-02 the negative growth was observed. Therefore, to raise the rate of growth of exports, recently new EXIM policy of 2002-07 has been announced. In this policy quantitative restrictions have been removed and several facilities have been provided to get the target of 11.9 per cent annual export growth rate. The main objective is to increase the share of India's exports in world exports from 0.7 per cent to one per cent by the end of 10th Plan in 2007. In this regard, product group-wise export projections have been proposed during the period 2000-01 to 2006-07 which have been shown in Table 4. This table reveals that the export of petroleum products and others is expected to increase by 604.91 per cent followed by gems and jewellery by 94.04 per cent, chemical and allied products by 82.65 per cent, engineering goods by 63.91 per cent, textile by 51.83 per cent, electric goods by 46.89 per cent, marine products by 37.23 per cent, leather and manufacturers by 33.98 per cent, agricultural and allied by 33.94 per cent, ores and minerals by 33.91 per cent, project goods by 33.33 per cent, sports goods by 14.71 per cent and plantations by 12.72 per cent respectively. So far as the compound annual growth rates for 2002-07 is concerned, it is the highest in case of petroleum products and others (39.39%) followed by jems and jewellery (11.67%), chemical and allied products (10.80%) engineering goods (8.96%), textiles (7.23%), electronic goods (6.96%), marine products (5.41%), agriculture and allied (5%), ores and minerals (5%), project goods (5%), leather and manufacturers (4.9%), sports goods (2%) and plantation (2%) respectively.

TABLE 4

Projections of Exports and Compound Annual Growth Rates in Percentage

(In Million Dollars)

Commodities	*Actual Exports 2000-01 (in Million Dollars)*	*Projected Exports in 2006-07 (Million Dollars)*	*Percentage Change*	*CAGR 2002-07*
Petroleum Products & Others	1893	13344	604.91	39.39
Gems & Jewellery	7384	14328	94.04	11.67
Chemical & Allied Products	6265	11443	82.65	10.80
Engineering Goods	5835	9564	63.91	8.96
Textiles	12060	18311	51.83	7.23
Electrical Goods	1141	1676	46.89	6.96
Marine Products	1394	1913	37.23	5.41
Leather & Manufactures	1951	2614	33.98	4.99
Agriculture & Allied	3869	5182	33.94	5.00
Ores & Minerals	1159	1552	33.91	5.00
Project Goods	27	36	33.33	5.00
Sports Goods	68	78	14.71	2.00
Plantations	692	780	12.72	2.00

Source: Government of India, *Economic Survey*, 2001-02.

It seems that increase in the percentage change in almost all the commodities except leather and manufactures, are directly related to annual export growth rates. Higher the percentage change higher will be the annual export growth rates. Lower the percentage change lower will be the annual export growth rate in case of all the commodities except one commodity. So far as the increase in percentage change is concerned, it is excepted to be the highest in case of petroleum products and others and lowest in case of plantations. Same is the case with annual exports growth rates also.

POLICY PACKAGE FOR THE FUTURE

India's exports performance is very poor not only in comparison with developed countries but with some developing countries also. Low productivity, higher costs, poor quality are the main hindrances in the way of export promotion. There is a target to increase the share of India's exports in world exports from 0.7 per cent to 1 per cent in 2007. In this regard improvement in the productive capacity, quality, marketing and research activities can play a vital role to enhance the export growth rates. No doubt, after the adoption of new economic policy, due attention has been given towards foreign direct investment even then more FDI needs to be attracted. Implementation of effective fiscal and monetary policy is the need of the hour. Infrastructure and timely financial facilities must be provided to the export industries. Indian exports have inelastic demand. To increase the demand developed as well as developing countries are required to be attracted. Competitive spirit in exports needs to be developed to compete the global market. No doubt, new EXIM policy of 2002-07 seems to be good to increase the rate of growth of exports on the one hand, and to get the target of 1 per cent share in world exports on the other, even then this target can be achieved only if this policy is implemented effectively.

CONCLUSION

Globalization has mixed impact on Indian's export performance. No doubt, the total volume of exports accelerated tremendously but even then the export growth rates fluctuated during the decade despite various steps taken by government to boost up the exports growth rates. So far as the percentage share of different commodities in total volume of exports is concerned, increasing trend has been observed in case of manufactured goods and minerals, fuels and lubricants whereas decreasing trend has been observed in case of agricultural and allied products and ores and minerals. With respect to the percentage share of India's exports in world exports, it is only 0.7 per cent, which is lower in comparison with the South-East Asian countries also. The target is to increase this share by one per cent at the end of 10th Plan in 2007 according to the new EXIM policy. To get this target various incentives have been given to boost up the growth rates of exports by 11.9 per cent per annum in new EXIM policy. But even then this target can be achieved only in case of all the measures together on the one hand and new EXIM policy on the other are implemented in a well planned and effective way in the present scenario.

21

Globalization and Consumption Pattern: The Indian Perspective

S. CHINNAMMAI

One of the indicators of a Nation's integration with the world economy is the participation in the world trade. There has been remarkable increase in international trade in recent years. Percentage of trade in goods to the PPP GDP (i.e. GDP measured in Purchasing Price Parity) has increased from 22.5% to 27.4% during the period 1989 and 1999 (World Development Indicators, 2001). The expansion was much faster in the high-income countries, which is slow in very low income, and lower in middle-income countries and it was less than one per cent (*Vyas*, 2002).

India is a small player in international trade, accounting for only about 0.6% of the world trade. But the economy of the country is globalizing fast. The ratio of international trade of GDP of the country increased from 15.6% in 1990-91 to 20.8% in 1999-2000. The ratio of foreign investment in the country to the exports increased from mere 0.6% in 1990-91 to 13.4% in 1999-2000. In absolute terms, the foreign investment inflows to the country increased from $103 million in 1990-91 to $181 million in 1999-2000 (World Bank, 2001). The annual growth rate of GDP picked up from 5.4% during 1980-81 to 1991-92 to 6.4% during 1992-93 to 2000-01, but the rise was mainly due to the rapid growth of service sector. The occupational structure in the country has also changed with agriculture and allied activities accounting for 59.8% (NSSO, 2000). These statistics represents the effect of before and after Globalization.

The Per Capita Income (Per Capita net national product at factor cost) in real terms, i.e. at 1993-94 prices has been estimated at Rs.10,204 for 1999-2000 as against Rs. 7,698 for 1993-94 registering a growth of 4.8% during the year. The percentage of per capita income decreased from 5.1% in 1993-94 to 3.5% in 2000-01.

TABLE 1

GDP and National Income

Year	*GDP*		*NNP*		*Per Capita NNP*	
	Current Prices	*1993-94 Prices*	*Current Prices*	*1993-94 Prices*	*Current Prices*	*1993-94 Prices*
1993-94	781345	781345	685912	685912	7698	7698
1994-95	917058	838031	805981	73458	8876	8088
1995-96	1073271	899563	941861	787809	10160	8499
1996-97	1243456	970083	1093961	852085	11601	9036
1997-98	1390042	1016226	1224787	890712	12772	9288
1998-99	1616033	1083047	1434456	948982	14712	9733
1999-00	1796459	1151991	1590301	1011224	16047	10204
2000-01	1978042	1211747	1765238	1063479	17350	10561
Per cent Growth over Previous Year						
1994-95	17.4	7.3	17.5	7.1	15.3	5.1
1995-96	17.0	7.3	16.9	7.3	14.5	5.1
1996-97	15.9	7.8	16.1	8.2	14.2	6.3
1997-98	11.8	4.8	12.0	4.5	10.1	2.8
1998-99	16.3	6.6	17.1	6.5	15.2	4.8
1999-00	10.5	6.4	10.9	6.6	9.1	4.8
2000-01	10.7	5.2	11.0	5.2	9.2	3.5

Source: National Account Statistics, 2001.

The economy in terms of GDP at 1993-94 prices has grown during 1999-2000 almost the same pace (6.4%) as that of the previous year (6.6%). This growth rate could be sustained mainly because of rapid growth in services, despite virtually no growth in agriculture.

In India the economic reforms which began in the year early 1990's still remain in controversy because, it touched the sensitive area of agriculture, labour, social development, consumer behaviour, etc. The country was not prepared for globalization with more than 100 crore population and the prevailing socio-political set-up, but the foundations of social changes can not be laid in a short span of time and globalization will continue without waiting for India to get ready to board the bus (*Balasubramanyan*, 2001). Globalization is not just an economic phenomenon. It is something much wider; there is nothing new about it, because the interaction between communities started a long time ago. When people began to trade, mercantilism, colonialism, capitalism all contributed to increase the international economic activities through the centuries. From the economic point of view, the present stage is only an advanced phase of economic activity, which started some 500 years back.

The characteristics of globalization as it is now unfolding are multifarious. It is influencing consumer behaviour as much as the economics of nation. While most attention is focused on economics integration of globalization and consumption pattern, this paper throws light on consumption expenditure and consumer behavior on or before globalization.

The ratio of per capita consumption figures from National Sample Survey [NSS] to the per capita expenditure figures from National Accounts Statistics [NAS] has been provided in Table 2. The table shows that the ratio of foodgrains consumption to that of availability declined from 1.2 in 1977-88 to around 0.9 in 1997-98, a decline of about one per cent a year. The ratio of estimated consumption of NSS to the private financial consumption expenditure of NAS shows that after an initial decline the ratio had stabilised after 1993-94.

Over the States it varied from an average annual decline of –0.92% in Assam to –5.61% in the case of Gujarat between 1987-88 and 1997-98. The growth rates of per capita net state domestic product also varied widely between the States. Again the least growth was recorded for Bihar 0.20% per annum and the highest 7.13% for Gujarat. This variation has been shown in Table 3.

TABLE 2

Estimates of Consumption Expenditure from NSS and NAS, All-India

(Consumption in Rs. Crores)

Year	*Per Capita Consumption (Rs.) (NAS)*	*Per Capita Consumption (Rs.) (NSS)*	*Ratio of NSS to NAS*	*Per Capita Consumption of Foodgrains (Kg.) (NSS)*	*Per Capita Availability of Foodgrains (Kg.) (Eco-Survey)*	*Ratio of NSS to (Eco-Survey)*
1977-78	92.42	74.36	0.81	14.34	12.13	1.18
1983-84	163.81	124.70	0.76	13.92	11.93	1.17
1987-88	244.87	179.05	0.73	13.63	12.69	1.07
1989-90	303.20	214.03	0.71	13.29	13.32	1.00
1990-91	341.50	232.09	0.68	13.25	13.53	0.98
1992-93	405.89	284.85	0.70	12.78	13.05	0.98
1993-94	483.96	325.18	0.67	12.76	12.93	0.99
1994-95	544.95	363.65	0.67	12.53	13.41	0.93
1995-96	604.74	409.62	0.68	12.34	13.62	0.91
1997-98	682.75	459.03	0.67	11.96	13.32	0.90

Source: EPW, March 24, 2001.

TABLE 3

Expenditure (NSS) to Net State Domestic Product between 1987-88 and 1997-98—Average Annual Change

(Percent)

State	*Per Capita Income*	*Ratio of Expenditure to NSDP*
Bihar	0.20	-1.09
Uttar Pradesh	1.90	-1.88
Orissa	2.15	-2.42
Assam	2.46	-0.92
Punjab	2.86	-2.93
Madhya Pradesh	2.88	-2.70
West Bengal	4.08	-3.00
Karnataka	4.09	-3.53
Haryana	4.10	-4.67
Andhra Pradesh	4.36	-4.03
Tamil Nadu	5.22	-4.32
Kerala	5.31	-3.44
Maharashtra	5.42	-3.46
Rajasthan	5.51	-4.18
Gujarat	7.13	-5.61
All India		-4.07

Source: EPW, 2001.

Globalization will also change food habits of Indian masses, likings to consume products in raw or semi-raw form (fruits, vegetables, foodgrains) will be replaced by greater likings for processed products, fast food and highly impressive packed pocket like uncle chips, maggi, ruffles, etc. This will be resulted in lesser consumption of nutritive products and cause a bad impact on health.

As per NAS data on private final consumption expenditure by object-wise in 1999-00 foods, beverage and tobacco stands first place on consumption expenditure. Transport and communication stands second place, gross rent, fuel and power stands third place, miscellaneous goods and services stands fourth place, clothing and footwear stands fifth, medical care and health services stands sixth, recreation, education and cultural services stands seventh place and finally furniture, furnishing appliance and services stands eighth place. This has been classified in Table 4 at 1993-94 prices. The bracket shows the percentage distribution of private final consumption expenditure.

Globalization is not, as a 'free of charge' or 'free and fair' phenomenon. The costs are paid by the poor nations and by the poor in all nations. The main problem is that, globalization does not address three core elements of development: Accountability, Equity and Democracy. There is a sift in focus from human to animals (*Cheriyan*, 1998). The effect of globalization would be the demise of small companies in developing countries and also mean the loss of normal independence. Economic gains have benefited greatly a few countries at the expense of many. The poor get poorer and the richer goes on rich. Globalization has brought about an economic growth of 6-7% in this country. But it has created only less than 2% increase in employment opportunities, along with devaluation and high inflation rates (*Cheriyan*, 1998). The rich and upper middle classes are benefited by the new economic reforms because all the consumer and luxury goods are at their doorsteps. But the condition of the poor and the marginalized has further worsened.

DIVERGENT TRENDS IN CONSUMPTION OF DURABLES

A variety of consumer goods, both durable and expandable, entered in the Indian market soon after liberalization. There was

TABLE 4

Private Final Consumption Expenditure Classified by Object (1993-94 Prices)

Item	*1993-94*	*1994-95*	*1995-96*	*1996-97*	*1997-98*	*1998-99*	*1999-00*
Food, Beverages and Tobacco	315243 (56.1)	325436 (54.1)	340124 (53.2)	369285 (53.6)	362475 (51.7)	404108 (53.8)	414078 (52.9)
Clothing and footwear	34999 (4.5)	34178 (5.7)	36181 (5.7)	38231 (5.5)	41572 (5.9)	38651 (61.)	41749 (5.3)
Gross Rent fuel and power	68239 (12.1)	70688 (11.8)	72907 (11.4)	75380 (10.9)	79862 (11.4)	82880 (11.0)	85656 (11.0)
Furniture, furnishing, appliance and services	17610 (3.0)	18181 (3.0)	20241 (3.2)	21755 (3.2)	23142 (3.3)	23520 (3.1)	24321 (3.1)
Medical Care and Health Services	19543 (3.4)	21770 (3.6)	24232 (3.8)	26878 (3.9)	29813 (4.3)	33079 (4.4)	36660 (4.7)
Transport and Communication	64993 (11.3)	71783 (11.9)	79568 (12.5)	87748 (12.7)	86758 (12.4)	88266 (11.7)	90595 (11.6)
Recreation, education and cultural services	17626 (3.1)	19494 (3.2)	20688 (3.2)	21868 (3.2)	25296 (3.6)	25903 (3.4)	29819 (3.8)
Miscellaneous goods and services	36519 (6.4)	39951 (6.6)	44997 (7.0)	48421 (7.0)	52196 (7.4)	55032 (7.3)	59186 (7.6)
Private Final Consumption in domestic market	574772 (100)	601481 (100)	638938 (100)	689566 (100)	701114 (100)	751439 (100)	782064 (100)

Source: National Account Statistics, 2001.

TABLE 5

Private Final Consumption Expenditure Classified by Types of Goods (at Current Prices)

Item	*1993-94*	*1994-95*	*1995-96*	*1996-97*	*1997-98*	*1998-99*	*1999-00*
Durable goods	11018 (1.9)	14832 (2.2)	19152 (2.5)	21313 (2.4)	19016 (2.0)	18753 (1.6)	18314 (1.4)
Semi-durable goods	45604 (7.9)	52531 (7.9)	63032 (8.2)	67371 (7.5)	74989 (7.7)	72891 (6.4)	79137 (6.3)
Non-durable goods	378108 (65.8)	437172 (65.8)	496886 (64.9)	601042 (66.5)	645512 (65.8)	780406 (68.4)	866800 (68.5)
Services	140042 (24.4)	159802 (24.1)	186727 (24.4)	213927 (23.7)	239278 (24.5)	269157 (23.6)	391181 (23.8)
Private final consumption expenditure in domestic market	574772	664337	765797	903653	978795	1141207	1355432
Add: direct purchases abroad by resident households	1475	2502	3521	3049	5340	7326	9268
Less: Direct purchases in the domestic market by non-households and extra bodies	7022	7420	9180	10232	10880	12604	13166
Private final consumption expenditure	569225	659419	760138	896470	973255	1135929	1351534

Source: National Accounts Statistics, 2001.

a consumer boom and the country witnessed impressive growth in the consumption of goods and services. The classified type of durable goods and its percentages has collected and tabulated by NAS. It has been presented in Table 5. Perhaps, NSS is not capturing these items adequately in its surveys.

There were a special tabulation on consumer durables covered in the 1987-88 and 1993-94 by National Sample Survey [NSS] and Market Information Service of Household [MISH] of NCAER survey. Estimates of consumption of these durables based on NSS and MISH along with the sales of these durables as available from various newspapers, reports and business magazines are present in Tables 6 and 7.

TABLE 6

Estimates of Consumption of Durables in 1987-88

(Rs. in millions)

Item	*NSS*	*MISH*
TV/VCR/VCP	8232	18808
Tape Recorder	779	2841
Electric Fan draw	1272	2359
Bicycle	2102	3360
Two-wheelers (motorized)	4229	10048

Source: EPW, 2001.

TABLE 7

Estimates of Consumer Expenditure on Durables in 1993-94

(Rs. in millions)

Items	*NSS*	*MISH*	*Sales***
TV	7997	29287	26000
Tape Recorder	1308	8506*	9400
Electric Fan	1551	6178	6600
Bicycle	2914	8354	10000
Two-wheelers (motorized)	10040	34201	34000

*Does not include music system; ** Production.
Source: EPW, 2001.

Consumption of these durables has been increased after globalization in India. There is an attractive purchase of these items now-a-days.

TABLE 8

Estimates Market Size of Consumer Durables

Year	*MISH**	*NAS*	*NSS*
1987-88	-53	70	54
1993-94	132	158	85
1997-98	268	320	202

*Only 20 selected durables.
Source: EPW, 2001.

DIVERGENT TRENDS IN CONSUMPTION OF EXPENDABLES

The market for expendables also expected rapidly in 1990's and MISH data show that the consumption of about 20 products covered in MISH more than doubled between 1987-88 and 1997-98. This has been shown in Table 9.

TABLE 9

Estimated Market Size of Expendables

Year	*MISH**	*NAS*	*NSS*
1987-88	152	224	
1997-98	305	283	223

*Only 20 selected durables.
Source: EPW, 2001.

Globalization will act as a slow poisoning process for Indian household industries and in Indian culture. It is also truly said that, globalization would be against principles of Gandhian economics. Rural industries also become a prey to globalization. Indian people will consume a large number of international standard goods and commodities and it will change their way of life. Thus, sprit of Swadeshi will be hurt. It will change the life-style of Indian people. No doubt, Globalization of Indian Economy will increase the job opportunities for Indian images through vast entry of Multinational Corporations. This will increase the purchasing power of the people and they may be able to consume high quality and quantity of goods. Thus, globalization proves to increase the living standard of the Indian people and will have an impact of their style. Consumption of luxury goods will increase not only due to high discretionary spending power, but also through demonstration effect. Multinational Corporations are using television media to advertise their products vastly. This has resulted in demonstration effect. High consumption of luxurious goods will be increased (*Gaur*, 2000). Everybody wants to increase their income and there is wider scope for malpractices like bribery etc. V.R. Krishna Iyer (1993) said that hi-tech foreign print media have gradually propagandized power to consolidate the western culture conquest. In time to come it is regarded that it will make Indians un-Indians and Indian politicians puppets welcoming economic re-colonizaation.

The survey of Indian investors by NCAER and SEBI has also collected the consumer durables in 1999. These durable has been classified under, refrigerator, washing machine, motorcycle, scooter, colour television and car. These durable has been presented under different income groups in Table 10. Particularly the data has been given per 1000 households for All-India, urban and rural level.

From above tables it is very clear that consumption of durables has been increased steadily from 1987-88 to 1999-00. This trend make children used to see advertisement on TV. They induce to show advertisement to the owners and even others. After seeing such advertisement, children press their parents; the immature kids become decision-making units in purchasing of many articles.

The consumption pattern of the bottom 17% corresponding to the population below poverty line is given in Tables 11 and 12. The poor spend more than they earn. In other words, they have negative saving and borrow for consumption. We can assume that their income is less than their expenditure.

The total market size of the 20 expendable products in MISH was Rs. 800 million in 1997-98. Of this about 7 per cent is consumed by the households classified as poor. Practically every one of them use toilet soap. Nearly 90% use washing cake and cooking oil. Footwear of one kind or other was bought by almost all. Vast majority also bought tea and hair oil. Only nail polish, lipstick and health beverages were bought by less than 5 per cent of these households.

TABLE 10

Penetration Levels of Consumer Durables

(Per 1000 Households)

Items	*Income Class (Rs.)*			
	Upto 5000	*Upto 10,000*	*Upto 15,000*	*More than 15,000*
Refrigerator				
All-India	60	199	411	429
Urban	158	340	589	616
Rural	20	60	145	141
Washing Machine				
All-India	16	83	278	303
Urban	45	151	428	462
Rural	4	16	57	59
Motor Cycle				
All-India	22	62	135	139
Urban	35	77	138	145
Rural	17	48	132	132
Scooter				
All-India	47	124	230	238
Urban	102	200	313	327
Rural	24	49	106	101
Colour Television				
All-India	52	164	356	372
Urban	122	261	476	506
Rural	23	69	177	166
Car				
All-India	—	24	204	226
Urban	—	47	322	355
Rural	—	2	27	28

Source: *Survey of Indian Investors—by NCAER and SEBI,* 1999.

TABLE 11

Consumption of Expendable Goods for Population below Poverty Line as Estimated from MISH, 1997-98

(Per cent users)

Product	*Urban*	*Rural*	*Total*
Toilet soap	95.3	95.1	95.1
Washing cake	88.8	87.3	87.6
Washing powder	67.7	49.4	53.3
Toothpaste	46.5	21.1	26.6
Tooth powder	62.2	40.8	45.4
Body Talcum Powder	39.8	20.9	24.9
Shampoo	18.9	4.7	7.8
Hair oil	78.5	69.8	71.7
Face cream	16.4	8.3	10.1
Nail polish	8.7	3.5	4.6
Lipstick	8.9	1.0	2.7
Edible oil	90.4	93.5	92.8
Packaged biscuits	27.3	15.5	18.0
Tea	86.6	78.2	80.0
Health beverages	4.5	0.9	1.7
Electric bulbs	56.2	29.4	35.1
Electric tubes	21.7	3.1	7.1
Sports shoes	20.1	13.4	14.8
Footwear-leather	44.3	26.2	30.1
Footwear-others	52.0	50.9	51.2
Cigarettes	18.9	13.0	14.3

Source: *EPW*, 2001.

Every tenth household bought shampoo and face cream. Nearly a fourth bought body talcum powder. About 15% bought packaged biscuits. (*Deepak Lal, Rakesh Mohan, Natarajan*, 2000-01) These are all the implications of globalization and people are educated through hi-tech media.

These households own a variety of consumer durables also. About three-fourth of the households owned a wristwatch. Bicycle and radios were owned by 40% and 30% of the households. Black and white television and tape recorders were owned by 10% and 16% respectively. Two per cent had a mechanized two-wheeler. Nearly a tenth had a sewing machine. (*Deepak Lal, Rakesh Mohan, Nataraian*, 2000-01)

TABLE 12

Ownership of Durables by Population Below Poverty Line as Estimated from MISH, 1997-98

(Per '000 hhs.)

Durables	*Urban*	*Rural*	*Total*
Transistor-Radio	423	309	319
Cassette Recorders	202	150	155
Pressure Cooker/Pan	260	76	92
Bicycle	419	410	411
Electric Iron	153	47	56
Electric Fans	582	220	252
Wrist Watches	1024	706	734
TV—B&W	312	79	100
Sewing Machine	98	54	58
Mixer Grinder	55	12	16
Colour TVs	43	7	10
Two-wheelers (motorised)	49	14	17
Washing Machine	12	0	1
Refrigerator	35	4	7

Source: EPW, 2001.

Also these are the households of whom more than 85% claim, according to NSS, to be getting two time meals a day throughout the year. The bottom 18% of households in India display such a consumption pattern it provides further evidence that the estimate of 37% being below the poverty line in India 1997-98.

CONCLUSION

The Indian economy is only marginally integrated with the world economy. There is little new capital formation in the economy with foreign financial resources. The development of foreign private resources is largely in "white goods sector", in automobiles and other luxury items catering to the needs of rising middle and upper middle class. Share of investment strategically important hi-tech sectors, or in consumer goods industries catering to the needs of the poor is not significant. Poor countries and the poor in these countries were left behind in the process of growth. In recent years, world has become much more unequal.

Technological changes and financial liberalization results in the dis-proportionately fast increase in the number of households at the extreme rich and without shrinking the distribution at the poor end. Till date the experience of globalization for the developing countries, including India is not happy. Whether one like or not people's aspirations have changed and it is a common desire to reach the standard at least the content, of western style of living. Thanks mainly to information technology, penetration of ideas and images to become all possible.

Globalization has not only promoted western outlook in countries like India but also wiped out small consumer by widening the gap between the rich and the poor. Globalization impact will be viewed as positive in the sphere of living standard, job opportunities, high consumption pattern, brotherhood at global level, etc. On the other hand, the impact is likely to be negative so far as commercialization and advertising blind aping", demonstration effects, malpractices, children's educational goals, household and rural industries, the feeling of swadeshi, five star culture, liberal education, Indian literary heritage, food habits, etc. are concerned (*Gaur*, 2000).

From above analyses we can conclude that even people do not have money to educate them or fulfilling the basic needs, they wanted to lead their life very comfortably and luxuriously. In early days people's attitude was to work hard and live simple and humble. But now they prepare to work less, feel happy and increase their life style. This type of attitude will lead to corruption, malpractice and terrorism extra. If we would like to avoid these type of reticules, first we should worship our nation and to buy our product, encourage our small producer and to remove fantasy of foreign goods.

References

Balasubramanyam, V.N., "*Conversations with Indian Economists,*" Macmillan, India, Delhi, 2001.

Cheriyan, George, "*Globalization—A Challenges to the Church,*" in R. Jegadish Gandhi and George Cheriyan (ed.) Bangalore, 1998.

Deepak Lal, Rakesh Mohan, Natarajan, I., "Economic Reforms and Poverty Alleviation—A Tale of Two Surveys", *Economic and Political Weekly,* March 24, 2001.

Gaur, G.L., "Globalization and Acculturation: The Indian Perspective," *Economic Affairs*, Vol. 45, Qr. 3, September 2000, p. 183.

Iyer, V.R.K., "Foreign Print Media Incarnating as Indian Fourth Estate," *EPW*, Vol. 29, No. 49, 1994, p. 3082.

"National Accounts Statistics, 2001," Central Statistical Organization, Ministry of Statistics and Programme implications, Governmental India.

NSSO, Government of India, *"Household Consumer Expenditure and Employment Situation in India"*, Round 50th (1994), 51st (1995), 52nd (1996), 53rd (1997), 54th (1998).

"Statistical Outline of India", 2000-01, Tata Service Limited, Dept. of Economics and Statistics, Mumbai, December 2000.

Vyas, V.S., "Globalization: Hopes, Realities and Caging Strategy," *Economic and Political Weekly*, Vol. XXXVII, No. 12, March 23-29, 2002 .

World Bank, *"World Development Indicators,"* Washington, D.C., 2001.

22

Transport Sector Pricing: A Model

Kanaga Sabesan Nagarajan

The reform process initiated in the aftermath of May 1990 balance of payment crisis, aimed at improving the productivity and efficiency of the system. In this process the private sector has been assigned a larger role. With much hope and expectation the power sector was thrown open to private sector investment, including foreign (FDI) ones. Few projects were launched with much enthusiasm. Almost all of them failed to take-off expect a few. Now there is a rethinking on the role of public sector in power development. In the recent conference organized by the union ministry of power it is observed that the central and state power utilities would add 23000 MW and 11000 MW, respectively, of the proposed addition of 44000 MW in the next five years.

While much debate is about the power utilities, less is said about the nationalized road passenger transport (corporation) sector. Probably, the poor financial performance of the transport corporations does not greatly bother the center. Most of the State Transport Undertakings are in existence for about five decades. These utilities, like the power utilities, suffer from the problem of losses due to frequent increase in cost of operation, inadequate tariff revision and irrational tariff structure. For example, the State Transport Undertakings of Tamil Nadu is burdened with the cumulative loss of about Rs. 2035 crores as on March 31, 2001 and an expected loss of Rs. 481 crores for the year 2001-02. The subsidy, which was about Rs. 387 crores in 1990-91, has risen to Rs. 165 crores in 2001-02.

The consequences are:

1. Inability to maintain the service, already 800 buses are off the road for want of spares and periodic maintenance.
2. Inability to replace the backlog of ever aged buses which is 4962 or 29 per cent of the fleet strength.

This raises the question as to whether we have failed to think and act on correct lines. The evidence, as found in the recommendations of the various committees set-up to study the working of nationalized passenger transport reveal that nothing is wrong is policy formulation. However, these recommendations were given a go-by by people in power for reasons well know to them.

Even international financial institutions such as World Bank and International Monetary Fund have been insisting on economic viability. World Bank in its Sector Policy paper on Transport, 1986, laid down viability as one of the criteria for evaluation of a public passenger transport system. This view is also reiterated in its Development Report on Infrastructure, 1994. Further, it observed that public ownership and public operation as one of the four institutional options available to improve the performance of infrastructural provision. For example, the Karnataka Road Transport Corporation, after reorganization, is able to earn profit in three out of four regions during 2001-02.

It is in this connection an attempt is made, by adopting Break-Even Concept, to formulate a fare model, applicable to State Transport Undertakings, taking stark realities like political decision into account. The various policy variables identified are capacity utilization, cost of operation, rate of return, concession and free rider. By manipulating these policy variables desired results could be achieved. In fact, the profile one gets is amazing.

For the purpose of model building, the State Transport Corporation catering to the mass transportation, needs Chennai Metropolitan Area, viz., Metropolitan Transport Corporation is considered. This paper consists of Section 1, A brief overview of MTC, Section 2, Price Model and Section 3, Conclusion.

METROPOLITAN TRANSPORT CORPORATION: AN OVERVIEW

Keeping with the ideas of time then, the Central Committee on Post War Reconstruction, as early as December 1944, recommended that public transport should be state owned and state managed. On this recommendation the City Bus Services in the Madras City was nationalized in stages and the process was complete by July 1948. These services were organized into a departmental undertaking. In 1972, based on the recommendations of The High Power Committee on Tamil Nadu State Transport Department, it was reorganized as State Transport Undertaking under the Companies Act, 1956. The growth of this organization is as given in Table 1.

TABLE 1

Sl. No.	*Item*	*Magnitude*	
		1976-77	*1998-99*
1.	No. of Depots	12	24
2.	No. of Routes	224	568
3.	No. of Services	1333	2547
4.	No. of Buses	1455	2806
5.	No. of Passengers (in lakhs)	6685	15629
6.	K.M. Operated (in lakhs)	990	2223
7.	Total Revenue (in lakhs)	2206	26384
8.	Total Cost (in lakhs)	2199	34010

Source: Management Information System, MTC, Chennai.

The major source of revenue to this Corporation is fare. Under the Motor Vehicle Act, the power to fix fare rests with state Governments. Therefore, interest groups exert pressures and enjoy concessions. It is evident from the concessions extended to monthly season ticket passengers and students. The fact that fare revisions are usually announced by the Government of Tamil Nadu, rather than the management of MTC, reveals that pricing policy is as much a matter of state craft as it is one of economic efficiency.

Similarly, the capability of MTC to minimize costs are severely constrained. Variable costs are determined by a number of exogenous factors such as conditions of roads, density of traffic, periodic occurrence of bottlenecks and traffic diversion. The trade unions of STU's are powerful as they are controlled by political parties. Hence, labour cost is exclusively a function of collective bargaining.

Thus political constraints operate on both the revenue and cost side. It is these constraints which restrain on organization like MTC from being viable.

PRICING MODEL

The objectives laid down at the time of formation of this Corporation, among other things are:

1. To function in accordance with sound commercial principles consistent with its responsibility as a public utility concern.
2. To manage an efficient, adequate, economic and viable system of transport services in its area of operation.
3. To meet the company's requirements of fleet replacement from internally generated cash resources, and to earn a minimum return of 6 per cent on capital investments after meeting interest charges and earmarking necessary funds for depreciation.

Despite these objectives an organization like MTC suffers losses for reasons beyond their control.

The aim of this paper is to formulate a comprehensive model of fare determination, taking stark realities into account, which would render the organization viable and self-reliant, i.e. generate resources for both replacement and augmentation. The various constraints of the model are:

1. The existence of concession seeking pressure groups, such as monthly season ticket passengers and students.

2. The political risk of increasing the fare of ordinary fare paying passengers.
3. The existence of powerful unions which impose strong restrictions on the possibilities of either wage reduction or employment reduction as a cost reduction exercise.
4. The general urban traffic conditions and other exogenous variables which determine the limit to reduction in variable costs.

With these constraints, there are three internal policy variables, which can be used by MTC to give itself some scope of adjusting costs to revenue. These are:

1. improving operational efficiency or capacity utilization,
2. reducing free riders, and
3. the rate of return on capital.

What follows that we develop a generalized accounting model of price determination for an organization like MTC, which is a state owned monopoly, which faces pressure group constraints relating to its costs as well as revenue, and which has to break-even in order to remain viable.

The Break-even condition is:

$$TR = TC \qquad \ldots (1)$$

where TR = Total Revenue and TC = Total Cost.

Expressing equation (1) in term of *average cost and average revenue per passenger kilometer.*

$$\sum_{i=1}^{N} T_i F_i = C \sum_{i=1}^{N} T_i \qquad \ldots (2)$$

where T_i is the number of passengers in the 'i'th group,

F_i the fare per passenger kilometer for the 'i'th group, and

C the average cost per passenger kilometer for all groups.

Introducing free-riders as an element of additional cost to the transporter, we have

$$\sum_{i=1}^{N} T_i F_i = C\,(1 + \lambda) \sum_{i=1}^{N} T_i \qquad \ldots (3)$$

Here $0 < \lambda < 1$ is the fraction of additional passengers traveling as free riders. Since, cross-subsidies exist from the normal-fare paying passengers to the other groups, we can re-write the RHS of equation (3) to give:

$$F\,[\,\beta_1 T_1 + \beta_2 T_2 + \ldots + \beta_N T_N] = C\,(1 + \lambda) \sum_{i=1}^{N} T_i \qquad \ldots (4)$$

where $\beta_1, \beta_2 \ldots \beta_N$ are coefficients of cross-subsidy from any one group to the remaining $N - 1$ groups. In case of the subsidizing group $\beta = 1$; whereas in other cases $0 < \beta < 1$. F is the 'normal-fare' per passenger kilometer. Introducing the capacity utilization variable 0 < 0 < 1;

$$\theta\, F\,[\beta_1 T_1 + \beta_2 T_2 + \ldots + \beta_N T_N] = C(1 + \lambda) \sum_{i=1}^{N} T_i \qquad \ldots (5)$$

Manipulating (5) we get

$$F = \frac{1}{\theta} \left[\frac{C\,(1 + \lambda) \sum_{i=1}^{N} T_i}{\beta_1 T_1 + \beta_2 T_2 \ldots + \beta_N T_N} \right] \qquad \ldots (6)$$

However, we are yet to consider long-run break-even conditions of the transporters. This involves replacement of capital stock. Let $0 < r < 1$ be the rate of return on investment, net of depreciation and let

$$R = r.k \qquad \ldots (7)$$

be the absolute returns on capital stock (k) which the organization would like to earn, in order to raise investible funds for keeping its capital stock constant.

Incorporating (7) in (3), we get

$$\sum_{i=1}^{N} T_i F_1 = C(1+\lambda)\sum_{i=1}^{N} T_i + r.k \qquad \ldots (8)$$

Thus normal fare per passenger kilometer is,

$$F = \frac{1}{\theta}\left[\frac{C(1+\lambda)\sum_{i=1}^{N} T_i + r.k}{\beta_1 T_1 + \beta_2 T_2 \ldots\ldots + \beta_N T_N}\right] \qquad \ldots (9)$$

CONCLUSION

Thus far we have made an attempt to develop an accounting model of price determination for a STU like MTC. This model recognizes that an organization like MTC has to function under structural constraints such as general objection to fare revision, pressure seeking concession, chaotic traffic condition and powerful trade unions. It also recognizes capacity utilization, free rider and rate of return as internal policy variables which can be used by MTC to give itself some scope for adjusting cost to revenue.

An important inference is that, economic efficiency cannot be viewed as being isolated from structural constraints that determine statecraft. Structural constraints involve a combination of market and non-market and non-market roles of price determination. Thus, it is needless to say, these constitute the historically given political back drop to economic process, irrespective of the form of ownership.

References

Brown, S.J. and Sibley, D.S. (1986), *The Theory of Public Utility Pricing*, Cambridge (Mass).

Farris, M.T. and Harding, F.E. (1976), *Passenger Transportation*, Prentice Hall, N.J.

Harper, D.V. (1982), *Transportation in America: Users, Carriers and Government*, Printice Hall, N.J.

Heyel, C. (ed.), (1979), *Concise Guide to Financial Management*, The VNR Concise Management Series, Van Norstrand Reinhold, NY.

Government of Tamil Nadu (1969), *Report of the High Power Committee on Tamil Nadu State Transport Department*, Madras.

Kanaga Sabesan Nagarajan (1987), "Tariff Structure, Revenue and Performance of Pallavan Transport Corporation", Paper Presented at the ICSSR Research Scholars' Workshop, ISEC, Bangalore.

Locklin, P.D. (1972), *Economics of Transportation*, Irwin, Homewood, Illinosis.

Nash, C.A. (1982), *Economics of Public Transport*, Longman, Harlow, Essex.

Sivakumar, S.S. and Batavia, B. (1995), "Some Theoretical Issues Relating to Regulation: The Quasi Autonomous State", *Indian Economic Review*, Vol. XXX, No. 1.

Sivakumar, S.S. and Kanaga Sabesan Nagarajan (1995), "On the Rationality of Break-even Pricing", (mimeo), Department of Econometrics, University of Madras.

World Bank (1986), *Urban Transport: A World Bank Policy Study*, Washington, D.C.

World Bank (1994), *World Development Report: Infrastructure for Development*, Washington, D.C.

23

Drugs and Pharmaceutical Industry in India in the Era of Globalization

INDERPAL KAUR

INTRODUCTION

Pharmaceuticals enjoy a special place as a major research-oriented and knowledge-based industry. Numerous drug formulations for various ailments are invented, patented, produced and marketed throughout the world ever year. India's Pharmaceuticals industry plays a major role not only as a contributor to the economy, but also by providing drugs at affordable prices. Nearly 95 per cent of the domestic demand for pharmaceuticals in India is met through indigenous production. Imports are limited to a few life saving drugs like anti-cancer, cardiovascular, anti-hypertensive and other newer drugs which are not yet cleared for indigenous production. At present, there are over 12,000 manufacturing units of which 2,900 are large scale units and the remaining are small scale of the large scale units, among them 45 belong to multinational companies.

Hence, the industry is truly described as life line industry signifying the crucial role its products play in alleviating the sufferings of diseased persons or controlling various ailments that afflict human beings. Inclusion of this industry in the core sector by the Indian planners in the year 1951 (i.e. the year of launching planned development in the country) was a manifestation of the above mentioned importance of the industry. In the present paper, one attempt has been made to discuss certain important aspects of this industry in India. The paper has been divided into three sections. The first section takes into account the nature and the structure of the industry, second discusses the growth and profitability especially after the initial years of liberalization in the country. Finally, the third and the last part of the paper deals with the policy issues and implications with regard to the Pharmaceutical Industry in India.

The present study is based on the secondary data as collected from various issues of 'Annual Survey of Industries' for the period 1980-81 to 1995-96 along with the data also taken from CMIE, Centre for monitoring Indian Economy Reports. The profitability ratios have been calculated for the period of 1991-92 to 1997-98.

I. NATURE AND STRUCTURE OF THE PHARMACEUTICAL INDUSTRY IN INDIA

The Pharmaceutical Industry produces two kinds of products, i.e. bulk drugs and secondly the formulations Bulk Drugs are active chemical substances in powder form, i.e. the main ingredient in Pharmaceuticals, formulations are the final preparations such as tablets, capsules, injectables and syrups sold as a brand organic product and eighty per cent of the industry's sales are formulations. Major bulk drugs produced in India are anti-biotics, sulpha drugs vitamins, corticosteroids, analgesics and others which treat the diseases like tuberculosis, Asthma, Cardiovascular ailments, diabetes and malaria.

Regarding the firm-wise composition and structure of the Industry, it includes the large firm sector small firm sector and the informal (unorganized) sector. The structure of the industry may be classified into the public sector, the private sector and the foreign sector. The indigenous sector of pharmaceutical industry, including small firms accounts for 90 per cent of production. The remaining 10 per cent is produced by the six companies covered by the Foreign Exchange Regulation Act. Their foreign company equity ranges from 51 per cent to 75 per cent. The locally owned firms have been the greater producers of bulk drugs than formulations. In 1992, most of the top twenty firms had foreign company equity. Multinationals have always been a significant part of the industry. India's NEP adopted in 1991 relaxed controls and foreign ownership. It has attracted new multinationals and triggered others to increase their equity in their subsidiaries to more than 50 per cent. With less protection and control and increased competition a few multinationals have exited in the country. Along with it, the sales of the industry have grown enormously in the last decades and imports too have steadily increased as the government has liberalized trade. The pharmaceutical industry world-wide is characterized by intense R&D expenditure but it has been quite low in India.

II. GROWTH AND PROFITABILITY OF DRUGS AND PHARMACEUTICAL INDUSTRY IN INDIA

Drugs and pharmaceutical is one of the India's most successful industries. State owned enterprises, locally owned private firms and affiliates of major multinational drug companies have enjoyed significant growth since independence. Success has come despite strict price controls and regulations and an intellectual property system that until recently recognized only process patents. In the present part of the paper an attempt has been made to examine the growth pattern in this industry for the period 1980-81 to 1995-96, with the help of the variables like fixed capital, value of output, net value added, total inputs, number of employees, profits, gross fixed capital formation, total addition in stock and total emoluments, etc.

As is visible from Table 1, that all the variables recorded a significant rate of growth, but it was also observed that the average annual compound growth rate for the whole study period was quite low in case of total number of employees and hence truly showed the capital intensity of the industry. Further, some fluctuations are apparent in the growth pattern of the industry but

TABLE 1

Year	*Fixed Capital (Value in Rs. Lakh)*	*Total Inputs (Value in Rs. Lakh)*	*Value of Output (Value in Rs. Lakh)*	*No. of Employees*	*Profits (Value in Rs. Lakh)*	*Gross Fixed Capital Formation (Value in Rs. Lakh)*	*Total Emoluments (Value in Rs. Lakh)*
1980-81	28056	93139	128860	104888	10695	6601	14392
1985-86	56885	190394	261766	117340	19040	12319	28201
1990-91	137977	452539	598945	133267	37933	45240	49340
1995-96	552997	1245995	1683129	204589	145090	147531	112058

Compound Growth Rate

Year	*Fixed Capital*	*Total Inputs*	*Value of Output*	*No. of Employees*	*Profits*	*Gross Fixed Capital Formation*	*Total Emoluments*
1980-81 to 1995-96	21.8	18.69	18.46	4.74	18.74	24.98	12.55
1980-81 to 1984-85	16.93	18.26	18.66	6.44	9.45	14.08	19.43
1985-86 to 1989-90	19.69	23.24	21.87	-9.61	17.22	25.26	14.41
1990-91 to 1995-96	31.59	22.15	22.80	8.23	34.75	25.77	23.30

Source: Various issues of Annual Survey of Industries.

still Drugs and Pharmaceutical Industry grew well for the period under study, i.e. 1980-81 to 1995-96. For example, the value of fixed capital in Rs. Lakh increased from Rs. 28056 to Rs. 552997 from 1980-81 to 1995-96, showing compound growth rate of 21.8 per cent for the whole period. Similarly, the value of output increased from Rs. 128860 lacs to Rs. 1683129 lacs in 1995-96 recording a compound rate of growth of 18.46 per cent for the same period. As far as total profits are concerned, it increased from Rs. 10695 lacs to Rs. 145090 lacs from 1980-81 to 1995-96, hence recording a compound rate of growth of 18.74 per cent for the period. Analysis has also been carried out at five yearly basis and it has been found (it is clearly visible from the Table 1) that the growth rates are quite significant for the period 1990-91 to 1995-96, i.e. 31.59 per cent for fixed capital, 22.80 per cent for value of output and 34.75 per cent for profits. The above trend clearly indicates the positive impact of liberalization on the industry.

Profitability is a simple and frequently used index of assessing business efficiency of a firm, it is highly sensitive economic variable which is affected by a host of factors operating through a variety of ways. Some of them affect the cost of production while other make changes in capital stock, size of the firm, market share and growth rate of firm. It also acts as one of the major indicators of an industry's performance along with growth rate, productivity, technological advance and investment.

The economists differ in their understanding of the nature and source of profit. However, whatever is the source of profit whether the implicit earnings of the entrepreneur and/or reward for risk, uncertainties and innovations, it is essential from business point of view.

With the purpose to see the profitability in Drugs and Pharmaceutical, industries are showing different profitability ratios which have been calculated and the analysis has been done for the period 1991-92 to 1997-98. Different concepts used in various profitability ratios are defined as used by Centre for Monitoring Indian Economy (CMIE) report. In the present study profitability has been measured and compared in two different ways: Firstly, PAT (NNRT) to Gross Sales is calculated in percentage terms and is denoted as P_1 and is taken as first measure of profitability. Here PAT (NNRT) represents Profits After Tax (Net of Non-Recurring Transactions) and gross sale is the income from main business like sales of goods and services, fiscal benefits, trading income. This ratio indicates the selling side of the Drugs and Pharmaceutical Industry and a high profitability margin would mean that company is increasing its profit by merely increasing the price which means the exploitation of consumers and passing on the burden to them only. Secondly, PAT (NNRT) on Total Assets is calculated in percentage terms and is denoted by P_2 and is taken as the second measure of profitability. Here PAT (NNRT) is the Profit After Tax (Net of Non-Recurring Transactions) and total written off. This ratio represents the production side of the Drugs and Pharmaceutical Industry. A high percentage signifies more profitable use of total resources and indicates the efficient use of the capital assets of the Industry.

By comparing P_1 and P_2, one attempt has been made to examine that, whether the Drugs and Pharmaceutical Industry has increased its profits by efficiently using the resources or by exploitation of its consumers. The comparison has been made from 1991-92 to 1997-98. In the first five years of the study period, P_2 is greater than P_1. In 1991-92 P_1 is 0.5 while P_2 is 0.7. In 1992-93, P_1 is 2.2 and P_2 is 3.4. In 1993-94, P_1 is 4.3 where as P_2 is 5.6. In 1994-95 P_1 is 6.3 while P_2 is 6.7. This comparison signifies that in the first five years of study period, profit margins have been increased by the efficient of the resources. But the last two years of study period represent that P_1 is greater than P_2 indicating more exploitation of the consumers. This becomes clear from Table 2 which shows that in 1996-97 P_1 is 4.0 whereas P_2 is 3.9 and in 1997-98 P_1 is 2.6 but P_2 is 2.5.

More or less it may be concluded that the "Drugs and Pharmaceutical" industry is using its resources in an efficient manner during the study period which is very healthy sign, keeping in view the fact that the Indian economy is already capital scarce developing economy. Therefore, the performance of this industry seems to be satisfactory from the profitability point of view.

III. POLICY IMPLICATIONS AND SUGGESTIONS

The "Drugs and Pharmaceutical Industry" is considered an important part of the core sector in India. It has been subject to a lost of government policies, some of which have been important

TABLE 2

Ratios	*Years*						
	1991-92	*1992-93*	*1993-94*	*1994-95*	*1995-96*	*1996-97*	*1997-98*
PAT (NNRT/Gross Sales or P_1)	0.5	2.2	4.3	6.3	5.1	4.0	2.6
PAT (NNRT/Total Assets or P_2)	0.7	3.4	5.6	6.7	5.2	3.9	2.5

Source: CMIE Report, May 99, Corporate Sector.

in the phenomenal growth of the industry. Though some of them have had an adverse effect on technological development. The industry is characterized by a large number of firms, i.e. small and large some of which are technologically dynamic but others are stagnant. The industry's technological status is mixed one, i.e. each of its major sectors, e.g. public multinationals, indigenous, organized and small scale has its own strength and weaknesses.

Generally speaking, it can be said that most firms in the industry lack the resources to conduct product and process research innovations. Research and Development activity is an important dimension of the firm's growth. In this context, finance is an essential requirement for R&D investment and future growth of the firm. To overcome the scarcity of resource firms may consider a variety of options, e.g. merger, collaborations and joint venture with other firms and technology supporting institutions. Moreover, in the changing post-WTO environment the success of the industry depends on its ability to develop cost effective processes for products patented abroad. The industry must therefore create training facilities and an environment supporting basic research, young and creative scientist should be encouraged to ensure the industry's long-term success. Firm pursuing basic research should focus on the treatment for tropical diseases and herbal drugs which would exploit India's variety of plants and its tradition to indigenous medicine.

Further in the changing economic environment and in the world of globalization given the growth of the industry, the government must support the expansion of services for diverse firms. It should urge the industry to be a partner in institution which could be oriented towards applied research. Until recently, the government has behaved like regulator rather than a promoter. In this direction the measures like funding of R&D concession loans to build research facilities, export incentives and progressive removal of price controls and restrictions on mergers where possible, would help the industry to move into the world market. The government should also encourage co-operation among applied technology institutions, universities, higher level scientific technology institutions and industry itself.

References

Dholakia, J.R. (1982), 'Finance of Pharmaceutical Cost: 1980-81', *The Economic Times* (Suppl.) Jan. 28, p. iv, Col. 1-8.

Felker, Greg, Chaudhuri, Shekhar, Gyorgy, Katalin with Goldman, Melvin, (1997), 'The Pharmaceutical Industry in India and Hungar—Policies, Institutions and Technology Development', World Bank Technical Paper No. 392.

Gupta, Amit (1996), 'Economic Reforms, Health and Pharmaceutical, Conferring Legitimacy to the Market,' *Economic and Political Weekly*, Vol. XXXI, No. 48, Nov. 30.

Madanmohan, T.R. (1988), 'Exit Strategies Experience of Indian Pharmaceutical Firms'.

Narayana, P.L. (1984), 'Indian Pharmaceutical Industry: Problem and Prospects,' *Margin*, Vol. 16, No. 2, Jan.

Ramachandran, P.K. (1972), 'The Pharmaceutical Industry in India,' *Economic and Political Weekly*, 26 Feb., Vol. 7, No. 9.

Vernon, J.M. (1971), 'Concentration, Promotion and Market Share Stability in the Pharmaceutcal Industry', *The Journal of Industral Economics*, Vol. 19, Nos. 2-3.

24

A Study on the Trends and Growth of India's Exports and Imports

V.S. GANESAMURTHY AND K. MARIAPPAN

In the modern world no country is self-sufficient. To meet their varied demands, countries have to trade and maintain International Economic Relations. India is no exception to this rule. Foreign trade and capital transactions constitutes a country's external sector.

IMPORTANCE OF FOREIGN TRADE

Foreign trade contributes to economic development in a number of ways. The primary function of foreign trade is to explore means for procuring imports of capital goods without which no process of development can start. It is also a means to price stability. The demand supply imbalance which are likely to be severe in the initial stages of growth can conveniently be corrected through the mechanism of foreign trade. Further foreign trade may help to maintain the tempo of fast rate of growth not only by maintaining the essential supplies but also by ensuring market for manufacturing goods.

Today India's external sector is relatively small. The share of India in international trade is less than one percent. With globalization, trade liberalization and export led growth policy, however India's external sector is presumably seeking its due importance under the new regime of liberalization, privatization and globalization policy. The external sector has strategic role to play in the process of economic development.

METHODOLOGY

In order to know the trends of exports and imports in India since the inception of planning, a time series data are collected from the published sources for a period of fifty years—1950-51 to 1999-2000. In order to know the trends and growth of exports and imports and share of the external sector, this analysis has been made.

The collected data is analyzed on the basis of the statistical tools:

1. Decadal analysis — 5 decades (50 years)
2. Pre-reform period — 1981-91
3. Post-reform period — 1990-2000
4. For the entire period — 50 years
5. Correlation analysis
6. Compound Growth Rate (CGR)
7. Annual Average Trend (AGR)
8. Co-efficient of variation
9. Projection analysis for the next 4 years (2001-04)

1. Decadal Analysis (5 Decades)

Analysis for Whole Period

The import trend value for pre and post-reform decades calculated were 19897.60 and 111618.20. It clearly showed that the large increase in imports were noticed during post-reform decade.

If we compare the trends in increase in imports between pre, post-reform decades period, import value has increased nearly $5^1/_2$ times. The large increase in imports has affected India's balance of trade and India continues to be in adverse balance of trade. In general imports have been always higher than exports. The gap between exports and imports is considerably widening and this has adversely affected the Balance of Payments and foreign exchange position of the country.

TABLE 1

Summaries of Exports by Levels of Decade

Variable	*Label*	*Mean*	*Std. Dev.*	*Cases*	*C.V.*
For Entire Population		22512.9800	41148.3410	50	182.78
Decade	I	597.7778	50.9038	9	8.51
Decade	II	876.0000	263.3224	10	30.05
Decade	III	3269.1000	1705.0227 1	10	32.15
Decade	IV	11050.6000	4290.2019	10	38.82
Decade	V	88028.3636	46408.5403	11	52.71

Note: For the year 1956-57, 1957-58, 1958-59, 1959-60 the data are as per the Fourteenth report of the Estimates Committee (1971-72) of the erstwhile Ministry of Foreign Trade.

Source: DGCI&S, The Hindu Survey of Indian Industry, 1998, p. 470.

Due to slower growth rate of exports against a faster rise in imports there has been not only meager earnings of foreign exchange, but depletion of foreign exchange reserves too.

CORRELATION ANALYSIS

In order to know whether there is any correlation between exports and imports during the pre-reform and post-reform periods. The correlation value is calculated and it showed positive correlation between exports and imports. The calculated correlation value is 0.99 both for export and import for both periods.

Analysis for Pre-Reform Period—I

Dependent	*Mth*	*Rsq.*	*d.f.*	*F*	*Sigf.*	*b0*	*b1*
Exports	LIN	.813	8	34.68	.000	2606.13	1921.54
Exports	COM	.931	8	108.65	.000	5593.58	1.1492
Imports	LIN	.861	8	49.60	.000	7815.13	2196.81
Imports	COM	.947	8	142.45	.000	10548.3	1.1118

Correlations: Imports
Exports .9900
(10)
P = .000

Analysis for Post-Reform Period—II

Dependent	*Mth*	*Rsq.*	*d.f.*	*F*	*Sigf.*	*b0*	*b1*
Exports	LIN	.993	8	1084.97	.000	14190.1	14522.8
Exports	COM	.964	8	216.65	.000	31942.5	1.1911
Imports	LIN	.979	8	369.82	.000	9952.13	18484.7
Imports	COM	.986	8	554.09	.000	36227.5	1.1986

Correlations: Imports
Exports .9936
(10)
P = .000

Analysis for Whole Period

Dependent	*Mth*	*Rsq*	*d.f.*	*F*	*Sigf.*	*b0*	*b1*
Exports	LIN	.527	48	53.39	.000	-29719	2048.33
Exports	COM	.946	48	835.07	.000	189.428	1.1322
Imports	LIN	.533	48	54.77	.000	-35487	2476.50
Imports	COM	.954	48	1001.21	.000	270.163	1.1298

Compound Growth Rate (CGR) and Average Growth Rate (AGR)

Pre-reform Period		**Post-reform Period**	
Export AGR	14.59	Export AGR	15.44
Import AGR	11.04	Import AGR	16.56

Overall Period

Export AGR	115.40
Import AGR	109.19

CGR Value

Pre-reform Period		**Post-reform Period**	
Export CGR	14.92	Export CGR	19.11
Import CGR	11.80	Import CGR	19.86

Overall Period

Export CGR	13.22
Import CGR	12.98

Year	*Exports*	*Imports*	*Fit#1*	*Fit#2*	*Fit#3*	*Fit#4*
1951	606.0	608.0	-27671.0800	214.47475	-33010.26820	305.21874
1952	716.0	890.0	-25622.7510	242.83387	-30533.76830	344.82386
1953	578.0	702.0	-23574.4220	274.94281	-28057.26840	389.56813
1954	531.0	610.0	-21526.0931	311.29738	-25580.76850	440.11840
1955	593.0	700.0	-19477.7641	352.45896	-23104.26850	497.22807
1956	609.0	774.0	-17429.4351	399.06318	-20627.76860	561.74828
1957	605.0	841.0	-15381.1061	451.82968	-18151.26870	634.64061
1958	561.0	1035.0	-13332.7771	511.57328	-15674.76870	716.99144
1959	581.0	906.0	-11284.4482	579.21653	-13198.26880	810.02809
1960	640.0	961.0	-9236.11918	655.80398	-10721.76890	915.13716
1961	642.0	1122.0	-7187.79020	742.51828	-8245.26896	1033.88516
1962	660.0	1090.0	-5139.46122	840.69845	-5768.76903	1168.04187
1963	685.0	1131.0	-3091.13224	951.86059	-3292.26910	1319.60673
1964	793.0	1223.0	-1042.80327	1077.72124	-815.76917	1490.83861
1965	816.0	1349.0	1005.52571	1220.22394	1660.73076	1684.28950
1966	810.0	1409.0	3053.85469	1381.56919	4137.23068	1902.84254
1967	1157.0	2078.0	5102.18367	1564.24847	6613.73061	2149.75497
1968	1199.0	2008.0	7150.51265	1771.08268	9090.23054	2428.70671
1969	1358.0	1909.0	9198.84163	2005.26574	11566.73047	2743.85516
1970	1413.0	1582.0	11247.17061	2270.41388	14043.23040	3099.89720
1971	1535.0	1634.0	13295.49959	2570.62148	16519.73030	3502.13919
1972	1608.0	1825.0	15343.82857	2910.52430	18996.23025	3956.57601
1973	1971.0	1867.0	17392.15755	3295.37110	21472.73018	4469.98045
1974	2523.0	2955.0	19440.48653	3731.10462	23949.23011	5050.00413
1975	3329.0	4519.0	21488.81551	4224.45341	26425.73004	5705.29157
1976	4036.0	5265.0	23537.14449	4783.03571	28902.22996	6445.60896
1977	5142.0	5074.0	25585.47347	5415.47708	31378.72989	7281.98977
1978	5408.0	6020.0	27633.80245	6131.54360	33855.22982	8226.89918
1979	5726.0	6811.0	29682.13143	6942.29268	36331.72975	9294.42982
1980	6418.0	9143.0	31730.46041	7860.24381	38808.22968	10500.46171

(Contd.)

Year	*Exports*	*Imports*	*Fit#1*	*Fit#2*	*Fit#3*	*Fit#4*
1981	6711.0	12549.0	33778.78939	8899.57189	41284.72960	11862.99933
1982	7806.0	13608.0	35827.11837	10076.32610	43761.22953	13402.33954
1983	8803.0	14293.0	37875.44735	11408.67773	46237.72946	15141.42419
1984	9771.3	15831.0	39923.77633	12917.20081	48714.22939	17106.17209
1985	11744.0	17134.0	41972.10531	14625.18975	51190.72932	19325.86525
1986	10895.0	19658.0	44020.43429	16559.01913	53667.22924	21833.58531
1987	12452.0	20096.0	46068.76327	18748.55090	56143.72917	24666.70658
1988	15674.0	22244.0	48117.09224	21227.59556	58620.22910	27867.43040
1989	20232.0	28235.0	50165.42122	24034.43422	61096.72903	31483.52767
1990	27658.0	35328.0	52213.75020	27212.40970	63573.22896	35568.82336
1991	32553.0	43198.0	54262.07918	30810.59603	66049.72888	40184.22612
1992	44041.0	47851.0	56310.40816	34884.55588	68526.22881	45398.52254
1993	53688.0	63375.0	58358.73714	39491.19887	71002.72874	51289.42492
1994	69751.0	73101.0	60407.06612	44719.75289	73479.22867	57944.72951
1995	82674.0	89971.0	62455.39510	50632.86399	75955.72860	65463.62497
1996	106353.0	122678.0	64503.72408	57327.84174	78432.22852	73958.17067
1997	118817.0	138919.0	66552.05306	64908.06917	80908.72845	83554.96677
1998	130100.0	154176.0	68600.38204	73490.59926	83385.22838	94397.04103
1999	139753.0	178331.0	70648.71102	83207.96240	85861.72831	106645.98050
2000	162924.0	204582.0	72694.04000	94210.21297	88338.22824	120484.33970
2001	162924.0	204582.0	74745.36898	106667.26460	90814.72816	136118.36130
2002	162924.0	204582.0	76793.69796	120771.42270	93291.22809	153781.05020
2003	162924.0	204582.0	78842.02694	136740.53690	95767.72802	173735.64570
2004	162924.0	204582.0	80890.35592	154821.18210	98244.22795	196279.54520

It is clear from (the above table) that the export trend has steadily increased. The respective export value for the five decades were 597.77, 876, 3269.10, 1150.60 and 88028.36 crore Rs.

The increase in the value of exports is high during the last decade. This may be mainly due to Liberalization, Privatization and Globalization policies, export promotion measures adopted by the Government.

The co-efficient of variation for the study period is calculated in order to know the stability trends in exports. This analysis shows variations in trends in export. The value remained low in the first decade 8.51 per cent and during the last decade 52.71 per cent. It clearly showed fluctuating trend in exports for the entire period. One can infer from this a raising trend of India's exports.

TABLE 2

Summaries of Imports
By Levels of Decade

Variable	*Label*	*Mean*	*Std. Dev.*	*Cases*	*C.V.*
For Entire Population		27663.9800	49452.1578	50	178.76
Decade	I	785.1111	144.6940	9	18.42
Decade	II	1428.0000	415.4069	10	29.09
Decade	III	3755.2000	2006.1830	10	53.42
Decade	IV	17279.1000	5490.9810	10	31.99
Decade	V	104682.727	58386.5848	11	55.77

Similarly the import trend also showed an uptrend during the study period. The decadal import values were Rs. 785.11, 1428, 3755.20, 17279.10 and 104682.72 crores respectively for various decades.

While comparing exports, India's imports has been very large over the decades. This may be mainly due to heavy imports of capital goods, fertilizers, petroleum and some other essential commodities. Further steep rise in import prices have contributed to the rise of imports in India.

The co-efficient of variation value showed that the imports have very high fluctuation during the third decade 53.42 per cent and in the last decade 55.77 per cent.

2. Pre-reform and Post-reform Decade Trend

TABLE 3

Summaries of Exports
By Levels of Decade

Variable	*Label*	*Mean*	*Std. Dev.*	*Cases*	*C.V.*
For Entire Population		22512.9800	41148.3410	50	182.78
Period		1774.9667	1773.7956	30	99.93
Period I Pre-Reform		13174.6000	6453.9694	10	48.98
Period II Post-Reform		94065.4000	44131.7311	10	46.91

TABLE 4

Summaries of Imports
By Levels of Period

Variable *Label*	*Mean*	*Std. Dev.*	*Cases*	*C.V.*
For Entire Population	27663.9800	49452.1578	50	178.76
Period	2268.0333	2150.9692	30	94.83
Period I Pre-Reform	19897.6000	7167.5213	10	36.02
Period II Post-Reform	111618.200	56567.4100	10	50.67

In order to compare the pre and post-reform decade period the trends in exports and imports analysis has been made. It is clear from the table that, tremendous increase in export value has been noticed during post-reform period compared to pre-reform period. The pre-reform period value of exports stood at 13174.60 crores whereas for post-reform period the value obtained was 94065.40 crores. So it is clear that the export value is almost increased by $7^1/_2$ times between pre and post-reform period. This may be due to changes in trade policy, new economic policy and the opportunities provided through WTO.

In order to know the stability in the trends of exports, the co-efficient of variations has been calculated for pre and post-reforms period. This analysis showed that the variations were high during the pre-reform 48.98 per cent and post-reform period 46.91 per cent.

The calculated CGR for exports during pre-reform period was 14.92 per cent, whereas, for post-reform period the CGR value was 19.11 per cent.

Similarly, the calculated CGR values for imports during pre-reform period was 8.11 per cent, whereas, for the post-reform period CGR calculated value was 19.86 per cent.

The AGR for exports during pre-reform period was 14.59 per cent, whereas, for imports the AGR value was 11.04 per cent. During the post-reform period the AGR value calculated for exports was 15.44 per cent but the import AGR value was 16.56 per cent. This period shows that the import growth trend value is higher when compared to export growth trend.

PROJECTIONS TRENDS

In order to know the projection trend on the basis of collected data linear model and compound growth model was used and the best fit model value is taken on that basis the projection value trends for the years 2001-04 export and import trend values. On the basis of the analysis, the best fit model is taken. On the basis of the projection value the trends for the years 2001-04 for exports were Rs. 106667.24, 120741.42, 136740.53 and 154821.18. Similarly, the import value trend projected were 136118.36, 153781.05, 173735.64, and 196279.54 crore. It is clear from the projection that, import value trend is higher than export trend values.

This clearly points out that imports should be reduced, export the promotion measures may be adopted so as to cover the trade deficit.

SUGGESTIONS

1. India's exports should be increased. Indian export should acquire a high degree of competitiveness in the world market.
2. Sound fiscal and monetary policies are needed to boost our exports.
3. Diversification of foreign trade is a must.
4. India depends on more developed countries for its major proportion of exports and imports. India's exports and imports from the developing countries doesn't grow at a significant rate.
5. Basic infrastructure facilities should be increased in order to boost exports.
6. Tax concession and incentives, capturing new markets, technology, up-gradation policies are essential for increasing exports.
7. Import value should be reduced, import reduction measures, product substitution policies are to be encouraged.
8. The Government of India took several steps for correcting the Balance Of Payment problems. Some of the important measures taken are:
   - Acquisition of foreign currency

- Downward adjustment of the exchange rate of rupee
- Remittances from abroad
- External commercial borrowing
- NRI deposit
- Foreign direct investment
- Trade policy reform

To sum up during the last five decades significant changes are noticed in the exports and imports trend. The value, composition, direction of trade has completely changed. These changes have been made with developmental needs of the economy. India faces two important problems in external sector, first, growing of deficits in the balance of trade, widening trade deficits are posing problems of resource mobilization. Second, India's share in world trade is very small. This tendency needs to be reversed, if India is to play a rightful role in the international division of labour.

9. India should encourage tourism by developing new tourist spots and improving the facilities at the existing ones—
   - Boosting software exports
   - India's export industries should be made more efficient and competent.

References

Dhingra, I.C. (1986), *The Indian Economic Problems*, Fourth Edition, Sultan Chand & Co., New Delhi.

The Hindu Industrial Survey, 1998.

Mithani, D.M. (1998), *International Economics*, Third Edition, Himalaya Publishing House.

P. Subba Rao (2001), *International Business*, Himalaya Publishing House.

General Studies Manual, 2002.

25

Local Developments and Exports in India

UDAY KUMAR LAL DAS

Development through local resources, institutions and people may prove to be a boon for India. Local Development is influencing the Indian exports as follows:

1. AGRICULTURE AND ALLIED RURAL INDUSTRIAL EXPORTS

The products of agriculture and rural industries and vegetables are a prosperous source of exports. The analysis runs as follows:

India's Agricultural Exports

Agriculture is the most crucial sector of local development and the Indian Economy. With 26.8% contribution to the Gross Domestic Product at current prices (GDPs), 18.5% to the total exports and providing employment to nearly 66% of the work force. Agricultural exports from an integral part of India's sustainable agricultural development strategy as well as overall economic development strategy and trade policies and strategies particularly after 1991. To make agricultural export more viable, various policy changes like abolition of minimum export price for all varieties of rice, introduction of market determined exchange rates, decrease in items under restricted list, negative list and items subject to licensing or QRs, decanalization, subsidy on air freight to facilitate exports of perishable products, easy availability of credit for agricultural exports, reductions in import duties on capital goods particularly for green house equipment, plant and machinery necessary for food processing industries. Apart from these internal measures, the most ambitious multilateral Trade Negotiations known as Uruguay Round was also successfully completed during April 12-15, 1994. Its Agreement on Agriculture (AOA) in the form of (a) reduction in tariff by 36 per cent over six years in case of developed countries and by 24 per cent over 10 years in case of developing countries; (b) Reduction in domestic support (AMS) by developed countries has significantly opened up new vistas for Indian agro-exports and these exports are expected to benefit from these changes.

For a number of years the three agriculture-based exports of India, namely, Cotton textiles, Jute and Tea accounted for more than 50% of export earning of the country. If we add the export of other agricultural commodities like cashew kernels, coffee, tobacco, sugar, Vanaspathi, etc., the share of agriculture rose around 70 to 75%. With the economic progress and consequent diversification of production base, the share of agricultural goods in total exports has consistently fallen. However, the Export-Import Policy 1993 placed special emphasis on increasing agricultural exports of horticulture, fish and preparations and agro-products. As a result, the share of agricultural export has increased from 17.6% in 1992-93 to 18.5% in 1998-99.

The Trends

The trend has been fluctuating and the export of these commodities amounted to only Rs. 931 crores in 1998-99 which invites proper policy measures, quality control and proper processing the packing activities. But despite these opportunities or the features of our agricultural exports, a smooth trend of export growth of agricultural and allied products is still not visible. On the one side, we have fluctuating trend of agricultural production and exportable surplus and on the other, changes in the world market, our exports situations have a definite impact on our exports. Being tagged with the global market have also to bear the brunt of international market situation. The slow down in the world economy has led to a declining trend in our exports in recent years.

India's Share in World Exports

India accounted for 16.2 per cent, 7.8 per cent, 7.7 per cent, 3.3 per cent, 3.1 per cent and 2.3 per cent share in world exports of commodities like tea and mate, rice, spices, feeding stuff for animals and unmanufactured tobacco in 1992. India has now emerged as an important exporter of rice and spices in 1998 with rapid increase in export share. Other items experiencing an increase in India's share in world exports include fish and fish preparations, cereals and cereals preparations and feeding stuff for animals. Tea and mate experienced decrease in share in world exports.

The Index

Country-wise export performance of agricultural and allied products show that South Africa experienced highest growth rate of 285% followed by China 119% and Bangladesh 66% in India's exports, indicating increasing importance of these nations. USA, Italy, Belgium and Indonesia experienced slightly higher growth rate (i.e. about 20%) than overall India's exports of agricultural and allied products to the world. Singapore experienced lowest growth rate of 0.28% only while growth of India's exports in U.K. and Germany was not impressive.

TABLE 1

Commodity Concentration Index

Year	*1992-93*	*1993-94*	*1994-95*	*1995-96*	*1996-97*	*1997-98*	*1998-99*	*Trend Value*
Commodity Concentration Index	29.6	31.36	33.83	29.94	26.94	27.83	29.40	-.519 1.272

Source: CMIE, Foreign Trade and Balance of Payments, July 1999.

TABLE 2

India's Exports of Agricultural and Allied Products

Year	*Total Exports (Rs. in cr.)*	*Exports of Agricultural and Allied Products (Rs. in cr.)*	*Percentage of Agro-Exports to Total Exports*
1992-93	53688	9081	16.91
1993-94	69748	12632	18.11
1994-95	82673	13269	16.05
1995-96	106352	20440	19.22
1996-97	118817	24362	20.50
1997-98	130101	24626	18.92
1998-99	13952	25224	17.81
Compound Annual Growth Rate (1992-93 to 1998-99)	17.57	19.58 (6.59)	.313 (1141)

Source: CMIE, Foreign Trade and Balance of Payments, July 1999.

Share of Commodity-wise Exports

The changes in composition of agricultural exports from India in terms of their values and percentages. Among the various agricultural commodities exported, the export of marine product constituted the highest with 18.57% in 1991-92 and this increased eventually to reach 23.22% in 2000-01 though the exports stood highest in the year 1994-95, which was slightly higher than one-forth of the total agricultural exports. Among the remaining commodities, Tea (15.60%), Oil meals (11.86%), Cashew (8.64%), Basmati rice (6.43%), Spices (4.79%), Coffee (4.21%), Tobacco (4.04%) and non-basmati rice (3.30%), where in the order of their increase. However, the order in the year 2000-01 has slightly changed for these commodities with a change in their share. For example, while the shares of basmati rice (7.81%), Spices (5.92%) and Coffee (4.34%) have increased slightly, the share have declined in the case of oil meals (7.46%), tea (7.20%), cashew (6.85%), non-basmati rice (2.86%) and tobacco (4.04%).

Commodities, namely, basmati rice, cashew, cotton raw including waste, marine products, processed fruit and juices, processed vegetables, sugar and mollases, tea, tobacco (manufactured and unmanufactured), though experienced lower growth than exports of growth than exports of group (19.58%), but witnessed double digit growth rate during period 1992-93 to 1998-99. Non-basmati rice recorded highest growth rate of 73.23%, followed by groundnuts (52.732%), floriculture products, guargumeal (each experiencing growth rate of 40%), pulses (32%), caster oil, coffee, spices, seasame and niger seeds, fruits/vegetable seeds, poultry and dairy products, miscellaneous processed items and meat and meat preparations.

The Prospects

The study reveals that, internal and external trade policy reforms though have succeeded in higher increase in exports of agricultural and allied products exports as compared to total exports, their diversification and spread of destinations: but bulk of India's agricultural export still conforms to traditional items. India's share in world exports of meat and meat preparations, fish and fish preparations, cereal and cereal preparations and in vegetables and fruits is very small. Importance of developed countries in exports of agricultural and allied products has also decreased during post-1992 period. The importance of developed countries has declined in country's exports due to increasing concern of quality to safeguard human health, plant and animal life. The country has been facing various sanitary and phytosanitary measures in non-traditional food items (meat, fish, fresh fruits and vegetables) due to lack of information about health and sanitary regulations of these products in target markets. Indian agricultural exports also face domestic constraints in production, storage, distribution, food security, price policy, etc. Higher domestic prices in comparison to international prices of products of bulk exports like sugar; wheat and rice make exports less competitive.

To boost the exports of dynamic agricultural commodities especially fruit and vegetables and flowers and herbs there is need for agricultural research, as agriculture is becoming more capital-intensive, knowledge and skill-based activity. Structural strengths of agricultural sector be improved by investing more in R&D activities, introducing organic farming and environment friendly cropping practices, establishing two-tier organization for production and processing co-operative arrangement for processing and improving contribution of agriculture marketing organizations (*Vyas, V.S.*, 1998). To meet the challenges of sanitary and phytosanitary measures, Indian exporters should be made fully aware of these standards and these standards should be adopted at initial levels (*Vasudeva*, 2000). The country should get the information about standards from enquiry points of trading partners. India should participate in international organizations developing international standards for the products and disseminate information to exporters. Technological and other facilities like inspection and approval procedures be encouraged. Agro-food processing industry needs improved raw material, packing and sanitary conditions.

To increase bargaining power in international market, India should co-ordinate with south developing countries, as trade may neither be free nor fair in future. Therefore, South co-operation should be encouraged. Finally, Agriculture should be given the status of an industry in term of price factors, so as to enable it to avail of various other incentives.

2. THE VEGETABLE EXPORTS

India is one of the important vegetable growing country. In almost all states of India, vegetable of one or another kind is grown throughout the year. It is also a major source of income for the farmers. According to Agricultural Produce Export Development Agency (APEDA), India is the second largest producer of fruits and vegetables in the world. It has a comparative advantage in growing a variety of fruits and vegetables throughout the year because of diverse agro-climate conditions and availability of skilled and cheap labour, while in many of the countries such opportunities rarely exist and growing fruits and vegetables is a clostly affair for them. The export of fruits and vegetables increased from Rs. 216 crores in 1990-91 to Rs. 1067 crores in 1997-98 and Rs. 1212 crores in 1999-2000. In fresh vegetables exported during this year, onion alone accounted 78% of export earnings. Onion is mostly exported to the Gulf-countries. It is necessary to find new international market such as Japan, France, etc. Japan requires yellow onion, while in France, and in Europian Countries thick skin onion is exported from Africa,

Turkistan, Holland, etc. India needs to produce these varieties of onion.

It is evident from that, onion among all other vegetable occupied first rank both in the quantity exported and the value earned in 1996-97. In processed vegetables, preserved cucumber, dried mashrooms accounted larger share. In this section of processed vegetables, also dehydrated onion has a significant share in export earnings. Onion is exported to Gulf countries—Malaysia, Singapore, Shrilanka, Bangladesh and Nepal. The non-traditional vegetables like sweet corn, french bean, cucumber, mashrooms, etc. are exported to Europian countries. There is a great potential for Indian Vegetables in Europian Market during the period from December to April when local production of vegetables is not available in this market. Whereas India produces variety of vegetables during the same period. Spices play a vital role in export of agricultural commodities. The export earning of spices increased from Rs. 239 crores in 1990-91 to Rs. 794 crores in 1995-96, Rs. 1633 crores in 1998-99 and Rs. 1702 crores in 1999-2000. Even in terms of dollars the increase has been recorded from #339 million in 1997-98 to # 393 million in 1999-2000, accounting for 7.2% of our total agri-exports. In future also, they can be an important source of export promotion.

TABLE 3

Area and Production of Some Vegetables in India

Vegetable	*Area ('000 ha)*		*Production ('000 MT)*	
	1995	*1997*	*1995*	*1997*
Potato	1089	1120	17942	18500
Tomato	330	330	5000	5000
Cabbage	220	220	4200	4200
Cauliflower	280	280	5000	5000
Onion	384	40	4058	430
Brinjal	310	310	3300	3300
Beans (Green)	145	145	390	390
Green Peas	148	148	2150	2150
Cucumber & Gherkins	17	17	114	114

Source: FAO, *Quarterly Bulletin of Statistics*, 1997.

TABLE 4

Export of Some of the Vegetables from India

Commodity	*1994-95*		*1996*	
	Qty. (MT)	*Value (Rs. Lakhs)*	*Qty. (MT)*	*Value (Rs. Lakh)*
Fresh Vegetables				
Onion	401281.52	20461.94	427011.77	26521.18
Potato	15755.37	669.30	24935.90	1715.79
Tomato	1072.47	62.94	690.09	41.96
Cabbage	—	—	—	—
Cauliflower & Lettuce	42.58	1.70	20.92	1.95
Carrot & Turnips	—	—	1.260	0.025
Cucumber & Gherkins	1101.37	178.05	9608.76	1448.93
Beans	—	—	1.090	0.33
Misc. Vegetable	40596.96	3500.58	36592	4385.54
	459833.27	24874.51	498862.69	34115.61
Processed Vegetables				
Mixed Vegetables (Frozen)	7694.94	728.70	6095.65	824.44
Dehydrated onions	1261.89	525.74	4124.52	1781.55
Flakes, Powder	67.29	34.84	744.93	246.10
Dehydrated garlic Powder				
Dehydrated garlic	95.15	34.73	233.94	87.85
Dried garlic	48.92	9.85	260.65	76.97
Dried Potatoes	133.05	18.77	899.17	103.22
Other Dehydrated Vegetables	822.88	47.13	52.38	168.01
Preserved Cucumber & Gherkins	6535.31	1178.26	15391.69	2690.19
Dried Mushroom	77.11	1195.72	106.03	2099.44
Preserved Vegetables	327.02	68.49	655.43	133.50
Canned Vegetables	1380.49	461.15	1066.12	455.61
Other Processed	47019.62	9549.03	58645.03	14440.66
Vegetables	—	—	—	—
	65463.67	14652.42	88675.54	23107.54

Source: APEDA.

TABLE 5

Exports of Agricultural Commodities

Commodities	*($ Millions) April-Nov.*		*Share in Total Exports (in Percent)*	
	1999	*2000*	*1999*	*2000*
Basumati Rice	274.0	318.6	1.15	1.12
Non-Basumati	187.9	101.4	0.79	0.36
Wheat	—	0.1	—	—
Other Cereals	1.1	5.3	—	0.02
Pulses	70.1	75.5	0.30	0.27
Sugar	2.0	42.1	0.01	0.15
Cashew	409.0	283.8	1.72	1.00
Coffee	215.8	140.8	0.91	0.50
Tea	303.2	249.3	1.28	0.88
Processed Fruit & Juices	59.8	75.0	0.25	0.26
Fresh Fruits	45.4	48.2	0.19	0.17
Processed Vegetables	28.7	32.0	0.12	0.11
Fresh Vegetables	44.9	61.1	0.19	0.22
Groundnuts	54.1	30.8	0.23	0.11
Castor Oil	171.7	132.6	0.72	0.47
Seasame & Niger Seeds	44.3	70.8	0.19	0.25
Spices	283.5	220.2	1.19	0.78

Source: CMIE, *Monthly Review,* March 2001.

TABLE 6

Export of Onion from India

Year	*Export ('000 M.T.)*
1990-91	2.89
1991-92	4.60
1992-93	3.96
1993-94	4.47
1994-95	4.10
1995-96	4.35
1996-97	5.13
1997-98	4.18

Source: NHRDF, Annual Report, 1997-98.

THE CONCLUSION

It can be concluded that there is large potential to vegetable export provided appropriate incentive and policy measures are undertaken by the Government. The other suggestions can be summarized as follows:

(i) Cooling and Storing facilities are *sine-qua-non* for agricultural commodities especially vegetables and fruits export. Hence, a substantial investment is needed to be made in this vital sector.
(ii) The high rate of air freight for agricultural commodities especially vegetables and fruits export and the non-availability of air cargo space are major draw-backs in exporting vegetables and fruits except onion. Therefore, special attention is required to overcome this drawback.
(iii) Proper grading, Packaging and Quality Control measure are required for agricultural commodities especially vegetables and fruits exports.
(iv) Research, extension, packaging and Quality Control measures are required for agricultural commodities especially vegetables and fruits exports.
(v) There should be consistency in the export policy of the Government.

A separate Price Commission of agricultural commodities especially vegetables and fruits should be set-up.

The immediate impact of rise in agricultural exports will be an increase in the prices of agricultural commodities in the national market. And if these commodities include wheat and rice or other cereals, the vulnerable section of the society will be hit hard. This will necessitate a more effective implementation of the Public Distribution System. This may also result in increase in food subsidies. One important way of solution is to develop and adopt cost effective technology for production of agricultural products. Reduction in the cost of production will surely keep the internal prices of agricultural commodities stable even when these are exported. In this respect, National Agricultural Research System (NARS) needs to be revamped.

There exists a large potential for increasing exports of quite a few agricultural commodities produced in India. However, despite the great potential for increase in agricultural exports, various economists suggest caution in completely freeing exports, especially of foodgrains to other countries. There is a need to regulate the exports, not only for reason of food security but also for some other politico-economic considerations. Specific steps have to be earnestly taken to generate this surplus. This implies development of infrastructure especially irrigation and power research, extension of new technology to uncovered crops and areas, development of market infrastructure and a more efficient use of existing resources. Further, in view of the increasing competition in the world market, it will also be necessary to pay special attention to the improvement in the quality of the products to be exported.

There is need to change the rural mindset on agro-exports. A farmer as well as a labour working in the field should be made to think about export and quality of the product. A rural infrastructure development fund needs to be established at every district level in the country to support the landless labourers and small marginal farmers.

On the whole, the above exports for local developments need a big push to compete with the International Standard.

References

Annual Report (1998), HHRDF, New Delhi.

CMIE, *Foreign Trade and Balance of Payment*, July 1999 and July 2000.

FAO, *Quality Bulletin of Statistics*, 1997.

Govt. of India, *Economic Survey*, 1993-94, 1994-95 and 1999-2000.

"Impact of Cost of Transportation on Price and Profitability of Onion Production in Nasik District," Ph.D. thesis (Unpublished).

News Letter, Vol. XVIII, April, June 1998.

Vasudeva, P.K. (2000), UAE Health Standards," *Economic and Political Weekly*, Vol. XXXV, No. 32, August 5-11.

Vyas, V.S. (1998), 'Agricultural Trade Policy and Export Strategy', *Economic and Political Weekly*, Vol. XXXIV, No. 13, March 27-April 12.

26

Prospects of Agro-Processed Food Exports under Globalization

V.P. Tripathi, V. Prakash and Arun Bhadauria

INTRODUCTION

India is an agricultural country as it is predominantly, the main source of livelihood for most part of Indian population. But last decade of economic reforms has witnessed the growth of agriculture as vital factor of economic development in India. Also in the last 50 years of planning, Agriculture has not only emerged as an industry, which has helped India to become self-reliant in food production and employment generation but has also helped it to earn foreign exchange. In true sense, Agriculture accounts for approximately 33 percent of India's GDP and employs nearly 62 percent of the population. Even after heavy industrialization, agriculture provides job for more than half of total population of the country. As an industry, it accounts for 18.56 percent of India's exports directly including rice, cashew nuts, coffee, tea, horticulture and floriculture products, etc. Since 43 percent of India's geographical area is being used for agricultural activity, it becomes pre-requisite to develop agri-business at priority basis, so as to satiate needs of huge population and to acquire a respectable status in world trade.

India, the second largest populated country in the world, has emerged to be as a big market for multinational companies especially after the start of new world order for global trade. Today every developed country wants to venture its products in Indian markets. Population explosion, a big hurdle in economic development of India, has proved to be a boon to multinational producers. Their goals have further been made easier by weakening cultural fabric of Indian masses, which has become victim of onslaught of western culture. It not only provides big market for their product directly, but they have also started making entry in Indian markets through mergers, acquisitions and collaborations with local manufacturers so as to encash the benefit of familiarity of them.

Since 1991, the government has initiated a series of radical changes in its policies relating to industry, trade, finance, foreign investment and fiscal finance. The structural adjustments, when put together, constitute the new economic policy, which marks a total shift from the previous policies. Consequently, government has announced several policy measures to make agriculture in general and agri-business in particular, globally competitive. As a result of that recently it has established several Agri-Export Zones (AEZ) on the lines of Special Economic Zones (SEZ) to promote agri-business both within and outside of the country.

In the age of globalization when whole world is emerging as global market, every nation has to open up its boundaries and has to participate in the global market. India has also become an active partner of this global market by accepting the membership of WTO (It is noteworthy to mention that India is one of the founder member of this world trading system), so it cannot escape from challenges, which has been put forth by many multinational companies by marketing the traditional Indian products in domestic market. The traditional mode of production and marketing needs reorientation to suits the need of global market. Agri-business, which in ancient India, use to be very rich in global market, can still be a potential foreign exchange earner. There is need to concentrate upon quality besides quantity in agri-business like all other vital sectors of economy. The time has come to reconsider potential of our agri-business to suit and serve our national interests in global trade in the changing world economic environment. India has great potential in many vital sectors of economy including IT, science & technology and agriculture as for as exports are concerned. There is need to have fresh look to redesign our strategy on agriculture production and trade. Indian agricultural sector like other sector of economy is also facing new challenges from globalization. The problem has further intensified after WTOs inclusion of agriculture. Under Agreement on Agriculture (AoA) in WTO constitution, despite protest from developing countries, the trading of agricultural products has been included in WTOs jurisdiction.

Therefore, this paper evaluates the state of agro-processed food industry of India and its place in global market. Global market unlike domestic market is boundaryless. Indian agriculture though advancing day-by-day, still lags far behind the mechanized agriculture farming techniques of developed countries. There is an urgent need to reform our agriculture, and recent policy changes in agriculture are well beginning in this direction. India possesses great opportunities in agro-food production. The identification of potential areas of agro-food and its promotion can put India on agro-food business map of the world in a respectable position.

Now one must ask the question why should India go for agri-business? The answer is the growing realization of the following intrinsic advantages:

1. It is one of the countries best blessed with a natural bounty in terms of flora and fauna.
2. India is the largest producer in the areas of fruits and vegetables, tea and jute and a closed second or third in other products.
3. A large coastline with a thriving fishing trade.
4. Varied Agro-climatic Zones.
5. A good area for Foreign Direct Investments.
6. Skilled and cheap Labour.

STATE OF AGRO-FOOD PROCESSING INDUSTRY

The first and foremost issue of agri-business in India is the quality of agro-products and the total capital investment in this sector. As far as investment is concerned, Table 1 shows the targeted cumulative investment of Rs. 720,000 million with the total turnover of value added products around Rs. 800,000 million. It is satisfactory if targeted output of food processing industry around Rs. 2,500,000 million upto 2008, is achieved by the end of Tenth Plan. Meanwhile quality in agro-products is a key issue that India must consider to enhance its exports to developed countries.

TABLE 1

Agro Products and Food Processing sector statistics

(In billion Rupees)

1.	Turnover	2,500
2.	Turnover of Value Added Products	800
3.	Investment (Targeted)	720

Source: Statistical Outline of India, 2000-01.

While India has been rapidly opening up its market and cutting down on quantitative restriction in imports, other countries were not as vigorous in opening up their markets. The major constraints of Indian food processing industry in this concern are firstly, high cost of packaged foods due to high local taxes on the total retail price and secondly restrictions, imposed by EU countries on imports from developing countries even from those countries who are registered with WTO on issues like social and environmental clauses, etc. Thirdly, low quality due to poor technology and malpractices of putting bottlenecks and middlemen between the farm-gate and the retail markets. In this concern, confederation of Indian Food Trade Industry (Affiliate to FICCI) promises to adopt following measures—

1. It will take up with the government the issue of reducing excise on packaged food products.
2. It will organize exhibitions with the CIDEX Ltd. for the

launch of new products, identifying marketing agents and joint venture partners and enhance public awareness.

3. Indian Institute of Packaging under the commerce ministry will organize the food technology conference where more than 200 exhibitors will be showing their products and services.

Following the measures taken by FICCI and other governmental and non-governmental organizations, food processing industry is estimated to reach a gross value addition of Rs. 5 lakh crores, but value added foods are expected to grow at a much faster rate, i.e. to expand from Rs. 80,000 crores to Rs. 2.25 lakh crores by 2005 A.D., some 20 crore people will move from subsistence foods, like cereals and pulses, to modern processed food which is better in quality in terms of basic nutrients. The expected growth of production of agro-food in general and agro-processed food in particular will not only enhance the domestic consumption level of such products, but it will also augment the share of India's global trade (It is estimated to be very low, i.e. around 0.6 percent of total world trade). It is widely believed that, if agricultural production of the country is brought near to global standards, the share of India in world trade might reach to 1 percent level.

AGRO PROCESSED FOOD MARKET—AN OVERVIEW

Agriculture is the backbone of the Indian Economy, as it contributes 33% of GNP. Two-thirds of the country's work force derives its livelihood from agriculture and allied sector. Economic reforms over the past few years have improved the profitability of agriculture. A lot has been done to modernize the pattern of agriculture by improving production technologies, including upgrading of handling and storage facilities, so as to make Indian Agriculture globally competitive.

The Food Processing Industry in India is one of the largest in terms of production, consumption, Export and growth prospects. The government has accorded it a high priority with a number of fiscal relief, and incentives to encourage commercialization, and value addition to agricultural production for minimizing pre/post-harvest wastage, generating employment and export growth. Important sub-sectors in food processing industries are: Fruit and Vegetable processing, Fish processing, Milk processing, Meat and poultry processing, packaged/convenience foods, alcoholic beverages and soft drinks and grain processing, etc. As a result of several policy initiatives undertaken since liberalization in August 1991, the industry has witnessed fast growth in most of the segments. As per a recent study on the food-processing sector, the turnover of the total processed food market is approximately Rs. 250,000 crores (US $ 69.4 billion) out of which value added food products comprise Rs. 80,000 crores (US $ 22.2 billion). Since liberalization in August 1991, and uptill Feb. 2000, proposals for projects of over Rs. 53,800 crores (US$ 13.4 billion) have been proposed in various segments of the food and agro-processing industry. Besides this government has also approved proposals for joint ventures, foreign collaboration, industrial licenses and 100 percent export oriented units envisaging an investment is over Rs. 9,100 crores (US$ 18.2 billion). Processed food exports were approximately at Rs. 13,500 crores (US$ 3.2 billion) in 1998-99. Out of these export, rice accounted for 46 percent whereas marine products accounted for over 34 percent.

India is the world's second largest producer of fruits and vegetables, but hardly 2 percent of the produce is processed. Size of semi-processed and ready-to-eat packaged food industry is over Rs. 4,000 crores (US$ 1 billion) and is growing at over 20 percent per annum. Exports from Agro-food processing sector in the country have gone up from Rs. 28.5 billion in 1991-92 to an estimated Rs. 107.7 billion in 2000-01. The agro-food-processing sector in India employs around 18 percent of the country's industrial force and it ranks fifth in terms of its contribution to the GDP. India's strength in the agro-processed foods sector includes supply of raw material as well as trained and cheap manpower.

Global buyers are seeing improvement in quality, quantity, variety and price of fresh and processed fruits and vegetables from India as a result of the policy initiative taken by government of India by creating product specific Agri-Exports Zones in various parts of the country. The AEZs help buyers to identify areas for sourcing specific products at more competitive prices. A total of

10 such zones already have been approved. Included are those for lychees in Uttaranchal, pineapples in West Bengal, gherkins in Karnataka, potatoes and mangoes in Uttar Pradesh, vegetables in Punjab and grapes/vines in Maharashtra. Other AEZs waiting to be approved are for walnuts and apples in Jammu & Kashmir, apples in Himachal Pradesh, ginger in Sikkim, passion fruit in Manipur, organic pineapples in Tripura, onions, potatoes and garlic in Madhya Pradesh, oranges, mangoes and pomegranates in Maharashtra and mango-pulp and vegetables in Andhra Pradesh. Because sporadic and disjointed efforts from various organizations are not enough to promote exports basis approach is being incorporated. Initiated by the Agricultural and Processed Food Products Export Development Authority (APEDA), the project identifies potential export products and geographical regions where they are grown. The next step involves intensive research on products to determine the difficulties encountered at each stage. This involves production, marketing and the shortcomings in the marketability of the item. Corrective time-bound measures will then be delegated to specific government agencies. The APEDA will ensure, that the measures are completed on schedule. Export of quality products will have specific niche, markets identified and will be promoted extensively the program companies, all the existing subsidies and incentives provided by control government agencies. It also introduces new scheme and incentive on case-study basis.

To draw exact conclusion about the status of agro-processed food exports in India, we conducted a brief survey of Agra Division, which happens to be one of the most fertile region of western U.P. and therefore a potential producer of agro-products, so a sample survey was conducted of the area to collect data about the production of agro-products. The major Agro-food products being grown in this region are pulses, groundnuts and other oilseeds (soyabean, sunflower and mustard, etc.), potato, tobacco and sugarcane, etc. Among these Agro Food Products potato has emerged to be a major crop being grown in the region. Though there are other crops, which can also be grown up in the region with larger production, but this is possible only if proper infrastructural support is provided. Though potato has not contributed much in Agro-Food Exports till last decade, but now it is emerging as main foreign exchange earner for the region. Total price of production is increasing at rapid rate in the first three years of Ninth Plan. During this period total price of production has increased two and half times. (Table 2) While its average production (Quintal per Hectare) has not shown much increment in absolute and relative terms, however its production (In Metric Tons) has increased by 25.6 percent. (Table 4) The increase in production of the crop has resulted because of increase in the area of cultivation for the crop. It has been observed that most of the cultivation of the crop in the region is undertaken by using traditional methods due to lack of proper infrastructural support. As a result of this, the average productivity of the crop in the area is far below than the major grower developed countries. The productivity of potato production in the region is 27.19 hectare per metric ton.

TABLE 2

Cost of Production of Potato of Agra Division

(In crore rupees)

Region	*1996-97*	*1997-98*	*1998-99*
Agra	40.27	33.97	100.71

Source: Divisional Statistical Superintendent, Agra.

TABLE 3

Total Irrigated Area under Potato Production

(In Hectares)

Period	*Total Area*	*Irrigated Area*
1996-97	68088	68088
1997-98	66482	66473
1998-99	84841	84841

Source: Divisional Statistical Superintendent, Agra.

TABLE 4

Total Average Production

(In Quintal per Hectare)

Region	*1996-97*	*1997-98*	*1998-99*
Agra	269.66	195.36	272.95

Source: Divisional Statistical Superintendent, Agra.

The region because of world famous historical monuments like Taj Mahal, Buland Darwaja, etc. are the main places for tourist's attraction and has well developed tourism industry along with shoe, carpet and foundry and forging industry. However, there has been lack of exploring the possibility of agro-food exports from the region inspite of its being a prospective and potential producer. Now it has better prospects for international trade due to its inclusion in Agri-Export Zones (AEZ) recently. The major problem related to potato exports and production in this area is more associated with infrastructural constraints of the region and less with the geographical and climatic condition. Till Dec. 2000, there were only 25 marketing co-operatives that were engaged in purchase and sale of Agro-products. Though facilities regarding irrigation are satisfactory as almost whole area under cultivation of potato is irrigated by using different means of irrigation. (Table 3) In 2000-01 the target of potato production was 22 lakhs metric tons while the actual production has been 21.21 lakh metric tons. Thus it can be concluded from the above observations that until unless there is marked improvement in the infrastructural support, there is less likelihood of desired growth in the production of the crop. In pursuance of the economic reforms, the government of U.P. has taken several measures including consultancy assistance to augment its export potentials. A great emphasis has been made to increase the exports to SAARC nations where trade restrictions are minimum. It is important to note that during last three to four years the exports of the state have significantly improved as a result of these measures.

As far as Infrastructural facilities are concerned, government is making arrangements for proper storage facilities. Significantly, the central government has announced several incentives to augment the food preservation potentials in the country. The subsidy on cold storage has been increased multifold, so as to attract investment in this field. Presently, about twenty-five lakh rupees subsidy is provided for constructive cold storage of cost not less than one crore rupees. Several other similar incentives have been provided to the people so as to enhance food preservation facilities. It is believed that setting up of AEZs will certainly help to provide basic infrastructure in this sector. At present, there are 96 cold storages in Agra district only with the storage capacity of 7.6 lakh tones. (N.H.D. and Director

Horticulture, Agra) Now Agra lies in Agri-Export Zone (with Kannauj, Baghpat, Ghaziabad, etc.), it has better chances for development of Agro-Food Exports in this region.

PROSPECTS OF AGRO-FOOD EXPORT UNDER WTO REGIME

Agriculture has been one of the most divisive issues in WTO, especially because EU and Japan were totally opposed to further liberalization of agriculture while USA was pressing for greater market access. The fourth ministerial conference held at DOHA, in its declaration, provides firstly for negotiations 'which shall aim', to eliminate tariffs including the elimination of tariff peaks, high tariffs and tariff escalation as well as non-tariff barriers in particular on products of export interest to developing countries, secondly, it gave a substantial clarification on the rights of the member-states to override the patent right in the interest of public health and access to medicine, thirdly, provide for negotiations on anti-dumping and anti-subsidy measures. Under the Agreement on Agriculture (AoA) market should be distortion free, which is perhaps in tune with the concept of *lassiez-faire* policy of classical economists. Accordingly greater market access is to be provided with greater competition by removing various restrictions on global trade. The major provisions of AoA are first, market access (Tarrification), second, reduction in domestic support and third, export competition. Thus AoA aims for ending the era of protectionism and it will lead to free, efficient and competitive world trade of agro-foods. Though the Indian representatives to Doha summit have claimed their visit as successful for having represented the case of developing countries in general and India in particular to provide safeguards in international trade in the interest of equity, yet for effectively facing the challenges put before our country, we have to have consistent and suitable EXIM policy. It is important to mention here that India's exports performance in three major world markets (EU, USA and Japan) though fluctuating, has increased in the post-Uruguay round era. (Table 3) As far as Tarrification is concerned, it refers to conversion of all Non-Tariff Barriers (NTBs) into equal tariff barriers. Developing countries like India where no item is under QRs, has to reduce tariff by 24% in 10 years. Therefore, fluctuating growth in export to major market may be superficial since all these markets belong to developed countries. The present condition of Indian exports seems to be satisfactory but this is only a superficial growth. It is worth-mentioning here that Indian exports in developed countries do not face tough Tariff and Non-Tariff Barriers (NTBs). The situation of exports may witness a downward trend in future when developed countries will replace their tariff barriers by NTBs especially after year 2005. It is also important to mention here that the nature of NTBs is such that it may even put blanket ban on some of our exports thereby causing hurdles to our exports. On the other hand, India will have to reduce its Tariff Barriers by 24% in next three years. While most of the QRs have already been removed, the exports of developed countries will therefore have easy access to Indian market. As a result of that, India has to face tougher challenges in global market after year 2005. In nutshell the Globalization has put a question mark on our export performances in the change scenario. Needless to mention here that many a times it has been outcry of many developed countries that they are coming forward to remove non-tariff barriers while countries like USA, UK are imposing restrictive impediments, viz. environmental concerns, labour standards, child labour and so on. Developing countries would opt all the necessary steps to overrides such restriction and also defend themselves.

TABLE 5

Progress of Potato Development in the Region in 2001-02

Particulars	*Target*	*Achieved*
Area (Hectare)	75450	78004
Production*	22.00	21.21
Productivity**	—	27.19

*In Lakh metric tons.
**In Hectare per metric ton.
Source: Director, Horticulture, Agra.

Another major provision of AoA is reduction in domestic support. It has suggested some (five) categories like Aggregate Measurement of Support (AMS). In India AMS has been found negative in last decade. It provides that Indian policy-makers are going on the right path to accept global challenge. Obviously WTO has therefore granted India freedom not to make any cut in subsidies. But there is high degree of discrimination when developed countries provide 30 to 45 percent Producer Subsidy Equivalent (PSE, a working alternative of AMS). Thus Indian Policy-makers will do everything to strengthen this sector but they must negotiate at WTO to sort out all such practices.

REFERENCES

'Trends in Agricultural Marketing in India' by Dipankar Guha.

Address of Mr. Muthiah, Senior Vice-President, Federation of Indian Chamber of Commerce and Industry (FICCI), 6th Feb. 2002.

Yojana, Jan. 2001, p. 34.

National Agriculture Policy, India.

Speech of Commerce Minister Mr. Murasoli Maran presenting EXIM Policy (2002-07) on 31st March, 2002.

Report of Ministerial Conference of WTO, Doha.

Yojana, Vol. 45, No. 1, Jan. 2001, pp. 12-13.

Md. Abdus Salam (2001): " Problems and Prospects of India's Exports under WTO regime: A study of Agricultural Commodities," IEA 84th Conference, Vellore, 28-30 Dec. 2001.

27

Implications of Intellectual Property Rights for Indian Pharmaceutical Industry: Revision of Balance between Patent Rights and Public Interest

B.P. Chandramohan

The interests of the Indian pharmaceutical industry and the indigenous communities are likely to be affected by the TRIPs agreement of WTO. TRIPs agreement is a part of globalization process by removing all the barriers of economic integration for economic interdependence. Unlike the other agreements of WTO, it is perceived that TRIPs ensures more power to control the activities of developing countries by financially powerful developed countries. Under this agreement it is mandatory to accept product patents, which will ultimately influence the growth of Indian pharmaceutical industry and the prices of drugs. Indian Patent Act, 1970 will be amended in lines with the TRIPs agreement and it will come into force from Ist January, 2005, completing the transition period of 10 years available to India under Article 65 of TRIPs agreement. In this paper an assessment is made on the growth performance of pharmaceutical industry in India and the possible impact of TRIPs on prices, employment and public sector. It also focuses on the evolution of patent, patent policy and patent policy shift in India. Finally, the opportunities offered by the TRIPs to the growth of pharmaceutical industry in India and the possibility of getting drugs available to the common man at affordable prices are also discussed.

PHARMACEUTICAL INDUSTRY IN INDIA

Pharmaceutical industry is largely a research-oriented and knowledge-based industry. India is sufficiently endowed with talented human resource to pursue improved inventions. At present the size of the Indian pharmaceutical industry is $ 3.8 billion ranking 12th largest in the world. It grew from a few MNCs in 1950's to 23,000 small, medium and large drug factories, which include 16,000 licensed pharmaceutical companies in 2002. It is one of the high skilled industries in India that has a comparative advantage over its competitors around the globe because of its skilled personal at relatively low wages.

COMPETENCE OF INDIAN PHARMACEUTICAL INDUSTRY

The United Nations Industrial Development Organization (UNIDO) has classified 190 countries into various categories based on the degree of development of pharmaceutical technology and industrial production.[1] Out of the 190 selected countries, no developing country represented in the category of countries with significant research base. The second category is countries with innovative capabilities which formed 17 out of the total 190 countries[2]. Among the 17 countries with innovative capabilities in pharmaceutical industry, only 5 countries represented from developing world that includes India, besides Argentina, China, Mexico and Republic of Korea[3]. India is not only self-sufficient but also self-reliant in the production of drugs. India has the technology to produce chemical intermediaries and raw materials for their needs but also export them at various competitive prices.

INDIAN PHARMACEUTICAL INDUSTRY PRIOR TO THE PATENT ACT, 1970

The pharmaceutical industry in India was merely engaged in producing formulations based on imported bulk drugs in 1947. At this period the value of drugs produced amounted to mere Rs.10 crores. However, it has achieved tremendous progress at the turn of the 21st century. It is because of a series of measures undertaken by the Government of India to enhance the growth of the industry since 1947. At the beginning, the Industrial (Development and Regulation) Act was passed in 1951, subsequently the pharmaceutical industry was brought under the purview of the Director General of Technical Development (DGTP). It had a development council to suggest various measures for fostering growth. A Pharmaceutical Enquiry Committee was formed under the Chairmanship of General Bhatia and it submitted the report in 1954. Its recommendations covered a wide range of aspects including licensing, foreign collaboration, production of bulk drugs and the sale and distribution of medicines. Since then, the industry registered a high tempo of growth during the 1950's and 1960's. The total investment in the industry grew at 8.8 per cent per annum between 1952 and 1962. The pattern of growth was the same for both the production of bulk drugs and formulations.

Even after Independence, the Indian pharmaceutical industry was controlled by a few MNCs functioned under the guidance of the colonial Patent and Design Act, 1911. They were mainly engaged in the import of drugs from their country origin. Between 1947 to 1957, out of the 1704 drugs and pharmaceutical patents in India 99 per cent were held by foreign MNCs. They controlled more than 80 per cent of the market share. The activities of MNCs during this period have shown that they did not come forward either to invest or to transfer technical assistance to establish drug production centres in India. The drug prices were also one of the highest in the world. Therefore, the Government of India wanted to take some measures to improve the domestic production of bulk drugs and formulations. Two important developments during this period were the establishment of Hindustan Antibiotic Ltd. Company (HAL) in 1954 with the assistance of WHO and UNICEF and the Indian Drugs and Pharmaceutical Ltd. (IDPL) in 1961 with the help of the USSR.

THE INDIAN PATENT ACT OF 1970

The idea of Intellectual Property Rights was thought over 500 years ago. The first national law on patent was the Venitian Law of 1474.[4] The history of patents in India, dates back to the first Indian Patent Law, which was enacted in 1856 in the same lines as the British Patent Act of 1852. There was no proper institution to administer the patents till the appointment of the Controller of Industrial Patents and Designs Act in 1911.

In order to study more about the patents two expert committees were appointed in the Independent India to provide suggestions on the type of patent system that India should follow. In 1948, the Patent Enquiry Committee (1948-50) was appointed and it submitted its report in 1950 which stated that "the Indian patent system has failed in its main purpose, namely, to stimulate inventions among Indians and to encourage the development and exploitation of new inventions for industrial purposes in the country so as to secure the benefits thereof to the largest section of the public."[5] The Government of India appointed the Justice Rajagopala Ayyangar Committee (1957-59) in 1957 and it submitted the report in 1959 which noted that the foreign companies acquiring patents not "in the interests of the economy of the country granting patent or with a view to manufacture there but with the object of protecting an export market from competition from rival manufacturers particularly in other parts of the world." Thus India, " is deprived of getting, in many cases, goods . . . at cheaper prices from alternative sources because of the patent protection granted in India[6]. The reports inferred that foreigners held 80 to 90 per cent of the patents in India and were exploiting the system to achieve monopolistic control of the market.[7] These committees recommended that the patent system of India should focus more on access to resources at cheaper prices to the people.

Based on the recommendations of Patent Enquiry Committee (1948-50) and Ayyangar Committee (1957-59) a bill was introduced in the Parliament in 1965, it lapsed in 1965 and in 1966. This bill was again reintroduced in the Parliament in 1967 and eventually passed as the Indian Patent Act of 1970. The rules of the Act were passed in 1971 and the act along with the rules came into force in 1972.

The Act does not encompass the product patents on medicines, agricultural products and atomic energy. Even the process patents in India is allowed for 5 to 7 years which is the most suited patent for the developing countries. This favourable aspect of the Indian Patent Act, 1970 helped India become self-sufficient in the production of basic drugs. Moreover, Indian scientists developed new process for 107 drugs. Many Indian companies successfully compete with the global players in the production of bulk drugs from basic stages.

The Industrial Revolution of England and subsequent industrialization in Europe on the lines of Free Trade provoked criticisms on patent laws. In Netherlands and in Switzerland debates and discussions resulted in cancellation of patent laws. However, the principle of public interest before commercial interest was strictly emphasised in the VIIIth Paris Convention. Under this, countries were free to decide on the areas of non-patentability, duration of patents and the exclusive rights given to the patent holders. Many of the developing and developed countries accepted the principle of Paris Convention while enacting their patent laws to serve as policy instruments for strengthening their pharmaceutical industry. These measures include exclusion of pharmaceutical products from patent protection, process patents only for a period of 7 to 10 years, patent protection only to the domestically manufactured drugs and imports not qualify for patent protection and compulsory licensing. The provision enshrined in the Paris Convention helped India along with Argentina, Brazil, China, Republic of Korea and Mexico to achieve spectacular growth in the pharmaceutical industry.

Countries with sophisticated pharmaceutical industry with significant research base once persistently resisted product patents citing the reason that a patent-free environment is indispensable for the technological development of pharmaceutical industry. This argument continued till they reached the stage of supremacy in international competitiveness in pharmaceutical industry. These countries accepted product patent only in the latter half of the 20th century. For instance, France in 1960; Germany in 1968; Japan in 1976; Switzerland in 1977 and Italy and Sweden in 1978. There is no logic in their protest because these countries once fully utilised the provisions of Paris Convention to strengthen their pharmaceutical industry now prevent the developing countries to enjoy the same privilege. The developed countries through the window of WTO strongly pushed the agenda to provide strong patent protection for their products and processes for 20 years.[8]

The Uruguay Round of GATT and the subsequent WTO regime accelerated the globalization process in India. As a result of it, the Government of India softened all checks and controls in order to invite Multi-National Corporations. MRTP and FERA acts have been diluted and amended. Customs duties and corporate taxes have been reduced. All these concessions are extended to the Multi-National Corporations and the biased policies showed an adverse impact on the domestic drug industry. The possible implication of it is that the availability of new drugs may be delayed as per the wishes of the patent holders. At present newer drugs are made available in the country within a period of 4 years.

A successful patent policy of any developing country is one that strikes a clear balance between protecting the rights of innovators and services at affordable prices to the population. India's patent policy so long has been in fact of protecting the interests of public more than that of the monopoly rights. India's patent policy based on Indian Patent Act, 1970 necessitated change after the emergence of TRIPs in the WTO. The Intellectual Property Rights (IPRs) were included under Uruguay Round of GATT and later it became formally a part of WTO. India initially resisted the inclusion of IPRs in the WTO but, ultimately it had to sign the agreement because WTO was a take it or leave it agreement[9]. It necessitated the amendment of the Indian Patent Act, 1970.

In a democratic country it is not that much easy to shift the policy against public interest. India was in a difficult situation of protecting people's interest at the one hand and fulfilling the WTO's agreement of TRIPs on the other. The commercial interest has to be protected to comply with TRIPs. A domestic policy shift enabled India to revise its patent laws in 1998-99, which laid the foundation for redefining the balance towards the rights of innovators. The change in India's policy shift occurred at various stages. The BJP Government continued the economic liberalization measures initiated by the previous Congress government.[10] Secondly, some of the important industry bodies in the 1990's began to advocate the need for greater patent protection in India. The Confederation of Indian Industry (CII) took the position in its statements before the Gujral Committee[11] that India was not able to get relevant technology due to the absence of product patents. Another powerful trade body ASSOCHAM (Associated Chamber of Commerce and Industry) stressed before the committee that India needed to strengthen patent laws in order to attract Foreign Direct Investment (FDI). The Industry bodies began to support the bill to amend Indian patent laws in conformity with the TRIPs. Another important development is the propagation of the slogan "Patent or Perish" by the Federation of Indian Chamber of Industry and Commerce (FICCI) and it established an International Institute of Intellectual Property Development in 1997 to serve the purpose.

Some of the domestic drug producers visualised significant avenues for profit from the new-patented regime. Dr. Reddy's Laboratories believes that it has a competitive edge in new drug discovery that will lead to its growth in the revised policy. India's top research and scientific institution, CSIR, felt that they could benefit more from patents rather than their publications. In General, people advocated that India can benefit more, if many of the traditional knowledge are patented.

PATENT AMENDMENTS

After signing the WTO it is obligatory to comply with the provisions specified in the TRIPs. It related to all areas of intellectual properties identified by TRIPs, which include enforcement of patent law, copyright, etc. Therefore, India need to amend the Indian Patent Act, 1970 in accordance with various provisions prescribed in the TRIPs. A comparison of IPA with TRIPs shows that, in the former only process patents are allowed in medicines and chemicals whereas in TRIPs both process and product patents are compulsory for inventions related to almost all fields of technology. Moreover, the term of patent in TRIPs was 20 years as compared to the 5-7 years in process patents in chemicals and drugs in IPA. Another difference is with regard to the licensing and rights. In IPA compulsory licensing and licensing of rights were allowed. But TRIPs possess only limited compulsory licensing and it has no licensing of right. Another most important advantage of Indian patent law is that it allowed the government to use patented invention to prevent scarcity of drugs in the domestic market. But in TRIPs there is only limited scope for government to use patented inventions.

PATENT FIRST AMENDMENT ACT OF 1999

IPA provides process patents to inventions relating to food and medicines. Therefore, India benefited from inventions abroad by imitating the products and selling the same product at relatively cheaper prices. It was justified that such inventions are life saving in nature and India has a large number of people living below the poverty line. Moreover, the alternative drugs produced in foreign countries are available in India at a higher cost. However, the comparative advantage of Indian pharmaceutical industry will decline because TRIPs ensures patent protection for any invention without discrimination. TRIPs obligates developing countries to provide a Mailbox Mechanism and an Exclusive Marketing Rights (EMR) to benefit the inventors during the interim period till 2005.

The Mailbox Mechanism should be available for the interim years (till 2005) or until the product patent is introduced. According to this provision any applicant is entitled to an EMR to a product that is granted patent by another member state. India was required to fulfil this obligation by January 1, 1995 and the ordinance become effective on the same date. The Patents (Amendment) Bill of 1995 aimed to give permanent legislative effect to the Ordinance 1995 and it was passed in Lok Sabha but lapsed in the Rajya Sabha. The sentiment over EMR was cited as the reason for the lapsing of the bill. The drug producers felt that, it is more constrictive than the product patent regime. However, the most important reason was the fear of cost escalation of medicines and the substantial elimination of domestic drug production. Such a delay resulted in Mailbox Dispute because India did not fulfil its TRIPs obligations within the stipulated time. Finally the Patent First Amendment Act was finally passed in December 1999.

The Chapter IVA of it, deals with EMRs. The Amendment under section 24 A(1) mandates that the controller to refer every application seeking an EMR. Unless the controller is satisfied, the specified product will not qualify for a patent. It also authorises the grant of an EMR for 5 years for inventions made in India after January 1, 1995. This provision is being criticised as discriminatory. It provides discrimination because India at present has only the process patent and this may be disadvantageous to the applicants. In the case of drugs, section 24B(2) provides that prior publication or use before filing the claim by the applicant in India or foreign will not cause EMR infringement but it excludes the use by third person. The amendment also allowed for applications for product patents in agro-chemical and pharmaceutical fields, which would be examined in 2004 and granted (if it meets the stipulations in 2005) EMR for these products. The main provision of change in the Amendment is the revision of balance between public interest with patents rights in India. Another important policy change reflects India's accession to Paris Convention and the Patent Cooperation Treaty, 1998. India for long did not join the treaty because of its too wide definition of intellectual property, national treatment clause, procedures for compulsory licensing and India's lack of knowledge over-screening patent filing.

SECOND PATENT AMENDMENT BILL

Even after the Patent First Amendment Act, 1999, India has to cross two more steps to pass the TRIPs barrier. One is to bring forth other changes related to the patent and the second is the introduction of product patents by January 1, 2005. The Patent Second Amendment Bill of 1999 was introduced in the Parliament but the Rajya Sabha could not pass it. This bill was referred to the selected committee. The selected committee could not give the recommendations before the deadline. India has already defaulted the first amendment on the deadline. The bill was designed to rise the term of patents to 20 years, to narrow the framework of compulsory licensing and to remove the licenses of right. The bill also tries to use exception provided in the TRIPs to exclude patents on animals and plants. In general, the bill provides stronger protection to patent holders and lesser to the general public.

The bill amends the definition of invention. According to the Second Amendment, the definition of invention requires that an invention should have an inventive step and is capable of industrial application. The current definition does not alter the requirements under old definition. The bill also amends the section 3 of IPA to be in line with the TRIPs, which provides a list of exclusions from the definition of invention. The new definition excludes, in sub-section 3, inventions whose use or commercial exploitation is contrary to law and morality. But this is contrary to Art. 27(2) of TRIPs, which limits exclusions from patentability to inventions, the commercial exploitation which is necessary to protect morality. The bill also amends the previous clause to exclude medical, surgical, curative, diagnostic treatments on plants and animals. However, TRIPs does not envisage such exclusion.

Although the first amendment to the IPA placed before parliament in 1994 and after significant pressure from WTO in response to complaints from US and European Union, it was passed in 1999. The first draft of the current bill was sent to a selected committee of parliament which submitted its report before the Doha ministerial declaration, partly explains why the current legislation does not make use of all flexibility now available in TRIPs. Nevertheless, the modified bill was passed in the Rajya Sabha and Lok Sabha with little discussion. The most contentious feature of the bill is its likely impact on accessibility to medicines and healthcare.

In order to expand the scope of compulsory licensing and to keep the definition of 'public health emergency' very flexible, the Second Amendment did not impose any limit on the royalty to be paid to patent holders. It incorporated the Bolar Provisions of the US Patent Law, which allows drug companies to begin work on drugs going out of patent before the expiry of the patent so that the original patent holder does not get undue extension simply because of the non-availability of the now-patented drug. The bill empowered the ministry to define a national emergency, however, it chose to at any point of time. This gave the government a great deal of manoeuvrability. For example, non-availability of critical drug would be defined as a public health emergency. Critics point out that, it would lead to endless litigation between the drug companies and the government.

The government incorporates three of five proposed revisions in the Second Amendment. It defines the conditions for the grant of compulsory license but sets no limits on royalty payment, allowing it to be fixed on a case-by-case basis. This may limit the scope of compulsory licensing provision to provide access to essential drugs if the government is unable to arrive at a reasonable royalty agreement with the original license perhaps making the drugs so produced in the country unaffordable. On the other hand, the government has argued that, by putting a limit on royalty payment, India may do itself out of a better bargain in an emergency. However, the bill's reference to 'reasonably affordable price' in the context of the issue of compulsory licensing is, experts point out, a contrary interpretation of TRIPs. The Doha declaration does not directly link prices to patents and this may be of some consequence even in industries other than drugs.

The bill fails to provide the government with enabling provisions for protecting its interest in the event of a dispute over the WTO treaty. The scope of Articles 7 and 8 of the treaty, which on the best interpretations would allow for greater protection of national interests and access to innovation has not yet fully exploited. Developing countries like Brazil and Argentina have done better jobs in the context of protecting the local interest than other countries. The new bill does not provide the scope of patentability (dosage forms that have been protected) because it does not specify whether the molecules or the dosage forms the drug that has been protected. It is also generally criticised that the phase working of a patent-one section states that, the same as importation, which is ambiguous on the point and member countries interpret this part differently. The third amendment expected to incorporate and address these issues.

Among the pharmaceutical companies Ranbaxy showed readiness to act in the new environment, while Cipla[12] have taken the issue to the government to postpone the introduction of product patent to 2016 instead of 2005.

The ability of Indian pharmaceutical industry to face competition in the environment of patent regime can be analysed by examining the growth and export of drugs during the late 80's and 90's of the 20th century. The impact of the changing rules of international trade and domestic economic reforms on the prices, employment and public sector of pharmaceutical industry will focus more light on the issue of IPRs on the Indian pharmaceutical industry.

DEMAND FOR DRUGS IN INDIA

The effective demand for drugs in India depends on many interrelated factors viz., increase in population, healthcare facilities, per capita income and employment opportunities. After Independence, the Government of India has taken a number of measures to improve the health conditions of people especially those who live at the bottom strata of the society. Increase of employment in the public and private sector undertakings, increased the demand for drugs because they provided healthcare facilities to their employees at subsidised rates. The demand for drugs in India between 1984-85 and 1999-2000 is given in Table 1.

TABLE 1

Demand for Drugs in India between 1984-85 and 1999-2000

(*Rs in Crores*)

Year	*Demand for drugs*
1984-85	2204
1989-90	4112
1994-95	8300
1999-00	15996

Source: *Chemical Business*, Vol. 14, No. 1, Jan., 2000, p. 22.

GROWTH OF PHARMACEUTICAL INDUSTRY IN INDIA

The Patent Act of 1970 accepting only the process patent for a shorter period inspired the growth of pharmaceutical industry and its self-sufficiency in the production of drugs. The Indian research institutes utilised the provisions of only process and not the product patents to reverse engineer technologies, build indigenous capabilities in them and disseminate them to the industry. The domestic industry could get alternative drugs just four to five years after the introduction of a new drug in the globe. The Indian patents structure enabled India to achieve almost self-sufficiency in the production of bulk drugs and to sell them at relatively lesser prices. It is feared that by allowing product patents, India would no longer be able to find alternative processes to produce drugs patented abroad. The total value of production of drugs and formulations in India between 1988-89 and 1998-99 is shown in Table 2.

TABLE 2

Production of Bulk Drugs and Formulations in India between 1988-89 and 1999-2000

(Value in Rs. Millions)

Year	*Bulk Drugs*	*Formulations*
1988-89	500	31500
1989-90	6400	34200
1990-91	7300	38400
1991-92	9000	48000
1992-93	11500	60000
1993-94	13200	69000
1994-95	15180	79350
1995-96	18220	91250
1996-97	21860	104940
1997-98	26230	120680
1998-99*	31480	13878

*Projected figures.
Source: Chemexcil's Annual Report, 1997-98.

DRUG EXPORT

Product patent regime will decelerate drug exports from India because the importing countries will be forced to purchase drugs from patent holders only.

The export of basic drugs and formulation from India between 1988-89 and 1997-98 is shown in Table 3.

TABLE 3

Exports of Basic Drugs and Formulation, 1988-89 and 1997-98

(Value in Rs. millions)

Year	*Formulation*	*Percentage of growth over previous year*	*Basic drugs*	*Percentage growth over previous year*	*Total percentage growth over previous year*
1988-89	1573	78	2429	4002	76
1989-90	3142	100	3505	6647	66
1990-91	3714	18	4134	7848	18
1991-92	5585	50	7226	12811	63
1992-93	5537	-08	8560	14097	10
1993-94	13108	137	5308	18416	31
1994-95	15055	15	7601	22656	23
1995-96	20448	36	11329	31777	40
1996-97	25092	23	15811	40903	29
1997-98	28050	12	21730	49780	22

Source: Chemexcil's Annual Report, 1997-98.

The item-wise export of drugs to different destinations from India is furnished in Table 4.

TABLE 4

Items of Pharmaceutical Export from India between 1995-96 and 1997-98

(Values in Rs. Millions)

Item	*1995-96*	*1996-97*	*1997-98*	*Destinations*
1	*2*	*3*	*4*	*5*
Cephalexin Formulations in capsules etc.	1139	1694	1396	Asia, W. Europe, USA
Menthol	648	2464	3037	USA, W. Europe, Asia and Latin America
Amoxycillin in capsules, injections.	994	790	1166	W. Europe, Asia and Latin America
Amoxycillin and its salts	909	1018	1013	W. Europe, Asia and Latin America

(Contd.)

1	2	3	4	5
Ibuprofen tablets	549	612	901	USA, W. Europe, Asia
Ampicillian in capsules, injections	1017	1091	696	USA, W. Europe, Asia
Ranitidine	229	155	652	W. Europe, Asia and Latin America
Ciphalexin and its salts	646	818	632	USA, Asia and W. Europe
Ampicillian and its salts	712	715	576	W. Europe, Asia and Africa
Sulphamet-Hoxazole	587	524	517	USA, Asia and W. Europe
Ciprofloxacine and its salts	277	293	362	W. Europe, Asia and Latin America
Eruthromycin and its salts	154	100	357	USA, W. Europe, Asia, Africa
Paracetamol in tablets . syrups	469	423	353	W. Europe, Latin America and Asia
Trimethoprin in tablets etc.	22	210	321	USA, W. Europe, Latin America
Ciproflocacine in capsules tablets etc.	117	103	307	Asia, West Europe, Africa
Total	8359	11010	12286	
As a percent of total exports of the panel	26	27	25	

Source: Chemexcil's Annual Report, 1997-98.

IMPACT OF TRIPs ON PRICES

In order to understand a clear picture of the impact of TRIPs on developing countries, it should be examined in the context of globalization. Globalization integrates consumer markets globally, which cause social and economic problems domestically. The social problems emanate mainly because of the breakdown of national boundaries. Moreover, various research studies revealed that, globalization concentrates only a portion of the population with disposable personal income and consumption patterns for preference to foreign brands. It is widely believed that after the implementation of TRIPs, the pharmaceutical market will identify a global middle class with preference for costly foreign brands leaving the millions without access to essential drugs to treat common illness. Therefore, they perceive globalization as the feast for rich and tragedy for the poor. As far as the pharmaceutical industry is concerned, abundance of branded drugs designed to meet the needs of the rich will flow into the drug market. There is a possibility of price stabilization but a few essential drugs to a large number of poor consumers may be in short supply, which can lead to a hike in prices of such drugs.

A consumer can purchase commodities according to his preferences in the product market. But in the case of patients, they have no preference and to abide by the prescriptions of his doctor. Hence, there is a tendency for the prices of drugs to increase at a higher level as compared to the prices of commodities. This is the basic reason why most of the drugs were brought under the control of Drug Price Control Order (DPCO). The DPCO was introduced in 1970 and 347 items were brought under price control. The number of drugs under its control reduced to 163 drugs in 1987 and further reduced to 73 drugs in 1994.[13] After the patent amendments there is a move for the complete decontrol of the drugs from DPCO[14]. All other drugs require no import license. Even in developed countries some of the drugs are under government control. Not only the prices of drugs, but also the profit level of individual companies are controlled by the government. In UK a drug company with excess profit is to reimburse a portion of the profit to the Department of Health.

Even before the implementation of new patent in compliance with the TRIPs agreement, there has been an observable tendency among the prices of life saving drugs to move up steeply. The DPCO was framed by keeping the ordinary people and their purchasing power in mind. But the present pattern of drug price fluctuations explains the eagerness of drug and pharmaceutical industry on making more profits. The impact of liberal policies of the government on the price of some of the essential drugs is shown in Table 5.

After the imposition of WTO agreement on product patent in India since January 1, 2005, the prices of new drugs will go up without respecting DPCO and they are accessible only to the richest population of the country. It is pertinent to show the prices of new drugs even before the imposition of product patent in India from the following Table 6.

TABLE 5

Price of some Essential Drugs

Name of drug	*For Treatment*	*Packing*	*Price in 1995*	*1998*	*Percent increase*
Diazepam	Depression	10	3.13	9.50	204
Ampicillin	Antibiotic	4	12.85	23.15	80
Cephalexin	Antibiotic	10	45.07	113.15	151
Ethanbutol	Anti-TB Drugs	10	5.92	33.00	457
Rifampicin	Anti-TB Drugs	10	24.00	64.00	167
Pirazinamide	Anti-TB Drugs	10	17.01	46.95	176
Lignocaine HCL	Anaesthetic	30 ml	4.16	12.40	198
Promethaxine HCL	Anti-Allergic	10	1.25	3.23	158
Antacid liquid	Gastritis	200 ml	13.00	23.00	77
Oxydedrine HCL	Angina pectoris	10	10.44	21.41	105
Discopyramide phosphate	Cardiac problems	10	16.50	50.46	206
Dipyridamole	Anti-angine	10	2.00	4.73	137

Source: Compiled from the information supplied by different drug companies.

TABLE 6

Prices of New Drugs

Drug	*Company*	*Strength*	*Pack*	*Price*
Sporanox	Ethnor	100 mg	4 tablets	173.00
Lumicil	Novertis	250 mg	14 capsules	1247.00
Spariex	Sun pharma	200 mg	6 tablets	154.00
Rispid	Panace	50 ml	1 mg/ml capsule	141.00
Livial	Infar	—	28 tablets	1225.00
Pipracil	Cyanamid	2G	Vial	215.78
Amate	Mescopharma	50 mg	12 tablets	180.00
Adnoject	Inca	3 mg	2 ml. Vial	210.00
Roxisara	Sarabhai	300 mg	6 tablets	165.00
Celex	Glaxo	250 mg	4 tablets	140.00

Source: Compilation from reports published in various newspapers.

Health for All by 2000 AD (WHO goal) was a distant dream

by taking into account the severity and intensity of the problem case of India. As technology progresses, new drugs are being introduced. Experts are of the opinion that very few of the drugs have advantages over the existing drugs. It was stated by a Federal Authority of the USA that 25 big drug companies of the USA between 1981 and 1988 introduced 348 new drugs. Out of which only 3 per cent made potential contribution while 84 per cent made a little or no potential contribution. Therefore, it is not correct to understand that all the new drugs developed are capable of curing diseases efficiently than the existing drugs.

PRICES OF DRUGS AND ACCESSIBILITY

The cost of most of the patented drugs largely depends on who makes them and where are they made rather than the cost of ingredients used to produce them. The cost difference naturally reflects upon the prices of drugs. The cost of drugs is estimated by including the cost of tableting, packaging, marketing, transportation and profits. The percentage of profit to the actual price of patented drugs in many countries is worked out as more than 1285. For instance, AZT (Zidovudine) in the USA can be purchased for 42 cents for 300 mg from worldwide suppliers and it is retailed at $ 5.82. The bulk purchase price reflects not only the profit of the manufacturer but also the middleman bulk buyer. An Indian company Cipla sells AZT capsule for $ 1.42 per 300 mgs. It earns 200 to 300 per cent profit margins with the drug. Most of the drugs manufactured in India by the pharmaceutical companies on an average 1000 to 4000 per cent cheaper than the same produced in countries like the USA.

In India there is wide inequality in income distribution among population sub-groups. On the average more than two-fifths of the population have very low income. In this context any move towards meeting the requirements of TRIPs, which should take into consideration the impact of higher drug prices on the poor consumers. In India consumers themselves pay more than 85 per cent of the cost of Pharmaceuticals. The drug prices in developed countries are very high and insurance companies at a very high premium predominantly fund the expenditure. Hence any hike in prices of drugs will have a negative impact on their accessibility.

The drug policy of 1978 was one of the factors determined the availability of drugs and medicines at a comparatively lesser prices in India. The drug prices in India are one of the cheapest in the world. For example, Ranitidine is sold by the Glaxo Company in Pakistan at Rs. 65 and in the USA at Rs. 545, while the same company sold the same quality of drug in India at Rs. 7.20. The prices of drugs will increase at least 5 to 10 times while comparing the prices of drugs available in India at present after the implementation of the TRIPs in January 1, 2005.

PROFITABILITY Vs. VALUES

Medical research and public policy measures can bring down the cost of life saving drugs for the people in developing countries. At present 95 per cent of the people in developing world cannot afford the prevailing cost of medicines. Unless the governments take measures to reduce the cost of drugs, unnecessary illness and deaths in the developing world will be on the increase. A world full of diseases will not be good for any country for any business. Today the world experiences new diseases like AIDS. A public policy is inevitable to treat curable AIDS-related diseases by making drugs available at an affordable price.

Profitability is the leading indicator of success of business in the era of globalization where the values are being substituted by competition and immediate pay-off. Private sector drug companies show less interest in investing huge funds for Research and Development in inventing medicines to treat diseases like AIDS, because either it will not give them an immediate financial pay-off or the sick people are too few and incompetent to pay for the cost of research. Therefore, the government should act as a compensating force between the short-term gain and long-term investment.

Epidemics such as HIV and its victims largely belong to the third world countries. Science could not be used immediately to invent drugs for such diseases because of the doubts about the immediate returns. Efforts were made to form a collaboration of private companies in the name of Inter-company collaboration of Aids Drugs Development. The experiment miserably failed because of the difficulty inherent in the collaborative efforts between competitors in a market driven context. The element of communality is missed as the central value of scientific enquiry and it is being replaced by profits. Mere profit motive fits in the poor corporate culture. Patenting and protecting discoveries for profits without communality run counter to the purpose of scientific enquiry. The profit motive in the social sector has its own limitations.

The campaign of developing countries who are members of WHO along with NGOs and consumer representatives framed a resolution on revised drug strategy against the WTO's TRIPs principle on pharmaceuticals. It was tabled at the World Health Assembly in Geneva in May 1998. Due to the opposition from developed countries, the resolution was referred back to the WHO for reformulation. The resolution was reformulated and presented in the World Health Assembly in May 1999. The provisions rewarded, urges countries to ensure that health interest are paramount in pharmaceutical and health policies. The resolution also strengthens WHOs mandate to study the effects of international trade agreements while addressing public health needs and priorities. For instance, countries that would like to use compulsory licensing for certain essential drugs under patent can call upon the WHO for assistance. This is a positive development in favour of public interest coupled with commercial interest, which is again back on the global agenda.

IMPACT OF TRIPS ON EMPLOYMENT

Though many drugs in India are cheaper, some drugs became unviable after the reduction of customs duties on foreign exports. As a result, they are closed down and their workers are out of employment. For instance, the loan producers of chloramphenicol such as Boehringer Mansheim and Parks Devis closed down their factories because its price in the international market is much cheaper than its cost of production in India. This is the fate of many other drugs such as vitamin C, paracetamol, metronidazole, ampicilin, etc. The imported drugs are available at a cheaper rate because of the lowering of excise duties. The impact of this policy is that, on the one hand the Indian factories producing these drugs closed down and the workers are without employment and on the other for the above drugs India has become dependent on foreign supply. In addition to the closure of the drug companies, some companies such as Pfizer, Rhone Poulene, Hoechst, Glaxo, etc. have reduced the number of workers. Some companies shifted to the third party manufacturing. Some others closed their large factories and started new smaller factories in new places by appointing contractual workers at low wages and more workload. Some companies opted for cost and freight agency system where the companies have no responsibility towards the workers.

It is estimated that during 1990-2000 around 15,000 distributing workers have lost their jobs and they are substituted by agency system. In marketing, sales representatives are facing severe challenges from franchise, co-marketing, appointment of communicators, etc. The latest is the casualization, sub-contracting and agency system that gradually substitute the permanent jobs in the drug industry. The details of the reduction of work force in different companies are portrayed in Table 7.

TABLE 7

Reduction of Workforce in Pharmaceutical Companies

Company	*Year*	*Reduction of workforce*
Glaxo	1995	1564
Hoechst	1996	1049
Knoll pharma (Boots)	1995	600 (All workers)
Smith Kline Beecham	1995	208
E. Merck	1995	194
Rhone Doulenc	1996	700
Hindustan ciba geigy	1993	907
Duphar Interfran	1996	154
Bayer	1996	590
Abbott	1996	All workers
Roche	1996	All 320 workers
Boxharinger Mannheim	1997	All 335 workers
Park davis	1997	All 650 workers
Pfizer	1995	215
Unichern	1997	All workers

Source: Annual reports of respective companies and the information elicited from trade unions.

IMPACT OF TRIPS ON PUBLIC SECTOR

The public sector drug companies like Indian Drugs and Pharmaceuticals Ltd. (IDPL), Hindustan Antibiotics Ltd. (HAL),

Bengal Chemicals and Pharmaceuticals Ltd. (BCPL), Bengal Immunity (BI) played a significant role in the development of drug industry in India. They were primarily responsible for selling the essential drugs and raw materials to the small-scale sector drug companies at affordable prices. But many of these companies face severe problems inclusive of closures. The IDPL, the biggest pharmaceutical plant in Asia was closed in 1996. When IDPL was established, it had strength of 15,000 workers. At present it has been reduced to less than 7,000. The penicillin plant of HAL (the biggest in India) is privatised. Such a sorry state of the public sector drug factories is due to mismanagement and corruption besides the lack of political will. The public sector drug factories are even capable of meeting the challenges from the MNCs in some of the modern areas like biotechnology etc. If the same trend continues, MNCs will control drugs market in India in the future. This is because of the Government's permission to the MNCs to come to India with 100 percent equity considering the wide gap of technological development between the poor and rich countries in the world.

CONCLUSION

The new patent law may lead to pauperization of the poor people by selling the drugs at higher prices. More than 85 percent of the patents are enjoyed by the Transnational Corporations of the developed world, could sell the drugs at a higher price in the new millennium by considering the enactment of new patent law by favouring the product patent and increased population growth which require more quantities of drugs. At present India has 16.1 per cent of the world population but it produces only 1.2 per cent of world drug production. Therefore, the developed countries act for the interest of their own manufacturing companies to capture market in other countries even at the cost of the interest of people there. They successfully included intellectual property rules in international trade. The TRIPs disregards public health considerations and forced dramatic changes in the intellectual property rules world over. The success of India playing the game of TRIPs requires a constructive reshaping of political and economic paradigms, which should take care of short-term economic gains and long-term self-interest.

Notes and References

1. The status of Indian pharmaceutical industry can be assessed on the basis of the nature of pharmaceutical technology and the degree of self-reliance in comparison with other drug producing countries. The status of technology of pharmaceutical industry is generally classified as: (i) Strong Research and Development base, (ii) Production of chemical intermediaries from basic chemicals, (iii) Production of raw materials (or bulk drug forms) from chemical intermediaries or fermentation or plant sources, and (iv) Formulation of dosage forms (finished products) from bulk drug form. The technology for the production of raw materials from chemical intermediaries (stage (iii)) is more sophisticated when compared to the formulation stage, because the former is capital-intensive and economies of scale are very critical. The technology involved in formulation of dosage form is very simple, less capital-intensive and economies of scale are not critical. Only ten industrialised countries (Belgium, France, Germany, Italy, Japan, Netherlands, Sweden, Switzerland, UK and the USA) have human, technical and financial resources with significant research base in their pharmaceutical industry (stage-1).
2. Each country in this group discovered and marketed at least one new chemical entity between 1961 and 1996.
3. This law placed public interest before that of the patent holder. It explicitly stated that the Government of Venice had the power to use any patented invention for the social welfare. It was the guiding principle in almost all national and international patent laws such as the French Patent Law of 1791, the Austrian Law of 1810 and the Paris Convention IV, V, VI, VII and VIII.
4. UNIDO, The World's Pharmaceutical Industries: An International Perspective on Innovation, Competition and Policy, Robert Balance, Janos Pogany and Helmet Forsteiner UNIDO, 1992.
5. Government of India, 1949.
6. Dhavan, *et al*, 1985.
7. FICCI, 1996, p. 8.
8. TRIPs was justified in the pharmaceutical sector by the developed countries because inventing drug is as a result of strenuous effort by conducting research over a longer period of time. Therefore, the pharmaceutical Research and Manufacturers' Association (PhRMA) gave tremendous pressure to the US government to force the third world countries to adopt various Intellectual Property Rules enshrined in the WTO agreement.
9. Either a member accepts all agreements or none, leaving no scope for sectoral agreement.
10. A section of the Congress party began favouring changes in patent laws. The BJP, once the opponent of patents, after coming to power in

1998, abandoned its opposition to patent reforms and adopted a pro-patent position.

11. A committee established by the Indian Parliament to solicit views and prepare a report on the impact of the WTO agreement on India.
12. Cipla is a company that provides medicines at affordable prices to poor countries.
13. The tariff rates on drugs have declined, since, India signed the WTO agreement. Import procedures are also simplified and as a result of which only Penicillin and its derivatives, 6APA, Tetracycline, Oxytetracycline, Vitamin B1, B2, Rifampicin and its intermediates and streptomycin require import licenses.
14. *Economic Times*, 28th September, 1998.

References

A Report on the Indian Drug Industry, 1980-2000. The Indian Drug Manufacturers' Association, Bombay, p. 45.

Agarwal Pradeep and P. Saibaba (2001), "TRIPs and India Pharmaceuticals Industry," *Economic and Political Weekly*, Septemper 29.

Chemical Weekly, Sept. 21, Vol. XLV, No. 4, p. 150.

Ganesan, A.V., *The Implication of Patent Amendment Ordinances, 1999*, Indian Council for International Economic Relations, February 1999.

GATT and the Gap: "How to Save Lives," *AIDS Treatment News*, # 307, November 20, 1998.

Ragavani, Srividhya, (2001), Patent Amendments in India in the Wake of TRIPs, *CASRIP Newsletter*, Winter.

Ramanna, Anitha, (2002), "Political Implications of India's Patent Reforms: Patent Applications in the post-1995 Era," *Economic and Political Weekly*, May 25.

Roport Balance, Janos Pogany and Helmet Torsteiner, UNIDO (1992), UNIDO—The World's Pharmaceutical Industries: An International Perspective on Innovation, Competition and Policy.

Shahari, Ranjit, (2002), "Issues in Patents (Second Amendment) Bill," *The Hindu*, June 23.

Vasant Desai, *Indian Industry: Profile and Related Issues*, Himalaya Publishing House, pp. 391-94.

Venkateswarelu, M. Address at the *50th Indian Pharmaceutical Congress and 13th Congress of Pharmaceutical Sciences*, January 1999 (transcript available at htt://w.w.w.rediff.com)

Wishvas Rane, (1997), "New Drugs at what Cost"?, *Economic and Political Weekly*, June 28.

28

Global Economic Integration: A Case Study of Euro and its Implications to India

GAJAVELLI V. SWAMY

INTRODUCTION

The European Union (EU) is the association of countries formerly called the European Community (EC) and prior to that known as the European Economic Community (EEC). The EEC became the EC when the issues handled in common moved from mainly economic and trade matters to include social and political aspects. EC became the EU when common tariff levels were applied by all members to outside countries and tariffs among the member countries were removed—EC transformed into a Customs Union.[1]

The European Union (EU), which came into existence on 1st January 1993, is a major event in international political and economic relations and has caught the attention of the world. The collapse of the erstwhile USSR and the dramatic turn of events in Eastern Europe have significant bearings on North-South Relations as the countries of South undergo fundamental changes. Against this backdrop, the construction of the EU and its impact on developing economies in the context of changing North-South relations provide an interesting agenda for research, which is beyond the scope of this particular paper.

"The process of construction of the Union involved radical changes in the economic, commercial, trade and external policies of the EU. These changes, although mostly internal, would have significant implications for all other countries in relation to the Community, the issues in contemporary North-South relations and trade prospects of emerging economies at large."[2]

Recently, the EU facilitated the transition of European currency (€) from a notional accounting measure to its acceptance as legal tender in twelve member states from January, 2002—with this EU transformed into a Currency Union. How big a deal is a currency union really? It is tremendous, say economists and analysts. A currency union goes much beyond a free trade zone or customs union like the North Atlantic Free Trade Zone (NAFTA) and does away with the very notion of fluctuations across currencies and exchange risk involved. The main objective of such arrangement being: *To create a unique European common market and bring-in the benefits of enhanced market competition and integration.*

Such European Integration will have far-reaching implications to India's foreign trade, capital inflows and growth prospects. Since the fifteen member European Union is India's major trading partner and source of investment and aid, ahead of Japan and the U.S. It is in this context, this paper is an attempt to address some of these issues from the point of view of emerging challenges and opportunities for India's foreign sector and its growth prospects.

The paper is divided into four sections. The first section gives an account of European integration and its impact on India's business and industry. An attempt is made here to assess the implications to exporters and importers, exchange rate movements, currency risk and hedging prospects and the relevant strategic considerations for Indian Corporates. The second section is an attempt to analyse the possible implications to India's foreign trade, investment flows and growth prospects. Also it gives an appraisal of India's preparedness in terms of legal, banking and IT-related changes. The third section examines the mega-implications of the European integration and macro-economic policies pursued by EU (for example, European Central Bank's monetary policy) to global economy, equity and bond markets in Europe and the rest of the world; and trade and investment flows into India. Also it focuses on the issues of growing regionalization of trade (such as EU, NAFTA, ASEAN and Mercosur in South America) and their implications to major currencies; and prospects for emerging economies like India in such an evolving scenario. The fourth section gives an appraisal of the expected benefits and risks arising out of euro for the EU itself. Also it critically examines the progress made by the union towards a true integration, apart from providing summary and concluding remarks.

I

1. European Union, the Euro and Indian Business

The implementation of European Monetary Union (EMU) and the introduction of the Euro, would significantly transform the way the business is done by companies, at both strategic and operational level. Though the Euro represents new business prospects, the companies must develop new skills and capabilities to tackle and effectively manage the changes in the areas of accounting, information technology, tax, treasury, legal and most importantly the financial and other information systems. Further, inadequate preparation to deal with the Euro may adversely affect the companies' very existence.

Some Issues Related to Business and Industry

Some of the challenges that the Euro will pose to the Indian Corporates are mainly with regard to the following, including an assessment of corporate strategies. Most corporates are already trying their best to adapt to the changing scenario.

(i) **Invoicing and Pricing:** Problems in pricing and invoicing occur when a company has to quote its products/services both in euro and the legacy currencies (or in-currencies). While one-fifth of India's foreign trade is with Euroland, less than 10 per cent is invoiced in the EMU currencies. The immediate effect of the EMU will therefore be moderate, though there may be pressures from counter-parties and banks to switch-over to the Euro. Besides, it will be necessary to assess pricing and marketing policies followed by corporates. As currency barriers completely vanish by July 2002, transparency and efficiency gains for the markets will be enormous. Euroland contributes nearly 17.5 per cent of world trade (compared to 15.9 per cent of the U.S.) and synergies will only improve their share in the world trade.

(ii) **Risk-monitoring and Hedging:** A common currency does effect transaction costs at the margins and influence trade and capital flows between India and Eurozone economies. It means, Indian and European exporters and importers as well as European investors now need to hedge risk in one currency only, the Euro instead of a multiple currencies like the DM and FFr. This clearly reduces the cost of foreign exchange risk monitoring and hedging. However, given the share of India's trade with Euroland and invoicing practices as mentioned above, the magnitude of this effect has been and is likely to remain moderate.

(iii) **Effect on Rupee:** There is not likely to be any significant impact on the rupee. We expect the U.S. dollar to retain the 'intervention currency' status for the foreseeable period. However, as invoicing shifts to the Euro and its importance increases, the Euro-Rupee rate will be monitored more closely. For instance, during 1st Jan. 2001 to 15th January 2002, the rupee has gained by Rs. 0.72 and the U.S dollar by about $ 0.05 against euro.[3] The result is that, the weakening of the Euro against the dollar has reduced the export competitiveness of Indian firms from the rupee's depreciation against the dollar.[4]

(iv) **Dollar-Rupee Risk Diversification:** The majority of Indian firms have atleast 80% of their foreign exchange transactions in US $s. This goes very much against the basic tenets of prudent, Risk Management and Diversification. For example, during mid-June to 11th August 2002, US$-Rupee rose 2.35%. An importer with

100% exposure to US $ saw its liabilities rise from a base of 100 to 102.35. Over the same period, when Euro-Rupee fell 4.63%, an importer with 25% exposure to the Euro saw its liabilities rise from a base of 100 to only 100.60. By diversifying into a more liquid market such as Euro-Dollar, the risk arising from the structure of the Indian rupee market (which is small, thin and illiquid with wide spreads) can be hedged. Trends in one strong currency, say US $, can be hedged by offsetting trends in another currency, say Euro.

(v) **Macro-environment, Forecasting and Budgeting:** It is very essential to understand the economic impact of the Euro to enable intelligent forecasting and to have an understanding of the overall economic performance of Euro-12 rather than individual economies. Euro involves following a single monetary policy and a largely similar fiscal policy across the member-economies; and also merging of capital markets.

The Euro's performance on the foreign exchange markets mainly depends on the underlying strength of the euro-zone economy. Over the past three years, 1999-2001, the US has been a better place to invest because its economy has performed well. Capital over-flowed into the U.S. from Europe in 2001 because, most investors thought the U.S. economy would recover from recession more strongly than the Euro-zones. Consequently, the dollar continued to strengthen against Euro, even though the Euro-zone did not show it as quickly as the U.S. This essentially reflects the role played by 'perceptions' of the market players about the macro-economic fundamentals of respective economies within the region.

(vi) **Re-conventioning and re-denominating:** Outstanding debt in the 'in-currencies' (pre-1st January, 2002 individual currencies and to be phased out by July 2002) need to be re-denominated into Euro only after 2002, but it will have to be re-conventioned in terms of floating rate indices, day count conventions, etc. The understanding is that the LIBOR (London Inter-Bank Offer Rate) for in-currencies will be replaced by the Euro

LIBOR and that PIBOR, FIBOR (Paris/Frankfurt), etc. will be replaced by the Euribor. The day count for bonds is expected to be Act/Act. These details should be agreed with one's counter parties. This holds good for derivatives as well. For option players, historical volatility measures for risk analysis are available, obtained by creation of a 'synthetic euro'[5], tracked over a period of time.[6]

(vii) **Corporates—Size and Business Strategy:** A currency union like the EU overcomes the trade barriers and the so-called 'home-country bias'[7]created by exchange rate risk and facilitate a truly integrated market. Trade and investment flow within the region pick-up with corporates and countries competing purely on the basis of competitive strength[8].

Firstly, the Euro will greatly enhance sales and procurement opportunities as, currency-related barriers to the movement of merchandise, services and factors of production within EMU region will cease.

Second, the Euro region will also be an attractive investment destination as it may serve as access points to all the member countries and also the newly emerging markets of Central and Eastern Europe.

Third, selecting a right business location in Europe will be easier for Indian corporates as exchange rate-related concerns no longer matter for the choice of a right business location. Corporates could concentrate on other critical parameters directly related to the main concerns of the company such as production cost, technology, proximity to market centers and infrastructure.

Fourth, for banks the process of integration brings a bit of bad news with good. The most significant impact for the Indian banks operating abroad is the elimination of exchange rate risk across the EMU region, which will encourage branches to buy/sell securities across the borders on a massive scale.

With the introduction of Euro, the notion of currency become redundant taking away captive markets for foreign banks *on par* wit' banks. The activity of M & As and restructuri can see in the European banking sector and their ramifications for their Indian subsidiaries (and also for Indian banks operating there) reflects this adjustment to a level-playing field.

Fifth, Indian firms with already established sales and production networks in Euro-zone will face more strategic challenges—in terms of the pricing of product and services. While on the one hand it will lead to larger local markets, on the other, the companies will come under pressure from newly emerging competition, as in the case of European banking sector, within the region. The increased price transparency in this market will have an impact on price discrimination and the prices charged by a business for its goods and services in different markets in the region. This in turn might impact on existing packaging and labeling of products and on new product development. Thus, cost-cutting and innovation will be prerequisites for competitiveness and the future market position in an evolving scenario.

II

2. Euro-Zone, the Euro and Indian Economy

The implications of Euro on India can be analysed in terms of its effect on trade, foreign aid, external commercial borrowings, FDI and portfolio flows, banking-related issues and technology.

2.1 Prospects for Foreign Trade

The EU is India's biggest trading partner and source of investment and aid exceeding the contribution of both Japan and the U.S. Nearly 25% of our exports go to the region and imports from there make-up for about 30% of the total.[9] Apart from the direct favourable impact on exchange rate risk monitoring and related costs (as mentioned in the above section), there is no immediate impact of Euro on India's exports and imports to, and from the Euro-zone.

However, going by the trends in European corporate sector, it is quite possible that European firms will become more and more competitive as they would rationalize, streamline and become cost-efficient competitors. Further, the evolving markets of a gigantic size as Euroland would enhance market access and open up new opportunities for commercial ventures. This would imply that Indian firms have larger opportunities to be proactive and competitive. Sectorally, there could be more scope for software exports to the Eurozone. As recent experience shows Indian software companies are already able to access and diversify exports to Euro-zone countries.

2.2 Trade Invoicing

Indian exporters and importers are currently invoicing nearly 80% of its total trade in US $s. Switching over to invoicing in euro by Indian firms depend on a number of circumstances. For example, POL products and fertilizers, which account for a major chunk of our imports, are denominated in US $s which is an international practice. Similarly, exporters and importers in other countries may still continue with US $ denomination. However, the European companies which were earlier invoicing in US $s prefer to shift to Euro. Indian firms would keep a watch on international practices, preferences of their trading partners, possible natural hedge opportunities and their own considerations in such a shift in invoicing from US $ to Euro.

2.3 Foreign Currency Accounts/Deposits

These are basically nostro accounts of banks, foreign currency accounts maintained in India by banks such as EEFC/RFC accounts and foreign currency deposit accounts (FCNR-B) in DM. During the period of transition (i.e. introduction of euro on 1st January, 2002 followed by complete withdrawal of national currencies by July 2002), banks can maintain nostro accounts in "in-currencies" or/and euro. Banks in India are already maintaining nostro accounts in Euro. With respect to foreign currency accounts, banks have been allowed to open accounts in euro also. Similarly, in the case of FCNR (B) deposits, banks were permitted to offer 'Euro accounts' in addition to DM during the transition phase. In the case of existing fixed rate FCNR (B) deposits, the interest rates will continue till maturity. For existing floating rate deposits, as they are linked to Libor, banks have been instructed to use Eurolibor, the successor index. And for new deposits, banks have been allowed to link their interest rates either to Eurobor or Eurolibor.[10]

2.4 Foreign Direct Investment (FDI) Flows

The Eurozone accounts for nearly 12% of the total FDI in India. Newly introduced Euro is unlikely to have an impact on existing investments, which are denominated in rupees. The investor can remit the funds in any convertible currency of his choice including euro. However, in the case of GDRs if they are denominated in any of the 12 national currencies, the issuer can re-denominate them into euro during the transition phase. As the physical arrival of the Euro will encourage Euro-zone governments to push-through much needed structural reforms and a broader and deeper Euro market would make the euro more attractive to investors.[11]

2.5 External Commercial Borrowings

The introduction of euro would go a long way in enhancing the financing opportunities for Indian firms who have been so far largely tapping the markets abroad in U.S $s in the form of bonds and syndicated loans . With Euro becoming attractive, competition between US $ and euro would become more intense and result in possible marginal reduction in spreads for Indian corporates. Moreover, Indian borrowers will now have greater access to euro-zone markets in view of the larger investor base and a common financial market. For long-term financing, those firms which have natural hedge in euro now find it attractive to borrow in euro and take advantage of lower costs. Also, there is scope for raising dollar denominated and euro loans in Euroland now.

2.6 Legal and Information Technology Issues

There are no difficulties as such in Indian legal system regarding continuity of contracts *per se*. Under the existing foreign exchange regulations, Reserve Bank of India (RBI) has notified euro as a permissible currency and hence settling payments in Euro is legal. However, a clause of continuity has been recommended for existing contracts which goes beyond 2002.

With regard to information technology, existing computer systems are already modified to recognize Euro, carry out and record relevant business transactions in the Euro. The modified systems must be able to provide a link between the in-currencies and the euro as all the in-currencies are connected through euro (atleast till July, 2002, when all in-currencies will be phased out). Thus, the systems will need to be made to handle orders in both the currencies which will require a thorough understanding of user interfaces with other linked sub-systems and ledgers to ensure consistency throughout the financial information system. The businesses may also require a system functionality to match in-currencies/euro receipts with national currency unit invoices.

The significance attained more prominence as the IT impact of the change-over to Euro coincided over broadly the same period as the Y2K problem.

Overall, the influence of the Euro and the underlying monetary union on the global economy, asset markets and the structure of international banking are anything but moderate. However, there are effects which Indian businesses, government and the banking sector need to monitor to explore the opportunities, given the size of the Euro-zone market.

III

3. European Union, the Euro and World Financial System: The Underlying Macroeconomics and Policy Implications

Going by the experience of the last two years, it would be too early to be able to assess accurately how important the euro will become in the international economy and financial system. It would take some more time for analysts, policy-markers, borrowers, investors and other financial market players to understand the euro and its relative importance. However, one can assess the possible advantages and implications of the Euro and the underlying macro-economics and policy.

First, the impression among market analysts is that the euro would become a more attractive currency for bond issuers. In fact, in the first month of its introduction in 1999, the euro was the most popular currency for bonds issued in the international markets. It accounted for nearly 55% of the volume of new bond issues compared with 40% for the US $. This was mainly due to initial euphoria about euro-denominated instruments.

Second, with euro, the notion of domestic currency become redundant and the dominant strategy for European banking heavy weights would be to increase market share in the par-European market. Thus, the persisting trend of M&As and consolidation is likely to continue in future. Size does matter, especially when domestic banks are loosing captive markets in the wake of Euro's introduction.

Third, indications show that the Euro is likely to become more attractive for the investment of Central Bank's official reserves. Currently, the US $ is by far the most important reserve currency world over. It is reported that well over half of official reserves are held in US $ denominated assets while about one-fifth are currently held in EMU currencies. Some major Central Banks may decide to keep a larger part of their reserves in euro. The People's Bank of China, the Bank of Japan, the Central Bank of Taiwan, and the Bank of England have all indicated that they may now divest part of their reserve holdings by acquiring the single currency[12]. The shift to euro assets by Central Banks around the world would be motivated by its strength, its increasing use as a transaction currency and the more liquid and deeper bond markets, among other factors. And there are indications of supporting factors that should help to boost the euro currency's value over both the medium-term and long-term. The euro zone's 'basic balance'—i.e. the sum of its current account balance plus long-term capital flows—is growing and this indicates that during the course of 2002, the Euro might at last appreciate.[13] Other factors are also supportive of euro like weaker oil prices, tumbling inflation rates, and an expected increase in the acquisition of euro-zone companies by foreign institutions.[14]

Fourth, the emergence of Euro, and the underlying EU will have far-reaching implications to major currencies (and the much-touted benefits of globalization) more particularly to the US $. Indeed, considering Regional Trading Arrangements (RTAs)—such as NAFTA, EU, Mercosur in South America and ASEAN, more and more of international trade is occurring within regions. Statistics show that between 1982 to 1998, the proportion of U.S. trade with countries in North, Central and South America increased from 29.31% to 37.1%, while Japan's trade with other Asian nations increased from 19.7% to 34.6%; and Germany's trade with other European countries which was already at a record high of 64% has increased to 77.6%.

This trend toward regionalization of trade has important currency implications, making it a paramount significance to international financial management. The Euro currency (earlier it was DM, which played a dominant role in Europe) is likely to become more dominant as the settlement currency in Europe, with the same being true for Japanese Yen in Asia. It is quite possible that the euro could also emerge as an important anchor currency for other countries, particularly among countries in Central and Eastern Europe by virtue of their geographical proximity and possible economic linkages. Some of these countries may find it useful to peg their currencies formally or informally to the euro or a basket of currencies with euro carrying large weightage. *As a result, the role of US $, which has been the dominant global currency for price quotations and settlement of international payments, likely to be diminished outside the Americas*[15] *in future.*

Fifth, the euro is likely to become an alternate currency for invoicing next only to the US $. Approximately 50% of the world exports is invoiced in US $s, almost four times the share of US in world trade. While nearly 20% of world exports are invoiced in EU currencies and 5% in Japanese Yen. In the long-run, it is possible that euro would become an important alternate currency for invoicing of international trade.

Sixth, it is quite possible that corporates would find euro as a preferred currency for financial transactions. Trade finance could be more easily accessible to corporates in India and abroad as the European banks compete purely on their competitive strength and able to extend loans at attractive rates. Further in the case of long-term financing those firms that have natural hedge in euro may find it advantageous to borrow in euro and take advantage of lower costs.

Also, with the elimination of exchange risk and the emergence of a single currency market, the scope for sector-specific funds expected to be more attractive. Therefore, raising funds for sectoral projects like financing of infrastructure projects become easier with the single currency.

Last, but not least, issue is with respect to the underlying macro-economics and policy implications of the euro on world trade, output and investments flows. With the advent of euro, national central banks of the member countries have ceded monetary control to the European Central Bank (ECB)—based at Frankfurt. The German Bundesbank heavily influences the ECB's 'monetary stance' with inflation control as the prime target. However, this is often at the cost of the real economy and its growth prospects. Inspite of clear signs of global and European slow-down since the middle of 2000, the ECB foiled an interest rate cut till May 2001—its second cut since inception.[16] While the Bank of England resorted to interest rate cuts thrice during the same period. For the Global economy in the long-term this kind of 'tight' monetary stance would imply that there would be an upward pressure on interest rates and consequent tightness in liquidity. This would dampen both the equity and bond markets in Europe and the rest of the world. For the world economy as a whole, it could mean that expansion/revival in output would be more moderate. This bound to affect trade and investment flows into India, and hence its growth momentum.

Thus, the implication to the global economy though difficult to assess accurately, the general perception is encouraging. How important is the role euro would play and how fast it would impact on the global macro-economy hinges on a variety of factors. More importantly, it would depend on how the expected benefits and risks evolve for all the players, and more particularly for the Euro zone economy itself, as examined below.

Benefits and Risks for European Monetary Union

There has been a lot of discussion about the possible benefits and risks arising out of euro for the EMU itself. There is even greater interest in the implications for the rest of the world. It may be useful to highlight the differing view points in this regard.[17]

Benefits

First, by eliminating different currencies, the euro eliminates foreign exchange risk, including to countries that are members of the EMU.

Second, an immediate implication of the introduction of the single currency is the reduction in transaction costs. The costs associated with converting one currency into another, cross-border transfers by companies and hedging of risks are reduced.

Third, the current nationally based bond markets are transformed into a single market with common norms. The integration of financial markets is expected to boost the supply of new issues and instruments.

Fourth, the new funding and investment possibilities in the euro-region are expected to become more efficient and competitive. As a result of increased price transparency and competition, financing costs of firms will probably scale down.

Fifth, the higher yield corporate debt market will in all likelihood become much large in the euro with the elimination of foreign exchange risk. This will enable corporate credit risks to be priced more accurately.

Sixth, elimination of exchange rate fluctuations between legacy currencies or in-currencies is expected to lead to a significant increase in trade and investment within the euro area.

Seventh, it is argued that giving other countries the ability to peg their currencies to a basket of hard currencies (say a mix of US dollar and euro) might stabilize fixed exchange rate regimes.

Risks for EMU

First, it is held that different economies in the EMU are at different levels of business cycle, and hence there may be occasions when a single monetary policy appears inadequate to tackle the problem of growth and employment—which is country-specific—in a desired manner.

Second, the 'stability and growth pact' provides an excellent in-built mechanism to ensure fiscal discipline among the EMU countries. However, it is felt among some that the in-built mechanism may come under some stress during the initial periods.

Third, some concern has been expressed by some regarding absence of clear rules on 'seignorage' sharing and open market operations.

Fourth, since introduction of the euro, there has been some degree of volatility and depreciation of euro, against the US dollar. However, it is too early to formulate any medium to long-term view based on €-US $ exchange rate movements in the short-term.

Fifth, it is conceded that there would be significant reduction in transaction costs, but there are doubts about the extent to which this will get translated into cost reduction and efficiencies—given the fact that product and factor markets are still regulated in the euro-zone economies to a significant level.

4. The Euro-zone and Prospects: Summary and Concluding Remarks

The primary objective of introducing a single currency is essentially to create a unique European common market and bring-in the benefits of enhanced market competition and integration for the Euro-zone economies. But the new currency has not really achieved the targeted objectives. Inspite of its initiation and experimentation over the years not really contributed to transform Europe into a vibrant economic entity. The governments resist to introduce structural/micro-economic reforms and industries are still protected from competition. Moreover, Europe's product and labour markets are highly regulated, which renders the very process of European Integration incomplete.

Coming to the macro-economic management issues of integration, the reality is that different economies within the euro zone are at different phases of business cycle, and therefore, ECB's uniform monetary policy proves, sometimes, inadequate to tackle the basic issues of low growth and unemployment (which are country-specific) in a desired manner. Especially since membership of the Union also comes with tight 'fiscal discipline' enshrined in the Maastricht criteria which sets upper bounds on government budget deficits and hence the ability to revive their flagging economies by pump-priming will be muted. The ECB refuses to lower interest rates and the member nations cannot raise public spending either since it might violate the Maastricht norms. In 2001, Ireland faced a similar situation. Its attempts to raise budget deficit attracted a severe reprimand form ECB. The Irish opposition did not loose the chance to criticize the government against the perceived 'loss of sovereignty'. The IMF advised the ECB to get a bit easy on fiscal targets.[18]

Another problem lies at the heart of Europe: Germany which is struggling to keep its budget deficit below 3% of GDP, inspite of impending recession. This is to adhere to 'the stability and growth pact' norms. The Pact, adopted at Germany's behest, provides that any country breaching the 3% ceiling could be subject to fines as big as 0.5% of GDP. Though there are let-out clauses for deep recessions, but Germany looks unlikely to qualify for such relaxations.

Is there a way out of this crisis-driven model of

integration?[19] Many eminent European leaders and policy-makers could come out with several solutions including a whole new round of political integration. One popular idea, promoted by both Lionel Jospin, the French Prime Minister and Romani Prode, the head of European Commission (EC), is the appointment of Mr. Euro who could represent the entire euro-zone in various international economic forums.[20] Other suggestions include the harmonization of corporate and other taxes and the creation of a bail-out fund to help countries in economic trouble. Because options open to countries with a national currency, notably devaluations and an independent monetary policy, are no longer open to members of the euro-zone. Hence Mr. Prodi suggests that the Union should greatly increase its central budget (implying that members pay taxes into a central pool), so that if a country hit by a shock specific to itself, then some of it could be transferred to help it tide-over the crisis.[21] This federal fiscal structure is considered as the key to the success of the U.S. often touted as the oldest and the most stable currency union.

Though many eminent European leaders think that the logical end to the integration process is that of a closer 'political union', but that is not to say that Europe must now proceed to closer political union. On the contrary, the union has a new currency to reckon with and a daunting task of adhering to the stability pact norms . In case if the breach of the limit norms went unpunished, the down-side risk is that the new currency could suffer a credibility loss. And the problem is that the stability pact, far from creating more of flexibility, actually creates less and out of the reach of a member country, as in the case of the recent German experience.

The true flexibility and endurance is that Euro-zone economy badly needs at this juncture can only come from removing remaining barriers to competition and further deregulating product and labour markets. More importantly, the governments including Germany's must go ahead with the structural reforms to make their economies more vibrant and contribute to the very process of heightened market competition and integration.

Notes and References

1. Levi, D. Maurice (1996): *International Finance: The Markets and Financial Management of Multinational Business*, McGraw-Hill International, New York.
2. Giri, D.K. (2001): *'European Union and India—A Study in North-South Relations'*, Concept Publications, New Delhi.
3. Many currency strategists now believe that the coming 12 months could see more strengthening for the euro, as it recovers ground lost since its launch as an electronic, accounting currency on Jan. 1, 1999. Measured on a trade weighted basis, the Euro has declined every year of its existence by 12% during 1999, 1% during 2000, and 2% in 2001. David Fairlamb (2002): 'A Real Currency with Real Impact', *Business Week*, Jan. 4, 2002.
4. Rohit (1999): 'Where do we go?' *Business India*, July 11, 1999. Economists at Credit Suisse First Boston in London now predict that the single currency will rise by 10% during 2002.
5. It is a synthetic (cross) rate, say between € and US $, calculated from the rates of these two currencies against, a third currency, say Pound Sterling £. It gives lower and upper limits on the direct quotes/rates between, say € and US $.
6. Jon Bowen (1999): 'What the Euro means for Indian Business', *The Hindustan Times*, Jan. 17, New Delhi.
7. It is the tendency on the part of coporates and households to invest more in domestic assets and buy more from domestic producers in the face of foreign exchange rate risk and related costs.
8. In the case of European Currency Union (ECU), the impact of this has been quite significant. In the second quarter of 1999, just three months after the introduction of Euro, cross-border mergers and acquisitions (M&As) in euroland increased by 43%, a trend that persisted since then. The rise of the Euro has also deepened the pan-European debt-market and increased the available risk instruments significantly.
9. Of these, the UK is the most significant but does not belong to the currency union (the Pound sterling, £ continues to exist). Excluding U.K. the Union's rank drops by a couple of points, but remains significant.
10. Development Research Group (2000): 'EMU, Euro and India', Reserve Bank of India (RBI), Mumbai.
11. David Fairlamb (2002): A 'Real Currency' with 'Real Impact', *Business Week*, January 4, 2002
12. *Op. cit.*
13. *Op. cit.*
14. *Op. cit.*
15. Include North America, Central America and South America.
16. Development Research Group (2000): *op. cit.*

Abheek Barua (2002): 'The Euro-Making it Work', *Economic Times*, 16, January, 2002.

17. This box item text is summary of a section from *op. cit.* note no. 16.
18. *Op. cit.*
19. The problem with this model is that, crisis by their nature are unpredictable.
20. Economist (2002): 'Europe's Big Idea—The Euro', *The Economist*, 5th January, 2002, London.
21. *Op. cit.*

References

Bairne, P.O. (1998): 'Managing Risk in Euro Currency Conversions', *IT Journal*, Volume XI, No. 6, June.

Meier, G. (1994): *Leading Issues in Economic Development*, Oxford Press, New York.

Ugur, M. (2002): *An Open Economy Macroeconomics Reader,* Routledge Publishers, London and New York.

Rajvade, A.V. (2002): "Issues in Asset Liability Management," *Economic and Political Weekly,* Vol. xxxvii, No. 9, March 2.

Euroframe Forecast (2001): 'Short-term Prospects for the European Economy—Evaluating the current slow-down and aftermath of the September 11th attacks on the USA, 9th November, 2001.

APPENDIX 1

What is the Euro? The Construction

With the arrival of the European Monetary Union on January 1, 1999 the European countries have begun replacing their national currencies with the euro, transforming the European Union (EU) into the world's largest single currency trade group. The union poses both challenges and opportunities to businesses which will now be operating in an open and transparent market.

Out of 15 nations which comprise the European Union (EU), only 11 (and later 12) adopted the euro in January 1, 1999. The EMU is the largest single currency zone in the world with a GDP of eight trillion dollars. The new block will be an economic might accounting for 19.4% of the world GDP and 18.6% of the world trade as compared to the US which accounts for 19.6% of world GDP and 16.6% of the world trade and Japan which contributes only 7.7% of world GDP and 8.8% of world trade. Also, the unification is expected to bring an additional growth in GDP (for the 11 member countries) of about 0.5-1% thus overtaking the US.

Key Statistics

1998	*Area (000 km²)*	*People (mn nos.)*	*GDP (mkt. pr.)*
EU-15	3191	376	7495
Euro-11	2364	292	5774
USA	9373	270	7592
Japan	378	127	3327

Apart from this the formation of EMU will rake in many other benefits such as:

- Lower business costs with a single currency.
- Rise in competition may reduce prices benefiting the consumers and making countries more competitive in the international markets.
- Centralized fiscal and monetary policy will provide interest and inflation rates which are stable and under control.
- Which will in turn encourage corporate investment.

Starting Jan. 1, 1999, the currencies of member countries (11 countries which joined the EMU include Austria, Belgium, Finland, France, Germany, Ireland, Italy, Luxembourg, Netherlands, Portugal and Spain) has been linked to the euro with a fixed conversion rate. The local currency and the euro will co-exist until July 2002 at the latest, after which the local currency will be replaced by the euro.

Entrance Criteria

The European Commission (EC), the EU's administrative body, has set-up entrance criteria to ensure the countries that joined EMU had a reasonable chance of succeeding in a single currency zone. These "convergence criteria" focused on stabilized inflation, exchange rate stability, sustainability of public finances and the ratio of public debt to GDP.

Qualification Test for EMU Members

Inflation rate should not exceed 1.5% above the average of best three Countries.

- Long-term interest rate not more than 2% higher than the average rate of 3 member countries with the lowest inflation rate.
- Budget deficit to be maintained within 3% of the GDP.
- Public debt not exceeding 60% of the GDP.

Appendix 2

Legal Framework

The main parts of the legal framework for the introduction and the use of the euro are laid down in two European Council regulations:

Introduction of the Euro

"The euro will be substituted for the currencies of the participating Member States at the fixed conversion rates applicable from 1 January 1999. During the transitional period from 1 January 1999 to 31 December 2001 national currency units become sub-divisions of the euro."

No Compulsion—No Prohibition

The fundamental principle applicable during the transitional period (1 January 1999 to 31 December 2001) is that, no enterprise or individual will be required to use the euro. The corollary will also apply; no enterprise or individual will be prohibited from using the euro in transactions where they deem it appropriate. Thus, obligations in legal instruments stipulating the use of one of the units possible, the national currency or the euro shall be performed in the stipulated unit unless otherwise agreed by the parties. This rule ensures that economic agents will only have to use the unit to which they have agreed. To further clarify, if an enterprise or individual chooses to use the euro and the counterparty of the transaction does not; the financial institution or bank is required, under European legislation, to convert to the chosen currency.

The principles of 'no compulsion' and 'no prohibition' concerning the use of the euro were established during the 1996 Madrid summit. There is an inevitable trade-off between the freedom of the economic agents and that of the Member States. As a result of these, tradeoffs, enterprises may be faced with the following situations:

- It may not be possible in all countries to file tax returns for income taxes, value-added taxes, and customs and duties, in euro from the start of the transitional period.
- It may not be possible in all countries to keep books and

records and to file accounts in euro from the start of the transitional period.

- Other transactions with government bodies and agencies, such as payments of registration fees or sales and purchases, may only be possible in the national currency unit during the transitional period. However, as explained above, it is the obligation of your financial institution to convert the euro to the national currency to effect the payment.

Payments in Euro during the Transitional Period

As from 1 January, 1999, any amount denominated either in the euro unit or in the participating member state national currency unit, can be paid by the debtor either in the euro unit or in the national currency unit.

The legal regulations enable debtors to settle their debts in book money (electronic form) by making a payment in either the euro or in the national currency. Banks are under an obligation to convert such payments into the unit of account of the creditor.

When a business only maintains a bank account in the national currency, receipts in euro must be converted into the national currency. The euro regulations do not expressly address the issue of charging for the conversion of amounts between the national currency unit and the euro unit. This will be subject to competitive forces.

Rounding

"Monetary amounts to be paid or accounted for when a rounding takes place after a conversion into the euro unit shall be rounded up or down to the nearest cent. Monetary amounts to be paid or accounted for which are converted into a national currency unit shall be rounded up or down to the nearest sub-unit or in the absence of a sub-unit to the nearest unit, or according to national law or practice to a multiple or fraction of the sub-unit or unit of the national currency unit. If the application of the conversion rate gives a result which is exactly half-way, the sum shall be rounded up." The resulting amount must be rounded to the nearest number in the smallest sub-division of the currency (i.e. 2 units to the right of the decimal). If the conversion results in an amount that is exactly the middle of the smallest sub-division of the currency, the amount is rounded up.

29

Liberalization of Agricultural Trade—What it Holds for India?

A.R. VEERAMANI AND K. RAMESH

INTRODUCTION

The economic reforms of 1991 introduced liberalization, privatization and globalization in pursuit of setting the domestic economy in order. It mainly altered the industrial sector, leaving the agricultural sector highly in tact. But the arrival of the World Trade Organization, at the end of the Uruguay Round, which has brought in new set of rules, (the Agreement on Agriculture) is going to affect the Indian agricultural sector as never before. AoA has new international rules like domestic support commitments, market access commitments and export subsidy reduction commitments. With the advent of WTO and the pressure of all the developed countries, the tropical (mainly the Third World) countries are in an unenviable position. These countries are being compelled to globalize their agricultural trade and commit themselves to AoA diligently. Though the impact of AoA on our agriculture needs to be experienced, this paper tries to assess the possible outcome of the new rules of the game.

THE EXPORT ARGUMENT

Not many empirical studies, with the help of primary data, are available to find out the impact of liberalization on the sector in particular, and the economy, in general. But, by using statistical tools and econometric models, it has been estimated that, liberalizing agricultural trade will lead to large export volumes of rice, wheat and cotton, while, cheaper import of pulses and edible oils. This might push up the price of rice, wheat, sugar and cotton, thereby benefiting the domestic producers and bring down the price levels of cereals, pulses and edible oils which would benefit the consumers.[1] Obviously, this will help to increase farmers' profitability and private capital formation. This also implies that, not only farmers, the total sector can grow enormously by reallocating resources to produce more exportables and thereby maximize efficiency (*Gulati* and *Sharma*, 1997).

CHANGING CROPPING PATTERN

The increasing domestic price levels of rice, wheat and maize would induce producers to reallocate their land in the pursuit of maximizing returns, resulting in cropping pattern changes. This trend has already started to happen in India. In the first four years after 1991, the percentage of change in area under coarse grains has come down by 11.08 per cent and pulses by 6.13 per cent. Though the change has been positive for rice and wheat put together, it is as low as 0.98 per cent. For cereals as a whole, the percentage share has come down by 2.95 per cent, and all this has benefited oilseeds' area of cultivation, which has gone up by 10.23 per cent between 1989-91 and 1991-95 (*Utsa Patnaik*, 1996).

In a region-wise study, it has been estimated that, this kind of changes in cropping pattern is fairly similar among regions. Data for the period (triennium ending) from 1962-65 to 1992-95 show that, except for North-Western region, in all the other three (Southern, Eastern and Central), the percentage share of area under non-food grains has gone up at the cost of food grains. The highest percentage of decline has occurred in the Southern region

(21 per cent) while, the national average was only 7.2 per cent. In Eastern, Central and Southern regions, the percentage share of oilseeds has gone up enormously—by 95, 66 and 89 per cent respectively. This is clearly higher than the national average of 44.5 per cent. This nature of cropping pattern change favouring non-food grains, particularly oilseeds, may not directly be attributed to trade liberalization. It was mainly due to the Government's effort to encourage farmers to shift over to oilseeds, which made it highly profitable. This is given here to explain the probable attitude of the producers when domestic and international prices are equated.

Cropping Pattern Changes—Region-wise (triennium ending 1962-65 to 1992-95)

(*in %*)

Region	*Rice*	*Wheat*	*Cereals*	*Pulses*	*Foodgrains*	*Non-food grains*	*Oilseeds*
North-Western	47.0	92.5	-47.0	-56.0	3.8	-14.7	-43.0
Eastern	-1.4	190.0	-35.0	-38.0	-4.5	34.8	95.0
Central	2.6	5.2	-22.0	5.1	-9.1	27.0	66.0
Southern	-5.7	-30.7	-43.0	25.0	-21.0	55.0	89.0
All India	4.7	61.0	-32.0	-14.0	**-7.2**	27.0	44.5

Note: Only oilseed is mentioned among non-food grains.
Source: Estimated from Bhalla and Singh (1998).

The developed countries' demand for complete opening up of the developing countries' agricultural trade will lead to restructuring of the latter's cropping pattern to suit that of the former's. This will be in direct contrast to the food habit of the developing countries. For example, the bulk of new demand from the developed countries is for vegetable oils, fruits and vegetable. The developing countries have to re-orient their agricultural practices to reap the so-called export advantage.

NET SOCIAL WELFARE

As noted, with liberalization, producers gain through higher prices for a crop while, consumers lose on that and *vice versa* in another crop. Calculation of net social welfare gives the total picture. This calculation (*Chand*, 1999) shows that, free trade in rice would result in a small net social loss to the country, while creating some gain in other crops. It should, however be mentioned that, though the net social loss is small, the consumers' loss is so huge that it more than offsets the enormous gain made by the producers.

DECREASING DOMESTIC AVAILABILITY

Generally, agriculture is featured with unique characteristics, and is different from industrial activities. With the help of a two-sector model, it has been proved that, a positive import tariff equilibrium would provide more manufacturing employment and a larger per capita food availability, than that of a zero level import tariff (*P. Patnaik*, 1996). A positive industrial import tariff would enlarge manufacturing output and reduce imports in that sector, and thereby, it would require only a small quantity of agricultural exports for a foreign exchange market equilibrium. This will increase per capita domestic food availability. The decreasing food availability with a zero import tariff along with higher domestic price level of food crops will, directly affect, not only the agricultural labourers and other rural labourers, but also, small and marginal farmers themselves. Since, they involve in contract farming, they too remain as net purchasers of food grains.[2]

INTERNATIONAL PRICE VOLATILITY

The outcome of linking domestic and international prices is, the problem of volatility of international price levels. World Bank report on world market price instability shows that, wheat is a moderately high instability crop, rice is a high instability crop and edible oil and sugar are very high instability crops. Hence, globalizing and liberalizing of Indian agriculture will create higher instability in the economy and also in producers' earnings. Moreover, price projections for major agricultural products for the year 2005 show that, price levels of rice, wheat, maize, edible oil and sugar all will decline moderately when compared to the price levels of 1990 and will fall hugely when compared to that of 1980 (*Gill* and *Brar*, 1996). This kind of instability has not yet been experienced by our farmers, who are well protected by the minimum support prices. Farmers' revenue expectations suffer because of the volatile price conditions. Small and Marginal farmers, who remain highly vulnarable to such problem, will have to give up cultivation once-for-all. Moreover, developing countries like India, when begin to export agri-products in this era, their export earnings too become highly unstable, which will also affect investment decisions. The inverse link between export instability and negative growth in per capita income and the rate of growth in the developing countries has also been proved (*Glezakos*, 1973).

India being a major producer of some crops, a mere export of five per cent of its rice output, for example, will increase the world supply by 25 per cent, worsening the problem of price volatility at the international level.

THE PREJUDICED POLICIES

The impact of changes in cropping pattern when influenced by international factors, become both extensive and intensive on all sectors of the economy. The same kind of economic liberalization, stabilization and structural adjustment programmes which are now being followed in India, are in practice in many African, Latin American and East Asian countries, atleast since the 1980's. These measures which never have been implemented in the developed countries themselves, are applied to the developing countries, whose benefits have accrued exclusively to the former. When the same set of polices are simultaneously pursued by all the developing countries, they compete among themselves for every export item and price begins to fall, which benefits Western customers and affects Third World producers.

NON-PRICE FACTORS AND AGRICULTURAL SUPPLY

Economic liberalization directly affects domestic industrial sector which leads to de-industrialization, and thus increases imports of manufactures. To balance this, on the payment front, agri-export should be increased. Though it is argued that, higher profitability in agriculture through higher domestic price, will increase private capital formation, it has been proved that, while, higher private investment is only a necessary condition to increase yield per acre, higher public investment, especially in rural infrastructure and market, is both necessary and sufficient condition. This also undermines the importance of better terms of trade for agriculture. Yield per acre becomes inelastic for any additional private investment after a point (*Desai* and *Namboodiri*, 1997). This explains why correcting the domestic terms of trade and bringing it in favour of agriculture alone is not sufficient.

THE FLAWED OPTION

The major advantages of liberalizing agricultural trade which seem to accrue, rely on many probable conditions. For example, India can export more of rice, wheat and cotton in which its international price advantage is higher and import more of edible oil, cereals and pulses in which the disadvantage is higher. This will lead to better use of resources and sectoral growth. But all these can happen only:

- If the developed countries change their attitude and become fair players of trade liberalization;
- If countries like the Europian Union and Japan heed to the plea of the developing nations for market access and others;
- If developed countries begin to reduce their tariff peaks without demanding any reciprocity from the developing countries; and
- If even after conceding on all the above, developed countries should refrain from inciting any special clauses like sanitary, phyto-sanitary and/or other similar conditions.

CONCLUSION

The following can be concluded as the possible outcome of this agenda:

(a) increasing domestic price levels, particularly that of basic food crops;
(b) declining domestic availability of agri-products will hit rural masses and urban poor, including small and marginal farmers, who remain net purchasers;
(c) to reap quick returns from a possible free exports, farmers would reallocate their land holdings to suit the Western countries' demand; and

(d) through highly volatile international prices, the total sector might become unstable, thereby chucking the small and marginal farmers, out of cultivation.

This explains why freeing of Indian agricultural trade is a flawed option and implies the heavy burden that rests upon the government in dealing with the AoA, without causing much harm to our farmers. Countries like India are treading on a very thin ice, and not much room is left to manoeuvre, particularly when, all the Western countries are pressurizing the developing countries for market access commitments. Fiscal constraints, and not AoA structures, compell India to reduce its agricultural subsidies, even though it is well known that its Aggregate Measure of Support is way off, from the permitted level.

SUGGESTIONS

The inevitable nature of the impact of globalization and liberalization on Indian agriculture can be redressed to a certain degree, provided the government takes some bold initiatives:

(a) agriculture being the prime sector still, all kinds of agricultural subsidies can be re-targeted by, clearly omitting the 'creamy layer' within the sector, and see to that, all subsidies are really appropriated by the needy-ones only;

(b) the significance of public investment not only in rural power, rural transport and marketing, but especially in storage (including cold storage), should be augmented immediately;

(c) the necessity of investing in Research and Development and extension services should not be under-estimated; and

(d) as India's export potential is larger in vegetables and floriculture, this kind of diversification should be encouraged, but without causing any serious damage to cropping pattern or availability of food crops.

Notes and References

1. Here it might be argued that, the export demand is going to be mainly for high quality products (of rice, wheat, etc.) and thus, only price levels

of these high quality varieties will go up. Hence, consumers of low and medium quality varieties need not suffer from globalization. But while, demand for high quality varieties will be coining from Europe and America, the Near East countries could be importing more of medium quality varieties. And this will push up the price level of rice in particular, atleast by 10-15 per cent (*Yap*, 1999).

2. P. Patnaik (1996) traces the historical evidence for the link between higher exports and decreasing domestic availability of foodgrains.

REFERENCES

Bhalla, G.S. and Gurmail Singh (1998), "*Recent Development in Indian Agriculture—A District Level Study*", Centre for the Study of Regional Development: Jawaharlal Nehru University, New Delhi.

Chand, Ramesh (1999), "Liberalization of Agricultural Trade and Net Social Welfare: A Study of Selected Crops", *Economic and Political Weekly*, 25, December.

Desai, Bhupat M. and N.V. Namboodiri (1997), "Price and Non-Price Determinants of Aggregate Agricultural Supply", in *Agricultural Development Paradigm for the Ninth Plan under New Economic Environment*, (Ed.) Bhupat M. Desai, Oxford and IBP.

Gill, S.S and J.S. Brar (1996), "Global Market Competitiveness of Indian Agriculture: Some Issues", *Economic and Political Weekly*, 10 August.

Glezakos, Constantine (1973), "Export Instability and Economic Growth: A Statistical Verification", *Economic Development and Cultural Change*, 21, July.

Gulati, Ashok and Anil Sharma (1997), "Freeing Trade in Agriculture: Implications for Resource Use Efficiency and Cropping Pattern Changes", *Economic and Political Weekly*, 27, December.

Nambiar, R.G. and Bhavani Sridharan (1997), "Trade Policy for a New World Agricultural Market", in Desai (1997), *op. cit*.

Patnaik, Prabhat (1996), "Should Domestic Prices be Equated to World Prices?", *Economic and Political Weekly*, special number, September.

Patnaik, Utsa (1996), "Export-Oriented Agriculture and Food Security in Developing Countries and India", *Economic and Political Weekly*, special number, September.

Vaidyanathan, A. (2000), "India's Agricultural Development Policy", *Economic and Political Weekly*, 13, May.

Yap, Chan Ling (1999), "The Impact of the Uruguay Round Agreement on Agriculture on the World Rice Economy and South Asia," in *Implications of the Uruguay Round Agreement for South Asia: The Case of Agriculture* (ed.) Benoit Blarel *et al*, Allied Publishers, New Delhi.

30

WTO and Indian Agricultural Development: A Case Study of Punjab

DAVINDER KUMAR MADAAN

World Trade Organization (WTO) was established on 1st January, 1995, by replacing General Agreement on Tariffs and Trade (GATT), which was in existence from 1947 to 1994 GATT was a multilateral treaty, governing trade in goods only, but the WTO has acquired a much wider and ever increasing scope and coverage. At present, 144 countries are its members including India and China. A Ministerial Conference that meets at least once every two years, directs WTO, till date, four Ministerial Conferences have been held in Singapore (Dec. 1996), Geneva (May 1998), Seattle-USA (Nov.-Dec. 1999), and Doha-Qatar (Nov. 2001) respectively. The fifth Ministerial Conference is to be held in Mexico during early 2003. WTO is based on the principles of non-discrimination, free trade, and promotion of fair competition among the member-countries. About 95 per cent of the global trade is governed by the rules and regulations of WTO. The Quad countries (USA, EU, Canada and Japan) with their share of 80 per cent of the global trade, dominate the decision-making of WTO. The WTO Agreements are permanent and ratified by members of Parliament. These are to be implemented till December 31, 2004.

Indian agriculture accounts for about one-fourth of the Gross Domestic Product (GDP) and is source of livelihood of more than two-third of the population. The increase in the foodgrains production has been more than the increase in population since the early 1950s. Now the problem is of excess supply over demand. Indian agriculture has been facing serious challenges and huge opportunities under WTO. During 1986-89, the base year of WTO, the international prices of most agro-products were more than the domestic prices and then, India was expecting the international prices to remain stable due to reduction of subsidies by the developed countries under WTO commitments. But international prices have declined except paddy and now domestic prices of India are more than international prices.[1] This resulted a threat to India's domestic market from cheap imports.[2] India's competitiveness in the agro-export markets has been lost due to large increase in Minimum Support Prices (MSP). During post-WTO period, the share of India's agro-exports in her global exports has declined from 16.2 per cent in 1995-96 to 10.4 per cent in 2000-01.[3] India's food stocks of wheat and rice has increased from 30.3 mn tonnes in January 1995 to 58 mn tonnes in January 2002 against the minimum norm of 16.8 mn tonnes[4]. As a result, WTO has become serious challenge to several food-surplus States of India including Punjab.

Punjab agriculture accounted for 21 per cent of wheat and 10 per cent of rice in India's production during 1999-2000. While the foodgrains production in Punjab increased from 3.16 mn tonnes in 1960-61 to 25.2 mn tonnes in 1999-2000, but its growth has come down from 5.84 per cent during 1967-81 to 2.98 per cent during 1981-99. With the increase in input intensity and fall of water table, the growth of total factor productivity also declined. As a result, the returns of various crops in Punjab have been reduced over the period. Hence the income of Punjab farmers has come down. The incidence of indebtness of Punjab farmers increased due to their poor financial conditions. As such, the farmer's suicides rate went up manifolds in the State. In fact, WTO agreements pose a serious threat to Punjab economy. This paper is an attempt to discuss the impact of WTO Agreement on Indian agricultural development in general and Punjab agriculture in particular, thereby suggesting some urgent steps in this regard.

AGREEMENT OF AGRICULTURE (AoA) OF WTO

Under GATT Accord of 1947, agriculture was the highly protected sector in the developed countries. As a result, the agricultural exports of the developing countries suffered a lot. AoA of WTO recognizes free and market-oriented trading system in agriculture. Its main features are as follow:

1. Tarification

It means conversion of all non-tariff barriers on trade such as Import Quota into Tariffs. Tariff bindings (commitment not to exceed a particular level of tariff) are to be reduced under this agreement. Developed countries were to reduce their tariff bindings by simple un-weighted average of 36 per cent with a minimum cut of 15 per cent for each tariff line over a period of six years (1995-2000). Developing countries are to reduce their bindings by simple un-weighted average of 24 per cent with a minimum cut of 10 per cent for each tariff line over a period of ten years (1995-2004). Least Developed Countries are exempted from tariff reductions.

India has indicated tariff bindings of 100 per cent on primary agricultural goods and raw commodities like wheat, rice, milk and cream, etc. 150 per cent on processed agro-commodities like cotton, etc. and 300 per cent on most edible oils. But, in practice, import duty imposed by India is as per Table 1.

India has revised the rate of import duty to 65 per cent on crude palm oil, and 92.4 per cent on refined palm oil in November 2001. India is now the world's biggest importer of edible oils, importing 45 per cent (5 mn tons) of the total requirements, of which palm products enjoy 61 per cent of total import requirements of edible oils. Edible oils have emerged as the second largest item in India's import bill after petroleum products.[5]

TABLE 1

Import Duties on Agricultural Products in India

(Per cent)

S. No.	*Commodity*	*WTO's Bound Rate (2001)*	*Applied Rate*
1.	Wheat	100	50
2.	Spelt Wheat	80	50
3.	Rice	70 & 80	70 & 80
4.	Pulses	1100	5
5.	Maize	60 & 70	50
6.	Sugar	150	60
7.	Oilseeds (Rapeseed/Sunflower)	75	75
8.	Raw Cotton	100	10
9.	Crude Palm oil	300	65*
10	Refined Palm oil	300	92.4

*Fixed tariff US$ 286/tonne w.e.f. 9/11/2001.
Source: Govt. of India, *Economic Survey*, 2001-02.

2. Market Access

Where tariff bindings are either too high or incomplete tariffication, current market access has to be maintained as the amount of exports to other countries at preferential tariff rates. However, where current access provisions do not prevail, minimum access to be provided, which is equal to 3 per cent of 1986-88 base level consumption, rising to 5 per cent till 2000 by the developed countries, and 1 per cent of the 1986-88 base level consumption, rising to 2 per cent in 1999 and 4 per cent in 2005 for staple in diet commodity by the developing countries. Market access provisions do not apply, when the commodity in question is a traditional staple in diet of a developing country. In case of India, wheat and rice are staple foods and hence their imports can be restricted.

3 Domestic Support

I. Aggregate Measure of Support (AMS)

AMS is the annual level of support in monetary terms extended to agriculture sector. It is the non-exempted support of following two kinds:

(a) Product-Specific Support

It is the market price support/subsidy given to the producer of specific crop.

(b) Non-product Specific Support

It comprises sum total of subsidies on inputs like power, irrigation, fertilizer and credit.

If AMS exceeds 5 per cent of the total value of agricultural production in the case of developed count lies (10 per cent for developing countries), these are to be reduced by 20 per cent over six years from 1995 (13.3 per cent over ten years for developing countries).

The AMS to Indian agriculture is still below 10 per cent in terms of WTO stipulations. The product-specific support under AMS to Indian agriculture during reference period (1986-89) TE on an average was -21.6 per cent of its agricultural GDP. It reduced to -38.6 per cent during 1995-96, which now might have increased due to recent fall in the international agricultural prices and rise in MSPs for wheat and rice.[6] The non-product specific support amounted to 4.04 per cent of agricultural GDP during 1986-89. It increased to 7.52 per cent during 1995-96 and 5.27 per cent during 1997-98. However, it could be reduced by almost 80 per cent, if India avails the exemption of input subsidies to resource poor farmers.[7]

II. Green Box Support

It is exempted support and is given on such items, which have minimal impact on trade like research, pest and disease control, training and advisory services, market intelligence and promotional services, infrastructure services, food security, buffer stock operations, relief from natural disasters, etc.

III. Blue Box Support

It is product-limiting subsidy and covers the fixed costs of the farmers indirectly. This support is exempted from reduction commitment under WTO and is related mainly to the developed countries.

IV. Special and Differential (S&D) Treatment Box Support

This support is related to the developing countries, and is exempted from reduction commitment under WTO. It includes:

(a) Investment subsidy to agricultural sector on farm development work (field, channels, land leveling, shallow wells, etc.), and

(b) Agricultural input services to low-income or resource poor farmers.

It is worthwhile to mention that the developed countries have not implemented fully their commitments for reducing domestic support. Rather agricultural subsidies have been increased during the post-WTO period. Though agriculture contributes a very high proportion to employment and GDP in the developing countries, resulting low productivity, yet this sector has become equally important in the developed countries in the process of economic development. Table 2 depicts the agricultural subsidies in selected OECD countries and India.

TABLE 2

Agriculture Subsidies in Selected OECD Countries and India

(US$)

S. No.	*Country*	*T.E. 1986-89 (WTO's Base Period)*			*1999*		
		Per Farmer	*Per Hectare*	*Total Subsidies (US $ in mn)*	*Per Farmer*	*Per Hectare*	*Total Subsidies (US $ in mn)*
1.	Canada	12000	75	5645	9000	52	3093
2.	EC	11000	707	95214	17000	831	114450
3.	Japan	15000	10048	53637	26000	11792	58885
4.	USA	17000	98	41890	21000	129	54009
5.	OECD	11000	187	246226	11000	218	282780
6.	India	11	8	1058	66	53	7247

T.E.= Triennium Ending Average per annum.

Source: Govt. of India, *Agricultural Statistics At A Glance, 2001*, Ministry of Agriculture.

The annual agricultural subsidies in OECD countries have

increased from US $ 246 2 bn during 1986-89 (base period of WTO agreement) to US $ 282.78 bn in 1999. India's agricultural subsidies were only US $ 1.06 bn and 7.2 bn during this respective period. While per farmer subsidy of USA increased rapidly from US $ 17000 in 1986-89 to 21000 in 1999, but in case of India, it increased from US $ 11 to US $ 66 only. Further, per hectare subsidy of Japan has increased from US $ 10048 to US $ 11792 as compared to US $ 8 to US $ 53 only of India during this period.

In fact, OECD countries are subsidizing their agricultural sector by increasing support under green and blue boxes. During 1995, green box support accounted for 33.11 per cent of agricultural GDP in USA as compared to only 2.34 per cent of India.[9]

4. Export Competition

In the area of export competition, countries are obliged to reduction commitments of their direct export subsidies. Developed countries are to reduce the volume of subsidized agricultural exports by 21 per cent and the value of subsidies by 36 per cent of the average base period 1986-90 within six years. Developing countries are to reduce the same by 14 per cent and 24 per cent respectively within ten years.

India is not giving any export subsidies On the other hand, the developed countries are giving as high as 90-100 per cent export subsidies.

PUNJAB AGRICULTURE

With a population of 2.43 crores in 2001, Punjab is basically an agricultural economy. However, the importance of agriculture sector in Punjab economy has declined over the period. But still two-thirds (66.05 per cent) of the population of Punjab is dependent on agriculture.[10] There is a growing trend of urbanization in the State as the share of urban population has increased to 33.95 per cent as compared to India's 27.78 per cent in 2001. Nevertheless, it is below the proportion of world urban population, which was estimated to 47 per cent in 2000.[11] Though the growth rate of Punjab population during 1991-2001 was 19.76 per cent, but urban population grew by 37.58 per cent. Slum population accounted for 13.97 per cent of the Punjab urban population. Punjab ranks 16th in terms of literacy among the Indian States and Union Territories. Its literacy rate has increased to 69.95 per cent, which is more than the national average of 65.38 per cent in 2001. 12.58 per cent of Punjab child population in the age group 0-6 is excluded in this figure as Census classified all children below 7 years as illiterates, but some of them might have been attending schools.

Though Punjab is only 1.5 per cent of the geographical area of India, but its contribution in terms of agriculture is remarkable. Punjab ranks second in terms of per capita income, which was Rs. 23,040 during 1999-2000. Table 3, depicts some important facts about Punjab and Indian agriculture during 1999-2000.

TABLE 3

Some Facts about Punjab and Indian Agriculture during 1999-2000

S.No.		*Punjab*	*India*
1.	Agriculture in total income (%, 93-94 prices)	28.06	24.7#
2.	Net area sown (% of total area)	84.18	46.60#
3.	Area sown more than once (% of total area)		
4.	Cropped area (% of total area)	155.91	62.17#
5.	Cropping intensity***	185	134.3
6.	Per capita electricity consumption by agriculture (KWH)	325.05	100.12 #
7.	Net Irrigated Area (% of Net Sown Area)	94.3	38.4
8.	Area irrigated by tube wells (%)	39.53	9.72 @
9.	Agricultural workers in total workforce (%, 1991)	55.26	64.70
10.	Agricultural labourers in total workforce (%, 1991)	22.76	40.00
11.	Average size of holdings per hectare (90-91)	3.61	1.55
12.	Marginal holdings: below 1 hectare (%, 90-91)	26.5	59.4
13.	Small holdings: 1-2 hectare (%, 90-91)	18.3	18.8
14.	Semi-medium holdings: 2-4 hectare (%, 90-91)	25.9	13.1
15.	Medium holdings: 4-10 hectare (%, 90-91)	23.4	7.1
16.	Large holding: above 10 hectare (%, 90-91)	6.0	1.6

= 1997-98 and @ = 1998-99.

***Percentage of Gross Cropped Area to Net Sown Area.

Source: Govt. of Punjab, *Statistical Abstract of Punjab, 2000*.

Agriculture accounted for 28.06 per cent in total Punjab income, which was higher as compared to 24.7 per cent of India during 1999-2000. The net area sown in Punjab was 84.18 per cent as compared to 46.6 per cent of India during this period. The total cropped area of Punjab accounted for 155.9 per cent of the total area as compared to 62.17 per cent of India. The cropping intensity of Punjab increased to 185 per cent as compared to 134.3 per cent of India which accelerated the agricultural production of the State. Punjab agricultural sector consumed more than three times per capita electricity of India. Punjab Government incurred loss of Rs. 1939 crore for free supply of electricity to agriculture sector during this period[12]. Irrigated area of Punjab was 94.3 per cent of net sown area as compared to 38.4 per cent of India. Agricultural labourers in total workforce of Punjab were about 23 per cent as compared to 40 per cent of India. At present, 33 lac farmers are land-less in Punjab. The size of Punjab operational holdings was more than double of India. The average size of holdings per hectare in case of Punjab was 3.61 as compared to 1.55 of India. About 70 per cent of operational holdings in Punjab were less than 4 hectare/10 acres during 1990-91, which however, decreased to 64.7 per cent in 1995-96. The State has contributed about 42.1 per cent rice and 55.4 per cent wheat to the Central Pool during 1999-2000.[13]

The contribution of agrarian economy of Punjab to Indian agriculture is praise worthy. Table 4, depicts the comparison of area, production and yield of agricultural products in Punjab and India during 1999-2000. The cropped area under foodgrains in Punjab accounted for 74.67 per cent as compared to 66.14 per cent of India during this period. However, wheat, rice and cotton constituted 82.4 per cent of the total cropped area of Punjab, as compared to 42.9 per cent of India during this period. On the other hand, Punjab's cropped area under sugarcane, oilseeds, fruits and vegetables was less than 5 per cent only during this period. It is clear that Punjab agriculture is more dependent on wheat, rice and cotton. The share of Punjab in foodgrains production of India accounted for 12.6 per cent during 1999-2000. However, in case of wheat, rice and cotton, Punjab contributed 21.05 per cent, 9.75 per cent and 5.69 per cent respectively in India's production during this period. In case of other agro-products, Punjab accounted for less than 3 per cent in India's production during this period. On the other hand, the picture of India in the global production of different agro-products is remarkable as per Table 4. While India occupied 1st position in the global production of pulses (24.6%), she got 2nd position in case of wheat (11.1%), rice (21.6%), sugarcane (22.2%), vegetable (9.2%) and fruits (8.7%) during 1999-2000. Further, in case of cotton (14.9%) and rapeseed and mustard (14.7%), India occupied 3rd position in the global production during this period. Average yield of Punjab's agro products except sugarcane as per Table 4 was higher as compared to India during 1999-2000. Nevertheless, the average yield of USA is more than that of Punjab in case of rice, cotton, sugarcane and maize during this period. But the average yield of Punjab wheat is more than that of USA. It is clear from this table that though Punjab agriculture is competitive at domestic level, but it is not so at global level due to its low productivity.

The profitability of the major crops in Punjab has been declining over the period. Punjab Agriculture University has calculated that paddy-wheat rotation in the Punjab agriculture gives an annual net return of Rs. 9000 per hectare.[14] Table 5, also depicts return per hectare over cost C2* of various crops produced in Punjab during 1998-99, a farmer of Punjab growing wheat earned Rs. 1943 per hectare (Rs. 324 per month) on all types of cost (C2). But in case of paddy, he earned Rs. 1312 per hectare (Rs. 219 per month) during this period. Clearly, paddy was less remunerative than wheat. The position of cotton was rather weak. Punjab farmer incurred loss in case of cotton during this period. However, he earned Rs. 257 per hectare at 95-96 prices for cotton. Nevertheless, CACP estimated that during 2000-01, Punjab farmer growing wheat and paddy earned Rs. 917 per month and a farmer growing wheat-cotton earned Rs. 1003 per month.

Punjab farmers have been facing the miserable economic conditions. Further, crop failures and indebtedness make their frequent losses, and are the basic causes of their recent suicides. During 2001, Punjab suffered a loss of one-lac bales of cotton due to American bollworm. In fact, price driven mechanisms such as Minimum Support Prices and subsidized inputs like free power for irrigation and concessional fertilizers have increased the cultivation against the agro-climatic conditions. The use of indiscriminate water has resulted in soil salinity due to water logging in some areas, and a fall in the water table.

TABLE 4

Area, Production and Yield of Agricultural Products in Punjab and India during 1999-2000

(Area in % of Gross Cropped Area, Production in Million MTs and Yield per hectare in Kgs)

S.No.	Commodity	Area		Production					Yield	
		Punjab	India	Punjab		India			Punjab	India
					% in India		% in World	Global Position		
1.	Foodgrains (wheat, rice & pulses)	79.67	66.14	25.2	12.06	209.8	10.7	3rd	4029	1627
	(a) Wheat	43.18	14.45	15.91	21.05	76.4	11.1	2nd	4696	2778
	(b) Rice	33.18	23.53	8.72	9.75	39.7	21.6	2nd	3347	1986
	(c) Pulses	0.78	11.68	0.04	0.03	13.4	24.6	1st	689	608
	(i) Gram	0.08	3.25	0.006	0.12	5.1	n.a.	—	974	833
	(d) Maize	2.08	3.36	0.42	3.66	71.5	1.7	—	2577	1792
2.	Cotton	6.07	4.90	0.95*	5.69	"5.7*	14.9	3rd	337	225
3.	Sugarcane	1.38	2.15	6.77	2.26	299.3	22.2	2nd	62685	70825
4.	Oilseeds	1.25	14.09	0.11	0.53	20.7	n.a.	—	1017	855
	(a) Sunflower	0.26	0.01	0.04	5	3.8	n.a.	—	1480	621
	(b) Rapeseed/Mustard	0.76	3.15	0.06	1.01	5.8	14.7	3rd	1117	960
5.	Vegetables (potatos, onion, topica)	1.56	2.33	n.a.	n.a.	56	9.2	2nd	n.a.	n.a.
	(a) Potatoes	0.97	0.68	1.56	6.25	24.7	8.5	4th	20705	18643
6.	Fruits (kinnow, mangoes, orange)	0.38	1.71	0.42	1.11	38	8.7	2nd	n.a.	n.a.

*Production in mn bales of 170 Kgs each.

Source: Govt. of India, *Economic Survey, 2001-02* and Govt. of Punjab, *Statistical Abstract of Punjab, 2000*.

TABLE 5

Returns to Punjab Farmers in Various Crops

(Rs./Hectare)

Crop	*Minimum Support Price (MSP)*	*Yield (Qtl./Hectare)*	*Gross Returns*	*Cost (C2*)@*	*Net Returns*
1	2	3	4=2×3	5	6=4–5
		1998-99			
Wheat	510.00	42.46	21654.60	19711.61	1942.99
Paddy	440.00	46.45	20438.00	19126.17	1311.83
Sunflower	1060.00	16.02	16981.20	12650.84	4330.36
Cotton	1650.00	4.56	7524.00	15459.22	-7935.22
Rapeseed & Mustard	940.00	8.31	7811.40	10208.43	-2397.08
		2000-01#			
Wheat	580.00	45.63	26465.40	19788.00	6677.40
Paddy	510.00	50.29	25647.90	21311.00	4336.90
Cotton	1825.00	10.95	19983.75	14619.00	5364.75

@ (C2*) includes all actual expenses in cash and kind incurred in production by the owner (Cost A1), rent paid for leased-in land, imputed value of Family Labour, interest on value of own capital assets (excluding land), and rental value of owned land after taking into account statutory minimum or actual wage whichever is higher.

#Estimated by CACP.

Source: Directorate of Economics and Statistics, Ministry of Agriculture, New Delhi.

IMPACT OF WTO ON PUNJAB AGRICULTURE

The Agreement on Agriculture of WTO is bound to influence Punjab agriculture positively as well as negatively. The globalization of Punjab agriculture would pose a new challenge to Punjab agricultural policy. The global agricultural trade would likely to become oligopolistic under WTO regime.

The positive impact on Punjab is in the sense that, WTO ensures level playing field to Punjab agriculture in the international market by reducing subsidies and thereby raising artificial lower prices of some rich countries. The WTO is for greater market access. Further, domestic subsidies to Punjab agriculture will not be reduced. Rather more subsidies can be given as AMS under WTO is below the upper limit of 10 per cent of agricultural production in India. The farmer is free to exchange seeds with his fellow farmer. He can retain his produce for personal use at the next sowing season. The WTO agreement merely says that the farmer can be a producer of grain, not seed. He is prohibited for commercial sale of a Patent variety. But if he does so, the provisions of WTO agreement will bind him. On August 9, 2001, India's Parliament passed the Protection of Plant Varieties and Farmer's Rights Act, 2001, granting breeders and farmers in India the right to claim intellectual property protection over their varieties. A farmer can save, use, resow, exchange, share or sell his farm produce including seeds of protected variety in the same manner as before except 'branded seed.[15]

On the other hand, the negative impact of WTO on Punjab agriculture can be seen from the following facts. *Firstly*, the productivity of Punjab agriculture is low as compared to the developed countries. *Secondly*, the high domestic support, export subsidies and denial of market access through various tariff and non-tariff barriers in the developed countries, have resulted a fall in global agricultural commodity prices in the post-WTO period. As such, India's agricultural exports have declined in this period. *Thirdly*, shifting of very high level of domestic support from non-exempted categories (Amber Box) to exempt categories (Green & Blue Boxes) by the developed countries provided their produce advantage over the produce of developing countries. In fact, AMS is the partial measure of support as about 60 per cent of total support is left out of the AMS calculations owing to exemptions prescribed in Article 6 and Annex. 2 of the AOA.[16] *Fourthly,* international quality standards are very difficult to be maintained by Punjab farmers in the WTO regime. *Lastly,* the patenting of hybrid genetically modified seeds under TRIPs would prevent Punjab farmers from retaining and exchanging their seeds. The Punjab farmers cannot afford to purchase seed for every sowing.

SUGGESTIONS

1. Agricultural productivity of Punjab can be improved by increasing public investment in irrigation, power, roads and agricultural research. The research under biotechnology can be promoted in State Universities. Bio-technology Park can also be set-up. The use of cost-reducing technology and internal liberalization of agricultural trade can also help in raising productivity.

2. Punjab must diversify its agricultural economy of wheat, rice and cotton. Alternative crops like oilseeds, pulses, horticulture, fruits and vegetables, which give higher returns, should be promoted. Punjab Government can give concession to farmers for sowing these higher return crops. Encouragement to food processing industries can promote the cultivation of fruits and vegetables, bringing higher returns to farmers, and thereby diminishing the subsidy burden arising out of food grains procurement.

3. Punjab should strengthen its marketing network. A basic problem of agriculture is the absence of reliable marketing mechanism. The fact is that the farmer receives a fraction of what the consumer pays. As such, middlemen eat away a big part. Therefore, it is must to ensure a remunerative price before asking the farmers to diversify high return crops like oilseeds, pulses, horticulture, etc. Modern marketing infrastructure and multifarious extension services should be provided to farmers.

4. Increased domestic support to agriculture can be given under Green, Blue and S&D Boxes of WTO, which are exempted from support reductions.

5. Punjab should explore export markets for its surplus agricultural production, which is causing financial loss and storage problems. Under WTO, developing countries like India

can give subsidies on export marketing costs, internal and international transport and freight charges.

6. Due to storage constraints, Indian government should issue wheat and rice under PDS at the rate of its export price by disbanding APL and BPL categories.

7. Punjab Government should insist on Union Government that the import of wheat and rice must be restricted as market access provision of WTO is not applicable to India for these staple food products. During post-WTO period (1995-2001), India imported 5.16 mn tonnes wheat and 62000 tonnes rice. It aggravated the situation of food surplus States including Punjab.

8. Punjab Government should start National Agricultural Insurance Scheme (NAIS), introduced by Union Ministry of Agriculture since 1999-2000 Rabi Season. 21 States/UTs are already implementing the scheme. It protects the farmers against losses due to crop failure. The small and marginal farmers (35.4% of total holdings in Punjab) are given 50 per cent subsidy in the premium, which is shared equally by the Union government and participating State/UT and phased out over a period of five years.

9. Punjab Government should promote the use of Information Technology (IT) in agriculture sector by giving special computer training to farmers. Through INTERNET access, farmers can learn the latest farming techniques in the world. They can get latest information on agricultural commodities prices in different countries. They can cheaply interact for the marketing of their produce after understanding the global demand and supply of farm products. They can know about the weather in advance.

10. Punjab has tremendous potential to develop food-processing industry, which besides reducing the level of wastage would also realize higher benefits for farmers. Though India is the second largest producer of horticulture crops and third largest food grains producer in the world, but it processes only two per cent of its annual production as compared to 45 per cent in Philippines and 23 per cent in China. About 40 per cent of the annual production goes waste due to lack of adequate storage facility for food processing industry. The biggest problem is our ignorance about the plantation of those varieties, which are suitable for processing purposes. It requires the seeds of processable varieties. It is desirable to reduce level of Sales Tax for food processing industry. Punjab should take advantage from

the new EXIM Policy of the Central Government for creating Agricultural Export Zones (AEZs) in order to promote the cultivation and processing of fruits and vegetables. Recently, one AEZ for vegetables is being set-up at Zirakpur (Punjab) with the investment of Rs. 26.77 crores. It would lead to an annual export of about Rs. 65 crores. This project will benefit about 1500 farmers and increase the employment opportunities in the State. It is desired to set-up more AEZs in Punjab for citrus fruits, grapes and potatoes.

CONCLUSIONS

Indian agriculture has been facing serious challenges and huge opportunities under WTO. Though India has become food surplus country, but its agriculture has been hit hard during post-WTO period (1995-2002). India's competitiveness in the agro-export markets has been lost due to large increase in Minimum Support Prices (MSP). The share of India's agro-exports in her global exports has declined during this period. As a result, WTO has become serious challenge to several food-surplus States of India including Punjab, which is the major contributor of foodgrains to India. During post-WTO period, agricultural subsidies of developed countries have been rather increased. Therefore, it is very difficult for India/Punjab to face global agricultural competitiveness. In this scenario, the global agricultural trade would likely to become oligopolistic. The returns of various crops in Punjab have declined due to increase in cost of production, slow growth of agricultural productivity, weak marketing mechanism, increase in input intensity and fall of water table. As a result, Punjab farmers have become highly indebted and resorting to suicides. The Agreement of Agriculture of WTO is bound to influence Punjab agriculture positively as well as negatively. The globalization of Punjab agriculture would pose a new challenge to Punjab agricultural policy. Hence there is an urgent need to chalk out a strategy to shift the labour force from agriculture to other sectors.[17] Further, it is suggested to improve agricultural productivity of Punjab by increasing public investment in irrigation, power, roads and agricultural research. The research under Bio-technology can be promoted in State Universities. Punjab Government should promote the use of

Information Technology (IT) in agriculture sector by giving special computer training to farmers for latest production techniques, marketing information, etc. Punjab must diversify its agricultural economy of wheat-rice/cotton. Alternative crops like oilseeds, pulses, horticulture, fruits and vegetables, which give higher returns, should be promoted. Encouragement to food processing industries can promote the cultivation of fruits and vegetables, bringing higher returns to farmers. Modern marketing infrastructure and multifarious extension services should be provided to farmers. New export markets should be explored for surplus agricultural production of Punjab. Lastly, Punjab Government should start National Agricultural Insurance Scheme, introduced by Union Ministry of Agriculture in order to protect the farmers against losses due to crop failure. The implementation of these measures would likely to make the economic sustainability of Punjab agriculture.

Notes and References

1. For Instance, during 1986-89 TE, India's domestic price of wheat was Rs. 174 per qtl. as compared to the international price of Rs. 354 per qtl. But during 2001-02, the economic cost of India for wheat was Rs. 839 (incl. Rs. 620 per qtl. as MSP) as compared to the international price of Rs. 415 per qtl.
2. Dhar, Biswajit (2002): "A Crop of Distortions", *Economic Times*, January 11.
3. Govt. of India (2002): *Economic Survey, 2001-02*.
4. *Ibid.*
5. *Economic and Political Weekly* (2001): October 20-26, 2001, p. 3957.
6. Gulati, Ashok (2001): *"Trade Liberalization and Food Security: Challenges to Indian Policy Makers,"* International Food Policy Research Institute (IFPRI), Washington DC, January.
7. Rao, C.H. Hanumantha (2001): "WTO and Viability of Indian Agriculture", *Economic & Political Weekly*, Vol. XXXVI, No. 30, September 8-14.
8. Chand, Ramesh & Phillip, Linu Mathew (2001), "Subsidies and Support in Agriculture", *Economic & Political Weekly*, Vol. XXXVI, August 11-17.
9. FAO (2001): *Production Yearbook, 2000*.
10. Govt. of India (2001): *Census of India, 2001*, Series 4, Punjab.
11. United Nations Commission Population and Development's working paper containing results of 1999 revision of world urbanization prospects.
12. Statement of Chief Minister in Punjab Assembly on June 12, 2002.

13. Govt. of Punjab (2001): *Statistical Abstract of Punjab, 2000.*
14. Sidhu, H.S. (2002): "Crisis in Agrarian Economy in Punjab: Some urgent steps", *Economic & Political Weekly,* Vol. XXXVII, No. 30, July 27-August 2, p. 3134.
15. Anitha, Ramanna (2001), "India's Policy on IPRs and Agriculture", *Economic & Political Weekly,* Vol. XXXVI, No. 51, December 22-28, p. 4689.
16. Gulati, Ashok (2000), "Indian Agriculture and the WTO: Preparing for the New Millennium", IEA Conference (83rd) Volume of the Millennium, Jammu.
17. Ghuman, Ranjit Singh (2001): "WTO And Indian Agriculture? Crisis and Challenges—A Case Study of Punjab", *Man & Development,* June, p. 94.

31

Impact of Globalization on Labour Utilization in India

S. VIJAYALAKSHMI

This paper attempts to analyse the impact of globalization on labour in India. The first section focuses on directives of the World Bank on labour policy. Section two presents the impact of globalization on labour in the organised sector. Section three gives agricultural labour scenario and section four points out the impact on child labour. The fifth section concludes.

The average annual growth rate of employment in the organised sector has been 0.83 per cent during the period 1991-99. Of this, public sector has recorded 0.405 per cent and private sector has recorded 1.63 per cent. Considering the backlog of unemployment and the new additions to the labour force, employment generation is meagre. In 1996 and 1998, the average annual percentage changes in employment in the public sector have been negative. Economic Survey, 2000-01 has stated that there is new and expanded opportunities in the service sector and in the unorganised sector. The survey is however silent about the nature, conditions and remuneration in the new and expanded opportunities in the unorganised sector. Due to various political and economic constraints workers in the unorganised sector (for instance weaving) are loosing their jobs.

1. DIRECTIVE OF THE WORLD BANK ON LABOUR POLICY

World Development Report (1990) has remarked that labour policies in many countries have been misguided in favouring those in good jobs at the expense of workers in rural and informal sectors and the unemployed. Further, it defines successful labour policies as those that work in harmony with the market and avoid providing special protections and previledges to particular labour groups at the expense of the poorest. It advises to construct a framework for labour policy that complements informal and rural labour markets, supports collective bargaining in the formal sector, provides safeguards for vulnerable and avoids biases that favour relatively well-off workers.

IMF and World Bank force Indian Government to introduce flexible labour policy which allows retrenchment of excess labour and employers' shift of workers from one unit to another.

2. LABOUR UTILIZATION IN THE ORGANISED SECTOR IN INDIA

2.1.1 Highly capital-intensive technology has become the order of the day for the Indian companies to match their MNC counterparts in the race of competition. According to one study,[1] 23 manufacturing companies sharing 17 per cent of the total sales of private manufacturing and having an employee strength of 2 lakh and 50 thousand in 1998-99 have cut the employee strength to 2 lakh and 9 thousand in 2000-01. Tata Steel and Tata Engineering taken together has cut 19,785 jobs just in two years during 1998-99 to 2000-01 (Refer Table 1).

2.1.2 Job cut in public sector has been larger. Through VRS route job cut in Coal India Limited is 90,000 and in SAIL it is 20,000. More than one lakh employees have been sent out by the same route from public sector banks. Within two years around 3 lakh employees have been axed. The organised sector intends to appear lean and fit to raise their profit margin at the cost of workers.

TABLE 1

Job Cuts in Some Private Sector Companies

Name of the Company	*Employee Strength*		*No. of Jobs cuts between 1998-99 and 2000-01*
	1998-99	*2000-01*	
Tata Steel	59,235	48,821	10,414
Tata Engineering	35,625	26,250	9,375
Bajaj Auto	18,585	13,819	4,766
Voltas	8,796	5,136	3,660
ACC	12,411	9,991	2,420

Source: *Business Standard*, August 18-19, 2000, p. 1.

2.2 In addition to retrenchment, lockouts, layoffs and closure of the units greatly affect labour community. During 1981-90, the percentage of mandays lost due to lockouts had been 46.2. It jumped up sharply to 61.2 per cent during 1991-97. As a result of 1,687 closures nearly 1.20 lakh workers have lost their jobs. The pity is that to reduce the permanent workers' component, some managements have used closure as a devise. Closing the unit in one location and starting a similar unit in another location and employing more of casual and temporary workers these managements have reduced labour cost to enhance profit margins unmindful of workers' sufferings. Moreover, layoffs have been frequently resorted during the lean period to downsize labour cost.

2.3 At present nearly 30 per cent of the workers in industrial units are out of the security net. Under the provisions of Industrial Dispute Act, the Government proposal to raise the threshold limit to 1000 employees would result in 75.4 per cent of the industrial workers going out of the safety net. (Table 2).

2.4 Structural adjustment and industrial restructuring programmes would add to the unemployment problem that the country is facing. While the Government is giving a red carpet welcome to MNCs, Transparency International (TI) has remarked that, "a large number of multinational corporations from the richest nations are pursuing a criminal course to win contracts in the leading emerging market economies of the world". Besides the entry of MNCs which is expected to bring in competitive environment and competitive strength to our companies has led to displacement of workers even in profit earning enterprises.

TABLE 2

Factory Sector by Size of Employment, 1997-98

Employment Range	*Number of Factories*	*Employment*	*Percentage to Total*
Less than or equal to 49	98,159	16,63,096	16.8
50-99	18,920	12,98,361	13.1
100-199	9,169	12,83,311	12.9
200-499	6,115	18,85,903	19.0
500-999	2,067	13,51,799	13.6
1000-1999	701	9,34,526	9.4
2000-4999	362	9,96,600	10.0
5000 and above	57	5,12,214	5.2
Total	1,35,551	99,25,810	100.0

Source: *The Economic Times*, March 6, 2001, p. 1.

2.5 Indian private corporations have not repaid Rs. 80,000 crore borrowed from the financial institutions and they are responsible for the huge non-performing assets piled up in the government owned by the financial institutions. On the other hand, in Employees Provident Fund Account only 40 per cent of the total demand for the year and arrears have been remitted by the employers till March 2001. On one side, they resort to retrenching of workers under the banner of industrial restructuring and on the other side they exploit the workers not retrenched by not remitting provident fund in their account. Moreover., they exploit the public sector financial institutions by not repaying the borrowings taken for industrial restructuring.

The irony is that, they participate in the disinvestment programmes of the Government through borrowings from public sector financial institutions and then pledging disinvested assets they take money from public sector banks to develop and restructure their own enterprises and retrench workers.

2.6 State Governments' employees numbering nearly 75 lakhs

(Table 3) are also facing threats to their jobs as the process of privatization of state owned enterprises have been initiated by many State Governments.[2] A public Enterprises Reform Programme has been taken up with assistance from World Bank and a State Renewal Fund for financing VRS and for providing retraining and redeployment support in Andhra Pradesh. Gujarat Government has closed down six loss-making undertakings and nearly 50 per cent of the remaining enterprises have been covered under restructuring programme. A public sector Restructuring Commission has been set-up in the case of Karnataka to identify the units for privatization and the remaining units are to be closed down. Madhya Pradesh is intending to disinvest 14 out of 26 PSUs availing assistance from Asian Development Bank. Kerala Government is not willing to continue support to loss-making PSUs. In Maharashtra five PSUs including State Electricity Board, State Road Transport Corporation and Small Scale Industry Development Corporation have been identified for disinvestment. There is going to be a large scale cut in the state governments' employment in industry.

2.7 The important recommendations such as recognition of unions, settlement machinery etc., of the First National Commission on Labour have not been implemented so far. Second National Commission on Labour has been set-up to suggest (i) rationalization of existing laws relating to labour in the organised sector, and (ii) an umberella legislation for ensuring a minimum level of protection to the workers in the unorganised sectors. The recommendations of the commission may form the basis for framing a flexible labour policy which is to be introduced soon.

3. LABOUR UTILIZATION IN AGRICULTURE

3.1 In 1999-2000, occupational distribution of labour force according to the Planning Commission's estimates is 60.41 per cent in primary sector, 12.42 per cent in industries and allied activities sector and 27.17 per cent in tertiary sector. Though employment in primary sector has declined from 67.4 per cent (in 1991) still it is the major employer of the labour force.

For unskilled agricultural labour who form the majority in agricultural sector the average annual percentage change in real

TABLE 3

Employment in the Public Sector by Industry

(Lakh Persons as on 31st March)

Sl. No.	*Item—By Branch*	*1981*	*1988*	*1989*	*1990*	*1991*	*1992*	*1993*	*1994*	*1995*	*1996*	*1997*	*1998*	*1999*
1.	Central Government	31.95	33.81	33.95	33.97	34.1	34.28	33.83	33.92	33.95	33.66	32.95	32.53	33.13
2.	State Government	56.76	67.81	68.29	69.29	69.79	71.12	71.9	72.93	73.37	73.37	73.55	74.14	74.85
3.	Quasi-Government	45.76	59.48	59.99	61.73	62.22	63.93	64.9	65.14	65.2	64.58	65.35	64.61	63.85
4.	Local Bodies	20.37	22.11	22.38	22.23	23.13	21.98	21.6	22.02	21.97	21.92	22.44	22.46	22.59
	Total	154.84	183.21	184.44	187.72	190.57	192.10	193.26	194.45	194.66	194.29	195.54	194.18	194.15

Source: Government of India, *Economic Survey*, 2000-01.

wage has been negative during the period 1993-94 to 1999-2000 in 12 out of 14 states considered in Economic Survey, 2000-01. In Tamil Nadu and Gujarat, real wage in agriculture has been continuously increasing throughout the period. In seven states real wage has fallen during 1998-99 and 1999-2000.

3.2 India has millions of small and marginal farmers for whom agriculture is not still a commercial venture. WTO agreement does not permit subsidies and concessions though they are essential to them. However, subsidies are provided on a greater scale under the provisions of Green Box in Europe and USA. Therefore, lifting of quantitative restrictions will have adverse effect on agricultural production and on all those who are engaged in agriculture. Agreement on Agriculture is biased in favour of the developed world. Imported good may become cheaper than home production in developing countries. Noble Prize winner (2001), Stiglitz (2002), has condemned the behaviour of the developed world and has remarked that "while preaching free market doctrines abroad, the U.S. bails out its airlines and increases agricultural subsidies at home. Even before these increases, subsidies to agriculture by the advanced industrial countries were enormous—exceeding the total income of Sub-Saharan Africa. The rich effectively closed many goods that represent the comparative advantage of the poor". Thus, the industrial countries demand trade liberalization and elimination of subsidies while maintaining trade barriers and subsidies for their own products. Hence, terms of trade worked to the disadvantage of the developing countries.

3.3 Besides, under the umbrella of WTO Agreement developed countries have denied market access to Indian agriculture. Trade barriers such as tariff barriers, anti-dumping and safe-guards have hit export of products like floriculture, textiles, Pharmaceuticals, marine products and basmati to European Union, carpet to Morocco, match to Egypt, mushroom to USA, sports goods and leather to the developed world.

3.4 Human Development Report, 2001 has pointed out that, the poor were not considered by the powerful nations when embarking on globalization. The Report has further stated that 40 per cent of the total population of India, Pakistan, Bangladesh, Nepal, Bhutan, Sri Lanka and the Maldives have only become poorer under globalization.

4. CHILD LABOUR

Developed countries insist that, every possible activity except the essential law-making, policing and judicial function are to be within the ambit of GAT's. Issues like social clauses, labour services, child labour, environmental protection, etc., have to be brought under the international control regime.

4.1 Child labour is prevalent not only in developing countries but also in USA, UK, Italy, Spain and Portugal. Europian Union boycott Bangladesh garments on the reason that, child labour is involved in manufacture. Export of Indian carpets is curtailed due to the same reason. The irony is that, out of 19 conventions on child labour, India has ratified 7 conventions, Germany has ratified three conventions and USA has ratified only one convention so far.

Thus, it is clear that the peasantry and the working class in the organised as well as in the unorganised sectors are greatly affected by the present process of globalization.

CONCLUSION

5.1 It is stated that the backbone of China's economic expansion in the 1980s and early 1990s were the township and village enterprises that were owned by local governments. These non-state enterprises created new jobs, provided valuable products for consumers and contributed to regional development. By the late nineties they had accomplished their objectives and are being privatised now. China's dynamism flows from its small and medium sized enterprises.

In India entrepreneurial talents are widespread and what is lacking is intensions. The Government could promote entrepreneurial talents by providing modern technology, training and retraining and adequate and timely finance and develop medium and small scale sectors. These sectors must be encouraged to produce quality and cost effective products to meet the local demands competitively in the beginning and later oft for export.

5.2 The difficulties in China's economy are related to the state sector's problems. However, the economy continues to grow due to the growth of non-state sector and financial and social stability are present as the state sectors' role is diminishing (refer Table 4).

TABLE 4

Trend in China's State Owned Enterprises Share in Output and Employment

(in per cent)

Year	*Industrial Output*	*Urban Formal Employment*	*Bank Lending*
1978	78.0	78.3	96.8
1988	57.0	70.3	90.0
1995	34.0	64.9	81.0
2000	23.5	38.1	77.6

Source: China Statistical Year Book quoted in The World Bank Publication 'Transition', May-June, 2002, p. 7.

Our central and state governments may attempt to reduce the role of PSUs gradually with a well planned deterministic view. However, profit earning competitive undertakings should not be used as a weapon to fill the budgetary gap through the process of divestiture. To further enhance the profit and the contribution to the exchequer what they need is professional management and complete autonomy without political interference of any sort and of course with accountability. In case disinvestment is a must, it must be broadbased. Chronically sick, small and unviable units could be completely privatised if there is taker or could be closed down. In the other units workers could be given a chance for revival by off-loading a part of the shares in favour of them. In the case of ADR and GDR issues a foreign-based advisory committee is inevitable.

5.3 Markets do not always have the necessary information. As Stiglitz has pointed out governments have to intervene to correct market failures. International financial institutions must realise that democratic governments should have the autonomy to decide the pace at which they engage with globalization with "a more human face". They cannot be directed by the modern versions of East India Companies in the form of MNCs or international institutions on what to do.

India need not yield to the pressure and whims and fancies of WTO and the interested groups in industrially advanced nations. While the World Bank preaches the governments of developing countries to avoid providing special protections and privileges to particular labour group at the expense of the poorest, WTO practices such preferential treatment by providing special protections and privileges to industrially advanced nations at the cost of poor developing world.

Above all, government programmes and policies concerning employment generation, entrepreneurial development and labour protection in the unorganised sector could succeed only when politicians and the administrative machinery at all levels work with clean-hands. In such a situation, people will not mind making sacrifices and introduction of flexible labour policy may become easier.

5.4 Unless 'globalization' ensures free flow of labour across countries' borders developing world's labour cannot get a fair deal under 'restricted globalization'.

Notes and References

1. A Study by Business Standard Research Bureau, *Business Standard*, August 18-19, 2001, p. 1.
2. *The Hindu*, September 1, 2002, p. 15.

References

Clairmont, F. and Cavanagh, H. (1994), "World's Top 200 Mega Corporations", Commentary, *Economic and Political Weekly*, February.

Government of India, Ministry of Finance, *Economic Survey* 2000-01.

Human Development Report, 2001.

Joseph E. Stiglitz (2002), *Globalization and Its Discontents*, W.W. Norton.

Nambiar, R.G., *et al.*, (1999), "Is Import Liberalization Hurting Domestic Industry and Employment", *Economic and Political Weekly*, February 13.

National Sample Survey, 55th Round, Employment and Unemployment in India (1999-2000), *Key Results*, December.

Papola, T.S. (1994), "Structural Adjustment, Labour Market Flexibility and Employment", *The Indian Journal of Labour Economics*, Vol. XXXVI, No. 1.

Ratan Khasnabis and Sudipti Banerji (1996), "Political Economy of Voluntary Retirement: Study of Rationalised Workers in Durgapur", *Economic and Political Weekly*, December 28.

Singh, G., "Who Needs an Exit Policy Anyway", *Economic and Political Weekly*, June 10.

Shyam Sundar, (2000), "Second National Commission on Labour", *Economic and Political Weekly*, July 22.

Sreeram Chaubia (2002), "Social Clause in WTO: Case for and Against", *Economic and Political Weekly*, February 16.

The Mahbubul Haq, Human Development Centre (2002), *Human Development in South Asia, 2001*, Oxford University Press.

The World Bank (1995), *World Development Report, 1995*, Workers in an Integrating World.

The World Bank (2002), *Translation: Newsletter*, Vol. 13, No. 3, May-June.

The Hindu, Various Issues.

The Economic Times, Various Issues.

TABLE A1

Annual Growth of Employment in Organised Sector

(*In Percentage*)

Year	*Public Sector*	*Private Sector*	*Total Organised*
1991	1.52	1.24	1.44
1992	0.80	2.21	1.21
1993	0.60	0.06	0.44
1994	0.62	0.01	0.73
1995	0.11	1.63	0.55
1996	–0.19	5.62	1.51
1997	0.67	2.04	1.09
1998	–0.09	1.72	0.46
1999	0.00	0.11	0.04

Source: *Economic Survey*, 2000-01.

TABLE A2

Trend in Number of Persons Employed Per 1000 Population in India

Year	*Rural*	*Urban*
1977-78	444	341
1987-88	434	337
1993-94	444	347
1999-2000	417	337

Source: NSS 55th Round, Employment and Unemployment in India (1999-2000), Key Results, December.

SECTION III

GLOBALIZATION AND SOCIAL WELFARE

32

Socio-Economic Consequences of Economic Reforms in India

A.P. PANDEY

Liberalization, privatization and globalization of Indian economy is now experiencing its second generation of Economic Reforms. It is quite but natural to have its impact on the socio-economic infrastructure of Indian economy. Yet, before drawing attention towards these consequences, let us have a bird-view over the evidences of globalization.

1. CONCEPTUAL EVIDENCES

The 'Neo-classical Model' of growth (that treatment of development economics separately from economics of rejects treatment of development economics separately from economic of advanced countries) got replaced by the emergence of 'New Economic Theory' (NET) during the late 80s and early 90s. Quite truly, over the last one decade example can be cited of high performances of industrializing countries of east Asia like, Hong Kong, Singapore, Taiwan, Korea and Japan. These countries are experiencing higher growth rates with their 'trade-openness' and outward-looking rather than 'inward-oriented' policies and thus extend empirical evidences of 'New Economic Theory' (NET). Prof. Amartya Sen also cited examples of these Economic. Yet on the other hand, he also cited low performances of many countries in Asia, Africa, and Latin America showing that it does not pay the government to mess much with market mechanism.

2. THE PARADOX

Interestingly, our modern world is experiencing two major phenomenon, namely, 'Globalization' and 'Regionalism', these two concepts are quite contrast with each other. On one hand, we have the era of 'Globalization' yet on the other hand, there are regional grouping that are getting stronger. The concept of liberalization has its root with Classical "Laissez-faire" who emphasized on free trade and market mechanism whereas, the concept of regional grouping is an outcome of the theory of 'protectionism', which is based on 'Infant Industry Argument'. However, one common point is that, within these regional grouping there exist free trade.

Nonetheless, as our matter of concern, we should not confuse liberalization as 'non-government intervention' concept of 'laissez-faire'. More specially, the main idea is based on Chicago School's emphasis on 'Market mechanism' to increase efficiency with competition.

3. THE CONNOTATION OF GLOBALIZATION

Let us now briefly understand the word Global dimensions:

(a) It means extension of market of each economy to globalization;
(b) It is extension of a more "outward-oriented" policy;
(c) It emphasizes elimination of anti-export bias, lowering of high tariff and lessening of import restriction;
(d) It is market-oriented development strategy with international competitive environment;
(e) It means, as per World Bank:
  (i) Gradual removal of import controls (including on consumption goods),

(ii) Reduction in import duty rates, and
(iii) Privatization of public sector enterprises.

To put the terms in logical sequence:

(1) Globalization implies economic integration with industrial economies in the field of finance production and trade.
(2) This thus means that 'Economic Openness' is an integral part of Globalization.
(3) Such 'openness' can be through liberalized policies adopted in finance, production and trade.

4. THE CORE OF ECONOMIC REFORM IN INDIA

Prior to July 1991, Indian economy was suffering from several severe imbalances. Larger fiscal deficits, wider BOP deficits, recession in industrial sector, stagnation in agricultural sector, mass unemployment, heavy level of poverty, etc. could found neither immediate nor long-term solutions. Consequently, the growth prospects got ultimately questioned. To come out of these severe problems, the Government of India in July 1991, introduced a package of policy programmes known as New Economic Reforms. It was based on two policy programmes, namely,

(i) Stabilization policies, and
(ii) Structural adjustment programmes. The former is short-term crisis programme (to correct fiscal and BOP deficits) and the latter is long-term Structural Reforms to improve upon the state of growth.

5. PREDICAMENTS OF ECONOMIC REFORMS

"Though economic growth is important, yet the ultimate objective is to expand the ability . . . to earn a decent living . . . by providing for a certain economic security to the poorest of the poor," says Prof. Amartya Sen.

Amartya Sen further says, to quote, "We should more

carefully note that a rise in income, may not adequately (or at all) extended one's entitlement to education, or entitlement to medical treatment, if there is no school or hospital in nearby village. A mere rise in income extend no such guarantees."

Hence, Economic reforms as applied in India raise some basic issues that must be answered before we proceed further with our second generation of reforms. These issues are:

1. Social Consequences of Economic Reforms

Historical experiences of Zambia, Brazil, Peru, Bolivia, Tunisia and Egypt (Streeten, 1987) have shown that their adoption of IMF-World Bank packages of economic stabilization and structural adjustment programme witnessed slowing down of employment opportunities, fall in real wages, withdrawal of food subsidies, rise in the prices of public services, and contraction of social expenditure by the government. Now the question rises, will also the economic reforms in India be under such heavy social costs? To what extent will India be able to protect the most venurable section of our society and mitigate their impact?

TABLE 1 (a)

I. Employment in Public and Private Sector

% share	*1991*	*1994*	*1995*	*1996*	*1997*	*1998*	*1999*
Public sector	71.3	71	70.7	69.6	69.2	68.9	68.8
Private sector	28.3	29	69.6	30.4	30.8	31.1	31.2
% change in total Emp. over previous year	—	—	0.5	1.5	1.1	-0.3	-0.2

TABLE 1 (b)

II. Average Per Capita Annual Earning of Factory

	1991	*1992*	*1993*	*1994*	*1995*
All India (% change)	—	(–)8.3	6.4	(–)3.2	0.05

TABLE 1 (c)

III. Consumer Price Index of Industrial Workers [(1982=100)(c)]

	1990-91	*1994-95*	*1995-96*	*1996-97*	*1997-98*
All India	193	284	313	342	366

Sources: Recent issues of *Economic Survey* and *Currency & Finance*, Govt. of India.

TABLE 1 (d)

IV. Function Classification of Total Expenditure of Government of India

Social services	*1985-86*	*1993-94*	*1994-95*	*1995-96*	*1996-97*	*1997-98*
Percentage share in total expenditure	7.3	9.5	9.9	10.2	9.4	10.0
% change over previous year	(+)22.8	(+)21.0	(+)18.2	(+)15.3	(–)7.8	(–)22.1

Sources: Same as before.

Here we mark that, there is very slow reduction in employment in public sector (i.e. from 71.3% share in 1991 to 68.8% share in 1999) as against the marginal increase in share of employment in private sector. Clearly, the economic reforms have failed to generate faster employment opportunities in private sector. What is more alarming is the slowing down of total employment opportunities specially from 1.5% increase in 1996 to a negative of 0.2% in 1999.

As against the slowing down rather increase in unemployment, the average per capita annual earnings of factory worker have also gone down and fluctuated widely. Further with the policy of the gradual withdrawal of subsidies, the situation is more precarious with high rise in the consumer price index of industrial workers (i.e. from the index of 193 in 1990-91 to as high as 366 in 1997-98). The final nail coffin is hammered by the falling trend in expenditure on social services by the government of India, specially from 21% increase in 1993-94 to (-) 7.8% in 1996-97 (with exception in 1997-98).

On the whole, the burden of structural adjustment has fallen more severely on the working class.

1. Inter-State Disparities

Due to natural, economic and technological reasons, the process of economic development all over the world is often characterized by inter-regional disparities (*Myrdal*, 1957 and *Hirschman*, 1958).

In India development of backward areas and a regionally balanced pattern of development have been one of the major objectives of the successive five year plans. But under India's policy of Economic reforms, with its emphasis on greater role of private sector and market forces, can the objective of balanced regional development be maintained? Will not be the flow of capital be more towards promising region then towards most needy regions? Will not the investments in big public sector projects that are located in backward region reduce? The combined impact of liberalized scenario on regional development can be seen through the pattern of investments.

6. STATE-WISE NDP (1980-81 PRICES)/PERCENT CHANGE OVER PERIOD

In Table 2, given below we may find percentage change in state-wise NDP classified under two periods. First from 1980-81 to 1990-91 and the second from 1990-91 to 1996-97 except for J&K, Kerala and Orissa, rest all other states have experienced slower rise in NDP during the post-reforms period. Even the leading industrialized states like Gujarat (66.7% during pre and 30.2% during post-reforms period then the pre-reform Maharashtra (79.5% during pre and 56.8% during post) were no exception to the trend of slower of post-liberalization period.

7. RANKED NDP/STATE-WISE [TABLE (3)]

Here, based on the levels of NDP, the states are ranked firstly, as the top ten states in 1990-91 and in 1996-97. Similarly, the states are also ranked from the lowest level of NDP also. Clearly, more or less, the top 10 states either maintained their positions by (Maharashtra, U.P.) or improve upon their position by getting richer during the reforms period.

TABLE 2

S. No.	*State*	*From 1980-81 to 1990-91*	*From 1990-91 to 1996-97*
1.	Andhra Pradesh	60.06	33.00
2.	Arunachal Pradesh	135.7	31.16
3.	Assam	49.08	19.9
4.	Bihar	61.5	(-)4.07
5.	Goa	80.3	23.6
6.	Gujarat	66.7	30.2
7.	Haryana	88.6	28.1
8.	Himachal Pradesh	59.2	23.3
9.	J&K	29.7	78.7
10.	Karnataka	63.1	41.8
11.	Kerala	37.7	41.1
12.	Madhya Pradesh	58.4	24.6
13.	Maharashtra	79.5	56.8
14.	Orissa	126.2	128.6
15.	Punjab	68.7	31.3
16.	Rajasthan	103.6	31.0
17.	Tamil Nadu	72.0	36.8
18.	Uttar Pradesh	62.6	18.6
19.	West Bengal	50.7	35.7

Data source: Same as above.

TABLE 3

Ranked as in 1990-91		*Ranked as in 1996-97*	
	THE TOP TENS		THE TOP TENS
1.	Maharashtra	1.	Maharashtra
2.	Uttar Pradesh	2.	Uttar Pradesh
3.	West Bengal	3.	Tamil Nadu
4.	Tamil Nadu	4.	West Bengal
5.	Andhra Pradesh	5.	Andhra Pradesh
6.	Madhya Pradesh	6.	Gujarat
7.	Gujarat	7.	Madya Pradesh
8.	Bihar	8.	Karnataka
9.	Karnataka	9.	Rajasthan
10.	Rajasthan	10.	Punjab

(Contd.)

Ranked as in 1990-91	*Ranked as in 1996-97*
FROM THE LOWEST ONES	FROM THE LOWEST ONES
1. Andaman and Nikobar	1. Andaman and Nikobar
2. Sikkim	2. Pondicherry
3. Arunachal Pradesh	3. Arunachal Pradesh
4. Nagaland	4. Meghalaya
5. Pondicherry	5. Manipur
6. Meghalaya	6. Goa
7. Manipur	7. Himachal Pradesh
8. Tripura	8. J&K
9. Goa	9. Assam
10. Himachal Pradesh	10. Orissa

Source: As given above.

But reverse is the case of poorer states. These states either remained poor or even got poorer, e.g. Pondicherry was fifth from the lowest in 1990-91, but occupied the second lowest position in 1996-97. Similar were with Meghalaya, Manipur, Goa, Himachal Pradesh, etc. Thus, clearly enough, despite of government's backward area-based programmes, the richer states continued to be richer while poorer states got further poor during the reforms period.

Here, based on the levels of NDP, the states are ranked firstly, as the top ten states in 1990-91 and in 1996-97. Similarly, the states are also ranked from the lowest level of NDP also.

Clearly, more or less, top 10 states either maintained their position by getting richer during the reforms period.

But reverse is the case of poorer states, these states either remained poor or even got poorer, e.g. Pondicherry was fifth from the lowest in 1990-91 but occupied the second lowest position in 1996-97. Similar were with Meghalaya, Manipur, Goa, Himachal Pradesh, etc. Thus, clearly enough, despite of government's backward area-based programmes, the richer states continued to be richer while poorer states got further poor during the reform's period.

8. POVERTY-INVESTMENT INTER-RELATIONSHIP

As a matter of our concern, our third issue is based on the linkage in between poverty-employment-investment inter-relationship. Conceptually, with the rise in the level investments in the states level of employment should also go up. As a result there should be alleviation in poverty level. Thus, our query is whether India's Economic reforms policies are providing helpful towards alleviation of poverty?

State-wise Poverty Position in India, 2001

State-wise level of poverty is presented here in Table 4. Interestingly, the top four rich states (as marked in transparency) namely, Maharashtra, U.P., Tamil Nadu and West Bengal are

TABLE 4

State-wise Poverty Position in India

States	*Rural*		*Urban*		*Total*	
	People in lacks	*In %*	*People in lacks*	*In %*	*People in lacks*	*In %*
1	2	3	4	5	6	7
1. Andhra Pradesh	58.13	11.05	60.88	26.63	119.01	15.77
2. Arunachal Pradesh	3.80	40.04	0.18	7.47	3.98	33.47
3. Assam	92.17	40.04	2.38	7.47	94.55	36.09
4. Bihar	376.57	44.30	49.13	32.91	425.64	42.06
5. Goa	0.11	1.35	0.59	7.52	0.70	4.40
6. Gujarat	39.80	13.17	28.09	15.59	67.89	14.07
7. Haryana	11.94	8.27	5.39	9.99	17.34	3.74
8. Himachal Pradesh	4.84	7.94	0.29	4.63	5.12	7.63
9. J&K	2.97	3.97	0.49	1.98	3.46	8.48
10. Karnataka	59.91	17.38	44.49	25.25	104.40	20.04
11. Kerala	20.97	9.38	20.07	20.27	41.04	12.72
12. Madhya Pradesh	217.32	37.06	81.22	38.44	298.95	37.49
13. Maharashtra	125.12	23.72	102.87	26.81	227.99	25.02
14. Manipur	6.53	40.04	0.66	7.47	7.19	28.54
15. Meghalaya	7.89	40.04	0.34	7.47	8.23	33.87
16. Mizoram	1.40	40.04	0.45	7.47	1.85	19.47
17. Nagaland	5.21	40.04	0.28	7.47	5.49	32.67
18. Orissa	143.69	48.01	25.40	42.83	169.09	47.15
19. Punjab	10.20	6.35	4.29	5.75	14.44	6.16
20. Rajasthan	55.06	13.74	26.78	19.85	81.83	15.28

(Contd.)

1	2	3	4	5	6	7
21. Sikkim	2.00	40.04	0.04	7.47	2.05	36.5522.
Tamil Nadu	80.51	20.55	49.97	22.19	130.48	21.12
23. Tripura	12.53	40.04	0.49	7.47	13.02	34.44
24. Uttar Pradesh	412.01	31.22	117.88	30.89	529.09	31.15
25. West Bengal	180.11	31.85	33.38	14.36	213.49	27.02
Union Territories						
1. Andman Nikobar	0.58	20.55	0.24	22.11	0.82	20.99
2. Chandigarh	0.06	5.75	0.45	5.75	0.51	5.75
3. Dadar & Nagar Haveli	0.30	17.57	0.03	13.52	0.33	17.14
4. Daman & Diu	0.01	1.35	0.05	7.52	0.06	4.44
5. Delhi	0.07	0.40	11.42	9.42	11.49	8.23
6. Lakshdweep	0.03	9.38	0.08	20.27	0.11	15.60
7. Pondicherry	0.64	20.55	1.77	22.11	2.41	21.67
India	1932.43	27.09	67007	23.63	2602.50	26.10

having higher percentage of poverty then the national average of 26.1% (with Maharashtra 25.02%, U.P. 31.15%, Tamilnadu 34.44% and West Bengal 27.02%). Consumer price index of industrial workers can be the three major attributed factors for higher level of poverty.

Further, we also marked a falling rate of expenditure on social services. This too accounts for such failure. In addition to these, it also held that, capacity of the government to generate employment directly through anti-poverty programmes remain limited. These programmes also suffer considerable leakage. Even financial institutions have experienced the high risk of non-recovery. To do away with these direct fallacies we feel it would be better if these anti-poverty programmes are directed towards creation of economic and social infrastructure by providing basic amenities. Higher industrial investment or even higher industrial growth does not necessarily guarantee decline in poverty. On the contrary industrial states are expressing more deficiencies in basic amenities. In short, improvement in Human Development Index (HDI) and Human Poverty Index (HPI) are more important.

9. BENEFIT FOR THE POOR

Finally, we would also emphasize the concept that, globalization is supposed to take care of the poor in two ways. Firstly, along with the faster growth of GDP, governments can carter larger resources at a low rate of taxation. Secondly, its stabilization policies would result in low rate of inflation. With these, thus, the benefits to the poor can well be extended.

In this regard, we also agree that the ultimate end or objective of any society is human development. The essential components of human development are: Income, Health and Education. Economic reforms in India are bound to have its impact on human development. We therefore raise our final issue here that, whether that section of our society who are still below the poverty line and are deprived of nutrition, health and education, be benefited by our reforms measures?

It is really alarming to the note that still today 19% of our population are without access to safe drinking water, 25% are without health services and as high as 71% of population are without access to sanitation 53% of our children below 5 years of age are under weight, 15.8% of Indian do not survive after 40 years of age etc.

Are these the economic growth we are talking about under second generation of economic reforms?

10. CONCLUDING REMARKS

(a) In a planned economic development, increases in productivity, standard of living and socio-economic equalization are the main attributes of ideal development of India.

(b) With our economic reforms, it is imperative to have a sound infrastructure. It includes those basic facilities which are essential.

(c) 'Public services' starting from law and order, through education and public health, to water supply, power information and communication, as well as irrigation treated as overhead capital in agriculture.

(d) It would be more appropriate to term these as socio-economic infrastructures. In fact, socio-economic infrastructure is the 'Wheel of Economic activity'. The success in providing it extended the true meaning of any economic reforms.

(e) Finally, today in India, we mark a shift from direct government provision of these services, to private sector provision. Precisely, this is the new way to increase efficiency and expand services, and it is expected that there will be poverty reduction and equality of environment as and when our private sector will extend greater access.

References

Ahroni, A. Yair, (1966), *The Foreign Investment Decision Process*, Harvard University, Boston.

Balasubramanyam, V.N. (1973), International Transfer of Technology to India, Praeger, New York.

Behrman, Jack N.A. (1970), National Interest and Multinational Enterprises: Tension Among the North Atlantic Countries, Prentice Hall Inc., Eagle Wood Cliffs, New Jersey.

Bhagwati, J.N. and Desai, P. (1970), India: Planning for Industrialization, Clarendon Press, Oxford.

Hamada, K., "Japanese Investment Abroad" in *Direct Foreign Investment in Asia and Pacific* (ed.), P. Drysdale, ANU Press, Canberra, 1972.

Hary Johnson (1964), *Economic Nationalism in Old and New States*, Chicago University Press, Chicago.

Govindarajulu, V. (1933), "Investment Approach to Generation of Indigenous Technological Assimilation Capability," *Journal of Scientific & Industrial Research*, Vol. 42, No. 9, pp. 477-83.

Satish, L. Rajkondawar (1992), "Globalization of Pharmaceutical Industry Opportunities and Challenges, *Chemical Weekly*, Vol. 37, No. 35, pp. 145-51.

Singh Kavaljit (2000), Taming Global Financial Flows: A Citizen's Guide," Madhyam Books.

Recent issue of *Economic Survey* and *Currency & Finance*, Govt of India.

Economic Times / Times of India / Hindustan Times / The Hindu.

33

Globalization and Decentralized Development: A Feminist Perspective

S.K. Mishra and I.D. Singh

In the 1960s, the state played major role in promoting the well-being of the majority of people in developing countries. Poverty reduction was at the center of development planning and there was an emphasis on an approach to development which was broad-based and integrated. All of this changed from the decade of 1980s onwards in the context of the debt crisis and the steep rise in the cost of living in industrialized countries, which made inflation and deficit reduction major preoccupation of the governments of those countries. Within a policy framework set by Washington, 'the Washington Concensus'; the role of status to promote broad-based socio-economic development was severely eroded. In many countries macro-economic policies and structural adjustment programmes took precedence over socio-economic development planning, and economic growth privileged over social development. In the decade of 1980s, the World Bank and the I.M.F. set the policy framework through a strategy of policy dialogue. From the beginning of 1990s, trade replaced development as the central policy issue. WTO now sets the policy framework based on epistemology that, liberalization of markets for goods and finance, small government and fiscal discipline is best for capturing the benefits of globalization.

However, international environment is far from enabling and those of us who are committed to the goals of sustainable human development have to fight disillusionment, despair and worst of all, cynicism in the form of deteriorating quality of life of poor in general and of women in particular.

Thus, the dramatic changes in power relations brought about by the globalization of financial and labour markets and by critical reinterpretations of modernity provide fertile ground for rethinking changing gender relations and development practice in the third world (*Feldman*, 1998).

The present paper aims at examining the impact of globalization on women in the form of its influences on women's awareness (literacy), physical capability (health) and autonomy (employment status). The paper also discusses the role played by feminists in countering the ill-effects of globalization on women.

A BRIEF ACCOUNT OF DEBATE ON GLOBALIZATION AND WOMEN'S STATUS

Globalization is touted as the panacea for the economic ills of the world. The free flow of capital, labour, goods and information without state and other forms of intervention is claimed to be the only path towards world prosperity promoted by various regional organizations like EU, NAFTA, APEC and world organizations such as GATT, WTO and financially sided by IMF and IBRD. Economic liberalism is sweeping the globe as it leaves millions of skeletons behind. Capital has become free to pursue the greatest profit wherever it may lead. Out flows often cause closures of plants and ouster of workers from job. Capital inflows lead either to greater exploitation of workers and plunder of natural resources, or to destroy nascent local industries and traditional enterprises due to severe competition. Both situations, while creating opportunities for some, drive more to destitution (*Lucie Cheng*, 1999).

UK government's white paper on Globalization of December, 2000—Making Globalization Work for the Poor—recognizes that "Globalization creates new opportunities for sustainable development and poverty reduction" and therefore opines that, "There is no alternative to globalization and we should learn to live with it". But, the paper also admits that globalization poses great threats to employment and livelihoods, to the environment and to human security in general—and so it argues finally that, "making globalization work for the world's poor is the greatest moral challenge facing our generation. The paper, however, does advocate intervention of the governments in the interests of equity and justice, for the benefits of globalization will not automatically reach poor people (*John Harriss*, 2001). Therefore, remedy to this challenge was perceived in decentralization, local development, and grass root initiatives that focused attention on the plight of the excluded—the rural landless, the urban poor, and women—and shift in development discourse to "meeting basic needs".

Boserup (1970), described the institutional barriers that limit women's productive capacity and competitive position in the market. To her, traditional values victimizing women, were associated with subsistence-based production. Rogers shared Boserup's commitment to market competition as the means for increasing gender equity. Though, Boserup and Rogers sought to improve women's status through participation in market-based exchange relations, they under estimated women's reproductive responsibility in status production.

Studies of women's resistence and intra-household bargaining have more recently been elaborated (*Sen*, 1990). However, patriarchal familiar relations between women and household limited women's voice and opportunity. Therefore, the policy goal was to free women from backward oppressive households and patriarchal relations which prohibited their participation in labour market. Hence, becoming wage labourers and self-reliant individuals then became the criteria for measuring women's status, mobility and achievement. It was further thought that, the availability of credit, in combination of new skills and training would transform subsistence and non-wage relations into marketable skills, enabling women similar to those of men.

In the last decade, the recent tide of globalization compelled countries to renegotiate their approach to development, a process that shifted national economic planning from import substitution and agricultural self-sufficiency to strategies of comparative advantage and export led growth. In the mean time, it was felt that the negative effects could be mediated by special programmes for women and children until economic equilibrium could once again be realized (*Cornia, et. al,* 1987). Despite the problems entailed in this analysis, the discussions non-the-less linked the costs of economic reorganization directly to poverty, motherhood, and the privatization of welfare institutions (*Cornia, et. al,* 1987; *Bakkar,* 1994).

This all led to a significant departure in 1990s from earlier researches with regards to women's development. Earlier, women's unequal status was attributed to their lack of access to resources, their limited skills, traditional cultural practices and their relationship to patriarchal household structures. In the 1990s, scholars recognized that women bear the unequal burden of reduction in social expenditure caused by introduced economic restructuring and social dislocation and concluded that these costs are not temporary (*Elson* 1990, 1992; *Feldman,* 1992, *Bakkar,* 1994).

GLOBALIZATION AND WOMEN'S STATUS IN OTHER ASIAN COUNTRIES

It is a general perception that women tend to bear the brunt of globalization. On the one hand, the general deterioration of living conditions and traditional patriarchal attitudes meant that they have had to take care of their families while generating an income. On the other hand, women are often the victims of plant closures.

In both Taiwan (China) and the Republic of Korea as the 'economic miracle' abated, a large number of textile, shoe, and garment plants, the labour-intensive manufacturing industries, closed leaving a millions of women workers jobless overnight, for these industries lost their competitiveness. These women struggled for compensation and the right to work.

In Masan, announcement of Japanese Sumida Company's withdrawal of capital caused loss of job by 300 women workers in 1990. In response to a long protest and struggle of the workers, the company promised a significant amount of economic compensation (*Lim,* 1998).

In Taiwan (China), textile, garment, shoe and electronic plants, women comprising more than 50 percent of their labour force, began to shut down one by one in the 1980s. To the report of Ministry of Economics more than 174000 companies and plants ceased to operate between 1993 and 1995, many leaving their workers without jobs, severance pay, or even back wages (*Huang*, 1998). Prevalence of low wages in Taiwan, compelled women in their 30s and 40s to seek employment—to supplement their family income. Most of them could not find comparable work for age-sex discrimination and had to take on food service or janitorial jobs, part-time, temporary contract, and other flexible work or suffer unemployment.

Likewise, many women workers in Philippines have also been victims of globalization. Development of a more sophisticated resistance movement, the organization like Gabriela in Philippines has gained an international reputation and is spear heading a transterritorial anti-globalization movement in the Asia-Pacific. In view of women in Philippines, the problem they face are related to their long colonial past as well as to the globalization of international capital (*Hsia*, 1998).

Committee for Asian Women Workers started in 1981 (CAW) with its head quarter at Hong Kong is an example of transnational labour activist group which arose to meet with the problem of brutal exploitation of women due to globalization. The CAW convenes conferences and workshops of Asian women labour organizers and also brings out a newsletter, carrying stories on women's labour conditions and their struggles in almost all Asian countries. Globalization and its impact on women workers in Asia have been a frequent topic since 1991.

GLOBALIZATION AND WOMEN IN SOUTH AFRICA

To South African Women, most government budgets are gender-biased, overlooking the ways in which programmes and policies either fail to address women's oppression, or exacerbate it (*Joanna Kerr*, 1999). They therefore take initiative to ensure that, every government department annually draws up its own 'women's budget', analyzing every line item for its impact on women. The success of the South African model is inspiring women elsewhere to create women's budgets as transformative tools for equality.

Women need a greater voice with this vision in mind, Gender and Economic Reforms in Africa (GERA) have been created to develop alternative and transformative economic policies and programmes that ensure gender equity and economic justice with the help of feminist economists, critical feminist researchers and activists who are able to analyse and influence economic policies and institutions—who can speak the language of economics.

ANALYSIS OF INDIAN EMPIRICAL EVIDENCES

Public expenditure on health and education; and state of women's health, education and work during pre and post-reform period in India and in developing countries on the whole have been demonstrated to evaluate the effect of globalization.

TABLE 1

Public Expenditure on Social Sector as Percentage of GDP in Pre and Post-Reform Period

Countries	*Expenditure on Health*			*Expenditure on Education*		
	1990	*1998*	*Change*	*1990*	*1998*	*Change*
India	0.9	0.6	–0.3	3.9	3.2	–0.7
Developing Countries	1.9	3.8	+1.9	3.5	3.8	+0.3
Difference	–1.0	–3.2	—	+0.4	–0.6	—

Source: UNDP, HDR-1992, HDR-2000 and HDR-2001.

Public expenditure on health and education in India is not only less in comparison to other countries but also shrinking influences of economic restructuring. The table shows that public expenditure on health and education as percentage of GDP reduced by 0.3 and 0.7 percent respectively in India, whereas it increased in developing countries in the post-reform period.

The difference in expenditures on health and education between India and developing countries increased sharply during this period. It clearly shows that the neglect of social sector in India is for more than that in developing countries.

SOCIAL DEVELOPMENT INDICATORS

Literacy

It is supposed to be a significant indicator of social development Indian position in literacy is shown in the following table.

TABLE 2

Adult Literacy in Pre- and Post-Reform Period in India

Countries	*Adult Literacy (In Percent)*							
	1990			*1998*			*TDL*	
	M	*F*	*GDL*	*M*	*F*	*GDL*	*M*	*F*
India	62	34	28	67.1	43.5	23.6	5.1	+9.5
Developing Countries	74	54	20	80.3	64.5	15.8	6.3	+10.5
S D L	12	20	8	13.2	21.0	7.8	1.2	1.0

GDL = Gender Difference in Literacy.
TDL = Temporal Difference in Literacy.
SDL = Spatial Difference in Literacy.
Source: UNDP, HDR-1992 and HDR-2000.

The Table 2 throws light on situation of literacy in population above 15 years of age. The female literacy has improved in post-reform period faster than that of males. However, India has much less than half literate adult females in comparison to nearly two-third of that in developing countries. Moreover, the gap in female literacy between India and other developing countries was 20 percentage point in pre-reform period which rose to 21 percentage point after economic reforms. Thus, India has not appropriately taken care of a very significant indicator of social development like female literacy.

Health

Availability of health facilities to the women may be

measured by Maternal Mortality Ratio, Expectation of Life at birth and also by sex ratio.

Maternal Mortality Ratio for India in 1998 was almost same as it was for overall average in all the developing countries a decade ago.

Life expectancy at birth for women in India has made substantial increase and now it is greater than that for men by 0.8 years (1998). However, the same figure of difference for overall developing countries is noted to be 3.2 years.

Sex Ratio, i.e., number of females per thousand males is a significant indicator of attitude of society towards females and the facility of health and nutritions given to them.

TABLE 3

Sex Ratio in Pre- and Post-Reform Period in India

Sex Ratio	*Census*		*Change over 1991*
	1991	*2001*	
General	927	933	+ 6
Child Population age 0-6 years	945	927	– 18
Population aged 7+	923	935	+ 12

Source: M.K. Premi, The Missing Girl Child, *EPW*, May 2001, p. 1875.

Increase in sex ratio in general population seems to be a matter of satisfaction. But, it conceals more significant facts than what it reveals. Increase in sex ratio is a result of tremendous rise in survivorship of elderly women. A sharp decline in sex ratio among the children of upto age six from 945 to 927 shows mass growth of foeticide and infanticide of girl child. This may be attributed to the realization of social attitude against the girl child into practice through foetus sex test. This action may not be considered that much immoral under the influence of globalization of thought at the social and individual level.

Status of Employment

Earning and workforce participation of women have been considered by UNDP as important factors to workout Gender Development Index. Globalization has significantly influenced women's WFPR.

TABLE 4

Women's (15+) Work Force Participation Rate in Pre and Post-Reform Period in India

Country	*WFPR of Women (In Percentage)*		
	Year		*TDE*
	1988-90	*1998*	
India	25.6	41.8	16.2
Developing Countries	32.5	55.6	23.1
SDE	6.9	13.8	6.9

TDE = Temporal Difference in Employment.
SDE = Spatial Difference in Employment.
Source UNDP, HDR-1992 and HDR-2000.

The table shows that Women's Work Force Participation Rate increased by 16.2 percentage point during the last decade which is far less than 23.1 percentage point, the rate of increase for overall developing countries. Likewise, Work Force Participation Rate for developing countries was higher than that for India by 6.9 percentage in 1990 which rose by double, i.e., to 13.8 percentage point in 1998.

One of the very disturbing features of growth pattern in the post-liberalization period is very low employment generating potential of growth in the secondary and the tertiary sectors. The result is concentration of work force in agriculture and a persistent deterioration of relative productivity and income of both male and female workers engaged in the primary sector (*G.S. Bhalla*, 2001).

In the wake of globalization, there has also been casualisation and information of labour market both for males and females (*Jeemol Unni*, 2001). However, this was comparatively more for females than that for males. Increase in percentage of casual employee has been by 2.4 and 3.3 percentage points for males and females respectively, whereas, there was reduction in percentage of regular employee by 1.7 and 1.1 percentage point for males and females respectively.

REMEDIAL MEASURES

The decade of nineties has been of paramount significance as regards to feminist research, strategy and advocacy. Attempts made by feminists to promote equality and women's empowerment have begun to bring fruition. Act of devoting an entire issue of the prestigious journal 'World Development' to gender and macro-economics in 1995, clearly indicates interest and seriousness of mainstream economists in feminist economic theory. Other remedial measures and their impacts are as follows:

INFLUENCING CORPORATE BEHAVIOUR

Corporations are the biggest players in the global economy and also the biggest winners. Foreign private investment in developing countries alone has grown five-fold and translates into investments of almost US$ 1 trillion (*Sutherland and Sewell*, 1998: 2). In comparison, the investment in development co-operation is a drop in the bucket.

Compaigns to make corporations more responsible, have been waged for decades for environmental protection, between working conditions for labour, ban on child labour, etc. Now, Southern Women's groups have become active on behalf of women factory workers. As a result of external pressure, some corporations are introducing voluntary codes of conduct, covering ethical, environmental, and labour practices in all their operations, both domestic and abroad (*Hibler* and *Beamish*, 1998). However, enforcement of voluntary codes of conduct needs independent monitoring. Moreover, most importantly, codes of conduct can not ultimately influence a global production system dependent on cheap and flexible female labour.

UN ENDEAVOURS

Institutions like the World Bank are increasingly seeing women as active agents of social, political and economic change instead of passive recipients of development. The 1995 UN World Conference on Women was probably the most visible and international focus on governments and their responsibilities. More than thirty-five thousand women from all over the world went to Beizing, many of them to share their experiences of working conditions, inadequate, health care, or lack of access to technology in the context of globalization. Non-governmental organizations had unprecedented access to government delegates attending the numerous preparatory meetings and Beizing summit, and they lobbied intensely for substantive changes in the final document—The Platform for Action. However, the Beizing summit does not seem to have gained ground. Firstly, sectoral approach adopted by UN denies any strategizing about the structural causes of gender discrimination. Secondly, the participants attending the summit mostly represented the 'minor' government ministries. Lastly, most of the Beizing recommendations addressing problem of globalization are vague.

PRESSURE ON GOVERNMENTS

The observations reveal that the globalization, well supported and strengthened by the government policies, has deteriorated the quality of life and work of women and disappointed to all those who are committed to the goals of sustainable human development. Nelson (1994), rightly says that it is women who have had to be the shock absorbers of the Structural Adjustment Programme (SAP). Therefore, government policies must have to pay due attention to the plight of those who are expected to be worsened by the globalization by extending some sort of safety net to them. For this, government need to be pressured and held accountable to these international commitments by the women's organizations, researchers and activists. Governments can be influenced to address the structural causes of poverty, or restructure the allocation of public expenditures—but unless feminist leaders show them how, it is unlikely to happen.

SUGGESTIONS

So, if development is to expand people's choices and guarantee their human rights, two things are necessary. First, global economic system must change and secondly, processes of change have to recognize gender imbalances to ensure that all people benefit from development. For this, feminist research and activism has to deepen its impact, expand its approach, and strengthen its alliances.

Deepening of impact means exposing and challenging vested interests and power structures—the historically rooted culture, principles, rules and procedures that underlie an organization. Simply adding women into existing structures is not going to serve the purpose.

Expanding of approach denotes our need to be more multi-disciplinary and holistic. Development objectives need to be informed by human rights, ecology, cultural studies, political science and so on. Economic growth will always supersede human welfare as long there is dominance of economics over other disciplines in defining development.

Finally, alliances need to be strengthened between women—North and South, East and West, rich and poor. We must be respectful to one another, taking care not to misrepresent the diverse positions of different women. The tensions that exist within international feminism need to be acknowledged and tackled. Global sisterhood can be replaced by a form of sisterhood which is both strategic and effective.

References

Bakkar, I. (ed.) (1994), *The Strategic Silence: Gender an Economic Policy*, London: Zed.

Bhalla, G.S. (2001), Political Economy of Indian Development in the 20th Century, Presidential Address at 83rd Annual Conference of IEA, University of Jammu, December 30, 2000 to January 1, 2001.

Boserup, E. (1970), *Women's Role in Economic Development*, New York, St. Martins.

Cornia, G.A. *et al.* (eds.) (1987), *Adjustment with a Human Face*, Vol. 1, New York, UNICEF/Clarendon.

Elson, D. (1990) "Male Bias in Macro Economics: The Case of Structural Adjustment" in Diana Elson (ed.), *Male Bias in Development Process*, Manchester, Manchester University Press, pp. 164-90.

Elson, D. (1992) "From Survival Strategies to Transformation Strategies: Women's Needs and Structural Adjustment", In Lourdes Beneria and Shelley Feldman (ed.) *Unequal Burden: Economic Crises, Persistent Poverty and Women's Work*, Boulder: West View, pp. 26-48.

Feldman, S. (1992), "Crises, Poverty and Gender Inequality: Current Themes and Issues," In Lourdes Beneria and Shelley Feldman (eds.), *op. cit.*, pp. 1-25.

Feldman, S. (1998), "Conceptualising Change and Equality in the Third World Context," In Nelly P. Stromquist (eds.), *Women in the Third World*, New York: Garland.

Harriss, John (2001), Globalization and World's Poor, *EPW*, Bombay, India, June 9, p. 2035.

Hsia, H.C. (1998), *'Awaking the Women who Nourished the Earth'*, Taiwan: Lihpao, April 1, p. 11.

Huang, C.H. (1998), "Economic Liberalism and Fate of Women Workers," Article presented at the Globalization and Asia Workshop, Taichung, July.

Kerr, Joanna (1999), 'Responding to Globalization', In Marilyn Porter and Ellen Judd (Eds.) *Feminists Doing Development*, London: Zed Books.

Lim, Y.I. (1998), 'Han Young Cases viewed from Korean experiences', Article presented at the Labour Rights and Labour Organizing in the Pacific Rim Conference, May 22, 1998, University of California, Los Angeles.

Lucie, C. (1999), Globalization and Women's Paid Labour in Asia, *International Social Science Journal*, UNESCO: Blackwell, June, p. 225.

Rogers, B. (1980), The Demistication of Women: Discrimination in Development Societies, New York: St Martin's.

Sen, A.K. (1990), "Gender and Cooperative Conflicts", In Irine Tinker (ed.), *Persistent Inequalities: Women and World Development*, New York: Oxford, pp. 123-49.

Sutherland and Sewell (1998), Quoted in Kerr Joanna, 1999, *op. cit*.

Unni, Jeemol (2001), Gender and Informality in Labour Market in South Asia, *EPW*, June 30.

34

Economic Reforms and Food Security for the Poor

ANIL KUMAR CHOUDHARY

Freedom from hunger has been described as one of the major feedoms that entails development (*Sen*, 1999). It is a tragedy, that despite such high aspirations, hunger and undernutrition is a real problem of the world today. The World Food Summit that took place in Rome from November 13 to 17, 1996 drew up an Action plan on the promise that "All people have the right to adequate food and to be free from hunger."

The question becomes interesting when considered in the background of globalization. Globalization, it is argued, will result in an efficient allocation of world resources and enhance human welfare. Removal of the threat of hunger and provision of food security seems to be one of the major ways in which welfare can be enhanced. However, globalization is essentially an expansion of world market. Since hungry people cannot but forward effective demand, market may remain completely insensitive to them. Infact, famine and hunger in large part of the world has been a direct impact of market forces through fall in effective employment or income manifested in entitlement failure. Public action is required to correct these distortions in market so as to enable a world secured from hunger.

This paper attempts to examine the dimensions of food security in the context of globalization and liberalization, focusing on changes to the Public Distribution System.

CONCEPT OF FOOD SECURITY

Food security means five things:

1. Food security is as much a matter of physical access to food as it is of economic access.
2. Food security relates to all people.
3. Food should be available to them all times.
4. Food has to be available in sufficient quantities.
5. Food has to be safe and nutritious which leads to a healthy and active life (*Economic Times*, Sept. 14, 2000).

In a dynamic and developing economy, food security changes with the stages of development attained by the society. From this point of view, the following stages of food security may be visualised:

Stage 1: The most basic need from the point of view of human survival is to make an adequate quantity of cereals available to all.

Stage 2: At this stage, we may think of food security as the adequate availability of cereals and pulses.

Stage 3: Food security should include cereals, pulses and milk and milk products.

Stage 4: Food security should include cereals, pulses, milk and milk products and vegetables and fruits, fish, eggs and meat (*Ruddar Dutt*, 1999).

The Government of India is committed to ensuring food security to its citizens. The approach paper to Ninth Five Year Plan urged in ensuring food and nutritional security for all, particularly the vulnerable sections of the society.

FOOD PRODUCTION

A number of studies exist that study foodgrains production

in India. These studies can be categorised into two groups. One group of study lump up various types of foodgrains by their values (*Bhalla & Singh*, 1997). Another type of studies focus on the individual crop pattern and foodgrains as a whole in terms of their physical quantity (*Saha and Swaminathan*, 1994). Both the methods have their relative merits and demerits. It would be worthwhile to consider foodgrain production in quantitative terms only.

Table 1 presents long-run linear growth rate of area, production and yield for 15 selected states of India over the period 1950-99.

TABLE 1

Linear Growth Rate of Foodgrains (1950-51—1998-99)

State	*Growth rate of*		
	Area	*Yield*	*Production*
North-West			
Haryana	0.43 (6)	4.07 (2)	4.52 (1)
Punjab	(-)0.12 (11)	4.26 (1)	4.14 (2)
Uttar Pradesh	0.38 (7)	2.62 (5)	3.01 (3)
East			
Assam	1.07 (1)	0.73 (15)	1.83 (12)
Bihar	(-)0.1 (10)	2.23 (7)	2.09 (10)
Orissa	0.99 (2)	1.23 (14)	2.23 (8)
West Bengal	0.51 (5)	1.91 (11)	2.44 (6)
Central			
Gujarat	(-)0.51 (13)	2.74 (3)	2.22 (9)
Madhya Pradesh	0.6 (4)	2.00 (9)	2.6 (5)
Maharashtra	0.002 (9)	1.73 (12)	1.73 (13)
Rajasthan	0.87 (3)	2.00 (10)	2.89 (4)
Southern			
Andhra Pradesh	0.54 (14)	2.63 (4)	2.07 (1)
Karnataka	0.07 (8)	2.29 (6)	2.37 (7)
Kerala	(-)1.1 (15)	1.45 (13)	0.34 (15)
Tamil Nadu	(-)0.41 (12)	2.03 (8)	1.61 (14)
All India	0.31	2.32	2.71

Figures in Parentheses give the relative rank.

Source: Atanu Sen Gupta, 'Food Security in India: A State Level Analysis', *Bhartiya Samajik Chintan*, Vol. XXIV, Nos. 1-4, Dec. 2001.

It is obvious from the table, in terms of both yield and production, North-Western states dominate. However, in terms of area expansion Eastern states seem to take an upper hand. Only way in which production can be further improved in this zone is through improvement of yield rate. This depends on the availability and adoption of improved technology which have usual limitations like environmental risks. So far as the central and Southern states are concerned, it seems they are more interested in the cash crops. Furthermore, large portion of these states face semi-arid conditions. Given the constraints in water supply, it is extremely difficult to enhance production in this area.

Since 1991, with the adoption of the policy of 'Economic Liberalization' and 'Structural changes', agriculture has become export-oriented. As a result, marked changes are observed in cropping pattern, agricultural diversification, output composition and domestic prices of foodgrains. Therefore, the slow growth rate in foodgrain productivity and export of foodgrain have mounted pressure on food prices and food security.

ENTITLEMENT FAILURES

The analysis is quite inadequate without proper emphasis on the failure of entitlement to food procurement for a large group of people. The nutritional status of population more particularly women and children belonging to vulnerable sections of the rural society has not been sufficiently improved. According to the recent reports of the UNICEF and the World Bank, 63 per cent of children in India are malnourished. Iron-deficiency anaemia is widespread among Indian girls and women.

From the point of view of an average calorie intake, it is declined steadily in rural and urban areas between 1972-73 and 1993-94. In rural India, average calorie intake fell from 2266 kcal in 1972-73 to 2153 kcal in 1993-94. In urban India, the average intake went down from 2107 kcal in 1972-73 to 2071 kcal in 1993-94. The two exceptions to this trend were Kerala and West Bengal.

A commonly used indicator of under nutrition among adults is Body Mass Index (BMI), defined as the ratio of weight (in Kilograms) to the square of height (in metres). If the BMI is taken as an indicator of under nutrition, then 48 per cent of men and women were chronically energy deficient in 1993-94.

It is then a concern why under nourishment and malnourishment persists in a country where foodgrain supply is adequate. The answer clearly lies in the entitlement failures as suggested by Dreze and Sen (1989). Growth of the economy has been extremely uneven. This leaves a section of the people at precariously low level of existence. With extremely poor level of income and wealth, they can not acquire enough entitlement over foodgrain that could save them from starvation and under nourishment.

GLOBALIZATION AND THE FOOD SECURITY

There are three key features of the policies being imposed by globalization on developing countries across the world including India. These are: a cut in subsidies-including subsidies for food, leaving distribution of food to the market with as little state intervention as possible and targeting to the 'Poorest of the poor.'

The burden of food subsidy has become central to the process of economic reforms. So far as India is concerned, the scale of food subsidies has grown in nominal in real terms but if food subsidies are viewed in relation to GNP or Government expenditure, the burden has not changed much over the last twenty years. In India, over the 33 year period, 1966-99, food subsidy averaged 0.60 per cent of GNP and 3.19 per cent of central government expenditure. It shows that even eliminating food subsidies totally will not solve the fiscal problems of the government (Table 2).

Another dangerous trend is that, the reformers wish to target to the 'poorest of the poor.' A world Bank study on the PDS in India suggested that the PDS be targeted to the 'very poor' or those with incomes less than three-fourths of the official poverty line.

PDS AND FOOD SECURITY FOR THE POOR

Distribution of foodgrains and its pricing is one of the vital dimension of food security in India. In India, The Public Distribution System (PDS) is one of the conspicuous programmes of poverty alleviation. Its basic aim was to provide essential commodities such as rice, wheat, sugar, edible oil, soft coke and kerosene at subsidised prices.

TABLE 2

Central Government Expenditure on Food Subsidy

	Expenditure at Current Price (Rs. Crores)	Percentage of	
		GNP +	Total Govt. Expenditure
1974-75	295	0.44	3.01
1980-81	650	0.53	2.89
1985-86	1650	0.71	3.11
1990-91	2450	0.52	2.33
1991-92	2850	0.53	2.53
1992-93	2800	0.45	2.22
1993-94	5537	0.78	3.80
1994-95	5100	0.61	3.01
1995-96	5377	0.61	2.90
1996-97	6066	0.61	2.89
1997-98	7500	0.53	3.23
1998-99	9000	0.61	3.19

Sources: Ruddar Datt (1999), 'Effectiveness of public distribution system as a provider of food security', *The India Journal of Labour Economics*, Vol. 42, No. 3, p. 395.

Since the mid-1980s PDS acquired the status of a welfare programme. The revamped PDS was later expanded to cover 1752 blocks with a high incidence of poverty covering 164 million persons.

Although rice, wheat, sugar, edible oil, soft coke and kerosene are sold through PDS outlets, four of these items viz. rice, wheat, sugar and kerosene, account for 86 percent of total PDS sales. This reflects general impression that the PDS commodity is weighted in favour of items supposed to be consumed largely by the relatively richer sections of the society (*Suryanarayana*, 1995).

Cereals consumption is an important indicator of food security. From the point of view of food security, it is necessary to bring the cereal consumption to the minimum cereal consumption norm of 11.58 kgs. fixed for subsistence level by ICMR. Presently for the poorest decile, consumption of cereals is in the range of 8 to 11 kgs. To reduce malnutrition among the poor, it is imperative that the consumption pattern of the poor, be altered in favour of nutritious non-cereal items.

The basic question, which needs to be probed, is whether PDS purchases are able to effectively help the poor. Radhakrishna *et al* (1997) concludes: 'The evidence shows that even now, the efficacy of PDS in distributing food to the poor seems to be as bad as in 1986-87. . ., obviously, there is mistargeting in the distribution of PDS foodgrains. He therefore, concludes: Impressive coverage and/or additional state-level spending on subsidy is no guarantee that the very poor are better served. The central issue, therefore is how to improve the efficacy of PDS in transferring food to the poor in a cost-effective manner'. (p. 31)

The introduction of targeting has led to large-scale exclusion of poor and vulnerable form the PDS. The method of targeting based on the income poverty line has already led to the exclusion from the BPL category of millions of undernourished people and people at the risk of undernourishment. Identification of beneficiaries on the basis of a narrow income poverty line is faulty conceptually and difficult to implement, resulting in large errors of exclusion. For example, one of the existing central guidelines for the targeted PDS is that a family with income above Rs. 20,000 a year should be excluded from the BPL category in UP, the government undertook a survey and began with a cut-off of Rs. 11,000 per annum to identify BPL families. Later the cut-off was reduced to Rs. 9000 per annum. In Maharashtra the government went one step further and issued BPL card only to households with income below Rs. 4000 a year.

A recent trend is the decline in off-take of cereals from PDS. Between 1991-92 and 1994-95, wheat off-take for PDS fell from 8.78 to 4.83 million tonnes and rice off-take from 9.94 to 8.0 million tonnes. The major factor responsible for a decline in off-take was the abnormal increase in the issue price of wheat in recent years. It has reduced the difference between issue price and on market price and has contributed to the shift of consumers from PDS to the open market.

As the off-take of cereals from the PDS felt, stocks of rice and wheat surpassed minimum requirements by large margins. Whereas, actual stocks in July 1992 were below the norm for that period. Since 1993, actuals stocks have been consistently higher than the norm in every quarter. In January 2001, there were 45.5 million tonnes of grain in the stocks, the current estimate is over 60 million tonnes. Thus the post-1991 period witnessed the cruels and irrational phenomenon of rising food stocks, on the one hand and falling food off-take from the PDS, on the other hand.

CONCLUSION

The Government of India is committed to achieving the goal of 'Food Security for All'. However, the achievement of food security for all amidst rising population is an arduous task. Poverty is a major threat of food insecurity. For the purpose of providing enduring food security to the poor, therefore it would be more appropriate to emphasize strategies, which reduce poverty. For this purpose identifying the poor is a basic problem. Political economic considerations are the major constraints that need to be considered in designing programmes. It is necessary to target those people and areas suffering mostly from hunger and malnutrition and identify causes and remedial action to improve the situation.

Policies offered by the Washington consensus as a part of the process of globalization have been disastrous for food security for millions of Indians. It is clear that the policies introduced since the early 1990 and particularly, the introduction of targeting in 1997, has weakened the PDS and are leading quickly to its eventual dismantling. Recent pronouncements on decentralization indicate that, the central government intends to give up its responsibility towards the PDS and food security.

In India, the PDS is one of the conspicuous programmes of poverty alleviation. Many empirical studies have shown that the poor were not benefitting much from the PDS. The faulty targeting in the PDS and narrowing gap between the PDS price and market price of foodgrains are two important problems of providing food security for all in rural India. Without ignoring the political economic considerations undermentioned policy options may be attempted: (1) The panchayati raj institutions should be assigned the task of identification of poor. (2) Commodities under the PDS, which are used by the non-poor, should be gradually shiffed to the open market. (3) To induce the poor to buy more from PDS, the gap between the issue price and the open market price should be sufficiently large. (4) NGOs committed to help the poor should be involved in supervising PRIs working. (5) The role of FCI should be limited to stabilization of food prices.

To sum up, the role of rapid economic growth with larger employment generation assumes crucial importance. To ensure that the gains of income to the poor are not eroded through rise of prices, the government should adopt price stabilization strategies.

References

Bhalla, G.S. and G. Singh (1997), 'Recent Development in Indian Agriculture: A State Level Analysis,' *Economic and Political Weekly*, Vol. 32, No. 13, March 29.

Dreze, J. and A. Sen (1989), *'Hunger and Public Action'*, Oxford University Press, New Delhi.

Datt, Ruddar (1999), 'Effectiveness of Public Distribution System as a Provider of Food Security', *The Indian Journal of Labour Economics*, Vol. 42, No. 3, July-September.

Economic Times, Sept. 14, 2000.

Sen, A. (1999), *'Development as Freedom*, Oxford University Press, New Delhi.

Suryanarayana, M.H. (1985), "PDS Reforms and Scope for Commodity Based Targeting', *Economic and Political Weekly*, Vol. 30, No. 13.

Sana, A. and M. Swaminathan (1994), "Agricultural Growth in West Bengal in the 1980s: A Disaggregation by Districts and Crops", *EPW*, Vol. 29, No. 13, March 26.

Radhakrishna, R., K. Subbarao, S. Indrakant and K. Ravi (1997), 'Public Distribution: A National and International Perspective', World Bank Discussion Paper No. 380.

35

People's Planning Programme and Social Revolution in Kerala

L. RATHAKRISHNAN AND N. KRISHNAKUMAR

1. INTRODUCTION

India has a long experience in the area of development planning next to Soviet Russia (which has been renamed as Commonwealth of Independent States, CIS). However, there exists a growing dissatisfaction among the people that the "trickle down" development strategy adopted since 1950 has not benefited the most needy people of India. Growth of national and per capita income is slow; poverty and unemployment have been aggravated; illiteracy and backwardness is a common phenomenon; rural-urban and regional imbalances have still widened; and also there is a co-existence of unexploited and unutilized natural as well as human resources in our country. One of the major reason pointed out in this context is that, the highly centralized nature of Indian planning system and the weak micro-level planning.

Development experiences of advanced countries on the other hand, show that decentralization, freedom, "laissez-faire" market economy, globalization, full employment, quality education, basic health, social security, adequate infrastructure facilities, and maximum use of natural resources have paved the way for economic development. The important lesson to be learnt from developed countries is that the plan should be people centered. Therefore, people's participation and involvement is an essential one for success of the plan objectives.

One of the specific objectives of the Ninth Plan (1992-97) of the Government of India is to promote and develop people's participation through Panchayat Raj Institutions (PRI), co-operative societies, and self-help groups. It has always felt that; panchayat raj system is the most suitable agency for democratic decentralization, which could be equipped with adequate powers and responsibilities. It is a strong media for strengthening the capabilities of the people. The slogans of "Power to the People" can be more meaningful only with the implementation of the system more effectively.

The Kerala Panchayat Raj bill was adopted by the legislative assembly on May 22, 1994, which seeks to replace the existing laws governing village panchayats and district councils, namely, the Kerala Panchayat Act, 1960 and the District Council Act, 1991. Now the State Government has introduced a revolutionary programme, "people's planning" through the three tire system—grama panchayat at the lower tier, block panchayat in the middle, and district panchayat at the upper tiers respectively. This paper examines how the people's planning programme introduced in Kerala has brought social revolution in the state through case study approach.

2. OBJECTIVE AND METHODOLOGY

The major objective of this study is to analyse and understand the people's planning programme with respect to various development schemes carried out by the panchayat and the pattern of fund utilization by the beneficiaries. Pallickal Gram Panchayat in Pathanathitta district, Kerala was selected for this study. Both primary and secondary data was collected from the selected panchayat union.

In order to understand fund utilization, 50 beneficiaries (out of 700) were selected. Data were collected with the help of well-framed interview schedule. The primary data was collected in the month of April 1999, and the secondary data was collected during the year 1997-98 mainly from plan documents, state planning board, and the office of the village panchayat.

3. LITERATURE BACKGROUND

Very limited studies have been conducted in the field of People's Planning Programme. Although the concept is a part and parcel of Panchayat Raj, very few studies have been carried out on this topic. Nevertheless, numerous Central and State Government's evaluation reports were available in the field of Panchayati Raj. Balvantray Mehta (1957), Ashok Mehta (1978), Rao (1985), and Singhvi Committee (1986) have carried out studies on Panchayat Raj Institution and offered a variety of suggestions for successful implementation of the programme. Some of the notable recommendations of these studies were: (i) reservation for SC/ST on the basis of their population; (ii) open participation of political parties in Panchayat affairs; (iii) allocation of more financial resources to the panchayat; and (iv) involvement of people in planning and development process.

Few individuals have also made some attempts on the issue of decentralized planning through Panchayat Raj Institution. Particularly Haldipur *et al.* (1970), Issac (1996), Jain (1997), Parmakar (1998), and Nanjundappa (1998) have carried out studies on some aspects of Panchayat Raj Institution in India. These studies have attributed the reasons for the failures and also gave some solutions. The reasons identified for failures of this programme were: skewed distribution of benefits, failure to evoke popular support from people, inability to achieve common acceptance of the decisions due to sections among the villagers, lack of spirit in leadership, dominance of rich and large farmers, undue and too much political interference in the work of the development functionaries, and paucity of funds. They have emphasized the need for integrated planning at different levels, the need for people's participation in the decision-making process at grass-root level, accurate identification, and effective utilization of leadership.

4. ANALYSIS AND DISCUSSION

Development Schemes Carried out by Gram Panchayat

As an initial step of people's planning programme, the Pallickal Panchayat have taken steps to identify development strategies, sectors, and also preparation of development projects. The funds have been allocated for two main purposes namely, General Sector Project and Special Component Project.

TABLE 1

Project and Sector-wise Fund Allocation (1997-2000)

(*in Rs.*)

Sl. No.	*Sector*	*General Sector Project*	*Special Component Project*	*Grant Total*
1.	Production	1872000	1179200	3051200
2.	Service	1404000	884400	2288400
3.	Infrastructure	1404000	884400	2288400
	Total	4680000	2948000	7628000

The State Planning Commission has allocated more than Rs. 76 lakhs for implementation of different development projects during the plan period out of which more than 61 per cent has been allocated for general sector project and the remaining 39 per cent has been spared for special component project, which is meant for the welfare of scheduled castes and scheduled tribes.

In the general sector project, agricultural schemes like promotion of betel cultivation, paddy cultivation, coconut cultivation, and vegetable cultivation received major share of funds. This also includes development of irrigation facilities like digging of new wells and protection of old wells. In the special component project, housing for SC/ST people, construction of latrine, development of drinking water facilities, help for re-thatching of houses, and electric connection to the houses of rural poor were included. To facilitate infrastructure development, a number of roads were repaired and tarred. Small culverts and bridges were also constructed during the study period.

In addition to the plan fund, a sum of Rs. 30 lakhs had been generated locally, which accounts for 28 per cent of the total plan outlay of the Panchayat. These funds have been mobilized through panchayat's own fund, voluntary services, and beneficiary contribution. Table 2, explains these particulars in detail. These funds have helped the Panchayat to identify and implement 47 development projects during the year 1997-98. Of which 34 projects were fall under general sector project, while 13 project were comes under special component project.

TABLE 2

Total Plan Outlay of the Panchayat (1997-98)

(in Rs.)

Sl. No.	*Particulars*	*Amount*
1.	Plan fund	7628000
2.	Gram panchayat own fund	64778
3.	Voluntary service	2221000
4.	Beneficiary contribution	74160
	Grant Total	10656938

Pattern of Fund Utilization by the Beneficiaries

Of the 700 beneficiaries, 50 respondents (7 per cent) were selected randomly, which constitutes 37 males and 13 females. Majority of the respondents fall under less than 40 years old age group. Surprisingly 14 per cent of the beneficiaries are illiterate. Similarly 86 per cent of the respondents are engaged in the agricultural sector and others are falling under daily wage earning group.

The selected respondents have received loan for agricultural development and also for service sector. As the panchayat does not have any provision to give loan to industrial sector no one had benefited under this scheme. It is found from the study that younger generations (less than 40 years old) have got major benefits.

Table 3, explains the fund utilization according to the purpose. About 60 per cent of the respondents have received grama panchayat loans for new house construction, latrine and electrification, construction of new wells, and protection of old wells. Only 40 per cent of the respondents have got their loan for agricultural purposes, namely, betel farming, paddy cultivation, vegetable cultivation, and protection of coconut trees. Although

86 per cent of the beneficiaries are agriculturists, only 40 per cent of them have received their loan for agricultural purposes.

TABLE 3

Sector- and Purpose-wise Fund Utilization

Purpose/ Sector-wise Fund use	*Respondents Age*					*Total Respondents*
	20-30	*31-40*	*41-50*	*51-60*	*61+*	
1. Agriculture						
Betel	3 (50)	2 (33)	1 (17)	—	—	6 (12)
Paddy	1 (20)	—	2 (40)	1 (20)	1 (20)	15 (.10)
Protecting Coconut	1 (20)	2 (40)	— (20)	1 (20)	. 1 (10)	5 (10)
Vegetable cultivation	1 (25)	—	2 (50)	1 (25)	—	4 (8)
Sub-total	6 (30)	4 (20)	5 (25)	3 (15)	2 (10)	20 (40)
2. Services						
New wells	6 (75)	—	1 (12.5)	—	1 (12.5)	8 (16)
Protection of Old Wells	2 (50)	1 (25)	—	1 (25)	—	4 (8)
Latrine	1 (11.1)	5 (55.6)	1 (11.1)	—	2 (22.2)	9 (18)
Electrification of house	2 (25)	—	3 (37.5)	1 (12.5)	2 (25)	8 (16)
New Houses	—	1 (100)	—	—	—	1 (2)
Sub-Total	11 (37)	7 (23)	5 (17)	2 (6)	5 (17)	30 (60)
Total	17 (34)	11 (22)	10 (20)	5 (10)	7 (14)	50 (100)

Note: Figures in the parentheses indicates the percentage to the total.

TABLE 4

Distribution of Samples According to the Amount Received

Amount Sector-wise Fund use		Respondents Age					Total Respondents
		20-30	31-40	41-50	51-60	61+	
Less than 15000		11	10	9	5	6	41
		(26.8)	(24.4)	(22)	(12.2)	(14.6)	(82)
	Rs.	16550	17300	7725	4600	6700	52875
15001-20000		6	—	1	—	1	8
		(75)		(12.5)		(12.5)	(16)
	Rs.	20080		15000		18000	53080
More than 20001		—	1	—	—	—	1
			(100)				(2)
	Rs.		20080				2008
Total		17	11	10	5	7	50
		(34)	(22)	(20)	(10)	(14)	(100)
	Rs.	36630	37380	22725	4600	24700	126035

Note: Figures in the parentheses indicates percentage to the total.

Table 4, shows the distribution of samples according to the amount received. 82 per cent of total beneficiaries have received less than Rs. 15,000. They have received a sum of Rs. 52,875. 16 per cent of the beneficiaries had a loan amount of Rs. 15,001 to 20,000 with the total amount of Rs. 53,080. The total amount received by all the beneficiaries together accounted for Rs. 1,26,035. Almost all the respondents have a opinion that the fund is not sufficient to meet their requirements.

As the selection of the beneficiaries are based on economic criteria, 82 per cent of the beneficiaries were satisfied with respect to loan amount distribution and the beneficiary selection criteria and the rest were dissatisfied. The satisfaction level is found to be high in the age group of 20-30. The reasons for dissatisfaction was unnecessary political intervention, providing funds to the close relatives of the authorities, and the neglect of deserved people.

5. THE PARTICIPATION OF PEOPLE IN THE PEOPLE'S PLANNING PROGRAMME

As a first step of ascertaining the involvement of local people in the planning programmes, maximum publicity has been given. This is mainly done in order to make sure that there is public presence in the gram sabha. The whole developmental problems are discussed in the grama sabha and people's opinion regarding its implementation is sought. And finally it is implemented on the basis of the views of the people. The entire programme is divided into two categories:

(i) Those developmental activities, which are being carried out through gram panchayat funds, and
(ii) The other development activities, which are done through people's full involvement, namely, through voluntary services.

The opinion regarding the people's planning programme reveals that the programme is a tremendous success during the first phase. The people are foreseeing dramatic changes in their economic as well as social conditions in the near future.

6. MAJOR DEVELOPMENT ACTIVITIES INITIATED BY THE PEOPLE

The involvement of people in the development activities of the panchayat are vastly appreciated by all sections of the people. The major attempts in this direction is with regards to the number of roads constructed and maintained during the year 1997-98. There are two new roads constructed in the first phase particularly in the backward areas (Laksham Veedu Colony and Priyadarshini Colony). As decided by the grama sabha, the people residing in the southern part of the Panchayat have cleaned the surroundings of the primary health center and they have also appealed to the panchayat to provide more infrastructure facilities to the health center. The major achievement in this respect is that the programme of vegetable cultivation within the premises of panchayat property. This programme is an ongoing one, which was started only in the final stage of the first phase.

It has been a long dream of the panchayat to construct a water tank near the pond Arathuchira. As a first step, with the involvement of the people, the pond was cleaned and deepended. The Panchayat has already sanctioned one and half lakh rupees for the construction of water tank. The total budget estimated for this purpose was three lakh rupees. A committee has been formed under the Chairmanship of the Panchayat President. In addition, a playing ground and construction of a stadium are also in the agenda of the Grama Panchayat for future implementation.

7. POLICY IMPLICATIONS

On the basis of the above results the study suggests the following points for further improvement of people's planning in Kerala.

(1) Voluntary agencies should be given greater importance in people's planning programme.
(2) The Gram Panchayat should take effective steps to organize 'Ayalkkoottams' (Neighbourhood Group) for strengthening the people's participation.
(3) Socially committed and honest people should be identified and encouraged to play a leading role in the development process.

REFERENCES

Ashok Mehta Committee Report (1978), *Panchayati Raj,* Government of India, New Delhi.

Balavantray Committee Report (1957), *Panchayat Raj Institutions,* Government of India, New Delhi.

Dubey, S.N. and Murdia (1976), *Structure and Process of Decision Making in Panchayat Raj Institutions,* Somaiya Publications, Bombay.

Gulati, I.S. (1994), *Decentralization and its Implications for Urban Service Delivery,* World Bank, Washington D.C.

Gangadhar Reddi (1998), "Panchayati Raj: The Challenge Ahead", *Kurukshetra,* 47(2).

Haldiput, R.N. and Paramahamsa, U.R.K. (1970), *Local Government Institutions in Rural India,* National Institute of Community Development, Hyderabad.

Jain, S.P. (1997), The Gram Sabha: Gateway to Grassroots Democracy, *Journal of Rural Development,* 16 (4).

Nanjundappa, D.M. (1998), "Panchayati Raj and Rural Development, (The Leadership Issue)," *Yojana*, 24 (4).

Prasad, Kanta (1993), *Integrated Framework for Decentralised Planning: Issues and Options*, Rawat Publications, New Delhi.

Padmakar (1998), "Panchayati Raj—A Look Back", *Kurukshetra*, 48 (3).

Rao, V.K.R.V. Committee Report (1985), *Panchayati Raj Institutions*, Government of India, New Delhi.

Singhvi, L.M. Committee Report (1986), *Panchayati Raj Institutions*, Government of India, New Delhi.

36

Social Sector, Social Security and the Underprivileged Class

S.K. Pant

The term social security in its broadest form refers to the retirement income, annuity, support, subsidy, payment, pension, allowances or survivors benefits. In other words, it is the protection that is given by the States to the socially in secured groups. Why was there such a need to provide social security, when the country was already practicing a planned model? The answer to it lies with the country's experience with decades of planning. It is no doubt, that it has attained self-sufficiency in many areas. However, it has also not with some glaring disappointments specially in the field of social sector development.

The persual of the profile of the planning shows that though the emphasize has been given to the development of both the economic as well as social sector, yet the achievement rate in the later has been quite slow and disappointing. What has really been the cause for concern is that the fruits of development have not percolated down evenly down to the grass root levels, as was being envisaged of them, and a sizeable chunk of population turn has remained isolated and marginalised from the impact of development which virtually undetermines the concept of holistic development (*Prabhu, S.*, 1998, *EPW Foundation*, 1994). This marginalised class mainly comprises people from disadvantaged group, females and children. Is it not ironical, despite the fact that during all the years, the country initiated a host of social sector development programmes?

The plausible reason for this hiatus may be traced back to the difference in the growth rate between the two sectors. While the growth rate in economic sector is faster and its impact becomes conspicuous even in short-term, the growth rate in social sector is painfully long and its impact is discernible only in the long-term. However, once the social development sets in, it provides sustenance to the overall process of development (*Panchmukhi, P.R.*, 2000). For this reason only, nations all over the world are paying increasing attention for developing their social sector.

In our country also adequate emphasis has been given for developing the social sector right since the inception of planning. However, on account of the mis-match between the growth rates of the two sectors, the country is inflicted with the high incidence of poverty, malnutritions, hunger, income disparities, high rate rural to urban migration (*Seventh & Eighth Five Year Plan*, 1992-93; *Swaminathan, D.*, 1996; *Economic Survey*, 1996), which have not only persisted with the time, but even have grown and become more sharp (*Arunugam*, 1999).

Concern over these issues, the government in an attempt to restore some parity, earmarked some programmes exclusively for the underprivileged classes. These programmes primarily focus on catering to their socio-economic and other requirements from the Fifth Five Year Plan onwards and were wrapped under the package of Minimum Basic Needs. However, with the passage of time it also became clear that the impact of these programmes has not reached the people uniformly and the benefits have been largely cornered by a small sections of their population (*Pant & Pandey*, 2000).

It is against this backdrop, an attempt has been made to study the performance of social sector programmes in the two districts viz. Varanasi and Saharanpur of Uttar Pradesh. Though both the districts belong to different economic regions of the State, however on development scale both qualified as socially developed districts.

METHODOLOGY

Five villages from each of the sample district were selected using stratified random sampling technique. As the focus of the study was to study performance of programmes on the underprivileged class of people, care was taken to select those villages where majority of these, the socially disadvantaged section resided. Accordingly, of the five villages selected, the first was from Gandhigram category, the second from Ambedkar gram category, the third from where female gram pradhan was elected and the remaining two villages were from the general category.

The basis of selecting those villages was to cover up as many social sector schemes as possible because as per the governments directives, maximum number of social sector schemes are in vogue in those villages only, where this deprived section resides.

After identifying the villages, the selection of beneficiaries was taken as at the next stage. It was decided to include only those set of households into over study who were living below the poverty line (BPL). The list of household was obtained from the block office and as the baseline survey was conducted by the block in 1998, validating and updating of the record became necessary and for this door to door listing of BPL families was undertaken. Thus, the study targetted only those households who were living below the poverty line. However, the exercise also revealed that there was a large number of other households who could not get the benefit of these schemes, though they too were living below the poverty line, hereafter called the non-beneficiaries. In order to provide a meaningful comparison, the study also included them.

The study analyses the performance of a total of fifteen social sector programmes and a majority of that fall under the ambit of Minimum Basic Needs, because it was increasingly being realised that the socially vulnerable group do not have the purchasing power, hence they should be provided these services that essentially take care of their consumption, shelter, sanitation and other vital aspects of human requirements. It was also envisaged that by providing convergence of these programmes to them, this vulnerable group may get more benefited and subsequently their socio-economic status would enhance. The perusal of the profile of these two programmes shows that they could also broadly be classified into two major groups based on their nature and coverage as specific and general programmes. The specific programmes were those programmes that targeted specific sections only like old age pensions, national welfare programmes, old age widow pension, etc. while the second contained general programmes like Jawahar Rojgar Yojana, Indira Awas Yojana, Employment Guarantee Schemes, etc. as their focus was on the general population.

The household selected under the specific programmes was limited on account of its low coverage, whereas, in general programmes was large. However, it was decided that the coverage for specific programmes was five percent of the total number subject to a minimum of five beneficiaries whereas for general programme, the coverage of beneficiaries was restricted to a maximum of 2.5 percent of the total subject to a minimum of 3 beneficiaries. The other details of the programme, beneficiaries and non-beneficiaries have been summarised in Table 1.

PROFILE OF SOCIAL SECTOR PROGRAMMES, BENEFICIARIES AND NON-BENEFICIARIES IN THE SAMPLE DISTRICTS

Objectives

The study primarily focuses on the performance of social sector programmes. The performance has been analysed at three levels, viz. first, at the level of the involvement of beneficiaries, the second, at the level of the involvement of programme functionaries and finally, it also studies the inter-programme linkages.

In view of the time and space constraint, the present study focuses on the performance of only two programmes, one drawn from specific category and the other from general category. Thus under the specific category, the performance of National Old Age Pension Scheme (NOAPS) and under general category the performance of public distribution system (PDS) have been analysed.

However, to study the inter-programme linkages, the principal programmes whose inter-programme linkages were studied were, Indira Awas Yojana, National Maternity Benefit Scheme, National Old Age Pension Scheme, National Widow

TABLE 1

Profile of Social Sector Programme, Beneficiaries and Non-Beneficiaries, in Sample Districts of Varanasi and Saharanpur

Social Sector Programme	*Total Beneficiaries*				*Sample Beneficiaries*			
	Varanasi		*Saharanpur*		*Varanasi*		*Saharanpur*	
	Beneficiary	*Non-Benefi.*	*Beneficiary*	*Non-Benefi.*	*Beneficiary*	*Non-Benefi.*	*Beneficiary*	*Non-Benefi.*
National Old Age Pension	25 (100.0)	27 (100.0)	105 (100.0)	37 (100.0)	10 (40.0)	15 (55.6)	23 (21.9)	16 (43.2)
National Family Benefit Scheme	4 (100.0)	10 (100.0)	4 (100.0)	5 (100.0)	2 (50.0)	10 (100.0)	4 (100.0)	5 (100.0)
National Widow Pension Scheme	51 (100.0)	23 (100.0)	13 (100.0)	45 (100.0)	19 (37.3)	13 (56.5)	7 (53.8)	14 (31.1)
National Handicapped Scheme	11 (100.0)	8 (100.0)	5 (100.0)	10 (100.0)	5 (45.5)	7 (87.5)	5 (100.0)	10 (100.0)
National Maternity Benefit Scheme	25 (100.0)	43 (100.0)	53 (100.0)	45 (100.0)	18 (72.0)	15 (34.9)	24 (45.3)	13 (28.9)
Employment Assurance Scheme/JRY	70 (100.0)	66 (100.0)	203 (100.0)	169 (100.0)	25 (35.7)	19 (28.8)	25 (12.3)	15 (8.9)
Indira Awas Yojana	71 (100.0)	44 (100.0)	46 (100.0)	25 (100.0)	13 (18.3)	17 (38.6)	18 (39.1)	11 (44.0)
Rural Domestic Cooking Energy	16 (100.0)	62 (100.0)	—	68 (100.0)	11 (68.7)	15 (24.2)	—	14 (20.6)
Rural Sanitation Scheme	23 (100.0)	69 (100.0)	46 (100.0)	53 (100.0)	12 (52.2)	15 (21.7)	13 (28.3)	14 (26.4)
Public Distribution System	121 (100.0)	16 (100.0)	225 (100.0)	12 (100.0)	121 (100.0)	16 (100.0)	225 (100.0)	12 (100.0)
Rural Electrification	29 (100.0)	116 (100.0)	95 (100.0)	229 (100.0)	29 (100.0)	116 (100.0)	95 (100.0)	229 (100.0)
Neo Literates (T.L.C.)	N.A.	—	811 (100.0)	—	48 (16.8)	—	49 (6.0)	—
Mid-day Meal	1508 (100.0)	—	695 (100.0)	—	25 (17.0)	—	26 (3.7)	—
Scholarship for Primary Education	296 (100.0)	—	353 (100.0)	—	42 (4.1)	—	22 (6.2)	—
Rural Water Supply	5 (100.0)	—	5 (100.0)	—	5 (100.0)	—	5 (100.0)	—
Total	2255 (100.0)	484 (100.0)	2659 (100.0)	698 (100.0)	358 (15.9)	263 (54.3)	591 (22.2)	390 (55.9)

Note: Figures in parenthesis denotes row percentage.

Source: For beneficiary data provided by block for non-beneficiary spot verification by the research team with the help of villagers.

Pension Scheme, National Handicapped Pension Yojana and Employment Assurance Scheme.

RESULT AND DISCUSSION

1. Analysis of Specific Programmes: The National Old Age Pension Scheme (NOAS)

The Programme

Under the programme old age pension of Rs. 125 per month is provided to persons of 65 years and above, who are destitutes and earn monthly income of Rs. 225 or less. The programme is sponsored by the Social Welfare Department and only those persons qualify for pension whose candidature is recommended by the Gram Pradhan and certified by Lekhpal. Finally, an applicant become entitled when his or her application is approved by the Deputy District Collector. The total amount disbursed as a pension to the beneficiary is Rs. 1500 in a year in two half yearly instalments.,

Profile of the Beneficiaries

The total number of beneficiaries selected were thirty of which ten belonged to Varanasi and the remaining 20 to Saharanpur district. The age-wise distribution of those beneficiaries shows that over 70 percent in Varanasi and about 52 percent in Saharanpur districts were between the age group of 60 to 69 years and the remaining 30 percent in Varanasi and over 48 percent in Saharanpur district were over 70 years of age. A majority of the beneficiaries were from the SC or OBC group in both the sample districts with the proportion of General Caste being very low.

Performance of Programme

The perusal of the selection of beneficiaries shows that the programme functionaries have, by and large, followed the selection norm as the representation of the deprives section was large. However, low awareness among the beneficiaries, regarding their selection, casts an aspersion on the fairness or genuineness on the selection process. A detail analysis to the methodology of selection reveals that the selection of some of the beneficiaries was decided by their proximity and connection with the influential group or programme functionaries. These incidences appeared to be more pronounced in Saharanpur district.

As the basis of selection for the scheme was that the person's income should be less than Rs. 225 per month which was too low for a developed district like Saharanpur. Since the scheme has limited slots, many of the households were found to have been using unethical means to gain the beneficiary status, thereby depriving some other genuine households.

Similarly, in a majority of the cases, in both the sample districts, the disbursement of pension was taking place on six monthly instalment basis, however in about 40 percent cases in Varanasi, the frequently of distribution of pension was quite uncertain. Likewise, though almost half of the beneficiaries in Varanasi and Saharanpur district were facing no difficulty in receiving the pension amount but about 30 percent in Varanasi and a small fraction of beneficiaries in Saharanpur districts were also experiencing uncertainty regarding their pension payments. Similarly over 10 percent in Varanasi and over 21 percent in Saharanpur districts also had to commute, too often, to the concern departments which caused a great deal of hardship to them. It was also found that about 10 percent of the beneficiaries in Saharanpur had monetarily obliged the programme functionaries. All these developments supplemented with huge backlog of non-beneficiaries, sustains our suspicious that the programme has been performing well only on paper, on the ground level, it has yet to make a genuine start.

Involvement of Beneficiaries

The involvement of beneficiaries could not be called to be high because the process of selection was too beaurucratic which the genuine beneficiaries found too en-cumbersome and tiring. The involvement of functionaries from different departments also encourages malpractice and blurs the element of transparency. The target-based approach followed by the government was also depriving a sizeable proportion of functionaries from participating in the programme. Lack of awareness on part of beneficiaries, many a times, deprived the genuine beneficiaries from participating and encouraged room from 'non-genuine' beneficiaries.

Involvement of Functionaries

The study of the performance of programme functionaries along with the analysis of the perception of beneficiaries and non-beneficiaries shows that the programme functionaries were only contended with following the norms of the programme superficially. Their ritualistic approach perhaps on account of their heavy workload, has encouraged many unscrupulous elements to take advantage of the situation. The incidence of beneficiaries, who are no more alive, receiving the pensions reflects both the level of corruption and total apathy towards the programme by the functionaries. Likewise, the lack of coordination between different departments, involved in the programme, has also contributed to its poor performance.

TABLE 2

Profile of Non-Beneficiary in National Old Age Pension Scheme

Particulars	*Varanasi*		*Saharanpur*	
	Number	*Percent*	*Number*	*Percent*
1	2	3	4	5
Age status				
60-69 years	13	78.1	6	40.0
70 years and above	3	18.7	9	60.0
Caste status				
SC	6	37.5	12	80.0
OBC	9	56.3	—	—
General	1	6.2	3	20.0
From which medium you got information about the programme				
Gram pradhan	15	93.7	12	80.0
Neighbourer	—	—	2	13.3
Relative	1	6.3	1	6.7
What was the reason of your not benefiting				
Do not know	7	43.7	1	6.7
Block officials informed that there was no budget	6	37.5	6	40.0
Did not provide the bribe	2	12.5	—	—

1	*2*	*3*	*4*	*5*
When form was filled up they were not present	1	6.2	1	6.7
Due to voting policy	1	6.2	4	26.7
Had no certificate of age as a proof	1	6.2	—	—
Due to corruption	—	—	4	26.7
What are the sources of your livelihood				
Wages	6	37.5	5	33.3
Other domestic work	2	12.5	2	13.3
Guard	1	6.2	—	—
Dependency on others	8	50.0	8	53.4
What other requirements that your source of livelihood could not meet?				
Medical expenses	9	56.2	7	46.7
Food grains and cloths	8	50.0	9	60.0
Travelling	1	6.2	1	6.7
How do you meet your day-to-day requirement of livelihood				
Dependency	10	62.5	9	60.0
Any how	3	18.7	5	33.3
Wages	3	18.7	1	6.7
Difficulties faced by you due to old age				
Unable to meet expense for the remedies	7	43.7	4	26.7
Unable to do wage work	1	6.2	2	13.3
Problem for livelihood	10	62.5	10	66.7
Ignored by family members	2	12.5	1	6.7
Weakness	2	12.5	2	13.3
Suggestions about the better life for old age				
Free hospital facility	4	25.0	2	13.3
More amount and for more people	8	50.0	9	60.0
Availability of food grains, cloths and housing without payment	9	56.2	5	13.3
Neutrality of pradhan and other officials	—	—	1	6.7
Providing job and economic benefits to old age	—	—	1	6.7
Total	16	100.0	15	100.0

Source: *Field Survey*.

ANALYSIS OF THE GENERAL PROGRAMME

The Public Distribution System (PDS)

Public Distribution System (PDS) is one of the key components of the government's food security system. It has been an instrument for ensuring the availability of certain essential commodities, at affordable prices, to the poor class. The government *via* Food Corporation of India (FCI), processes and stocks food grains which are realised every month for the distribution purpose through the PDS network across the country. The principal commodities distributed through PDS are rice and wheat, however, sugar, edible oils and kerosene is also disbursed. The PDS till recently, had been a general entitlement scheme. However, the monitoring food subsidy bills, increase in the Minimum Support Price (MNS), etc. and the pressure of New Economic Policy (NEP) to curtail the subsidy and other forms of non-plan expenditure forced the government to abandon the open ended coverage. However, coverage for poor people continued under Targeted Public Distribution System (TPDS) (Eighth Five Year Plan, 1992-97).

The public distribution system can be called as the general category programme because its coverage extends to all sections of society and classes viz. household living below the poverty line as well as the households lying above the poverty line. The sample contained a total of 346 households from beneficiaries categories and 28 household from non-beneficiaries categories. The study sample also contained those who were the public distribution shop owners, the programme functionaries from the block and the district besides households from focussed group.

Performance of the Programme

The study of the working of Public Distribution System in both the sample district reveals that its performance suffered from many accounts, and cannot be called to be good. The first being the selection of beneficiaries. It was found that the list of beneficiaries, identified to be living below the poverty line, by the block office was not accepted by the supply office who, in turn, pursued their own list of beneficiaries. Their list contained grossly inflated number of persons believed to be living below the poverty line because the list was tampered by influential local people, teachers, panchayat members, etc. and could not be relied upon. For analysis purpose, the list provided by block with minor modification was used. All this also isolated and further marginalised many genuine households from availing the benefits of PDS. Likewise the performance also suffered on account of the distance between the PDS shop, which was generally located in gram sabha, with other revenue villages, which many a time was found to be far. This often affected the dissemination of information regarding the arrival of food stock to the shop. The result of all this was that the benefits of PDS were largely localized and villages or habitations that were located in its proximity or where that information had reached were benefited at the cost of these villages that were located at distant places. It was also found that there was no fixed day meant for the distribution of food articles by PDS shop and after operating for two or three days of the arrival of food stock, the PDS shop owner declared that the articles have been exhausted, thereby depriving many prospective consumers, whereas the ground reality was quite different. It was also found that many of the articles which were stored in his residence later found their way to the market place fetching him higher returns.

The consumers were also found to be ignorant regarding the volume or amount of articles they were entitled to collect against their card which also benefited the shop owner. It was observed, in many cases, that the quantity of articles supplied to the customers was lesser than the amount declared in the card. Another disappointing part has been the declaration made by PDS shop owner that with the exception of kerosene, none of the food items like wheat, rice, sugar, etc. arrived regularly every month in the PDS shops. It was only during the Hindu and Muslim festivals that these items arrived and got distributed. However, in actual practice, it was discovered that arrival of all items to the PDS shop was a regular feature which was sold in the open market with the active connivance of concerned people and functionaries. Similarly, the PDS shop owners were also found to be manipulating their registers and showing all articles to have been distributed, on their own, and whenever a card beneficiary brought card to him, for purchase of articles, it was surreptitiously completed even for those months in which no distribution of articles had taken place, and this was done without the knowledge of card owner. Likewise the quality of articles supplied by PDS shops were reported to be of extreme poor quality for which shop owner blamed the district supply office. Here again, it was found out that the PDS shop owner and market business nexus operated to siphon of the good quality of articles to be replaced by the inferior ones.

Involvement of Beneficiaries

The poor performance of the programme often finds its manifestation in the level of involvement of beneficiaries. The study revealed that the level of involvement of beneficiaries was quite low because the selection process itself deprived many genuine focus group of households from joining the programme supplement with the complete dominance of PDS shop owners over the distribution of food articles. The ignorance of beneficiaries about the volume of articles they received or about the arrival of items at PDS shop, etc. also reflected their poor level of involvement.

Involvement of Functionaries

The performance of the programme also depends on the involvement level of functionaries. It was found that the functionaries had not carried out any physical verification exercise either of the PDS shops of their area or of beneficiary cards. The plausible reason for this being that many of the PDS shop owners were either the village pradhans or were their relatives or someone who belonged to influential family. It was also revealed that for availing the food articles from the supply departments to their godowns, the owner had to pay twenty to twenty-five thousand rupees in advance which the poor person could hardly afford to pay.

The analysis also showed that many of the households were availing benefits by assuming different names or getting the PDS cards from two different gram sabha which could not have been possible and the physical verification exercise been carried out. Similarly, it was also found out that many beneficiary households, whose family size had undergone change and who had also applied for updating of their cards through village level functionaries was also not being attended. All this clearly goes on to show the poor involvement of programme functionaries.

INTER-LINKAGE PATTERN AMONG SOCIAL SECTOR PROGRAMME

The impact of these programmes on the beneficiaries could only be fully realised if these programmes have an inter-programme linkage provision. The term inter-programme linkages refers to the mobility of beneficiaries from one programme to others. The higher will be the level of inter-programme linkages, the faster will be the beneficiaries access to basic services and higher will be the beneficiaries socio-economic level. In other words, if the national social assistance programme could be linked with poverty alleviation programmes and basic minimum needs programmes its impact would substantially be higher. Similarly, the benefits of the Integrated Rural Development Programme, Jawahar Rojgar Yojana could also be extended to the beneficiaries of national benefits schemes who have suffered the loss of primary bread. In other words, convergence of programme has to be matched by the integration. The size major programmes whose linkages have been studied are: (a) Indira Awas Yojana, (b) National Benefit Scheme, (c) National Old Age Pension Scheme, (d) National Widow Pension Scheme, (e) National Handicapped Pension Scheme, and (f) Employment Assurance Scheme/Jawahar Rojgar Yojana.

Further, linkages level has also been scaled into three categories, viz. strong medium and low. The low or poor level of linkages refers to that situation when the overall linkage level of principal programme with other supporting programme is upto 39 percent. The medium level of linkages refers to that situation when its level ranges between 40 percent to 60 percent, and finally when the linkage level exceeds 60 percent mark it is termed as high or strong. Further, for studying the inter-programme linkage pattern, the beneficiaries from these 9 principal programmes were randomly selected and their participation level in other programmes have been studied.

The first major programme whose linkages with other programmes have been studied was Indira Awas Yojana whose linkages were studied with: (a) sanitation programme, (b) smokeless chulha, (c) drinking water programme, (d) rural electrification, (e) public distribution system, (f) medical care or health services programme, and (g) programme on literacy or education. The total number of beneficiaries randomly selected from the principal programme were thirty-one of which about 42 percent were from Varanasi district and the remaining 58 percent from Saharanpur district.

The study shows that of the seven programmes, only two programmes viz. sanitation and public distribution programmes had strong linkages with the principal programme with their levels being worked out as over eighty percent and cent percent respectively, thereby implying that the beneficiaries of principal programmes were major players in these two other programmes whereas its linkages with other five programmes largely of poor levels. Thus, the overall success rate was merely about 29 percent which could be termed as poor, which reflects the principal programmes inability to reach out to the people and also strike a coordination with other programmes as well.

The national maternity benefits programmes linkages have been studied with the following nine programmes: (a) ICDS programme, (b) Balika Samridhi Yojana, (c) Early Child Care Scheme, (d) Drinking Water Programme, (e) Rural Electrification, (f) Public Distribution System, (g) Supplementary Nutrition, (h) Immunization Programme, and (i) Health Care Programmes. A total forty-two beneficiaries from the main programme were randomly drawn out of which over 45 percent belonged to Varanasi and remaining about 55 percent were from Saharanpur district. The perusal of the linkages of main programme with drinking water and public distribution system programmes was worked out to be about 62 percent and cent percent respectively. However, its linkages with other programme were largely of poor level except for health programme where its linkages were about 41 percent. Thus with the principal programme managing to forge strong linkages with just two of the nine programmes, its overall success rate stood at merely around 22 percent.

Likewise in the case of National Old Age Pension Scheme whose linkages were studied with the four following programmes viz. (a) health care, (b) drinking water, (c) rural electrification, and (d) public distribution system. The total number of beneficiaries drawn from the principal programme were thirty-three of which 30 percent belonged to Varanasi and remaining 70 percent to Saharanpur district. The analysis of the main programme's linkage with other four programmes shows that except with public distribution programme its linkages with other remaining three programmes were either of medium level or were of low to poor levels. Hence, with strong linkage with just one programme, its overall success rate was estimated to be just twenty-five percent.

In the case of National Widow Pension Scheme whose linkages were studied with the following eight programmes: (a) National Family Benefit Scheme, (b) Health Care Programme, (c) Rural Drinking Water Programme, (d) Indira Awas Yojana, (e) Rural Electrification, (f) Sanitation Programme, (g) Smokeless Chulha, (h) Public Distribution System. For studying the inter-programme linkage pattern, a total of twenty-six beneficiaries from the main programmes were randomly selected. Of these over 73 percent belonged to Varanasi and remaining 26 percent to Saharanpur district respectively. The study of inter-linkage pattern shows that the main programme's linkage with drinking water supply programme and public distribution system were strong and with the remaining six programmes it were of either weak or poor level. Thus, the overall success rate of the programme was worked out to be around twenty-five percent.

National Handicapped Pension Scheme was the other programme whose linkages have been studied with the following eight programmes namely: (a) Health Sector Programme, (b) Indira Awas Yojana, (c) Sanitation Programme, (d) Smokeless Chulha, (e) Drinking Water Facility, (f) Literacy Programme, (g) Public Distribution System, and (h) Rural Electrification. A total of ten beneficiaries, five each from Varanasi and Saharanpur districts were randomly selected. The study of inter-programme linkage pattern shows that the main programme could establish strong linkages with only two programmes, viz. distribution system where the linkage level was observed to be cent-percent each. However, for health sector programme its linkages were of moderate level while in the remaining five programmes they were of poor or weak level. The overall success rate was found out to be just twenty-five percent only.

The other main programme whose linkages with other social sector programmes was studied was Employment Assurance Scheme/Jawahar Rojgar Yojana. Its linkages were studied with the following seven programmes viz. (a) sanitation programme, (b) smokeless chulha, (c) health sector programme, (d) drinking water programme, (e) public distribution system, and (f) rural

TABLE 3

Social Sector Programmes and their Linkages Pattern

Principal Name of Programme	*Linkage with other Programme*	*Varanasi*		*Saharanpur*		*Total*		*Overall Success Rate (%)*
		No	*%*	*No*	*%*	*No.*	*%*	
1	*2*	*3*	*4*	*5*	*6*	*7*	*8*	*9*
	Sanitation Scheme	12	92.3	13	~72.2	25	80.6	
	Smokeless Chulha	11	84.6	11	35.5	—	—	
Indira Awas	Drinking Water	6	46.2	5	27.8	11	35.5	
Yojana	Indira Awas Electrification	2	15.4	5	27.8	7	22.6	
	Public Distribution System	13	100.0	18	100.0	31	100.0	28.6
(31)	Health Services/Medical Care	2	15.4	12	66.7	14	45.2	
	Neo-literate/Literacy Programme	5	38.4	1	5.5	6	19.4	
	Total (7)							
	ICDS Programme	5	26.3	6	26.1	11	26.2	
	Balika Samridhi Yojana	3	15.8	5	21.7	8	19.1	
National	Early Child Care Scheme	2	10.5	2	8.7	4	9.5	
Maternity	Supplementary Nutrition	5	26.3	3	13.0	8	19.1	
Benefit	Immunization Programme	4	21.1	6	26.1	10	23.8	22.2
Scheme	Health Service/Care	4	21.1	13	56.5	17	40.5	
	Drinking Water	—	57.9	15	65.2	26	61.9	
(42)	Electrification	4	21.1	6	26.1	10	23.8	
	Public Distribution Systems	19	100.0	23	100.0	42	100.0	
	Total (9)							

National Old	Health Service/Care	2	20.0	14	60.8	16	48.5	
Age Pension	Drinking Water	3	30.0	8	34.8	11	33.3	
Scheme	Electrification	2	20.0	6	26.1	8	24.2	25.0
(33)	Public Distribution System	10	100.0	23	100.0	33	100.0	
	Total (4)							
	National Family Benefit Scheme	2	10.5	4	57.1	6	23.1	
	Health Service	4	21.1	5	71.4	9	34.6	
National	Drinking Water	12	63.2	5	71.4	17	65.4	
Widow	Indira Awas Yojana	1	14.3	1	38.5	—	—	
Pension	Electrification	4	21.1	1	14.3	5	19.2	25.0
Scheme	Sanitation Scheme	—	14.3	1	3.8	—	—	
	Smokeless Chulha	—	—	—	—	—	—	
(26)	Public Distribution System	19	100.0	7	100.0	26	100.0	
	Total (8)							
	Health Service	1	20.0	3	60.0	4	40.0	
	Indira Awas Yojana	—	—	2	40.0	2	20.2	
National	Sanitation Scheme	—	—	1	20.0	1	10.0	
Handicapped	Smokeless Chulha	—	—	—	—	—	—	
Pension	Drinking Water	5	100.0	5	100.0	10	100.0	25.0
Yojana	Literacy Programme	—	—	—	—	—	—	
	Public Distribution System	5	100.0	5	100.0	10	100.0	
(10)	Electrification	1	20.0	1	20.0	2	20.0	
	Total (8)							

(Contd.)

TABLE 3 (*Contd.*)

1	*2*	*3*	*4*	*5*	*6*	*7*	*8*	*9*
	Indira Awas Yojana	6	24.0	5	20.0	11	22.0	
	Sanitation Scheme	1	4.0	3	12.0	4	8.0	
Employment	Smokeless Chulha	1	4.0	—	—	1	2.0	
Assurance	Health Services	5	20.0	16	64.0	21	42.0	
Scheme	Drinking Water	15	60.0	13	52.0	28	56.0	14-3
	Public Distribution System	25	100.0	25	100.0	50	100.0	
(50)	Electrification	4	16.0	5	20.0	9	18.0	
	Total (7)							

Note : Figures in brackets denote the number of beneficiaries.
Source : *Field Survey.*

electrification. The sample contained a total of fifty beneficiaries drawn randomly, from the principal programme. The distribution of beneficiaries shows that each district contributed twenty five percent. The study shows that EAS/JRY programme could develop strong linkages only with public distribution system programme and middle or moderate level linkages with health service programme and drinking water programmes its linkages were of low level. Thus, the overall success rate was worked out to be just around fourteen percent. The performance of social sector programmes has been disappointing and attributes factors like lack of coordination between various departments, poor involvement of programme functionaries which also provided room for local middlemen to middle in the selection process, poor functioning of block on account of their own heavy work load, lack of element of transparency in the functioning of panchayats, etc.

CONCLUSION

The analysis of the social sector programmes has clearly brought to the fore that their performance has, by and large, been disappointing on account of which the programmes have also failed to strike strong inter-programme linkage with other programmes thereby depriving the socially underprivileged class to move up in social hierarchy.

The other factors, contributing to those programmes poor performance was the poor level of involvement of programme functionaries which, many a time, permitted the local middlemen to meddle in the selection process. All this naturally invited many other unethical means by which non-genuine beneficiaries could also find their way into the programme.

The lack of coordination among various departments who were following their own policies, programmes and objectives that often criss-crossed each other boundaries and blurred the overall objective. Similarly, the other factors could be identified as block level functionaries departmental work load that often prevented them to participate in these programmes fully, their non-trained status, in-experience, etc. (as many of them had been given field posting just after recruitment or for the first time).

Another fact that the study clearly highlighted was that

functioning of block needs to be toned because at the sub-district level it is the most important administrative unit which is responsible for executing and implementing schemes. Its inability to perform the task has to be understood by the problems it is facing in its day-to-day functioning.

It was also found that the block office besides performing its own duties/work was also asked to implement other development programmes and being a lower subordinate unit it could not refuse the higher official at the district level. As such these institutions were overloaded with work. Though the blocks are provided personnels but they are drawn from various departments. These officials prime duty, for which they could be held responsible, is to pursue their respective departments programmes and policies. This additional work does not motivates them and though they could not refuse, they many a time loose the interest which lowers their involvement level in the programmes.

Further, the block offices were found to be short of their own staff. Many of the vacancies have not been filled for quite some time because of indifferent attitudes of the officials at the district level, which was also contributing to poor performance.

The poor involvement of the beneficiaries could also be attributed to their lack of information about various social sector programmes, absence of coherent, specified and uniform guidelines, target specified approach of the programmes which was not in conformity to the local needs or requirements and absence of connecting physical verification and evaluation of the programmes by the higher authorities. It was observed that the panchayats office house meetings were seldom being attended by the representatives of different departments which also lower the beneficiaries involvement level.

SUGGESTIONS

On the basis of the analysis of the programme, a number of suggestions could be made to streamline the performance of the programme. These suggestions could, broadly, be classified into three categories: (a) on how to improve the involvement level of programme functionaries, (b) on how to enhance the participation level of beneficiaries and finally (c) on how to improve the inter-programme linkages so that the impact of the programmes on beneficiaries optimizes.

(a) Improvement in the Involvement Level of Programme Functionaries

(i) at the block level, coordination be established between all the concerned departments dealing with social development programmes. Efforts be made to ensure that their meetings are held regularly like the one at the district level where each department unfolds and discusses their prospective strategies so that a uniform and comprehensible plan be formulated at the block level,

(ii) at the village level, provision should be made to train all department level functionaries from time to time. It is also suggested that these functionaries should not be unduly burdened with additional work load. Their work also needs to be evaluated at regular intervals,

(iii) efforts may also be made to fill the vacant posts at the earliest and creation of the post of BDO and other functionaries of the block should now be based on the demographic norm and not on the number of villages or panchayat,

(iv) uniform policy, at all levels, be maintained by all the concerned departments dealing with social sector schemes whether for identifying the focus group of households or maintaining the family register and other records, and

(v) the district level functionaries be involved to ensure that proper departmental coordination was being maintained in the execution and implementation of programmes at the block levels. Likewise, their intervention could also be sought to resolve the problems timely.

(b) Improving Involvement Level of Beneficiaries

It was also observed that the functioning of panchayats at the village level, was not upto the mark. It is quite ironical to see that while the government on one hand was trying to empower these grass root level institutions through Panchayatiraj Acts, these bodies, many a times, were found to be totally unaware of their duties and responsibilities. Their work also lacked an element of social consciousness while performing duties as a local self-body. Hence, it becomes quite imperative to attach some Non-Government Organizations (NGOs), were requisite experience, in disbursing their duties more effectively and in the right direction. Besides this, the other task of such NGOs could also be to provide assistance to those institutions to identify local problems and demands and provide solutions to it. They should also be required to act as a liaison between various departments and helps the panchayats to carry out the task of monitoring and evaluation of social sector programmes, this way the NGOs would also sensitize the panchayat and encourage them to work for total integrated development of the villages. Similarly, the help of NGOs could be sought to develop close rapport between blocks and village identify and train potential group, at the village level, so that it may take up their place at an appropriate time.

(c) Improving the Inter-Programme Linkages

The social sector programmes are primarily meant to assist the focus group of households who have so far development. If those households are provided assistance in isolated and sporadic manner, it is unlikely to break their vicious circle of poverty. For their holistic development, the strategy should incorporate an array of social sector programmes that enables the beneficiaries to move from one programme to another thereby improving their socio-economic status.

Therefore, it is suggested that:

(i) the blocks be given the same status as the DRDA agency at the district level and their identified focus group of households be accepted by all concerned department;

(ii) the focus group of households also be provided BPL card specifying the benefits they have received. The card should also include information related to what other benefits the households require;

(iii) the procedure in the selection of beneficiaries be simplified and made uniform so that genuine beneficiary does not feel unduly harassed. The NGOs could also be taken up;

(iv) while deciding the target for each programme

separately, concerned departments should focus on the linkage aspect of those programmes so that they may have converge at some point of time to provide maximum benefit to the focus of households.

References

Arumugam, P. (1999), "Determinants of Health Status and Indian Development", in *Social Sector and Development* (Ed.) by A.K. Das, Deep & Deep, New Delhi.

Bhaduria, Mridula Dr. (1999), "Some Issues of Women's Health, Social Welfare", Vol. 46, No. 1, April, New Delhi.

Dadibhavi, R.V. and Vaikuntha, L.D. (1990), "Infrastructure for Rural Development: A Case Study of Regional Disparities", *Journal of Rural Development*, Vol. 9 (3), NIRD, Hyderabad.

Datta, Anindita and Sinha, Sachidanand (1997), "Gender Disparities in Social Well Beings: An Overview", *Indian Journal of Gender Studies*, 401, Sage Publication, New Delhi.

Dreez, Jean and Sen, Amartya (1995), *India Economic Development and Social Opportunity*, Oxford University Press, Delhi.

Economic and Political Weekly Research Foundation (1994), "Social Indicators for Development for India—IInd Inter-State Disparities", *Economic and Political Weekly*, May 21, Mumbai.

Economic Survey, (1992-93), Government of India, Ministry of Finance, New Delhi.

Eighth Five Year Plan, (1992-97), Planning Commission, New Delhi.

Ghosh, P.K. (1998), "Disparity and Some Possible Determinant of Rural Literacy in Education", *IASSI Quarterly*, Vol. 17, No. 3, New Delhi.

Guhan, S. (1996), "Social Expenditure in the Union Budget", *Economic and Political Weakly*, Vol. 30, No. 18 & 19, Mumbai.

Kulkarni, P.D. (1997), "Integrating Social Development" in *Social Sciences in Development*, (Ed) P.D. Kulkarni and M.C. Nanavatty, Uppal Publishing House, New Delhi.

Mahendra Div, S. (1999), "Social Society in India: An Overview of Performance and Issues", Social Security in India, Seminar Papers, organized by Institute for Human Development, New Delhi, April 15-17, 1999.

Majumder, M. and Vaidyanathan, A. (1994), "Access to Education in India: Retrospect and Prospect", *Journal of Educational Planning and Administration*, 7 (4), New Delhi.

Mehta, A.C. (1995), *Education for All*, Kaniska Publishers and Distributors, Delhi.

Nayyar, Deepak (1990), Quoted in *Social Sector and Development, Experiences and Challenges* (Ed.), by D.K. Das, Deep & Deep Publication, New Delhi.

Panchmukhi, P.R. (2000), "Social Impacts of Economic Reforms in India: A Critical Approach", *Economic and Political Weekly*, March 4, Mumbai, 836-47.

Pandey, Janak and Pant, S.K. (2001), "Performance of Social Sector Schemes in Rural Areas of Uttar Pradesh", Final Report, G.B. Pant Social Science Institute, Allahabad.

Pant, S.K. (2002), *Gender Bias in Girl Child Education*, Kanishka Publishers & Distributors, New Delhi.

Pant, S.K. and Pandey, Alok (2000), "Social Choice: Its Manifestations on Minimum Needs Programme", in Datt, Ruddar & Divendranath Konarkh, "*Social Choice and Development*", Deep & Deep Publications, New Delhi.

Papola, T.S. (1984), "Rural Poverty Issues and Options," by J.L. Bajaj and C. Shastri, Print House (India), Lucknow.

Pillai, G. (1992), "Akshar Keralam, Total Literacy Programme in Kerala: A Case Study", *Journal of Educational Planning and Administration*, 6 (3), New Delhi.

Planning Commission (1996), *Draft Mid-Term Appraisal of the Eighth Five Year Plan 1992-97*, Government of India, New Delhi.

Prabhu, Seitha, K. (1998), "Social Sectors in Economic Development", *Journal of Social and Economic Development*, Vol. I, No. 2, July-December, Bangalore.

Rajeev, P.V. (1999), *Planning to Social Reforms: The Key to Economic Progress*, Deep & Deep Publications Pvt Ltd., New Delhi.

Rajula Devi, A.K. (1990), "Poverty Alleviation Programmes in Rural India", *Journal of Rural Development*, Vol. 9 (3), NIRD, Hyderabad.

Ramchandran, V. (1998), "Engendering Development: Lessons from Social Sector Programmes in India", *Indian Journal of Gender Studies*, 5:1, Sage Publication, New Delhi.

Rao, Hanumantha (1995), "Attack on Poverty and Deprivation: Role of Structural Change and Structural Adjustment", The Presidential Address at Indian Labour Conference at Punjabi University, Patiala, January 5-7.

Rao, Sudhakar and A.C. Moss (1999), "Government Budgetary Expenditure on Social Sector in India: Allocation Priorities During Pre and Post-Reforms Period", in *Social Sector and Development* (Ed.). D.K. Das, Deep & Deep, New Delhi.

Rout, H. (1998), "India's Health Sector: Past and Present", *Vision*, (Vol. XVIII, No. 1-2), Jayaprakash Narayan Institute of Social & Economic Studies, Bhubneshwar, Orissa.

Sengupta, Keya (1999), "Trends in Educational Expenditure and its Impact on Indian Economy", in *Social Sector and Development* (Ed.) by D.K. Das, Deep & Deep Publications, New Delhi.

Seventh Five Year Plan (1985-90), Planning Commission, Vol. 1, New Delhi.

Shah, Anil C. and Sudarshan, Iyengar (1998), "The Contribution of NGOs to Development: Some Issues and a Case Study", *Social Change through Voluntary Action* (Ed.) Dantawala, M.L., Harsh Sethi and Parvin Vasaria, Sage Publication, New 'Delhi.

Singh, Surendra (1999), "Paradigm Shift in Social Development in India: A Critique", *The Indian Journal in Social Work,* Vol. 60, Issue-I, January, Mumbai.

Singh, K.M., Verma, V.K. and Singh, D.K. (1989), "Optimization of Social Service Function: A Case Study of Kachhona Block of Hardoi District (U.P.)", *Journal of Rural Development,* Vol. 8 (2), NIRD, Hyderabad.

Singh, L.R. (1987), *Planning Atlas of Uttar Pradesh,* Planning Department, Government of U.P., and G.B. Pant Social Science Institute, Allahabad.

Swaminathan, D. (1996), "Inaugural Address", National Seminar on Rural Water Supply and Sanitation, Sponsored by Rajeev Gandhi National Drinking Water Mission, and Organized by Centre for Development Studies, Thiruvananthapuram, June 20-22.

Visaria, P.D., Gumber, A. and Vasaria, L. (1993), "Literacy and Primary Education in India: 1980-81' to 1991, Differentials and Determinants, *Journal of Planning and Administration,* 7(1), New Delhi.

37

Welfare of Disabled Persons

S.P. Saha, V.S. Paswan and Supriya

Global estimates have indicated that nearly 10 per cent of the population suffers from one or more of the disabilities—mental, physical, hearing and visual. The figures of incedence and prevalance however depended on the definition of disabilities. In order to ensure that the meagre resources for rehabilitation and assistance reach the more needy among the handicapped population in India, stricter definitions of disabilities and handicapped have been adopted. In the context of our definitions approximately 2.1 per cent of population of the country suffer from one or more disabilities. A National Sample Survey, 58th round, was carried out in 2001 census. This survey includes those having physical or sensory disabilities which includes visual, speech, hearing and locomotor disabilities. Estimates of disabled persons are available mainly from population sample and National Sample Survey carried out by the National Sample Survey Organization (NSSO). The estimated total number of disabled persons for the year 2001 was about 19 million in the country.

FIGURES AT A GLANCE

The analysis first attempts to disaggregate the data of disabled people. Such disaggregation of data helps one to identify the priority areas where the incidence of disability is of a more serious nature. There is a considerable variation in the incidence of various disabilities by the types of disability, the region (rural-urban) and gender (male-female). The aggregate estimates of the physically disabled in rural and unban India are given in the different types of disabilities, the number of persons with locomotor disability was the highest in both rural and urban India by the number of persons with all types of disabilities. (Table 1)

TABLE 1

Estimated Number of Disabled Persons by Types of Disability (in '000)

Types of Disability	*NSS 47th Round (July-Dec. 1991)*		*NSS 58th Round (July-Dec. 2001)*	
1. Locomoter (With or without other disability)	11982	(52.24)	8939	(49.24)
2. Visual	5928	(21.66)	4005	(22.06)
3. Hearing	3641	(11.26)	3242	(17.86)
4. Speech	3100	(14.84)	1966	(10.83)
5. Estimated Number of cases of physically handicapped	24651	(100.00)	18152	(100.00)
6. Estimated Number of Physically disabled persons (at least one of four disabilities)	20241		16154	
7. Percentage of disabled persons having more than one (i.e. multiple) disability	1027		12.37	

Figures in brackets give percentage to the estimated number of cases of physical disability.

Source: *The Hindustan Times*, 'Population Control & Social Change', 11 July, 2002.

In the following Table 2, the difference in the prevalence of disability by region can be seen. In the country as a whole, between the two sexes (male-female), the prevalence of disability was marginally higher among males than among females. The rate for males was 2-3 per cent and 1-8 per cent while that for females was 1-7 and 1-4 per cent in rural and urban India respectively. The inter-state variations in prevalence rate are significant in both the sectors.

TABLE 2

Number of Disabled Person per 1,00,000 Persons by Sex

	Rural			*Urban*		
	Male	*Female*	*Persons*	*Male*	*Female*	*Persons*
Andhra Pradesh	2640	2354	2498	2092	1712	1903
Assam	1408	947	1200	1390	948	1186
Bihar	1973	1125	1573	1740	1071	1436
Gujarat	1786	1557	1676	1720	1566	1648
Haryana	2290	1665	1988	1603	1105	1374
Himachal Pradesh	3580	2157	2870	1268	995	1144
Karnataka	2368	1891	2131	1662	1307	1494
Kerala	2280	1638	1945	1927	1587	1755
Madhya Pradesh	2281	1794	2051	1805	1113	1475
Maharashtra	2437	1927	2700	1787	1408	1610
Orissa	3191	2166	2306	2025	2077	2049
Punjab	3418	2384	2936	2025	1558	1807
Rajasthan	2141	1355	1767	1594	1168	1126
Tamil Nadu	2541	2201	2372	2075	1669	1874
Uttar Pradesh	2269	1441	1879	1779	1210	1519
West Bengal	2069	1484	1788	1690	1243	1505
All-India	2277	1694	1995	1774	1361	1579

Source: *The Hindustan Times*, New Delhi, Population Control & Social Change, 11 July, 2002.

The difference in prevalence of disability by types of sex and region can be seen in the following Table 3, of which all four types of disability have been focussed. The estimated number of visual disabled persons per 1,00,000 population for the major states and all India has been presented in such table. On the basis of this table, prevalence of visual disability among females was higher than among males in both sectors—rural and urban—in India. In rural sector, highest prevalence in visual disability was reported by Orissa (820) followed by Andhra Pradesh (806) and Himachal

Pradesh (629). In the urban sector also, the rate was quite high for Orissa (444) followed by Assam (441) and Kerala (388).

TABLE 3

Number of Persons with Visual Disability per 1,00,000 for each Sex

	Rural			*Urban*		
	Male	*Female*	*Persons*	*Male*	*Female*	*Persons*
Andhra Pradesh	668	746	806	326	445	385
Assam	405	355	382	520	371	441
Bihar	333	349	341	220	232	225
Gujarat	327	423	373	185	357	266
Haryana	538	710	621	335	399	364
Himachal Pradesh	661	809	629	332	319	326
Karnataka	494	632	562	309	370	338
Kerala	400	435	418	293	480	388
Madhya Pradesh	424	646	529	222	258	329
Maharashtra	478	620	549	241	290	264
Orissa	733	908	820	349	550	444
Punjab	526	682	599	301	353	325
Rajasthan	375	502	435	212	298	253
Tamil Nadu	547	704	625	332	423	377
Uttar Pradesh	490	549	518	269	358	310
West Bengal	381	411	395	280	371	321
All-India	471	584	525	263	346	302

Sources: *The Hindustan Times*, New Delhi, Population Control & Social Change, 11 July, 2002.

The prevalence rate (per 1,00,000 persons) of persons having Hearing disability is given in the following Table 4 for each sex separately for rural and urban regions of major sates and All-India basis. It was 339 in urban regions and as high as 467 in rural regions. Prevalence of Hearing disability among females was higher than among males in both areas in India. The rates were 435 and 355 respectively for females in rural and urban India, the corresponding rates for males were 498 and 325 respectively.

The prevalence rate (per 1,00,000 persons) of persons having speech disability is given in the following Table 5 for each sex separately for rural and unban regions of major states and all-India. It was accounted same as visual and hearing disablity had.

Speech disability is comprised with higher rate among females in comparison to male members in both the regions in India. As is shown in following Table 5, the rates were 208 and 192 respectively for females in rural and urban India, the corresponding rates for males were 333 and 285. Among the states Bihar reported the lowest prevalence rate in both the areas. The rates were 255 and 225 respectively in the rural and urban areas.

TABLE 4

Number of Persons age 5 yrs. and above with Hearing Disability per 1,00,000 for each Sex

	Rural			*Urban*		
	Male	*Female*	*Persons*	*Male*	*Female*	*Persons*
Andhra Pradesh	657	662	660	476	526	501
Assam	358	273	319	410	311	364
Bihar	335	177	260	241	182	215
Gujarat	352	389	370	293	344	317
Haryana	477	460	469	423	338	384
Himachal Pradesh	1601	672	1108	233	242	237
Karnataka	603	585	594	346	318	332
Kerala	513	501	506	314	436	376
Madhya Pradesh	479	421	452	339	220	282
Maharashtra	554	503	529	319	432	372
Orissa	765	632	698	486	621	548
Punjab	466	398	435	275	179	230
Rajasthan	329	207	271	204	188	196
Tamil Nadu	722	724	723	483	553	518
Uttar Pradesh	307	266	288	231	220	226
West Bengal	633	502	570	341	386	361
All-India	498	435	467	325	355	339

Source: *The Hindustan Times*, New Delhi, Population Control & Social Change, 11 July, 2002.

As far as locomotor disability is concerned, the prevalence of locomotor disability per 1,00,000 persons is the highest. The rate was as high as 1074 and 962 respectively in rural and urban India. As is shown in the following Tables 5 and 6, among males, the prevalence was much higher than among females, 1345 and 1170 for males as against 784 and 728 for females (per 1,00,000) in rural and urban areas respectively. At the state level, the all-India pattern is reflected. Among the states, the prevalence of locomotor disability was the highest in Punjab (1974 per 1,00,000 persons) in the rural areas and in Kerala (1203 per 1,00,000 persons) in the urban area, whereas Bihar accounted 255 persons/lakh in the rural areas and 224 per 1 lakh persons in urban areas so far.

TABLE 5

Number of Persons of age 5 yrs. and above with Speech Disability per 1,00,000 for each Sex

	Rural			*Urban*		
	Male	*Female*	*Persons*	*Male*	*Female*	*Persons*
Andhra Pradesh	403	288	345	426	291	359
Assam	334	174	261	28	81	191
Bihar	323	179	255	300	130	224
Gujarat	211.	128	171	282	136	213
Haryana	208	113	162	103	122	112
Himachal Pradesh	668	271	457	232	160	200
Karnataka	424	282	353	280	177	231
Kerala	517	321	414	401	255	327
Madhya Pradesh	287	164	229	241	115	181
Maharashtra	327	204	266	244	206	226
Orissa	288	223	256	297	248	274
Punjab	286	229	259	282	243	264
Rajasthan	274	116	199	297	141	156
Tamilnadu	399	286	343	407	203	306
Uttar Pradesh	291	140	221	226	127	181
West Bengal	358	283	322	259	194	230
All-India	1345	784	1074	1170	728	962

Source: *The Hindustan Times*, New Delhi, Population Control & Social Change, 11 July, 2002.

Having discussed the data-based study of different types of disability more important and interesting disaggregation is by gender. There is no prior pattern of gender bias which can be presumed. In the case of visual disability the incidence is higher in the case of females than in the case of males. In the locomotor disability the pattern is reversed. The main reasons for higher number of cases of the girl child to immunization facilities and to nutrition. These differences are important but we see a lot of problems are being faced by all physically disabled persons.

TABLE 6

Number of Persons with Locomotor Disability per 1,00,000 for each Sex

	Rural			*Urban*		
	Male	*Female*	*Persons*	*Male*	*Female*	*Persons*
Andhra Pradesh	1490	1028	1260	1361	833	1098
Assam	533	282	419	552	275	424
Bihar	1243	571	926	1168	649	932
Gujarat	1125	822	979	1229	939	1092
Haryana	1402	727	1077	935	459	716
Himachal Pradesh	1651	1060	1356	692	501	1106
Karnataka	1339	841	1091	1064	708	895
Kerla	1347	750	1037	1304	744	1203
Madhya Pradesh	1469	914	1207	1245	679	975
Maharashtra	1462	944	1206	1254	789	1037
Orissa	1137	804	970	1160	1058	1112
Punjab	2494	1378	1974	1375	993	1197
Rajasthan	1393	701	1063	1100	712	916
Tamilnadu	1336	892	1116	1207	803	1007
Uttar Pradesh	1434	690	1983	1247	660	978
West Bengal	1123	637	890	1046	600	844
All-India	1345	784	1074	1170	728	962

Source: *The Hindustan Times*, New Delhi, Population Control & Social Change, 11 July, 2002.

Problems

The problems of the disabled are to be viewed from the perspective of the socio-economic condition in the society and the attitude towards the disabled. Substantial number of persons or families are below poverty line and have very little for the paper maintenance of their families. Those who are relatively better-off, i.e. the middle class also have a number of constraints. Only a handful of persons are capable of taking special care of the abnormal situations in the family. Under such circumstances the disabled, mostly for no fault of them, has to suffer agony in the society. Those who are disabled since birth are looked after shabbily or mercifully since the beginning of their life. They are very often isolated even by the parents and treated as if they are unwanted. Most of them do not receive proper attention both medical and educational, primarily because of lack of medical facilities within access and financial constraints of parents though psychologically parents have soft corner for such children. The social stigma as well as cloud of uncertainty mostly force the parents to leave such children to their luck. Those who have become disabled at later stage suffer from different psychological problems. They get dejected and feel helpless. Every action by others which has an iota of sympathy regularly pinches.

WELFARE MEASURES AND REHABILITATIONS

As the very out-let it has to be understood that a person is disabled because he/she is unable to perform functions which a normal person can do. It is item specific, i.e. a disabled person may not be able to do a particular item/items of work but is equally capable for the rest of the items like a normal human being. The welfare measures of the disabled persons are therefore to be conceived from the following consideration:

1. Providing medical and related facilities to the disabled so as to make them improved persons;
2. Educating them with general education, vocational training and the job-training which help them in finding out suitable wage-paid employment or self-employment; and
3. Rehabilitating them with suitable jobs or self-employment so that they can be economically self-independent.

Scenario

The survey carried out by the National Sample Survey Organization (NSSO) in 2001 gives the distribution of the disabled persons as per usual activity status. If we utilise this distribution, we find out, of the 19.5 million disabled persons, as may as about 12.6 million were out of labour force. This distribution of these persons are shown in following Table 7.

What is interesting to note here is the number of disabled persons categorised under others which include old persons. Children yet to go to schools and those who are either not capable of doing any work or doing odd jobs like prostitution and like. A large number fall in beggers category.

The estimated number of disabled persons who were working were only 5.1 million in rural areas and about 1.2 million in the urban areas. Their distribution as observed is given in following Table 8.

TABLE 7

Estimated Number of Persons

(in million)

	Areas	*Rural*	*Urban*	*Total*
1.	Attending educational Institutions	1.82	0.81	2.63
2.	Attending Domestic duties	2.11	0.67	2.78
3.	Beggers	0.12	0.08	0.20
4.	Others	5.00	L99	6.99
	Total	9.05	3.55	12.60

TABLE 8

Estimated Number of Persons

(in million)

		Rural	*Urban*	*Total*
1.	Self-employed in agriculture sector	2.21	0.13	2.34
2.	Self-employed in non-agriculture sector	0.84	0.48	1.32
3.	Regular employees	0.62	0.31	0.93
4.	Casual Labour	1.43	0.28	1.71
	Total	5.10	1.20	6.30

The employment scenario in rural areas was dominated by self-employment in agriculture and casual work. In urban areas, they were self-employed in non-agriculture or employed on regular basis.

The unemployed disabled persons constituted only 0.60 million (0.45 in rural areas and 0.15 in urban areas). This was only about 0.15 per cent of the disabled population or about 4.1 per cent of the labour force.

The gravity of unemployment problem is thus less as compared to the general employment in the country which was about 6.5 per cent in 2000-02.

REHABILITATIONS

Rehabilitation of the disabled consists of two parts namely, (i) taking care of those who are either beggers or categorised as others in the labour force, and (ii) providing the unemployed with salaried jobs and/or making avenues for self-employment. These coming under category first (quite large in number) suffer from typical problems.

They in a large number of cases are considered as burden to the society and to the households. Their case hence deserves to be taken up on priority as a welfare measure whereby they are assured of resonable life. Reformatory Centres, remade homes (for those involved in undesired activities like begging and prostitution), old age homes, etc. already existing should serve them in a better way.

Not Serve

The unemployment problem, as perceived, is not that severe among the disabled persons. Rehabilitation of disabled suggests adequate provision of regular jobs again can be mainly provided in the Government sector since limited absorption can be expected from the private sector. The reservation of jobs for the disabled in Government sector if implemented fully may be sufficient to absorb a large number of them. But the basic problem is their illiteracy and making them suitable for jobs. Unless they receive certain basic general education subsequent vocational training cannot be imparted in proper perspective and in most cases they are found to be not suitable since most of the Government jobs stipulate a minimum general education. Therefore, attempts should be made to give them atleast minimum required education if not maximum general education. A dedicate effort is therefore necessary in this background on the part of the Government.

The employment exchange, special employment exchange, for Handicapped and Vocational Rehabilitation Centres run by the central and state Governments play a major role in providing them with suitable employment or self-employment. Some of the non-Governmental and also the Government organizations other than those indicated above do help them in finding out suitable employment but the exact number of persons actually rehabilitated by them are not known.

NORMAL EMPLOYMENT EXCHANGES

Employment exchanges register the job-seekers with disability alongwith other candidates for placement against normal vacancies and against vacancies reserved for the disabled. During 1999-2000, a total number of about sixty-five thousand and seventy thousand disabled job-seekers respectively registered themselves with these employment exchanges. As against this, the placement made were 5200 and 5800 respectively. Out of the total placement of 5800 in the year 2000 about 2700 were against reserved vacancies and remaining 3100 were against normal vacancies. At the end of the year 2000, a total number of about 5.1 lakh job-seekers with disability were on the live register and most of them were below matric. The number of job-seekers on the roll of employment exchange appear to be very large number might pursuing self-employment activities or may be already employed. One of the major problem in providing job is their educational qualification.

SPECIAL EMPLOYMENT EXCHANGES

Special employment exchanges are 23 in number and responsible for registration and placement of the handicapped persons only. During the year 1999 and 2000, a total number of 14420 and 15143 job-seekers respectively registered themselves with these Special Emploment Exchanges (SEEs). The corresponding placement made during years were 1504 and 1707 respectively. At the end of 2000, a total number of about 74 thousand job-seeker were on the live register. Since inception of these SEEs and till Dec. 2000, a total number of about 2.69 lakh disabled persons registered and out of these about 70-75 thousand were placed in jobs. The achievement was of the 28 per cent. The educational distribution of job-seeker shows that about 92 per cent of them were undergraduates and about 57 per cent were below matric. Graduates and above it constituted only 10 to 15 per cent of the job-seekers. This again reflects that educated and disabled persons perhaps do not face serious problems in getting the job. It is only those not so educated who are really facing problems.

VOCATIONAL REHABILITATION CENTRES

Vocational Rehabilitation Centres are 17 in number and are located at Mumbai, Hydrabad, Jabalpur, Delhi, Ludhiana, Kanpur, Kolkata, Chennai, Ahmedabad, Thiruvanthapuram, Bangalore, Guwahati, Bhubaneshwar, Jaipur, Varodara, Patna and Agartala. These centres evaluate the disabled persons, impart suitable training and finally try to rehabilitate. During the year 2001, about 32,000 handicapped persons were admitted and about 8000 persons rehabilitated. By the end of December 2001, since their inception, the Vocational Rehabilitation Centres admitted about 3.12 lakh but rehabilitated about one lakh only. Therefore, about 31 per cent of the clients who came to vocational rehabilitation Centres were rehabilitated and hence their performance was quite satisfactory compared to the unemployment situation prevailing in the country. Overall registration and rehabilitation—As on 31st December, 2000, a total number of 3.65 lakh job-seekers were on the live register considering both normal employment exchanges as well the special employment exchanges for the handicapped. Forty-five to fifty thousand disabled persons are registering every year where as the total rehabilitation of the physically handicapped persons in a year was around 10 thousand (4 to 5 thousand by employment exchanges and about 6 thousand by the VRCs). The job-seekers were mostly (more than 90 per cent) undergraduates.

The Ministry of Social Justice had made a provision by introducing individual disabled Act, 1995 to rehabilitate the highly qualified disabled persons including technical degree-holder disabled persons. Vacancies in Government sectors for such highly qualified handicapped are created by this central ministry to rehabilitate by appointing them as techno-persons.

APEX CENTRES

There are four National Institutes in each major area of disability, under Ministry of Welfare. They are:

1. National Institute for the orthopaedically Handicapped, Kolkata.
2. National Institute for the Visually Handicapped, Dehradun.

3. National Institute for the Mentally Handicapped, Secundrabad.
4. Ali Yavar Jung National Institute for the Hearing Handicapped, Mumbai.

These Institutes are designed to be apex organizations for training of professionals, production of education materials and other aids for the handicapped, conducting research in rehabilitation and development of suitable model services for the handicapped. These institutes work in coordination with each other and other training centres in the country, leading voluntary organizations state Governments as well as international agencies. Besides, in order to provide timely correct information to the disabled, their families and the professionals, Government of India has set-up a National Information and Documentation Centre at New Delhi. The centre is being computerised and will have total information about various aspects of disability and its management.

PERSPECTIVE

In consonance with the objective of the Welfare State, not-withstanding the paucity of resources. Government has accorded top priority to welfare of weaker sections including the handicapped. Welfare of the handicapped has been included as an item in the 20 points programme which is an agenda of priority items for the Government. Government is also considering setting up National Trust for the Mentally Retarded which would provide guardianship and rehabilitation services to the mentally handicapped children and can even inherit property on their behalf. UNICEF has also assisted eight district rehabilitation centre projects which has been referred for welfare of disabled children.

CONCLUSION

The management and rehabilitation of disabled largely depend upon the socio-economic conditions as well as the willingness of the family. Poverty is the root cause due to which proper treatment as well as education are not being received by the disabled. Infrastructure facilities already created by the

Government and the voluntary organizations have not been very useful so far since they have not been able to motivate or impart vocational training and rehabilitation.

Some rehabilitation professionals are of the view that individual attitudes and prejudices lead to discriminatory behaviour against handicapped. They advocate a comprehensive legal package prohibiting discrimination against the less abled citizens, on the pattern of the untouchability Act. The opinion was also voiced in the National Conference on Welfare of the Disabled held in December 2001 in New Delhi.

A purely welfarist approach is bound to be highly resources intensive given the large numbers involved and is unsustainable in the long-run. The preventive approach, although resource efficient and desirable in itself may be limited in its scope as far as affected population is concerned. For them the possiblity of integration into mainstream society needs serious consideration. Resource efficiency considerations are only one part of the strategy of integration. The social and organizational factors provide the other part. These need further investigation in terms of the legal, institutional and infrastructure input available in the country and the need to argument these.

References

Kulkarni, V.M., Welfare of Handicapped, *Quarterly Journal of Labour Economics*, Vol. 13 (20), June 1997, p. 42.

OECD, *The Role of NGOs for Welfare of Disabled*, New Delhi, 1998.

Paper entitled 'Welfare measures for the Disabled' presented by India at the 26th World Congress of Rehabilitation International, held in Japan in Sept. 1997.

Jha, Surirang Kumar, Empowering the Disabled, *Journal of Welfare Economics*, Vol. 12 (17), Sept. 1999, p. 24.

Roy, P.K., Disabled and their Rehabilitation, *Yojana*, 101 40(5), May 1996, p. 18.

38

Globalization and Inequality: The Role of Foreign Trade and Investment: A Note

NIVEDITA CHATURVEDI

This article addresses the influence of foreign trade and investment on inequality or, more generally, on the distribution of income, with a focus on developing countries. The influence on economic growth of economic openness to the rest of the world has been a topic of scholary debate. Since growth affects the level of poverty and the distribution of income, the trade growth nexus is also addressed.

Does globalization lead to the world becoming a more equal place, or does it lead to the rich getting richer and the poor getting poorer? This question has assumed ever-greater importance with the emergence of the World Trade Organization as a force for trade liberalization throughout the world, with the increased economic integration of Europe, with the collapse of communism and the opening of previously autarkic economies, with the renewed speculation about the formation of a pan-American free trade area.

Distribution of income has different meanings, apart from the different measurements used to describe it. Economic theory has been concerned mainly with the functional distribution of income, with the returns to identifiable factors of production and their respective snares in total income of a particular country, such as the share of labour income in national income. Popular and political discourse is more concerned with the size distribution of income, such as the fraction of national income accruing to the top or bottom 10 percent of residents, and with changes in inequality. In recent years, concern with the size distribution of income has extended to its global distribution, with observations by country grouped by per capita income, rather than by individuals.

INFLUENCE OF FOREIGN TRADE ON GROWTH, INEQUALITY AND POVERTY

In a country open to the world economy, the level and composition of its foreign trade, like GDP, distribution of income, growth of output, and a host of other variables, are determined by the underlying social and political structure, technological possibilities, factor endowments, and household and government preferences across available consumption possibilities. Thus trade is endogenous, like many other economic variables, and jointly determined by the structure and exogenous variables affecting the economy under consideration, where "exogeneity" is itself determined by the ambition of the structural characterization of the economy. Thus it is not possible in such a framework to discuss the influence of trade on the distribution of income; both are jointly determined by other factors.

Since one purpose of the annul World Bank Conference on Development Economics is to discover what policy guidance the World Bank and other advisers should give developing countries, we will take an easier route of considering the incremental consequences of liberalization a country's imports by eliminating import quotas or reducing tariffs—or both. This act of import liberalization is the exogenous change.

Consider a small increment to imports made possible by tariff reductions (for concreteness, think of imports of cut flowers into Europe and the United States). The exogenous change opens up a new range of choices. This development inevitably makes those who initially take advantage of it prospectively better off; otherwise they would not knowingly have taken advantage of it. (If the purchases were merely exploratory, those who initially took advantage of it will stop if purchasers do not like the results.)

The gain is initially in (usually non-measurable) utility or satisfaction. There is no necessary impact on the level of output, much less on the rate of growth.

What about the distribution of income? The new possibility for trade enlarges the menu of choice, often but not always by lowering price. If the price of goods falls, that benefits consumers, but it hurts domestic producers of the good or of close substitutes for it thus domestic producers of close substitutes will experience a worsening of their terms of trade and hence of their real income. Inequality will increase if these produces are poorer than average; it will decline if they are richer than average. Poverty will rise if the domestic producers are initially just above the poverty line.

Over time, resources my be reallocated and the structure of domestic output altered as a result of this new trade. Domestic producers may exit production of the import competing product in favour of now more lucrative productive pursuits. In doing so, they will certainly improve their position with respect to their condition after arrival of the imports, and they might even improve their position with respect to the *status quo ante*, before the new imports arrived. This depends on how lucrative the new pursuits are, which in turn will depend among other things on the new export opportunities opened up—indeed made necessary by the requirements for restoring macro-economic equilibrium, e.g., through depreciation of the currency.

If the country is freshly importing a new product, one or more other countries must be exporting it, and that will affect relative prices and the distribution of income there as well, and usually output.

ECONOMIC GROWTH

With a reallocation of resources, the level of the country's output will rise when measured at world prices. When measured at pretrade domestic prices, it may actually fall, but need not. (This important distinction is usually neglected in empirical work on trade and growth). GDP at the new prices will of course rise as the reallocation takes place. But once the reallocation occurs, this GDP growth will cease unless it is sustained by one or more of five factors:

- The redistribution of real income raises the national savings rate, leading directly or indirectly through the capital market to a higher rate of investment.
- The relative price of investment goods is reduced, so that a given level of national savings finances greater real investment.
- Productive foreign investment flows into the country in greater amounts on a sustained basis.
- The redistribution of income or new competitive pressure leads people to attain higher levels of economically useful skills.
- The efficiency of labour and capital is continually improved as a result of the new imports, which may convey useful information from abroad as well as exerting greater competitive pressure on domestic producers (leading domestic producers of cut flowers to improve their efficiency in production or to discover new products to sell.)

The first four of these factors could, of course, have negative signs, leading to a reduction in subsequent growth, following the gains from the initial reallocation of resources.

This discussion assumes that there are no serious market distortions. Market distortions can either reinforce or weaken the impact on output of an exogenous change. With market distortions, incentives may guide the behaviour of both firms and households—which are assumed to respond to the actual incentives they face in the wrong direction for maximizing output.

However, there is an alternative view relating trade, in particular exports to growth. The view stresses that growth may be constrained by inadequate demand or inadequate availability of foreign exchange. This is an old model, not intellectually fashionable these days, but not wrong for that reason.

Export growth can be the leading sector of a growing economy, stimulating investment. Exports can growth because world demand for them is growing smartly or because the country in question is able to increase steadily its share of the world market through a suitable combination of competitive price and quality.

Export production is constrained in the short-run by installed capacity and labour force. But it need not be constrained in the medium run if the supply of relevant labour is elastic; the supply of investible funds is responsible to the public demand for them, either through national savings or funds from abroad; and any serious bottlenecks can be broken by imports of material inputs, machinery or technology.

An effective policy for growth would that:

- Exports are competitive, with strong implications for exchange rate policy.
- Supplies of relevant labour and capital are adequate, with implications for policies toward transportation, education, housing, and financial intermediation.
- Requisite imports are readily available, not subject to high tariffs or import restrictions.

As a rough generalization, these seem to be the policies pursued by such rapidly growing economies as the Republic of Korea, Taiwan (China), Singapore, and more recently Mexico and China—each with significant national idiosyncrasies. Some high-income countries have also relied heavily on export-led growth.

CONCLUSIONS

The result of theory and evidence are inconclusive, perhaps leading to an agnostic view on the relationship of foreign trade and investment with world economic growth and its distribution. There are no compelling theoretical reasons to believe that trade promotes growth as distinguished from an increase in real income, and the empirical work purporting to make a connection at the country level has been heavily criticized on methodological grounds. The theoretical case that foreign investment should stimulate growth, and even diminish world and host country inequality of income, is stronger, but the history of foreign assistance, some of it supposedly targeted on improving growth, is disappointing. And FDI historically has been drawn by natural resources, trade barriers, and low domestic competition which gives confidence that FDI has enhanced growth or reduced inequality in income distribution.

Despite the overall ambiguity of theory and evidence, it strains to believe that trade liberalization did not play a significant role in the growth of the world economy in the second-half of the 20th century. As a whole, this period offers the best economic performance in human history, far better than the often-cited second does—half of the 19th century does. More people, and a higher proportion of them, were lifted out of poverty than ever before, as reflected in the sharp decline in the proportion of workers engaged in agriculture.

Inequality, especially global inequality, should not be a focus of great interest. Undesirable consequences may well flow from greater inequality in particular circumstances in particular locations, especially if the growing inequality lacks legitimacy because of the way it was generated. The focus then should be on the most efficacious ways to avoid the undesirable consequences or on the lack of legitimacy, not on the inequality as such. Greater global inequality, on the usual measures, is a natural consequence of uneven growth. Even growth is not possible since not all countries are ready to sustain it at the same time. Uneven growth is better than no growth. The key questions are whether people lives are improving and whether they can look forward with hope to further improvement for themselves and their children. That is the perspective of most individuals, who are not concerned with aggregate statistics on global inequality.

Index